PLANTS & PEOPLE
IN
ANCIENT SCOTLAND

For Kate and Peter

Watercolour of Meadowsweet by K. Pickles. The pollen of this beautiful plant was first recognised from Scottish archaeological layers by Camilla Dickson (see chapter 4)

PLANTS & PEOPLE
IN
ANCIENT SCOTLAND

CAMILLA DICKSON & JAMES H. DICKSON

TEMPUS

First published 2000

PUBLISHED IN THE UNITED KINGDOM BY:

Tempus Publishing Ltd
The Mill, Brimscombe Port
Stroud, Gloucestershire GL5 2QG

PUBLISHED IN THE UNITED STATES OF AMERICA BY:

Arcadia Publishing Inc.
A division of Tempus Publishing Inc.
2 Cumberland Street
Charleston, SC 29401
1-888-313-2665

Tempus books are available in France, Germany and Belgium
from the following addresses:

Tempus Publishing Group	Tempus Publishing Group	Tempus Publishing Group
21 Avenue de la République	Gustav-Adolf-Straße 3	Place de L'Alma 4/5
37300 Joué-lès-Tours	99084 Erfurt	1200 Brussels
FRANCE	GERMANY	BELGIUM

British Library Cataloguing in Publication Data.
A catalogue record for this book is available from the British Library.

ISBN 0 7524 1905 6

Typesetting and origination by Tempus Publishing.
PRINTED AND BOUND IN GREAT BRITAIN

Contents

List of illustrations   7

Preface   9

PART 1

1   Plants and archaeology in Scotland   12
Investigations from the nineteenth century till 1970
Climatic and vegetational change

2   Mesolithic: the first woodmen?   30
Immigration of trees and animals after the Ice Age
Gatherers, hunters and fishers
The Inner Hebrides, Arran and the mainland
The Outer Hebrides and the Northern Isles
Irish and other European sites
Edible roots, green parts and berries

3   Neolithic: the earliest plant-rich middens   47
Six-thousand years ago: the first farmers and the elm decline
The stone village at Skara Brae, Orcadian Mainland
Other sites on the Northern Isles, the Outer Hebrides and the mainland
Twenty trees from Skara Brae: woodland loss from the Northern Isles and the Outer Hebrides
A unique wooden hall at Balbridie, Kincardineshire: Breadwheat and Flax

4   Bronze Age: funerary flowers, mead or ale?   69
The Inner Hebrides, Arran and the mainland
The Outer Hebrides and the Northern Isles
Pollen analysis and burial practices
Climatic deteriorations

5   Late Bronze Age and Iron Age: brochs and crannogs   86
Crannogs: Outstanding sources of waterlogged plant material
The broch at Howe, Orcadian Mainland: fire produces rare evidence
Other brochs on the Northern Isles: immersion preserves human coprolites
Brochs on the Inner Hebrides and the mainland
Other sites on the mainland

6   Roman invasions: foreign foodstuffs, weeds and medicines   114
Foreign foodstuffs, weeds and medicines
The landscape of central Scotland about 2,000 years ago
The sewage-filled ditch at the Bearsden Fort
Other Roman forts in Scotland

7   Early historic period: Roman spices still in use   128
Diversity of peoples and religion
Dundurn, Perthshire: A Pictish stronghold
Buiston Crannog, Ayrshire: foreign spices
Ecclesiastical communities: Iona and Whithorn, Wigtonshire
Edinburgh Castle and Easter Kinnear, Fife

8   The Norse versus the Northern Picts   143
    Caithness and the Northern Isles
    Norse sites in the Hebrides
    Landscape and farming
    Medicinal and spice plants

9   The Medieval period: productive cess-pits and drains   179
    Three ancient burghs
    Four other burghs
    Paisley Abbey: a neglected drain reveals monastic life
    Other Medieval sites

10 The present achievement and the future   204

PART 2 SOME PARTICULARLY NOTEWORTHY PLANTS   220

Alder (Alnus glutinosa), Birches (Betula spp), Bogmosses (Sphagnum spp), Bracken (Pteridium aquilinum), Broadbean (Vicia faba), Cereals: Barley (Hordeum vulgare), Cereals: Oats (Avena spp), Cereals: Rye (Secale cereale), Cereals: Wheats — Bread Wheat (Triticum aestivum), Emmer (Triticum dicoccum) and Spelt (Triticum spelta), Cloudberry (Rubus chamaemorus), Common Mallow (Malva sylvestris), Coriander and Dill (Corinadrum sativum and Anethum graveolens), Corncockle (Agrostemma githago), Crab Apple (Malus sylvestris), Deadly Nightshade (Atropa belladonna) and Henbane (Hyoscyamus niger), Fig (Ficus carica), Flax (Linum usitatissimum), Guelder Rose (Viburnum opulus), Hawthorn (Crataegus monogyna), Hazel (Corylus avellana), Heather (Calluna vulgaris), Hemp (Cannabis sativa), Lesser Celandine (Ranunculus ficaria), Mace (Myristica fragrans), Meadowsweet (Filipendula ulmaria) and Dropwort (F. vulgaris), Monk's Rhubarb (Rumex pseudoalpinus), Mosses (especially the weft- and fan-forming species), Oaks (Quercus spp), Opium Poppy (Papaver somniferum), Ramsons (Allium ursinum), Scots Pine (Pinus sylvestris), Sloe (Prunus spinosa), Walnut (Juglans regia), Woad (Isatis tinctoria), Yew (Taxus baccata)

Appendix 1: Archaeobotany   286
    Nomenclature and level of identification
    Large (macroscopic) remains of plants
    Microscopic remains of plants

Appendix 2: Archaeolozoology   295

Appendix 3: Dating   296

Appendix 4: List of formal names of plants discussed in the text   297

Appendix 5: List of formal names of animals discussed in the text   301

References   303

Index   318

List of illustrations

1   Drawing of the excavation at Lochlee Crannog, Ayrshire
2   Drawing of a fringe of Hairmoss found at the excavation of Lochlee Crannog
3   Miscellaneous wooden objects from Bar Hill Roman Fort
4   Implements from Newstead Roman Fort
5   Woodland cover of Scotland at about 4500 BC, before woodland clearance had begun
6   Judith Turner's pollen diagram from near South Flanders Farm, Flanders Moss East
7   Susan Ramsay's pollen diagram from Walls Hill
8   A modified version of O'Sullivan's pollen diagram from Loch Garten in Abernethy Forest on Speyside
9   A modified version of Jane Bunting's pollen diagram from Quoyloo Meadow, Mainland of Orkney
10 A modified version of Julie Fossitt's pollen diagram from Loch a'Phuinnd, South Uist, Outer Hebrides
11 Chronological Table
12 Map of some Mesolithic sites in Britain and Europe
13 Map of sites on Oronsay
14 Digging stick from the Storebælt
15 Map of Neolithic Sites
16 Plan of Skara Brae
17 The first excavation of Skara Brae
18 Pieces of the underground stem of Yellow Iris
19 A. Skin of a Puffball fungus from Skara Brae. B. A drawing to show the appearance of the Puffball when alive
20 Crowberry rope from Skara Brae
21 Wooden handle from Skara Brae
22 Knap of Howar houses
23 Reconstruction of the Knap of Howar houses
24 Berriedale, Isle of Hoy, Orkney
25 A reconstruction of the house at Balbridie
26 Map of Bronze Age sites
27 Plan of Lintshie Gutter 1
28 Plan of Lintshie Gutter 2
29 Lintshie Gutter. Reconstruction of the house that was built on Platform 13
30 Ashgrove cist
31 Westbank cist
32 Map of Iron Age sites
33 Milton Loch Crannog
34 Crannogs in Loch Tay
35 Structural timbers made of Alder from Oakbank Crannog

36 Reconstructed crannog at the east end of Loch Tay
37 Early illustrations of the broch at Dun Telve, Inverness-shire
38 Cross-section of Dun Telve Broch
39 Howe. Plan of the Early Phase 7 broch tower: wallhead and floor plan
40 Howe. Early Phase 7
41 Warebeth coprolite
42 Map of Roman sites
43 The Antonine Wall, as it may have looked when under construction
44 Plan of Bearsden Fort
45 The outer east annexe ditch showing the Roman and later in-fills
46 The Bearsden fort after the excavation and open to the public
47 A. Fragments of Wheat/Rye bran from the sewage produced in Bearsden about 145 AD.
    B. Fragments of Bread Wheat bran from faeces produced in Milngavie in AD 1978
48 Latrine in use
49 The stone base of the Wall under excavation at Bearsden
50 Map of Early Historic sites
51 Plan of Dundurn
52 Buiston Crannog
53 Hairmoss from Buiston Crannog
54 Plan of Whithorn 1
55 Plan of Whithorn 2
56 Plan of Norse sites
57 Plan of Freswick
58 Plan of the sites at Birsay Bay
59 Plan of the Biggings
60 Map of Medieval sites
61 Locations of the excavations at Perth
62 Plan of Aberdeen
63 Reconstruction of Aberdeen
64 Medieval herbalist
65 The Paisley Abbey drain
66 A species of Alnus
67 Map of Alder
68 A tree Birch
69 Map of Downy Birch
70 Birch bark rolls
71 Drawings of the Bogmoss, *Sphagnum palustre*
72 Map of Bogmoss
73 A single leaf of *Sphagnum* from the early fifteenth century silts in the Paisley Abbey drain
74 Mass of compacted Bracken fronds from Dundurn

75	Map of Bracken
76	Broadbean
77	Remains of Broadbean
78	Ears and spikelets of Barley
79	Carbonised ears of Naked Six-rowed Barley from Howe Broch
80	Fragments of carbonised awns of a Barley and a Wheat, from Old Kilpatrick crannog
81	Oats
82	Carbonised Oats from Paisley Abbey
83	Carbonised florets of Wild Oat, showing the horseshoe scars, from Old Kilpatrick Crannog
84	Rye
85	Partial ear and spikelet layout of Rye
86	Drawings of carbonised Rye grains from Scottish sites
87	Complete ear and spikelet of Breadwheat
88	Balbridie Breadwheat
89	Emmer
90	Carbonised partial ears of Emmer, from Old Kilpatrick Crannog
91	Spelt
92	Carbonised grain of Spelt from Lyne Antonine Fort
93	Cloudberry from Lightfoot's Flora Scotica (1777)
94	Map of Cloudberry
95	Pips of Cloudberry from Oakbank Crannog
96	Common Mallow
97	Map of Common Mallow
98	A pollen grain of Common Mallow from the Roman in-fill of the east annexe ditch at the Bearsden Fort
99	Coriander
100	Map of Coriander
101	Remains of Coriander from the Bearsden Fort
102	Dill
103	Remains of Dill from the Bearsden Fort
104	Corncockle
105	Map of Corncockle
106	Seeds of Corncockle
107	Apple
108	Map of Crab Apple
109	Two pips of Crab Apple from Skara Brae
110	Deadly Nightshade
111	Map of Deadly Nightshade
112	Henbane
113	Map of Henbane
114	Fig
115	Map of Fig
116	Fig pips from Paisley Abbey
117	Flax
118	Remains of Flax from the Bearsden Fort
119	Guelder Rose
120	Map of Guelder Rose
121	Arrow from Fyvie
122	Hawthorn
123	Map of Hawthorn
124	Branch fragments of Hawthorn from the Bar Hill Fort
125	Hazel
126	Map of Hazel
127	Hazelnuts
128	Coppiced Hazel
129	Heather
130	Map of Heather
131	Remains of Heather basket from the later Phase 7 of Howe Broch
132	Hemp
133	Lesser Celandine
134	Map of Lesser Celandine
135	Tubers of Lesser Celandine from Howe Broch
136	Mace
137	Mace from Paisley Abbey
138	Map of Meadowsweet
139	Dropwort
140	Map of Dropwort
141	Monk's Rhubarb
142	Map of Monk's Rhubarb
143	Remains of Monk's Rhubarb from Paisley Abbey
144	Map of Hylocomium splendens
145	Map of Neckera complanata
146	Neckera complanata carried by the Tyrolean Iceman
147	Sessile Oak
148	Map of Sessile Oak
149	Ring of Oak trunks at the west end of Mugdock Wood
150	Opium Poppy
151	Map of Opium Poppy
152	Seeds of Opium Poppy from a well in the Roman fort at Welzheim in southern Germany
153	Ramsons
154	Map of Ramsons
155	Carbonised bulbs of Ramsons from the Fairy Knowe Broch
156	Scots Pine
157	Map of Scots Pine
158	Map of ancient Scots Pine stumps in peat
159	The dated stump from Loch Sloy
160	Ancient Scots pine stumps exposed by peat erosion on Coire Riabach, Banffshire
161	Sloe
162	Map of Sloe
163	Stone of Sloe, opened by a Bank Vole, from Old Kilpatrick Crannog
164	Walnut
165	Map of Walnut
166	Woad
167	Yew
168	Map of Yew
169	Fortingall tree as published in Pennant's 1774 volume
170	Drawings of pollen grains and spores frequently recognised in samples from British peats, lake muds and archaeological layers
171	Phytoliths

Preface

This book depends very heavily on the latter part of the scientific career of my late wife Camilla who died in 1998. Camilla did not begin writing till after she knew in October 1996 that she was terminally ill but sadly passed away before her task was complete. Most of the chapters had been written to the first draft level.

We shared a great interest in the interplay of botany and archaeology ever since we first met in 1959 in Cambridge and worked together in Professor Sir Harry Godwin's laboratory in the Botany School. Camilla was the Professor's already very experienced technician identifying seeds and counting pollen and I was one of his last research students, working on Ice Age mosses. It proved very felicitous that, in the early 1960s, the first archaeological plant remains we investigated together came from the Bronze Age cist grave at Ashgrove, Methilhill, in Fife. This was not just because of the Scottish location, but because the interpretation of the results as funerary flowers, mead or ale has aroused much interest, which still continues. Subsequently, we devoted much of our scientific energy to the investigation of the archaeobotany of Scotland when we were based from 1970 in the University of Glasgow, my alma mater.

Camilla had carried out the first of her Quaternary palaeoecological and archaeobotanical studies, eventually totalling about 75 publications, before we met. The first famous archaeologist that I worked with was Professor Sir Graham Clark when, in 1960 at the request of Sir Harry, I gathered peat samples during the re-excavation of Shippea Hill in the East Anglian Fenland. The resulting radiocarbon dates helped push the Neolithic back many years and trebled the duration of that period in Britain. Furthermore, from a strictly botanical point of view, the peat samples from beneath the Fenland clay were noteworthy because they yielded a flower of the Broad-leaved Lime, a tree which at that time was still regarded as dubiously native in Britain.

This book sets out to show how all types of useful plants, and to some degree animals too, have been exploited in Scotland from Mesolithic to Medieval times. Investigations of pollen and larger remains from archaeological sites reveal how plants were used for fuel, construction, dyeing, medicine and both liquid and solid consumption. The story stops at about AD 1500 by which time documentary evidence fills in much, though by no means all, of Scottish history.

Archaeobotany has much of interest to say about diet. Though with no critically minded appreciation of the identification of animal remains, we have felt it necessary to refer, usually only briefly, to the faunal evidence, otherwise the reader would gain only a partial, unbalanced knowledge of ancient eating habits.

The story of the human impact on Scotland's flora and vegetation is a complex one, going back to 8000 BC when the first firmly dated Mesolithic folk arrived. Woodland clearances began at differing times at different places and the first such impacts were either strong or weak. The woodland history of Orkney is very different to that of the Isle of Arran, or to that of the west-central mainland. Various crops were introduced, some to disappear long ago, others to continue being cultivated almost to the present time. Humans were well acquainted with the differing properties of woods and other plant materials way back in the Mesolithic period and the uses of medicinal herbs were certainly appreciated in Scotland by the Neolithic period and, if then, why not already long before?

Thousands of Scottish archaeological sites have been examined, crudely or expertly, over the years, but only a small proportion have been examined for plant remains by the intensive and rewarding botanical methods developed during the last few decades. An even smaller number of investigated sites have yielded waterlogged, rather than carbonised, plant macrofossils. We have dealt mainly with such permanently wet sites because by preserving delicate plant parts, even petals, they have revealed much that is new, and waterlogged layers often contain remains of plants from a greater range of environments, as will be revealed in the text. Sites with less aqueous conditions have not been neglected, particularly not those that have been especially thoroughly sampled or have outstanding attributes such as faeces, human or canine, often produced but exceedingly rarely preserved as discreet lumps. Pollen analyses have been discussed, especially when they provided insight into the immediately local conditions of the site in question but they cannot reveal the full richness of the former wildwood, of which so very little is now left. Identification of wood and charcoal as well as seeds and other remains of herbaceous shade-loving plants can help to provide a fuller picture of past woodland floras.

In our experience, archaeologists have often been unaware that their samples, when sent for biological analyses, had become contaminated in ancient or modern times, or else they were resistant at least initially to the thought that such a happening was only too possible. In the 1960s when we identified as Yew the Neolithic long bows from the Somerset peats for Professor Sir Graham Clark, he shortly afterwards came to us thinking that an arrow shaft had been found from the same site. Microscopic examination quickly showed it to be a rattan cane, one of the variously useful products of a palm. It was not part of the gear of an archer of 5,000 or more years ago but probably the stick of a walker of Victorian or later times. On opening a large bag of midden material of Neolithic age from Skara Brae in Orkney there were fruits of Sycamore, an alien tree in Britain introduced in Medieval times. On opening a purpose-made wooden box containing the moss-rich layers of a cess-pit from Viking Dublin there was a loose, intact, long pod of Vanilla, the Orchid used as flavouring, brought into Europe after Columbus; this still leaves me astonished at the improbability of such a contamination.

Camilla intended that this book should be written not just in such a way as to be accessible to the general public with an interest in archaeology but also to draw to the attention of professional archaeologists the great value of botanical investigations in all their varied forms. In completing it I have reduced some sections and expanded others, as I feel sure Camilla would have done had she lived long enough to revise the whole typescript thoroughly, and I have written much of both the first and final chapters. Particularly appropriately, I believe, for a book written by botanists for archaeologists, I have placed extended accounts of some plants in Part 2. Camilla had dealt to some extent with these plants, such as Flax, Hemp and Woad, but I felt they deserved fuller treatment. They are all plants which were of economic or ecological importance or both during the periods in question. Moreover, they are all plants which have relevance to many areas outwith Scotland. In making these rearrangements and additions, I have in no way changed the concept of the book that Camilla had and I hope that her aims have been achieved. Chapter 1 is very largely mine, chapters 2 to 9 were very largely written by Camilla, chapter 10 is very largely mine, Appendices 1 to 3 Camilla, Appendices 4 and 5 mine and Part 2 very largely mine.

Acknowledgements. As Camilla wrote the chapters she sent copies in a still far from finalised state to a variety of archaeologists and lay people interested in the subject. In finishing the book, I too have sought help from various people. For their helpful comments and assistance in various ways the following are thanked: Dianne Aldritt, Jacqueline Andrews, John Arthur, Beverley Ballin Smith, Colleen Batey, Carole Biggam, David Breeze, Lonwin Edwards, Bill Gauld, Laurence Keppie, Andrew Kitchener, Barry Juniper, Liz and Clive Mason, June McKay, Jennifer Miller, Margaret Paxton, Susan Ramsay, David Ritchie, Ian and Lekky Shepherd, Philip Tallantire, Judy Turner, Robert Will, Gay Wilson and Bernie Zonfrillo. In particular, I must mention particularly Beverley Ballin Smith and Philip Tallantire, who have been especially supportive. I am very grateful to Jane Croft and Chris Page of the Biological Records Centre of the Institute of Terrestrial Ecology at Monks Wood for supplying the dot distribution maps of those species discussed in detail. Staff of the Special Collections of the Library and of the Photographic Unit of the University of Glasgow were most helpful. Historic Scotland funded much of the work that Camilla carried out in Scotland and I here put on record our thanks for this support and also for giving us free access to some illustrations.

Completed in Dartmouth, Nova Scotia, July 2000
James Dickson
Professor of Archaeobotany and Plant Systematics
University of Glasgow

PART 1

1 Plants and archaeology in Scotland

Investigations from the nineteenth century till 1970

Long before scientific archaeology was established, Scots wondered about the ancient landscape and about the food and drink of their distant forebears. Although obviously with no evidence from excavations, Sir Robert Sibbald in 1711 discussed the environmental conditions encountered by the Romans. In 1792, Sir James Foulis wrote 'An enquiry into the beverage of the Ancient Caledonians...'. He discussed ale but specifically excluded mead; see chapter 4 of this book, *Bronze Age; Funerary Flowers, Mead or Ale?*

The identification of plant remains from archaeological contexts in Scotland goes back to the middle of the nineteenth century if not before. When an ancient cist was opened in Aberdeenshire 'Some remains of a darkish fibrous-looking substance like dry moss were found beside and under the body' (Christie 1864, p363) and, in 1865, Stuart noted perfectly preserved Bracken and Heather found when crannogs in Wigtonshire were investigated. When the magnificently preserved plant remains from the Swiss lake villages were published in 1865 the potential benefit of combining botany and archaeology became very clear (Heer 1865).

John Sadler of the Royal Botanic Garden, Edinburgh, was the first professional botanist in Scotland to identify archaeological material. From the broch at Levenwick in Shetland he recognised wood of Scots Pine and a hardwood such as Alder or Elm (Smith 1871). However, the first substantial Scottish archaeobotanical study carried out professionally was by Professor Bayley Balfour of the University of Glasgow. It appeared in Robert Munro's *Ancient Scottish Lake-Dwellings or Crannogs* in 1882. Both Lochlee (**1**) and Buiston Crannogs in Ayrshire were excavated by Munro, a local medical doctor and antiquarian. He set out to record crannogs, more and more of which had become obvious following the drainage of many lochs. The pottery Munro found places the occupation of Lochlee as late as the sixth century AD (Ann Crone, personal communication). The plants from Lochlee that Professor Bayley Balfour listed and discussed were as follows.

Wood from the log pavement:
Birch, Hazel, Alder, Willow.
Wooden artefacts:
Elm and Ash.

1   *Drawing of the excavation at Lochlee Crannog, Ayrshire. It shows many timbers, some very substantial. From Munro (1882)*

[The excavator, Munro, says that he himself recognised Oak artefacts but did not send them to Balfour.]

Debris above the log pavement:

Two mosses: *Hylocomium splendens* and *Polytrichum commune.*

[These are both very common large mosses which are often encountered in excavations; the latter had been made into fringe-like objects (**2**); see account of Mosses in Part 2].

The fern, bracken, and 'rhizomes of fern'.

[Large amounts of Bracken are recovered from many excavations; see the account of Bracken in Part 2]

Bovista nigrescens.

[A puffball, discussed in the account of medicinal plants at Skara Brae, chapter 3.]

Daedalea quercina and *Fomes ignarius.*

[These two are bracket fungi, the latter used as tinder, as the name implies; Ötzi, the Tyrolean Iceman, had the related tinder fungus *Fomes fomentarius* with flints and pyrites, his fire-making kit, in his body belt. Bayley Balfour's discovery of three large fungi, the puffball and the two bracket fungi, from one Scottish site remains unique.]

Portions of Birch bark in strips rolled together like a ball of thread, Hazelnuts 'one knawed by a squirrel?', Heather stems and several masses containing 'roots and root leaves of a monocotyledonous plant'.

[Remains of Birch, Hazel and Heather are recovered again and again from Scottish sites; see the accounts in Part 2.]

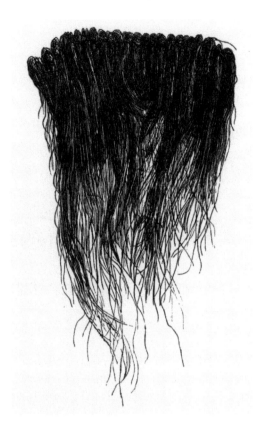

2   Drawing of a fringe of Hairmoss found at the excavation of Lochlee Crannog. About one third natural size. Other than timber or smaller wooden remains, this is the earliest illustration of plant material from a Scottish excavation. From Munro (1882)

Balfour set a good example by being cautious about his limits in determining those samples which were badly preserved. He is explicit about not finding any Beech [This is no surprise, as that tree is not native north of the Chiltern Hills.] nor any 'fir' [meaning Scots Pine, again no surprise; by *c.*1,500 years ago there would have been few if any such trees in Ayrshire. Moreover, with exemplary good sense, he sought second opinions from suitable experts on the mosses and fungi.]

Over 25 years later, the book *The Roman Forts on the Bar Hill Dunbartonshire* was published by James Macdonald and Alexander Park (1906), who discussed the numerous organic remains revealed by the excavations, especially from the well, including much leather and artefacts of Red Deer horn. Bones identified by Dr T.Y. Bryce belonged to Dog, Fox, Horse, Domestic Cattle, Pig, Red Deer and Sheep as well as to Humans (ankle, wrist, toe and finger bones — 'the relics of the work of either the surgeon or of the executioner', p128).

Remains of woody plants, many of them from the well and identified by a person or persons unspecified, were Alder, Ash, Birch, Elm, Hawthorn, Hazel, Oak, Pine, Rowan, Walnut, Whin and Willow. The authors give few details of the plant identifications, nor any formal names. By Whin some people mean Broom but others mean Gorse and so there is a state of uncertainty. Found totally intact in one of the refuse holes was an iron-rimmed chariot wheel, the felloe of which was made of a single piece of Ash, the spokes were of Willow and the nave was 'probably of Elm' (p94). Some of the wooden artefacts

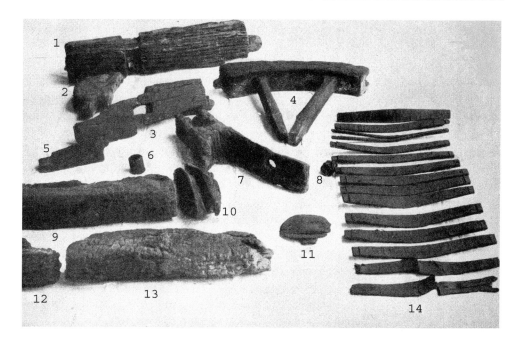

3   Miscellaneous wooden objects from Bar Hill Roman Fort. 1, 9, 12 and 13 are oaken structural timbers, the last three charred. 2, 3, 5 and 11 are parts of a wheel nave. 4. Section of an oaken wheel felloe. 6. Small round box of Willow. 7. Overhead beam from the well. 8. Piping. 10. Pulley from the well. 14. Oaken barrel staves. Modified from Macdonald and Park (1906)

from Bar Hill are shown in figure **3**. From another refuse hole, there was a six-foot length of Hemp rope, wrapped up in a large piece of leather, which may have been an apron; this find of Hemp rope is unique in Scottish archaeology. From the bottom of the well 'came the skin of a common puff-ball (*scleroderma*)'; again there are no details and so some doubt must attach to the identification.

From the point of view of richness of animal and plant remains, the first century Roman fort at Newstead, near Melrose, was even better than that at Bar Hill. Careful sieving might have produced bones of small mammals, but such a procedure was seldom carried out, if at all, 100 years ago. Large pits yielded a mass of bones of large mammals which were identified by J.C. Ewart and published in J. Curle's book (1911). Domestic cattle of Celtic short horn and crossbreeds, some polled, were recognised. Sheep were of two types, Soay and those small breeds common in Scotland up to the end of the eighteenth century. Goat bones were less common and Pigs were both Domestic and Wild Boar. Two Horse skulls were taken to be those of an unimproved native Pony and a crossbreed. R.G. Linton thought that there were five different types of skulls of dogs, presumably kept for hunting. Apart from the Wild Boar, there were bones of Red and Roe Deer, Fox, Badger, Hare and Elk, the last named now long extinct in Britain.

Harry F. Tagg was the pioneer of the archaeobotany of Scottish Roman sites. He identified about 60 different species, a lengthy list unsurpassed in Scotland for over 50 years. There was an unfinished 'basket' of Hairmoss from the bottom of one of the ditches of the early Fort. Sample C consisted of '... a closely caked mass of vegetable remains composed almost entirely of wheat chaff. It appears to be the discarded refuse after winnowing and gleaning the grain.' The processing of the cereals had taken place within the fort, as Tagg fully realised. Unfortunately, he gave no details concerning any of his identifications of cereals or other plants. Those were the days when, archaeobotany not being very advanced, one cannot be sure that he did indeed find wheat rather than any other cereal, though it is likely that he did. He found numerous seeds of Corncockle, the weed of cereal fields, in that cereal sample. In Sample M '...were a few grains of wheat and one or two grains of what I believe to be barley'. According to Curle (p109) 'Husks of wheat and barley were found in many of the pits'.

There are some other of Tagg's identifications that may be questioned. He listed '*Polygonum fagopyrum*? fruits'. The modern synonym is *Fagopyrum esculentum*; this is Buckwheat, a well-known food plant in Central and Eastern Europe, and if correct, this would be the one and only occurrence in Scottish archaeology. Perhaps he had found Black Bindweed, a cornfield weed, with many archaeological occurrences, which has similar if smaller seeds. Tagg identified a hammer handle and a gauge shaft as Rowan ('*Pyrus aucuparia*' = *Sorbus aucuparia*) but also recorded '*Pyrus aria*'. This last is *Sorbus aria* (Common Whitebeam, which is not at all common in Scotland now). That he could have recognised it from the wood of 'some branches of fair size'(presumably leafless) stretches credulity.

Many of the 60 species he listed were those of grasslands or heathlands: Buttercups, Lady's Mantle, Tormentil, Marsh Lousewort, Sheep's Sorrel, Soft Rush, 'several' Grasses, including '*Festuca ovina*? leaves' [though Sheep's Fescue is very common in Scotland and could very well have been some 2,000 years ago, again it is hard to believe such unexplicit precision]. These plants could have been gathered as hay for the animals. One of the remarkable things about Newstead is the great array of metal tools, including the very tools used by haymakers: sickles, scythes and a wooden rake with iron prongs (**4**). Carried out nearly 100 years ago, Tagg's study of the plants from Newstead was a fine achievement.

The fort at Mumrills near the eastern end of the Antonine Wall was investigated for bones and molluscs, but not for plant remains (MacDonald and Curle 1929). James Ritchie found bones of Shorthorn Cattle to be the most numerous and almost all were those of adults. There were only very few Sheep and Pig bones. Three Horse bones resembled those of the Ponies found at Newstead. Antlers and a solitary bone of Red Deer pointed to hunting and a single bone of domestic fowl may have been part of a gaming bird. A skull fragment proved to be Wolf and another interesting find were footprints of Wild Cat impressed on a brick while still drying. To identify Wild Cat from a Domestic Cat on the basis of footprints seems rather hazardous; the pads of the Wild Cat are the larger but not by much and, according to Bouchardy and Moutou (1989, p146) considering prints, '. . . it is practically impossible to distinguish one from the other'. These are not the only animal prints to be found at a Roman site in Scotland. Tiles and bricks, found by field walking at Newstead, revealed footprints of Dog, Sheep/Goat, Mouse/Shrew and Pig (Elliot 1991). Also at Mumrills, apart from the remains of mammals, were many Oyster shells.

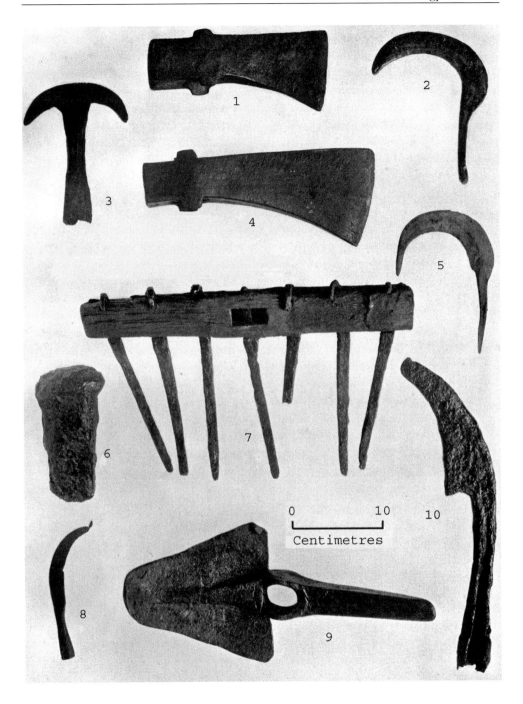

4   *Implements from Newstead Roman Fort. 1 and 4 Axes. 2 and 5 Sickles. 3 Turf cutter. 6 Heavy wedge. 7 Wooden rake with iron prongs. 8 and 10 Small and large socketed sickles. 9 Hoe. Modified from Curle (1911)*

The fort and temporary camp at Oakwood, 5.5km southwest of Selkirk, was excavated by Steer and Feacham (1954). No fewer than 11 main gateway timbers were found to be well preserved (up to almost 1m long and up to 0.35m across the base). They were identified as Oak by P.S. Green and M.Y. Orr, who carried out many archaeological wood identifications in the 1940s and 1950s but never published any summary. One of the trunks had 70 annual rings and, like the others, represented a tree that had not been of much greater girth. Some of the trees had been cut down by axe alone but others had first been notched by an axe then sawn down. The best preserved were pointed distally; this suggests that the fort gates had been destroyed by fire.

Elizabeth Knox was a pioneer of pollen analysis from archaeological layers in Scotland and she made various analyses from Scottish sites excavated in the 1950s. At Oakwood, from the fill of a ditch in the temporary camp, she found 30% Birch, 16% Hazel, 12% Alder, 5% Oak, 6% Willow, 16% Heather and small variety of pollen from non-woody plants.

In 1961, sand and gravel quarrying revealed both a native Iron Age site and an adjacent Roman annexe on the army's route to the north, just north of the Antonine Wall and the Roman fort at Camelon, Falkirk (Proudfoot 1978, with archaeobotany by Geoffrey Dimbleby and Joan Sheldon). This was a good opportunity to investigate the economy of a fortified native site, which, from the finds, appears to have been occupied during the late first and second centuries AD. The Roman fort is thought to have superseded the two circular superimposed houses, which made up the native dwelling. Unfortunately time permitted only partial examination of the site. Charcoal, from various features, identified by Joan Sheldon, was dominated by Hazel, with Birch, Oak, and Willow or Poplar. A rectangular pit, used for clay daub and rubbish, contained some charred grains of Hulled Barley. A single pollen count revealed very high grass values (76%) but with only 3% Ribwort Plantain and very low percentages of trees and tall shrubs and Heather. The few calcined bone fragments were not identifiable. The analyses of the site show that native farmers must have co-existed with the Romans, but as far as can be ascertained, maintained their native crops uninfluenced by the more exotic food eaten by the occupying forces.

In one of the first few phytolith analyses from a Scottish site (see Appendix 1), the result was summarised as (p126) 'The opaline phytoliths in this sample are supporting evidence for a grass cover, but do not enable us to determine the species involved'. This is a minuscule finding, barely worth the trouble, as assessed in Appendix 1 for more recent work in Scotland.

Published in 1964, the book *The Roman Fort at Castledykes* (in north Lanarkshire) by Anne Robertson, contains a section on wood identified by Donald Brett, who listed Ash, Beech, Birch, Elm, Hazel, Oak, Pine, Rowan, Service, and Willow or Poplar. No formal names are given, nor are any confirmatory details, and so it is hard to know what is meant by 'Service'. Perhaps Wild Service-tree was intended but that small tree is not a Scottish native and so it would be a remarkable discovery, unique in Scottish archaeology. Perhaps some other tree of the genus *Sorbus* (which includes Rowan, Whitebeams and Service-tree) was intended; this makes one think of the common Whitebeam from Newstead (on which aspersions have also been cast). Beech is not a Scottish native and Brett wondered if the solitary charred scrap was a modern contaminant.

Dr A.S. Clarke identified 'tiny fragments of bone' as Domestic Cattle, Pig, and Sheep/Goat as well as Fallow Deer ('dubiously identified', p158). The last is not a Scottish native but there are Roman records from England (Yalden 1999).

The Roman fort at Birrens, near Ecclefechan, was manned in both the first and second centuries AD and excavated by Anne Robertson in the 1960s. Large mammal bones (identified by Margaret Scott and Alison Macartney) were of Horse, Pig, Red and Roe Deer and Sheep/Goat and, as at Castledykes, a single bone was tentatively identified as Fallow Deer. Gay Wilson (1975) identified the seeds. An early Antonine well produced a diversity of seeds of plants derived from cultivated ground and waste places, although plants of healthy ground were the most numerous including five species of Sedge. The cereal remains were not studied in great detail (Barley and Bread Wheat were recorded and Emmer and Spelt may have been present) and Corncockle was found. A pollen count from the well included, among the trees, high proportions of Alder, Hazel-type and Birch and, among the non-trees, grasses, Heather, Sedge and Devil's-bit Scabious. Charcoal, studied by Cynthia Crewe (1975) and JHD, represented 11 different trees or shrubs: Alder, Ash, Beech, Birch, Elm, Hazel, Holly, Lime, Oak, Pine and Willow/Poplar. The most notable was a fragment of a writing tablet made of Beech and Lime, the latter not usually thought of as native in Britain north of the English Lake District.

The fort at Rough Castle on the Antonine Wall, between Bonnybridge and Falkirk, was excavated from 1957 to 1961 and the results published in 1981 by MacIvor *et al.* Wood and charcoal was investigated by John Barber who found Ash, Birch, European Silver Fir, Hornbeam, Oak and Scots Pine. The Fir was the remains of a radially split plank and the Hornbeam was a serrated disk; both of these were imports. It is clear that wood of trees not native in Scotland is to be expected at Roman sites. Recognised by Ian Hodgson, the only bones were of Domestic Cattle and Horse.

These short accounts of the findings from Roman forts excavated before 1970 convey much, but not all, of the archaeobiological achievements in Scotland till then. The pre-1970 excavations at Jarlshof and Clickhimmin in Shetland by Hamilton (1956, 1968) produced interesting botanical discoveries, but they will be discussed in the chronologically appropriate later chapters. In the 1940s, the Danes Knud Jessen and Hans Helbæk summarised cereal finds from British archaeological sites, including those in Scotland, and Helbæk can be considered the first specialist archaeobotanist to have studied Scottish material. He investigated the plant remains from the Milton Loch Crannog in Kirkcudbrightshire (Pigott 1955) and listed charcoal of Alder, Hazel, Oak and Willow as well as Hazelnut fragments and seeds of Carnation Sedge, Common Club-rush, Common Spike-rush, Pale Persicaria and Redshank. Elizabeth Knox made a pollen count of the peat from Milton Loch and she found sparse tree pollen including that of Lime but it cannot be taken as an indication of local growth. The Lime pollen could have come from not-too-far-distant trees in the English Lake District. She also recorded pollen of Lesser Bulrush, which is a rarity now in Scotland, but known from Kirkcudbrightshire.

In 1956, Sir Harry Godwin published the botanical analyses by Camilla Lambert [later Camilla Dickson] from the famous Neolithic tomb at Maes Howe on the Orcadian Mainland (Childe 1956). CD carried out both pollen and seed analyses from the same samples of turf and ditch fill. To pursue pollen analyses of archaeological layers without associated seed analyses is to greatly limit the scope for interpretation. On Scottish samples, this was the first time that such combined analyses had been carried out.

In the 1960s, there were published the first detailed pollen diagrams from Scotland that had been specifically prepared to reveal, from the earliest times, the long-term sweep of human effects on the vegetation. The pioneer of such detailed work was Judith Turner who analysed the deep peats of the raised bogs at Flanders Moss East in the upper Forth Valley and at Bloak Moss in northern Ayrshire; see the next section. Now, very many such diagrams exist, not just from peats but also from lake muds, from all parts of Scotland.

It has become completely routine that many scientific disciplines, not just botany and zoology, are fully integrated with post-excavational programmes. From 1970 onwards, there have been very substantial archaeobotanical and archaeozoological studies from all periods in Scotland, including some periods unrepresented, or virtually so, in the earlier studies, notably Neolithic and Medieval times.

Preserved plant remains are diverse in types and sizes; ranging from microscopic pollen and spores to much larger remains, such as wood and charcoal, seeds and fruits, and including the very important cereal grains, and leaves, budscales and other vegetative fragments and mosses. Consequently, such is the detailed knowledge and experience needed to be at the forefront of research, that the archaeobotanist now tends to specialise in particular plant categories (see Appendix 1). Though rarely encountered, seaweeds and large fungi have their own especial relevance; as indicated above, the latter were a marked feature of Bayley Balfour's early report, which also dealt with flowering plants, ferns and mosses.

Climatic and vegetational change

The Earth's Orbit

It is well known from a variety of sources that the Earth's climate has changed greatly and often abruptly many times throughout the Quaternary period, from warm to cold conditions, with major ice advances called Ice Ages separated by spells of milder, interglacial conditions. Such massive changes are commonly considered to have resulted from changes in the Earth's orbit, as first proposed by Milankovitch (Dawson 1992). At the Late-glacial to Holocene transition, some 11,000 years ago in Scotland, the climate suddenly warmed up and, during the present interglacial, the climate has varied both with regard to temperature and precipitation. On the extreme western fringe of Eurasia and much influenced by the huge expanse of the Atlantic Ocean, Scotland has a cool, windy and wet climate, with a large number of rain days; such conditions are conducive of soil impoverishment, of the spread of peat and of the flourishing of a rich flora of ferns and bryophytes (Birks 1997). The Scottish climate is not stable by the decade, the century or the millennium. Graeme Whittington and Kevin Edwards (1997) have recently discussed the diversity of ways (pollen, peat stratigraphy, insects, deuterium analysis) that have been used to deduce the changing Scottish climate since the last ice age. They state (p14),

Current thinking confirms earlier ideas both on the fast rate of temperature and precipitation increase between 10 000 and 7000 BP (5840 cal BC), and also by the latter date Scotland would have been drier and warmer than at present. Since that time, however, it is argued that changes in climate have been only minor.

Nonetheless, minor changes, or sudden even if short-lived changes, can have substantial effects for humankind. The varying climate affects plants, vegetation, soils and crops and consequently people.

The Medieval Warm Period and the Little Ice Age

That the climate has varied within the last thousand years enough to have greatly affected people is shown very convincingly by the times known as the Medieval Warm Period and the Little Ice Age. There are many documents and even paintings which directly or indirectly tell of these recent climatic changes in Europe. The late tenth to twelfth centuries experienced hot, dry summers and rather cold winters, and the twelfth and thirteenth centuries were described by Hubert Lamb (1982) as a golden age in Scotland, with farming established at a higher level on hillsides than at present. According to Brian Fagan (2000, p183) 'Average temperatures in the British Isles between 1140 and 1300 were up to 0.8 Celsius higher than those of 1900 to 1950'. This warm period with its good harvests was also when monastic sheep farms were instigated and the feudal estates initiated by David I. The population increased, housing and more agricultural land was needed and woodland was cleared for farms and housing. Plagues began in the fourteenth century, the Black Death reached Scotland in 1349 (Ziegler 1969), and in the 1430s severe shortages and famines were recorded for the first time in the records for Dunfermline.

From about 1420, according to Lamb, the climate became colder; the Little Ice Age had begun. The growing season was shortened by up to three weeks so that parts of northern Britain, which are borderline for the cultivation of cereals, suffered harvest failures. The severest effects of the Little Ice Age took place after 1500, outside the time covered by this book. There were famines of the 1590s and 1690s (Lamb 1982, Smout 1969), and by 1600 the upper limit of cultivation in the Lammermuir Hills in southern Scotland had dropped by 200-225m (Parry 1975). The book *Times of Feast, Times of Famine* by Emmanuel Ladurie (1971) shows paintings revealing how much further forward glaciers were in the Alps during the eighteenth century than now and discusses how great were the consequences for people of the severity of climate during the Little Ice Age. Jean Grove (1988) provided a very thorough summary of all aspects of the Little Ice Age.

Volcanic Eruptions

Very sudden climatic change can be caused by large volcanic eruptions and by large objects in space striking the Earth. In the last ten years or so years it has been a popular topic to investigate the possible effects of Icelandic eruptions on Irish and Scottish vegetation and climate (Baillie 1988, 1989, Birks 1994, Blackford et al. 1992, Dugmore 1989, Hall et al. 1994). It is known from contemporary accounts in Britain, France and Germany that in the month following the Laki fissure eruption in Iceland in 1783 considerable damage was caused to the vegetation. Tree leaves and cereals withered and pasture dried and shrivelled overnight. This damage is consistent with the acid deposition of industrial origin which affects plant growth in parts of Europe at the present time (Birks 1994).

It has been suggested that large eruptions can cause marked climatic change. Two particularly large Icelandic eruptions have been recorded, Hekla 3, at *c.*1159 BC and Hekla 4 at *c.*2310 BC. Such large eruptions result in thousands of tonnes of dust and sulphur dioxide being thrown into the atmosphere, severely altering both local and global climate. The reflection of sunlight by the dust would have resulted in cooler, wetter weather conditions in northern Britain. Mike Baillie (1988) has recorded spectacularly narrow bands of tree-rings in Oaks growing around lakes in Ireland, beginning in 1159 BC and lasting until 1141 BC. This has been attributed to the Hekla 3 eruption, causing a climatic downturn producing stress and therefore retarding growth.

The eruptions have also been registered in peat bogs in the form of thin layers of tephra, volcanic glass, thrown out high into the atmosphere during the eruption and settling up to many hundreds of km from Iceland. Tephra particles measure less than 140 microns in diameter and are identified microscopically after acid digestion of the peat. Electron microprobe analysis can identify the geochemical constituents; the relative abundance of the different chemicals can sometimes be used to pinpoint the specific eruption.

The Hekla 3 eruption has been recorded from tephra in northern Scotland, the Western Isles and Shetland by Andrew Dugmore. Ash from Hekla 4 has been found in Scandinavia, the Faroes, Shetland and the Mourne Mountains of Ireland. Dates are known of fallout from Icelandic volcanoes for the last 1000 years and a tephrochronology for the British Isles is being prepared by Valerie Hall and co-workers in Ireland.

The potential effect of the climatic upset caused by major eruptions is considerable and it has been suggested that the climatic deterioration of the later Bronze Age could have been the result of the 1159 BC eruption. The decline in Scots Pine from northern areas around 4,000 years ago is thought in some places to be correlated with Hekla 4, but in others it seems to slightly pre-date the Hekla 4 eruption. Changes in peat bog stratigraphy in northern Europe have been linked to major volcanic eruptions. It is clear that accurate dating is needed either to correlate with or exclude volcanic activity from vegetational changes.

It is possible that farming in marginal areas of northern Scotland may also have been affected by a volcanically induced, climatic deterioration, resulting in pressure on increased populations to move into other areas. Such potential movements of people could also have resulted in cultural changes. Although Oaks growing in marginal situations in Ireland seem to have been affected for some 18 years, it has yet to be shown conclusively that these eruptions changed the climate for long enough to result in substantial movements of populations and to effect cultural changes. See the article by John Birks (1994) as cautionary criticism.

On the evidence of narrow Oak rings, Baillie (1988, p155) considered that in AD 540 'A major dust veil event [was] likely to have had environmental consequences followed by Justinian plague'. This idea has been expanded into the book *Catastrophe* by David Keys (1999) who argues that global climatic change had resulted from a massive eruption of

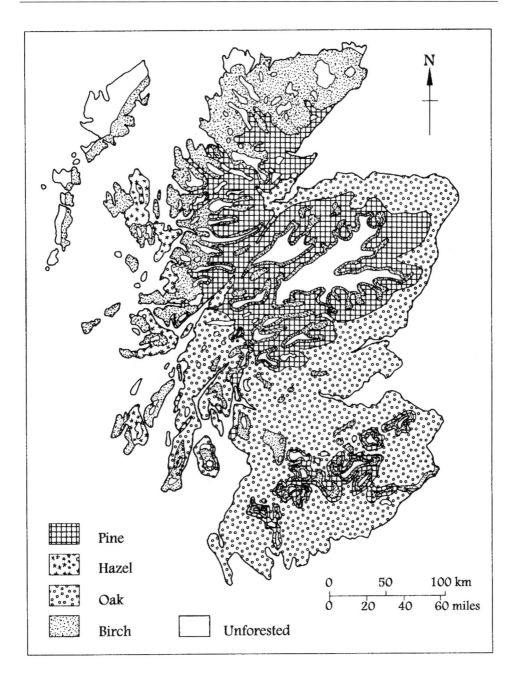

5   *Woodland cover of Scotland at about 4500 BC, before woodland clearance had begun. In Britain the timber line is low, compared to those in areas of more continental climate. In the Southern Uplands and Highlands exposure to the very strong winds of westernmost Europe kept the woodlands away from the hilltops as well as reducing tree cover in the furthest west and north, even at low altitudes. Modified from Lowe (1993)*

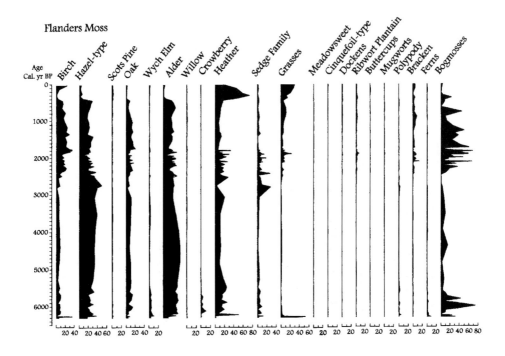

6 *Judith Turner's pollen diagram from near South Flanders Farm, Flanders Moss East. The Elm Decline can be seen near the base of the diagram*

Krakatoa in south-east Asia; this is the volcano famous for the enormous eruptions of 1883 Thornton (1996). The climatic downturn encouraged the spread of the plague during the reign of the Roman Emperor Justinian and the social consequences were very great in Britain, the rest of Europe and elsewhere. Again arguing basically from the firm evidence of tree rings, Baillie (1999) has written further on this topic in *Exodus to Arthur Catastrophic Encounters with Comets* and makes the case that in addition to volcanic eruptions there have been widespread, major effects of the impacts of comets and meteors hitting the Earth and disrupting human societies. He argues that the AD 540 effects were caused by a comet landing in the Celtic Sea.

Pollen Analysis

The methods and practice of pollen analysis and the related, complementary study of macroscopic fossils are outlined in Appendix 1. *Macroscopic* fossils, such as seeds, charcoal and leaves, are large — the opposite of *microscopic* pollen grains and spores. Pollen analysis has been outstandingly successful in revealing woodland history throughout the world, with Scotland as no exception. Since 1960, the great achievement relevant to this book has been to reveal in time and space how great the effects of humankind have been in reducing the woodland cover for arable and pastoral agriculture. This brief section outlines something of the regional diversity of the initial woodland cover within Scotland, for

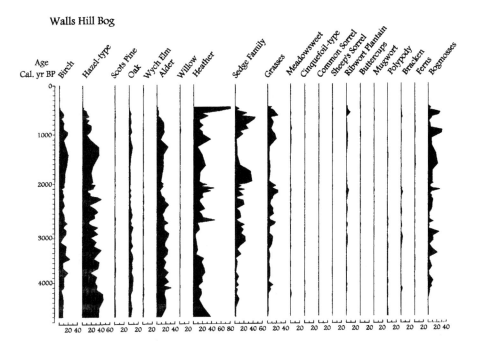

7   Susan Ramsay's pollen diagram from Walls Hill

reasons of differences in climate, topgraphy, soil and times of arrival of the different trees in the millennia after the retreat of the glaciers and, in particular, the differing regional histories resulting from human exploitation in the last several thousand years.

On the basis of the then sparse pollen diagrams from Scotland, combined with their knowledge of the remaining wildwood fragments and soil preferences, the noted plant ecologists Donald McVean and Derek Ratcliffe in 1964 published the large volume *Plant Communities in the Scottish Highlands*. A pocket in the back contains two maps, one showing the woodland cover of Scotland before human disturbance, the other giving the situation at the present day. At 6,000 and more years ago trees grew wherever it was physically possible for them to do so and the woodland cover was very extensive and divided into three big regions. In the south, in the central lowlands and extending well into the low-lying parts of the Highlands, the woodlands were dominated by Oak (see Oaks in Part 2), while in the Highlands the principal tree was Scots Pine. On the Outer Hebrides and on the Northern Isles (the latter omitted from the maps) tree Birches and Hazel predominated. Though the details can be questioned, the now many Scottish pollen diagrams have confirmed the broad picture. In the fashion of McVean and Ratcliffe, Keith Bennett (1989) published a map of the woodland cover of Britain and John Lowe (1993) has republished the Scottish part, which is here reproduced as figure **5**.

The pollen diagram from Flanders Moss East, in the upper Forth Valley (**6**), originally published by Dr Judith Turner in 1965, was one of the very first diagrams, not just from Scotland but for Britain as a whole, prepared especially to reveal in as much detail as

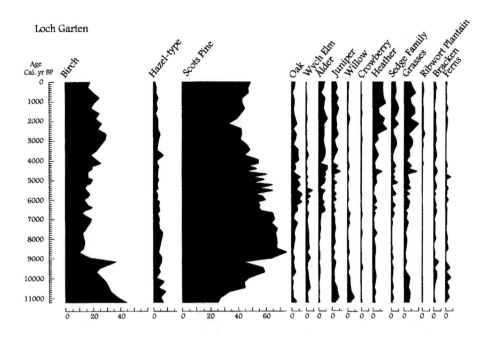

8   A modified version of O'Sullivan's pollen diagram, as reproduced in Bennett (1995), from Loch Garten in Abernethy Forest on Speyside (Steven and Carlisle 1959)

possible the effects of humans in clearing the landscape for agricultural purposes. There were also some radiocarbon dates obtained at a time when dating facilities were very few in Britain and elsewhere. As published at that time, the diagram was presented in a way now outmoded and it did not include all the many pollen types she had counted. Dr Turner has very kindly given permission for the diagram to be republished with some details not seen before and with the pollen types expressed as percentages of total pollen and spores from land plants (as distinct from aquatic plants) and excluding Bogmoss (which is expressed as a percentage of the land plants plus itself), as is usual now (**6**). For all the pollen diagrams figured in this section only selected pollen frequency curves are shown. Modern pollen analysis involves the recognition of very many pollen and spore types. Those shown here have been chosen for their appropriateness concerning the particular points being made.

Being in its present reduced configuration roughly circular and more than 3km across, Flanders Moss East is the largest remaining fragment of raised bog in the lowlands of Britain. At the site where the cores were taken by Judith Turner, JHD and Neil Alexander in 1959 (near South Flanders Farm) there are some 4m of Bogmoss-Heather-Cottongrass peat overlying several metres of coarse clay deposited when the upper Forth Valley was inundated by the sea in early to mid Holocene times. At the base of the sequence there is abundant Grass pollen which had come from the Reeds that had formed a large swamp, as the salty conditions gave way to brackish then fresh water. At a depth of 3.20m the quantity of Wych Elm pollen suddenly drops to less than 1%; that is the Elm Decline

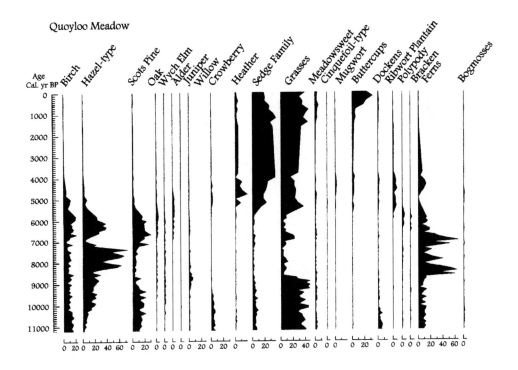

9 A modified version of Jane Bunting's pollen diagram (1994) from Quoyloo Meadow, Mainland of Orkney

which is known to have occurred about 5,800 years ago (on the basis of many calibrated radiocarbon dates) and the three radiocarbon dates straddling that very level at Flanders Moss are of that very period. The diagram shows pollen frequency of Ribwort Plantain, a rosette-forming herbaceous plant, which does not grow on very poor, markedly acid soils. It is connected exceedingly strongly with pasture and other vegetation types created by humans; see chapter 3, first section. That being the case, the occurrences of this pollen can be taken as indicating agricultural activity. That there is very little pollen of Ribwort Plantain at the level of the Elm Decline at Flanders Moss is not surprising because there have never been found any substantial traces of Neolithic people in the vicinity.

However, in the upper Forth Valley, there is much evidence of remains of Bronze Age, Iron Age and Roman occupation and in the uppermost 1.8m of the peat, formed in the last 3,000 years, indications of fluctuating human activity are very great: pasture and weedy Grasses (Gramineae, more usually now called Poaceae), very sparse cereal pollen, Ribwort Plantain and Bracken. Furthermore, the great diversity of pollen from plants other than trees is very striking and the pollen of many such plants would have been derived from agricultural ground: Fat Hen and related plants, Mugwort, Dockens and Sorrels and Cabbage family species are good examples. Not all of these are shown on figure **4**. The diagram shows that the pollen of Heather is very important, just as it is in very many Scottish pollen diagrams, particularly during the second half of the Holocene.

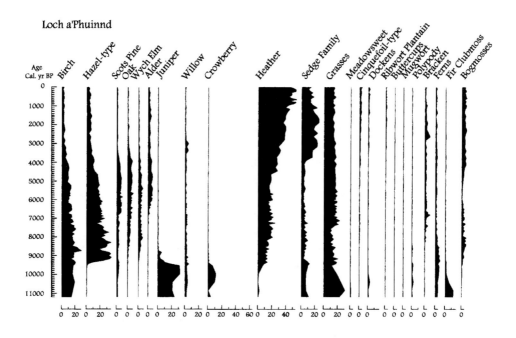

10 A modified version of Julie Fossitt's pollen diagram from Loch a'Phuinnd, South Uist, Outer Hebrides (1996)

The three radiocarbon dates of peat from the uppermost layers as published by Judith Turner are not now to be trusted, but to judge from well radiocarbon-dated diagrams (from hand-picked remains of Bogmosses from thin layers of peat) elsewhere in central Scotland, the first high peak of Grass pollen which coincides with the highest value of Ribwort Plantain (at 0.9m depth) will have resulted from pre-Roman woodland clearance by the Iron Age inhabitants. It is very desirable that the upper layers of peat at Flanders Moss should be reinvestigated and dated by the recent accelerator method. Judith Turner's other important Scottish diagram from Bloak Moss in north Ayrshire also has unsatisfactory radiocarbon dates from the uppermost 1m of peat.

Like the diagrams from Bloak Moss and Flanders Moss, the pollen diagram from Walls Hill, in Renfrewshire about 5km southwest of Paisley, comes from the area of Oak dominance (**7**). The analysed material was the topmost 2m of a Bogmoss-Heather-Cottongrass peat from a large, drained raised bog at the foot of the Hill. There are the remains of a large Iron Age fort on the top of the Hill. As in the cases of Bloak Moss and Flanders Moss, the work was carried out to investigate human disturbance but in particular to study in detail the period of some 2000 years ago so that the landscape in immediately pre-Roman, Roman and post-Roman times would be revealed. Walls Hill lies only some 14km north of Bloak Moss and the parallels between the two diagrams are very striking. There are series of small temporary clearances before the Iron Age and then extensive clearances. The radiocarbon dates from Walls Hill can be trusted and they put these extensive clearances in the pre-Roman Iron Age. See chapter 6 for a detailed discussion of the nature of the landscape in Roman times.

Only a little to the west of Walls Hill, at Machrie Moor on the Isle of Arran, also in the Oak zone, there were extensive clearances already in the Bronze Age (Robinson and Dickson 1988). That alone makes the point forcefully that regional differences in the woodland history in Scotland were very marked. In the Cairngorm area in the eastern Highlands, the woodland history was very different from that of southern Scotland even before human disturbance. The pollen diagram from Loch Garten, in Abernethy Forest, Speyside (**8**), comes from the heart of the Scots Pine region and the very striking result is the long dominance of that tree well up to the present day and the weak indications of human activity (low values of Grasses and Ribwort Plantain).

Very different again are the many pollen diagrams from Orkney and Shetland. The diagram shown here comes from the Orcadian Mainland at Quoyloo Meadow (**9**), the pollen analysis having been the work of Jane Bunting (1994). She analysed 2.6m of marly sediment. The very marked contrast with the diagrams from the Scottish mainland is the very early disappearance of the woodland cover which may never have been very dense, even if, with Alder, Oak, and Scots Pine, more diverse than argued by earlier pollen analysts such as Terry Keatinge and JHD (1979). Birch and Hazel were the principal trees and very few of those remain today, especially in the case of Hazel (see the Part 2 accounts of Birch and Hazel). The values of all the trees and tall shrubs decline from about 6,000 years ago and by about 5,000 years ago are all at very low values which never recover. Concomitantly, Grass, Ribwort Plantain and Heather pollen rise and Grass stays high right up to the present.

From the Outer Hebrides come the diagrams made by Julie Fossitt (1996) and the one shown here is from Loch a'Phuinnd on South Uist (**10**). She analysed about 2m of lake mud. Again, like Orkney, the woodlands are now thought to have been more diverse than was formerly considered (with Alder, Ash, Elm, Oak and Scots Pine) but, once again like Orkney, the present treelessness was established early. At Loch a'Phuinnd the tree pollen values all decline away gradually from some 5,000 years ago and by about 2,500 years ago are all at very low values. The Heather values are the reciprocal of the tree values; over the last 5,000 years Heather pollen has become the principal type. The Outer Hebrides in general were mainly treeless by some 2,500 years ago (see chapters 2 and 3).

In the lowlands of the Scottish mainland and in much of the Highlands the familiar treelessness, so dramatically shown on the map by McVean and Ratcliffe (1964), finally emerged within the last 1,000 years. As JHD wrote in 1992 (p159) 'A mere 1% [of the woodland cover] can be thought of as ancient semi-natural, some approximation to the wildwood, however distant'. At present the total woodland cover of about 14.5% is the result of large-scale planting, mainly coniferous, in very recent times (Roberts *et al.* 1992). On the Outer Hebrides and the Northern Isles the bleakness engendered by lack of trees and great stretches of blanket bog was already well developed in prehistoric times.

2 Mesolithic: the first woodmen?

Immigration of trees and animals after the Ice Age

By 9250 BC the British Isles were recovering from the effects of the last Ice Age, during which complex, sometimes abrupt, climatic changes affecting both temperature and precipitation had had severely testing effects on animals and plants (**11**). The climate rapidly warmed up and very soon became warm enough for most tree species to flourish, reaching one or two degrees warmer than at the present time. Because most trees had survived only far in the south and southeast of Europe, it took thousands of years for some to migrate back, dependent on wind, water or animals to disperse their seeds. Most of the familiar native trees re-colonised Britain while it was still joined to the continental mainland, before the Straits of Dover and the southern North Sea formed some 7400 years BC. Those herbaceous plants, dwarf shrubs and Birches, which were present already during the final cold period, spread very quickly, as did Willows and Junipers.

By about 8250 BC Hazel had arrived in some parts of Scotland and quickly colonised the better soils. Scots Pine arrived at different times in different areas and spread to form large woodlands. Oaks, which are very tolerant of soil conditions, and Wych Elm, which grew on the better soils, had arrived by about 7000 BC. Alder was the last major woodland tree to arrive in Scotland. It colonised the wetlands and, in places where other trees had died and left spaces in damp woodland, Alder became established.

Mammals quickly migrated, negotiating the fens which once covered the southern North Sea as well as crossing the short route of the then dry English Channel. Aurochs (wild cattle), Beaver, Elk, Brown Bear, Wild Boar, Wolf and Lynx have since died out at the hand of man (Kitchener 1998). Red and Roe Deer, Fox, Otter and Pine Martin and the smaller mammals such as Hedgehog and Red Squirrel also made their homes in Scotland.

Gatherers, hunters and fishers

Though humankind had inhabited England and Wales for hundreds of thousands of years, even if only intermittently, evidence for Palaeolithic (Old Stone Age) people in Scotland is so very insubstantial and vague as to need no consideration in this book. The earliest people to have colonised Scotland were Mesolithic folk. Some would have come overland from Europe before the sea broached the English Channel. Those travelling from the east would have come along slow flowing rivers before the southern North Sea was formed. Their transport could have been dugout canoes. Such a canoe was found last century in

11 *Chronological Table*

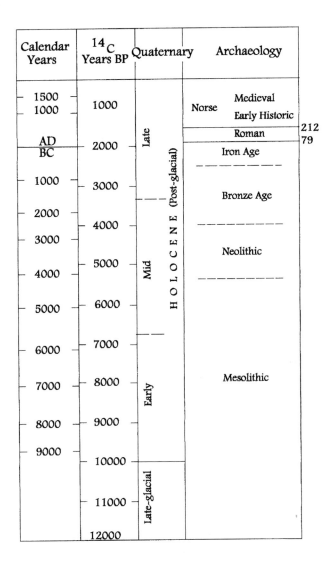

Calendar Years	^{14}C Years BP	Quaternary	Archaeology	
1500	1000		Norse — Medieval	
1000		Late	Early Historic	
AD	2000		Roman	212
BC			Iron Age	79
1000	3000	HOLOCENE (Post-glacial)	Bronze Age	
2000	4000			
3000			Neolithic	
4000	5000	Mid		
5000	6000			
6000	7000			
7000	8000		Mesolithic	
8000	9000	Early		
9000	10000			
	11000	Late-glacial		
	12000			

clay diggings near Perth; it seems from its reported position in the clay that it dates from the later Mesolithic period. Dugout canoes are unsuitable for the open sea and curraghs (skin boats) would have been used, as is discussed later in this chapter.

Scotland with its many rivers, long coastline and islands would have been an attractive place for hunter-fishermen. The western islands had lighter woodland, the growth of trees limited by the salty winds, and would perhaps have been settled by these intrepid sea voyagers in preference to the mainland with its dense forests. However, traces of Mesolithic people have been found far inland, as on Ben Lawers, in Perthshire, at the very heart of mainland Scotland.

The people were not just hunters and fishers but gatherers living mainly in temporary shelters. They had no cultivated crops to necessitate their staying in one place all the year round. The remains of their culture which survive are generally only the most durable

31

kind. Flints, post-holes, pits and hearths with charred patches, shell middens and the very common Hazelnut shells are the main finds so far from Scotland. But from Scottish pollen analyses and rare waterlogged finds from Europe we can build up a picture of the environment and peoples' exploitation of its resources between about 8,000 and about 4000 BC, the period that Mesolithic people inhabited Scotland.

Both seasonal and more permanent encampments were established to exploit the abundance of fish and shellfish. The general impermanence of dwellings is indicated by the post-holes set in a semicircle where pole framed tents were covered with whatever windproof material was to hand, skins, bark or brushwood. Stone hearths were made both inside and outside these simple shelters and sometimes remains of the last fires can be seen. These burnt layers, also found in rubbish mounds along with shells and bones wherever the soil conditions were not too acid, are the only clues we have as to the plant resources used. Wood was available in abundance, dry dead timber and twigs a ready source of fuel. Some wood charcoal, removed as large pieces during excavations, has been identified in the laboratory. Careful sieving will often reveal smaller pieces; even those of only a few mm diameter can often be identified.

Hazel scrub was extensive both on the islands and mainland until succeeded by taller trees. Some of the windswept islands, especially on their western sides, did not develop dense high woodland and the Hazel was still fully illuminated and, though in a cloudy climate, produced nuts freely.

The Inner Hebrides, Arran and the mainland

4,000 years on Rum

One of the Hazel-rich areas sought out by Mesolithic peoples was the eastern side of the island of Rum (**12**), where radiocarbon dates have provided the earliest evidence for humans in Scotland, almost 10,000 years ago. Caroline Wickham-Jones (1990) has shown by dating of Hazelnut shells that people stayed there intermittently for 4000 years. For such a long period of settlement the basic needs of food and of stone for tools must have been met. The bloodstone found on Rum provided abundant raw material and thousands of tools and waste flakes have been found. Animal bone has not survived at the excavated site but hunting and fishing would have provided much of the basic food.

Pollen analyses (Hirons and Edwards 1990) show that when humans first arrived, they would have found a sparse Birch-Hazel woodland, with Willows by the streams and on the hillsides a few shrubby or dwarf Junipers. The most windswept areas would have had an open vegetation, with sedgy mires, the habitat of Bogmosses and Horsetails. Crowberry grew on drier areas of grassy heath. In early summer, flowers of Buttercups and plants of the Dandelion family will have made the grasslands colourful, and well into late summer Meadowsweet flowered along damp streamsides.

Willows began to replace some of the Sedges and in shady places Ferns were prominent. Some 2,000 years later Alder took over from the Willows, and Royal Fern grew in wet places while Hazels still flourished and fruited abundantly. For about the next 250 years, Alder and Hazel became less in evidence and there was an increase in both Grasses

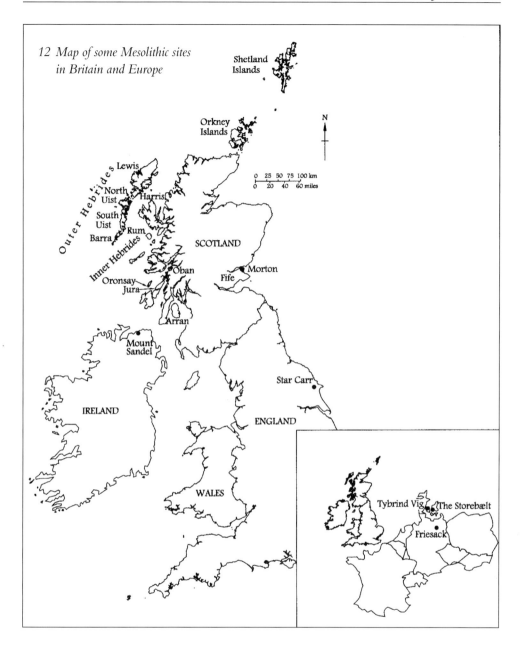

12 Map of some Mesolithic sites in Britain and Europe

and Bracken. High concentrations of charcoal were found in the pollen samples. This would seem to indicate that human fires were influencing the vegetation, but we can only speculate as to whether this burning represented a new influx of people, with consequently more wood used for domestic fires, or whether the environment was deliberately altered by burning. In this part of Rum the vegetation recovered, with possibly occasional Scots Pine, Ash or Rowan seeding in the woodland gaps. Honeysuckle clung to the trees and Ivy to trees and cliffs. An occasional Holly berry was brought in by birds and took root. The woodland remained open and both Devil's-bit Scabious and

Tormentil grew on drier slopes, perhaps in wetter habitats also, and other herbs, including Meadowsweet, flourished.

Oronsay

Signs of habitation by Mesolithic people have been discovered on many of the Scottish islands, not just on Rum. On Oronsay, the tidal island off the southern end of Colonsay, extensive shell middens of Cockles, Limpets, Mussels and Scallops, investigated by Paul Mellars (1987), now lie some distance inland, because the land has risen since the shore line activities of the ancient inhabitants occurred, as it recovered from the weight of the melting icesheets (**13**). Pollen analyses by John Birks *et al.* (in Mellars 1987) showed that, at the time of the Mesolithic occupation, Birch-Hazel scrub or woodland was widespread on both Oronsay and Colonsay and that Hazelnuts could have been collected locally on Oronsay.

Red Deer bones were retrieved by the excavators. The antler tines had been used to make Limpet scoops; Roe Deer were also caught. Wild Boar was represented mostly by selected bones of adult swine brought over from the mainland. Otters may have been caught for their pelts. Grey and Common Seal and bones of a small cetacean were identified. An excavation in 1881 and 1882 produced bones of Great Auk, Guillemot and Razorbill; subsequent work revealed the presence of Cormorant, Shag, Goose, Water Rail, Tern and Gull. Fish identified were Wrasse, Mullet, Dogfish, Skate, Tope, Angel Shark, Haddock, Black Sea-bream, Sea-bream and Spiny Dogfish; smaller bones of birds and fish were not identified. Found last century, harpoon heads of bone or Red Deer antler have since been lost. A variety of shellfish included Common Limpet, Periwinkle and Flat Winkle. The deep water Edible Crab was found.

Carding Mill Bay, Oban

A shell midden in a rock fissure at Carding Mill Bay was discovered during construction work and excavated by the Lorn Archaeological Society. Sieving for plant material produced charcoal, identified by Anne Crone, predominantly of Elm, Oak and Hazel; Willow, Rowan, Birch, Alder and Ivy were also represented (Russell *et al.* 1993). Remnants of similar species-rich woodland still exist in mid-Argyll. The other charred plant remains, identified by Sheila Boardman, mainly consisted of fragments of Hazelnut shells.

Mammal bones, identified by Finbar McCormick, include one Red and two Roe Deer bones and a single Pig's tooth, presumably of Wild Pig. Red Squirrel bones were also found; all are woodland animals. Small numbers of fish and bird bones were identified by Sheila Hamilton-Dyer, who considered that some of the fish bones may have represented the remains of Otter food. However, there were also burnt bird and fish bones and one Razorbill bone was both cut and burnt; this, together with Gull and possible Guillemot bones, were all probably part of the human diet. Cod, Saithe or Pollack, Whiting and Eel may represent both Otter and human food. The shells of the Common Limpets dominated the collection, although 18 species in all were identified by Nancy Russell. Land snails, identified by Stephen Carter, were from rock face, scree and woodland habitats. The presence of the latter throughout showed that the woodland was not greatly modified during the period, of unknown duration, when the shell midden accumulated.

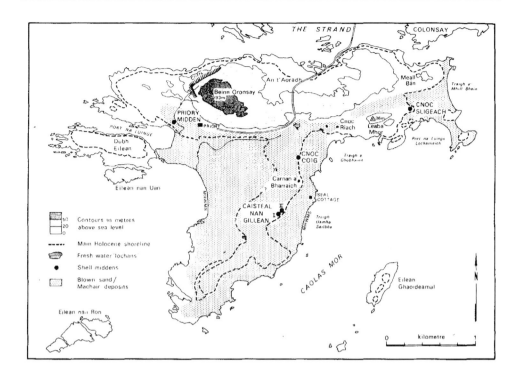

13 Map of sites on Oronsay. From Mellars (1987)

The culture of Carding Mill Bay and of other shell midden sites, confined to coastal areas of western Scotland, are called 'Obanian' and the sites have been provisionally interpreted by Clive Bonsall as special-purpose processing camps. Lacking microliths, Obanian sites consist primarily of shellfish and fish remains and range in age from the end of the seventh to the mid-fourth millennium BC. Not all shell middens are of this early date and only radiocarbon dating can provide a secure chronology.

Jura

From Glen Lussa a very late microlithic industry, investigated by John Mercer (1974), produced charcoal of Oak, Hazel, Elm, Ash and probable Willow and Sloe and Birch, identified by M.Y. Stant of the Royal Botanic Gardens, Kew. The charcoal came from the upper, shallow layer of the site which was a leached, brown, friable loam containing occupation material evenly distributed throughout. In addition, burnt Hazelnut shells, a Bramble pip and a few burnt acorn husks were identified; acorns, of course, need roasting to make them edible for humans. Acorns would not have been be an annually reliable source of food because, if the fruiting of Oaks was then as it is now, a heavy crop would have been available only at intervals of several years.

Arran: dispersed charcoal

Mesolithic presence on Arran is attested by the discovery of hearths and tools at

Auchareoch at the south of the island (Wickham-Jones 1994). Elsewhere some Mesolithic activity has been recorded in pollen cores. No artefacts were found at the site, which is Machrie Moor on the west side of the island. David Robinson (1983) showed that charcoal from a radiocarbon-dated core gave a long period of 2,000 to 3,000 years of settlement. Careful examination of the charred fragments revealed most of them to be of the Common Reed. As well as having derived from domestic fires, this herbaceous charcoal is thought to have resulted from deliberate burning of the reedswamp to drive out game and wildfowl. Temporary reduction in tree pollen, excepting Hazel, and increases in Heather and Bracken, both fire-resistant species, occurred in the two main periods of occupation. The earlier occupation is thought to have been on a seasonal basis and the later one of a more permanent nature, extends through to the Neolithic period. Frequent burning of the reedswamp during the Mesolithic occupation of Star Carr, in Yorkshire, has recently been discussed by Dark (1998).

Morton, Fife

A long period of habitation is known from mainland Scotland at Morton, in northeastern Fife, where the site was excavated by John Coles (1971). At the time of its occupation, the site became an island at high tide. Radiocarbon dating showed the presence of humans for nearly 2,000 years. Here conditions were good for bone preservation and both Red and Roe Deer, Aurochs, Wild Pig and Hedgehog bones were recognised. Sea birds were culled from nearby cliffs; Fulmar, Gannet, Cormorant, Shag, Razorbill, Guillemot, Puffin and Gull featured on the menu. Large Cod was a particular favourite and a few bones of Haddock, single bones of Turbot, Sturgeon and Salmon or Sea Trout were also recovered. The Cod, which ranged from 0.5 to over 1.0m in length, would have lived in deep water, necessitating fishing from a boat. A great range of seashells was identified, especially Common Cockle and Baltic Tellin (a cockle-like mollusc), but also including Limpet and Winkle. Edible Crab was also found. All of these are still to be found on the nearby seashore at the present time.

Hazelnuts were numerous at one site and charcoal from hearths and the extensive middens was used for dating. Unfortunately the charcoal was not identified, except that Hazel was noted, or we might have been able to reconstruct the composition of the woodland in the vicinity. Seeds of plants which are now considered arable weed seeds are a somewhat surprising addition as Mesolithic people are not known to have tilled the ground. It seems probable that these seeds had percolated down through the shallow sandy soils which underlie the present-day plough soils. Perhaps they were assisted on their downward journey by the burrowing of moles and earthworms, or were ingested and expelled by worms.

The Outer Hebrides and the Northern Isles

Boats and clothing

So far no artefacts of unequivocal Mesolithic origin have been discovered on the Outer Hebrides or the Shetland Isles. We will consider the proxy evidence from botanical sources shortly. Firstly we need to know whether suitable materials for shelter, clothing and boat repairs were available on the islands. Animal skins would have been a necessity for clothing and were probably also used to windproof rough wooden shelters. Wood and hides would also have been needed for boat repairs. There is no indication that sealskin was used in the northwest European Mesolithic, as in the Inuit cultures. No tree known to have grown in Mesolithic Scotland could have provided bark fibre suitable for clothing, like the Cedar bark used by native peoples of northwestern North America or the Small-leaved Lime Bark of the Tyrolean Iceman's cape.

How would animals have crossed to these remote islands? Was there suitable food and woodland shelter there for them? The question of how land mammals colonise islands has caused considerable discussion. Finbar McCormick and Paul Buckland (1997) point out that a land bridge existed between the Scottish mainland and Orkney shortly after 9000 years BC. Deer are known to swim between the mainland and Inner Hebrides of Scotland but the exposed waters between Skye and the Outer Hebrides and from Orkney to Shetland via Fair Isle present much greater problems. Red Deer, as it will be shown, were present on both the Outer Hebrides and Shetland in the Neolithic and it is generally agreed that they could have been trussed and transported there with domestic animals in skin boats. Specialists in ancient boat technology, Johnstone and McGrail (1980), consider that skin boats were used by Mesolithic hunters. Skin boats made from cowhides sewn together over a wooden frame have been shown from a recent experimental voyage by Tim Severin (1978) to be seaworthy in the open seas of the Atlantic ocean, although the technology used by Severin was based on that available in the sixth century AD.

The ability then to transport Deer to the Outer Hebrides would seem to have existed. Deer would have been an excellent source of protein and the skins, presumably smoke-tanned as was done by Neolithic folk, would have provided clothes, covers for shelters and hides for boat repairs. Deer are naturally woodland animals; what evidence is there for woodland on these islands in Mesolithic times?

Tree remains in the blanket peat

Did woodland exist on the now very largely treeless Outer Hebrides in the Mesolithic? The question is an important one as wood was crucial for shelter and fuel. From the now barren island of Lewis, a pollen diagram, published in 1979 by John Birks and B. Madsen, taken from the west side of the island, showed only very low tree pollen values. This suggested to the authors that only Birch and Hazel scrub were growing on the island and that other tree pollen had blown in from the mainland about 100km distant. D. Wilkins (1984) was not satisfied with that explanation and, encouraged by reports of Pine stumps of 'unknown age and provenance' on Lewis and Harris, set out to look for such stumps. In 1980 he traversed the roads across Lewis inspecting sections through the peat exposed in the peat cuttings; because the inhabitants of the Outer Isles have been dependent on peat for fuel for many centuries, he found many such cuttings. He noted 40 sites scattered across the island where tree remains were buried deep in the peat, mainly up to 20cm from the bottom but occasionally up to 50cm of peat growth lay beneath them and the base of the peat. He found wood of Birch, Scots Pine and Willow (the last named, however, need not necessarily have had the stature of trees). Small branches of Birch were buried in the peat and these and Willow branches, stumps and roots were all recovered from various sites. Large Scots Pine stumps of up to 50cm in diameter were still in the position in which they had been growing. One of the sites resembled the remains of an entire wood and Wilkins noted that 'the visual impression of an actual wood overtaken by a relatively sudden catastrophe was very strong'. As only one of these stumps was radiocarbon-dated we still do not know, however, if these trees were coeval. John Birks (1991) considered that there need be no disparity between the pollen data just mentioned and the wood remains in the peat discussed by Wilkins. Both these lines of evidence, he states (page 35) '. . . can indicate small areas of scrub in *local*, sheltered situations and a predominantly treeless *regional* vegetation'.

Remains of stumps, logs and branches of trees in peat bogs have been preserved by the water-logged, often strongly acidic peat which inhibits those organisms causing rapid decay under better oxygenated conditions. So-called because it appears to blanket the ground, blanket peat accumulates under the cool, cloudy climate with many rainy days that prevails throughout the uplands of the British Isles. Over thousands of years, the highly decomposed blanket peat may reach depths of only a few metres. Its rate of accumulation is slow and it is dark in colour and greasy in consistency with detailed plant structure hard to discern with the naked eye or even with a hand lens. It has formed the fuel still dug in the more remote Highlands and islands of Scotland. The exceptionally fine preservation of Scots Pine stumps, which often remain very hard with bark still adhering, is perhaps due to the preservative quality of the resin, typical of many conifers.

Julie Fossitt (1996) continued the search for trees and extended it to the other islands, recording a further 40 sites on Lewis, Harris, North and South Uist and Barra, with wood and associated remains identified. Like Wilkins, she had a representative selection of wood radiocarbon-dated. She also pollen-analysed two long cores going back to the Late-glacial and compared them with similar cores from Lewis and South Uist analysed by other workers. All were radiocarbon-dated at levels which showed changes in the vegetation. Alder and Hazel (nuts) were additions to Wilkins' wood identifications from Lewis. Pollen of insect-pollinated woody plants which shed very little pollen into the air and which must therefore have grown locally were Rowan and Ivy (the latter only on South Uist). Though wind-pollinated, Ash and Aspen were found in small amounts, as is usual, but perhaps enough to indicate local growth. At her site on the less exposed east side of South Uist, Oak and Elm pollen achieved sufficiently high values to show that these more warmth demanding trees had been growing in the vicinity of the pollen site; see figure **8**, chapter 1.

The extent of woodland present at any one time varied considerably in different parts of the islands, with Birch-Hazel predominating throughout. Julie Fossitt considered that early woodland was at its maximum from about 8000-7000 BC and then declined in west Lewis in less than 100 years. Blanket mires began to develop there at about 6800 BC. Other woodland trees established themselves in scattered areas. Oak and Elm seem to have been confined to the sheltered east side of South Uist where there is free drainage i.e. where blanket bog did not develop; see chapter 1. Woodland cover would have been patchy; Fossitt (p192) considers that 'In upland areas and on windward slopes, the proportion of tree-covered land would have been considerably less'. Pollen of all these trees declined between about 4000 and 2500 BC, concurrently with a spread of blanket mires until by about 600 BC peat covered much of the Outer Hebridean landscape. Neolithic settlers had arrived by the time of the tree decline.

The radiocarbon dates for the wood from the blanket peat divided into two groups. Wood tends to be preserved in blanket bog when conditions are unfavourable; this is usually when increased wetness, often due to climatic deterioration, accelerates the growth of the peat. Waterlogged ground kills most of the trees and parts of them become buried in the developing peat; the fact that they are then no longer taking up water accelerates the peat growth. Unfortunately when conditions are most favourable for tree development they are unlikely to be preserved, as Fossitt observed. The sudden decline in woodland, such as that seen in western Lewis at about 6800 BC, is not accompanied by an increase in charcoal until well after the decline was under way. The presence of charcoal is, by some, thought to indicate Mesolithic disturbance. Fossitt notes (p190) that 'Trees appear to have been killed by some disturbance event of high magnitude but short duration. An increase in the frequency and severity of westerly gales over several growing seasons could have made tree survival impossible in the most marginal areas'. Fossitt suggests that natural disturbance occurred at that time. It may be recollected that a hurricane swept through the west-central Scotland on 15 January 1968 felling many trees in a 20 mile wide swathe. Some, such as Oaks, have put up new branches from their horizontal positions, but the Scots Pines have died.

The second tree decline affected the whole of the Outer Isles beginning in different places between 4000 and 2200 BC, with the almost total replacement of woodland by peat growth by about 600 BC, as previously stated. Fossitt suggests that more than one cause is probable. The decline coincides with the early Neolithic period, so Neolithic settlers may well have been responsible. The sea level was rising and coastal areas becoming submerged; subfossil wood has been noted at low tides along the western side of the southern islands. It has also been suggested that an increase in precipitation occurred in western Scotland at about 2900 BC.

The interpretation of tree decline in areas marginal for good arboreal growth is therefore complex, and such declines cannot always be attributed to human intervention. The decline of trees and replacement by blanket mires has been noted also in the Shetland Islands, although the history of trees by examination of peat cuttings has not been undertaken there.

The presence of Hazel-Birch woodland throughout the period we have been considering has been shown in Fossitt's pollen analyses. Other trees were scattered throughout the islands and wood for fuel and shelter would have been present in all but the most exposed areas; this suggests that suitable areas would have been available for Mesolithic settlers. The west side with its machair (sandy beaches merging into fixed dunes) would have encouraged settlement. Even assuming that sufficient Deer were present to provide some meat, there would have been a heavy dependence on marine resources and sea birds would also have formed a large part of the diet. Settlements would therefore have been coastal. As we have noted, the rising sea level may have submerged sites, with associated flints, shell middens, rubbish pits and stake holes, by the early Neolithic. Sites on higher coastal ground would have been covered by the constantly shifting sands of the machair or encroachment of the peat. We need to be able to distinguish possible man-made decreases in tree pollen from natural changes, to know where to begin to search for signs of these elusive people.

Fires, natural or man-made?

Kevin Edwards (1996) has examined radiocarbon-dated pollen sites in both the Outer Hebrides and the Northern Isles of Orkney and Shetland, where microscopic charcoal has also been quantitatively recorded on pollen slides. An increase in charcoal means an increase in fires, which could pinpoint the presence of people in the area. He has been able to correlate a decrease in tree pollen with an increase in charcoal in some instances. He also suggested that heathlands may have been created or maintained as a grazing resource, as has been argued for England. A transect of sites across South Uist has shown a circumstantial link between charcoal and high Heather pollen in the Mesolithic period and at other times. All in all, Edwards considered that people are most likely to have been responsible for the fires.

Richard Tipping (1996) has discussed some of the same sites and has pointed out that periods of drier climate between about 7000 and 3800 BC are indicated by drier phases in peat bogs and lower lake levels in northern Britain. This suggested to him that some of the fires may have been natural; lightning strikes would not have burnt the deciduous woodland. Of native British trees, only Scots Pine is readily combustible, but the Heather which covered increasingly large areas of blanket peat does burn readily. Can this charcoal be attributed to Mesolithic folk or is it of natural origin? Can we distinguish charcoal from the wood of domestic fires? It has also been suggested that early peoples may have cleared part of the woodland to encourage grazing animals to feed on the resulting increase in herbaceous plants growing in the clearings. In the Outer Hebrides, as we have seen, the woodland does not seem to have been sufficiently dense to have needed opening up in this way. In Shetland it is thought that there was even less woodland. Nevertheless, supposing clearance was required, how could the woodland have been cleared? Ring barking is, of course, possible but the trees take some years to die. Fallen deciduous trees are very difficult to burn. There is as yet no evidence to show that Mesolithic peoples cut down trees, although dugout canoes could have been hollowed out with axes presumably using flint or antler blades. At Star Carr, the celebrated Mesolithic site in Yorkshire, apparent axe marks on logs have, on closer inspection, been shown to have been made by Beavers, as was demonstrated by Coles and Orme (1983).

One of the problems in interpreting the charcoal on pollen slides is that we do not know what types of plants produced it. Can some be traced to Heather? Were Grasses involved? Although charcoal on pollen slides is tiny and usually not further identifiable, larger fragments may be present in the pollen washings, the relatively coarse material remaining on the sieve when the polleniferous material has filtered through. Wind-blown charcoal can be up to 3mm in diameter and, in some instances, may be identifiable. Burnt Heather and other Heaths, with leaves, flowers and fruiting capsules, together with Heather wood, may all be preserved. Heather can be distinguished from other woods using a suitable high-power microscope with direct illumination as described in the first chapter. Other burnt herbaceous material, especially grasses, can often be identified to some degree. If heath or grass fires are suspected from an analysis, careful matching of dated, closely spaced samples from pollen cores from one area could show this on a regional basis; this would increase the likelihood of such fires being of natural occurrence or, if southern parallels are taken into account, would represent deliberate firing. If on the other hand these are shown to be wood fires, presumably of domestic origin, it is the task of the archaeologist to find the sites!

Whatever the outcome of our search for Mesolithic people in the Outer Hebrides, it seems that, at the very least, there were patches of scrubby woodland here and there on these islands and, even if only very locally, woodland with Oak, Wych Elm and Alder for the Mesolithic people to exploit.

Orkney

Hunter-gatherers spread as far north as Orkney and chance finds of flints have been made on Mainland, the largest island of the Orkney group, as well as on Papa Westray, a tiny island to the north. These windswept islands, now practically devoid of native trees (though recent planting has been made) once had flourishing woodland in sheltered areas. Pollen analyses, by Jane Bunting (1994), through the deep peat of the mires at Quoyloo Meadows on Mainland show that by about 7000 BC, Birch-Hazel scrub with some Willows and a Fern-rich understorey had developed; see figure 7. At about 5450 BC trees, Hazel in particular, showed a reduction in pollen, and Ferns and Grasses responded to the increased light as the woodland became reduced in extent. Charcoal increased slightly which may reflect local fires. The woodland decline took place over a few hundred years and is thought by Bunting to have been due to human activity. Birch regained its earlier status and Alder migrated into wetter areas but Hazel never recovered its former importance.

It would appear then, from these pollen-analysed sites, that habitation, although it may have been seasonal, continued over hundreds or even thousands of years. Furthermore, it may be that Mesolithic people had a longer lasting effect on the vegetation of lightly wooded islands than has previously been thought.

Irish and other European sites

Huts at Mount Sandel, Ireland

Since there is as yet only limited environmental evidence for Scotland, and England for that matter, it is informative to examine the evidence from a few important sites in Ireland and the north-west European mainland. At Mount Sandel, in Co. Londonderry, Peter Woodman (1985) excavated, from 1973 to 1977, the oldest Mesolithic dwellings so far found in the British Isles. They were set up on a bluff overlooking the river Bann, some distance from the sea. The occupation lasted about 500 years. The approximately circular houses, of which there were at least seven, were of two sizes, 3m and 6m in diameter. Posts had been driven into the soil to about 20cm in depth at a 60° angle pointing inwards.

Woodman considered that saplings could have been bent inwards and fastened together in the top of the dwelling. This would have avoided the need for separate roof

41

supports; flexible stems could then have been woven in and out to provide a wind and rain-proof shelter. Each hut had a central hearth dug into the soil; stake-holes found round the hearth could have provided a structure to support a skin cooking container. Rubbish, including burnt bone, was disposed of in pits.

Hazelnut shells and White Water Lily seeds were also found in the pits. Woodman has estimated the quantity of nuts required to provide four families with 20% of their food requirement for 125 days; 100g of unshelled nuts would have provided 100 calories and 625 kilos would be needed for these families. These nuts could have been collected from the Hazel scrub growing on the slope down to the river, within a 0.5km radius of the camp. This quantity would almost fill one of the pits where, Woodman suggests, they were stored for winter use. The Water Lily seeds could have been similarly stored but as Woodman points out they are very bulky in relation to their calorific value.

The bones were sieved through a fine mesh and identified by Louise van Wÿngaarden. Only heavily calcined bone had survived and 2,192 very small fragments were identified. Wild Boar had provided most of the meat, with a few bones of Mountain Hare and one of Wolf or Dog. Nearly half the Wild Boar bones were of juveniles and, assuming they were born in April or May, van Wÿngaarden suggests they had been hunted in winter. As the large herbivores, Aurochs, Elk, Red and Roe Deer were absent from Mesolithic Ireland, Wild Boar would have been an important food resource for inland hunters.

The bird bones consisted of 79 fragments; most were of Duck, with Red Grouse, Coot, Rock-dove and Song Thrush. All these are present-day residents. They were identified by Rik Maliepaard who noted that the Red-throated Diver, also recorded, only frequents the Irish coasts from October to April. Other records are of Capercaillie and Golden Eagle, which in Britain are now only Scottish residents and Goshawk, now a vagrant in Ireland, which would have been caught in traps in the woodland. Duck and Coot could have been caught in the nearby river.

1,784 fish bones were identified by Pauline Kelk who recorded 84% Salmon and Trout, 7% Eels, 8% Bass and 1% Plaice or Flounder. Salmon would have been easiest to catch in the summer and Trout would have been caught on their summer migration; both could have been smoked for later use. Eels migrate in September and October. Summer and autumn fishing is envisaged.

Before the technology of making and firing clay pots was brought to Britain by the early Neolithic peoples, meat would have been cooked mainly in a skin or paunch. John Coles (1971) has discussed experimental cooking and reported that cooking meat in water suspended in a skin is a feasible, if somewhat tricky operation. Coles quoted Herodotus (1V, 61) who describes the Scythian method of cooking meat in the animal's paunch when a cauldron was not available. As Scythia was by then treeless, the animals bones provided the fire lit beneath the suspended paunch. Coles recounts instances of the use of animal skins, suspended on four stakes, to cook beef over an open fire; this was recorded from sixteenth-century Ireland and a similar method is reported from fourteenth-century Scotland.

Although Herodotus was writing in the fourth century BC, there can be little doubt that this cooking method, known to have been used over 2,000 years later, was also used further back in time. The calcined bones from Mount Sandel suggest that they too were used for fuel, their remains later discarded in a pit. The woodland around Mount Sandel would have provided fuel from fallen trees and brushwood; perhaps readily available firewood was sometimes in short supply. It certainly suggests a disregard of, or insensitivity to, the pungent smell of burning bones! The absence of stake holes around other Mesolithic hearths may imply a different method of cooking meat. Animals can also, after disembowelling, be cooked in their skins as described by Coles. They would have been sewn up (with thongs made of sinews or strips of skin) and the skin bag roasted in the hot embers and heated sand; apparently the skin hardened and retained the juices, although meat cooked in this way was usually on the rare side.

Can we deduce whether this was a seasonal or all the year round occupation? Pigs would have provided the largest quantity of flesh per kill but may have been difficult to capture, because, as van Wÿngaarden points out, Wild Boar are solitary animals requiring a large territory of 20-200 ha, although in winter this would be reduced. Young Wild Boar would have about half the body weight of adults. Good winter Wild Boar hunting, eked out with Ducks and winter migrants and the store of Hazelnuts, would feed the community during the winter months. Nesting duck and birds, and probably their eggs, would have provided food in spring and early summer. Snaring birds, and fishing in summer, could have been supplemented with the starchy rhizomes of Water Lilies, these would have been available all the year round but would have been easier to locate when the floating leaves appeared. Woodland margins and natural clearings formed by fallen trees would have produced a crop of berries in the autumn. Fresh Hazelnuts and doubtless fish and wildfowl would have provided autumn food. Altogether, this could have been a site which was occupied all the year round, rather than seasonally, as is usually suggested for the Mesolithic period.

Careful sieving of the deposits from other Irish sites has revealed White and Yellow Water Lily seeds, some charred, and Wild Pear/Apple, in addition to Hazelnuts, all identified by Michael Monk and Jan Pals. A waterlogged site produced worked Pine and Hazel wood, broken and used as firewood; the wood may formerly have been employed as weapon shafts for hunting or fishing. The few English sites published have also produced Hazelnut shells.

Acorns, Raspberries and Yellow Water Lily seeds have been identified from Denmark and Water Lily, Water Chestnut and Apple from Sweden. From the late Mesolithic in the Netherlands, Water Chestnut, acorns and Wild Cherry have been recorded. Marek Zvelebil (1994) has compiled results which include other northern European countries. At all these northwest European sites, however, Hazelnuts are the most commonly recovered plant foods.

Tybrind Vig and the Storebælt, Denmark

Apart from food plants, there is some knowledge from northwest Europe of which plants were exploited to construct useful objects; particularly noteworthy remains were found off the coast of Tybrind Vig, in northern Jutland, Denmark, by an amateur diver in 1978 (Andersen 1987). There, rubbish thrown into Reed beds between about 5,500 and about 4000 years BC had remained continually waterlogged, protected by accumulating sediments. Two dugout canoes, one of them measuring 10m in length, were made from Lime trunks; one has a fitted stern board. Chopping marks are visible on the inner surface, made with a stone axe or adze. Even more remarkable are three ashwood paddles each carved in one piece with a heart-shaped blade on its shaft. Patterns have been cut into the wood and filled with a brown colouring matter which contrasts with the whitish wood. 'Pencils' of ochre were found at Morton, in Fife, and similar earth colours would have been mixed with animal fat to form the striking patterning. The underwater excavation produced many organic remains which showed the skilled use of plant materials for fishing. A trap similar to a lobster pot had been made from split Alder branches woven together with *Viburnum* (probably Guelder Rose) twigs. Fish spears, known as leisters, were made of Hazel wood; one was found with two prongs of Hawthorn still attached to the Hazel shaft with twisted plant fibre, probably of Nettle. A fishing line of plant fibre was still attached to a hook of Red Deer rib. Fine basketwork, textiles of plant fibres and plaited rope have been found and conserved. The workmanship of these items is of amazingly high quality.

Domestic Dog makes its first appearance with humans in this part of Europe and the hunted animals from Tybrind Vig include, in particular, Wild Boar, Red and Roe Deer; fewer bones were found of Aurochs and Wild Horse. Fur-bearing animals were represented by Fox, Pine Martin, Polecat, Otter and Wild Cat. These bones were found in clusters, each representing a single animal, the remains of animals skinned for their furs. Birds nesting and feeding in the Reed beds would have been Red-necked Grebe, Dalmatian Pelican, Greylag Goose and various Ducks. Whooper Swan would have been a winter visitor. Quail would have frequented open rough ground. Marine resources were represented by Grey Seal, White-beaked Dolphin and Killer Whale. Shellfish remains consisted of Oyster, Mussel, Clam and Periwinkle. Fishing was for Herring, Mackerel and Plaice or Flounder; with small Cod of 30-50cm in length particularly common. Salmon and Eels would have been caught in fresh water.

The presence of these remains indicates that summer, autumn and winter occupation was likely but further analysis is needed before all-year-round occupation can be confirmed.

Fish stew was on the menu, with plant material mixed up with Cod bone, skin and scales; fortunately some was burnt and the remains were found inside a pot. This was in the upper part of the deposit and marks the period of the earliest ceramics in south Scandinavia in this later part of the Ertebølle culture.

Recent excavations along the Storebælt, between the islands of Fyn and Sjaelland, (Pedersen *et al.* 1997) have added substantially to the fine results from Tybrind Vig. There are two exciting claims, the first being that Hazel coppicing was being carried out for the production of enough withies for making long fish traps, and the second a find of a digging stick, from about 6,500 years ago at Lindholm. Apart from its use for digging up palatable plants, it '. . . may also have been used as planting stick. If so, it represents an early form of 'agriculture' or 'gardening' . . .'(Dencker 1997). Similar lifestyles must have operated throughout the maritime areas of north-western Europe. Until the southern North Sea and the English and Irish channels were formed, by about 5500 BC, access to the British Isles would have been easier. Also from Denmark, at Skateholm, one burial was interred within a wooden or bark coffin. From an early Mesolithic site in Sjaelland, the floor of a rectangular building was covered with layers of Pine bark.

14 *Digging stick from the Storebælt. Right, the complete stick 117cm long, with three cross-sections. Left, detail of the bottom 22cm. The point has been worn by digging, probably for edible roots and worms. The large number of grooves across the facets are 'evidence of notches in the edge of the axe which was used to cut these faces'. Modified from Pedersen et al. (1997)*

Friesack, Germany

The inland Mesolithic site at Friesack in eastern Germany (Gramsch and Kloss 1989) yielded a paddle (made of Rowan wood), rope, nets, Birch bark floats and a container and an axe haft of Alder wood. Bast, the usable inner bark from trees such as Lime, was used to bind bone points onto a wooden shaft, some other points were secured with pitch. A carrying handle of twisted withies was found, net fragments were recognised and a hundred wooden artefacts of Alder, Hazel, Pine and Aspen/Poplar included a wooden trough-like vessel, with pointed ends, as well as arrows and spears.

Some of the many other recently excavated European wetland sites of Mesolithic times have been discussed in books by Bryony and John Coles (1989, 1996).

Edible roots, green parts and berries

In addition to the digging stick mentioned above, antler mattocks have been recovered from coastal and riverine situations in Britain and Europe. It has been suggested that one of the uses of these mattocks was to dig up the underground parts of plants for food.

The use of wooden implements to obtain food may well be worthwhile in the tropics but when we come to consider the edibility of roots, rhizomes and tubers in north-western Europe there are few that are palatable, nutritious and readily acquired in any quantity. All the European edible tubers are small and those of Pignut are difficult to grub up; they range from pea to chestnut in size and used to be eaten by children even in modern times. Tubers of Pignut (or perhaps those of Great Pignut) were found with a Bronze Age cremation in Oxfordshire (Moffett 1991). Bitter-vetch has small edible tubers but these are even more elusive than those of Pignut! In his travels around the Highlands in 1768, James Robertson noted that on Mull the inhabitants ate Bitter-vetch tubers to prevent intoxication and on Skye to allay thirst and faintness (Henderson and Dickson 1994). The large starchy rhizomes of Waterlilies can form a thick interwoven mass in shallow to deep water. These are known to have been eaten by Finns and Russians and any charred remains should be recognisable in the ashes of long-dead fires. Wild Carrot is mainly a coastal plant. Its thin roots used to be eaten in the Hebrides. The slender roots of Silverweed are edible and, when the plant grows on the sandy seashore, it is not too difficult to dig them up; boiled or roasted they are said to taste like Parsnips and have been eaten in the Hebrides in times of scarcity. In the opinion of the present authors, the considerable expenditure of energy involved in digging and preparing such roots would scarcely have been made up by the calories gained in eating them. However, the First Peoples of northwest North America certainly did dig up and eat the roots of Silverweed; see chapter 10.

More profitable will have been the gathering of berries during the limited season when they ripen. Spread in the droppings of various animals which enjoy these tasty fruits, Brambles would have colonised cleared areas and margins of woodlands The berry season is short in Scotland, beginning with Bilberry in heathy and lightly wooded places in July, occasional Wild Strawberry, then Wild Raspberry, another woodland margin plant, and Brambles in August and September. As the climate was a little warmer then, the danger of losing many of the Blackberries to early frosts may not have been so prevalent and in coastal areas, in particular, Brambles may have continued to ripen until the Hazelnut harvest was ready. Other fruits such as Cranberries and Crowberries are edible but less widely available. The small seeds of all these plants should be looked for in the charcoal dust although most will have been eaten raw, leaving no trace in the fossil record. In spring and summer various wild Cresses would have grown in waterside and woodland clearings. Many are edible, as are young tree leaves and Wych Elm fruits but the only significant source of plant protein would have been Hazelnuts.

3 Neolithic: the earliest plant-rich middens

Six-thousand years ago: the first farmers and the Elm decline

Around 4000 BC new cultures (New Stone Age people) began to spread throughout Scotland. Incomers from Europe arrived bringing with them cultivated seedcorn, domesticated animals and round-bottomed pots for cooking and storage. They still used flaked stone tools, but they also now made highly polished axes, mace-heads and knives for ceremonial as well as practical purposes. It can only be speculated as to how they may have mixed with the Mesolithic peoples, with whom they must have overlapped in many areas. The Neolithic farmers spread throughout not only the low-lying areas of mainland Scotland but also the islands including Arran and the Outer Hebrides as well as Shetland and Orkney where they left some of the most impressive stone monuments in Europe (Barclay 1997).

Pollen diagrams from that time in Britain, Ireland and adjacent Europe, including Scandinavia, frequently record a readily recognisable change in the amounts of Elm pollen. Whether the results are expressed as percentages or in absolute terms, Elm pollen values show a very sharp drop (**4**, chapter 1). When Elm is discussed in a Scottish prehistoric context in all likelihood the species is Wych Elm and that species alone. In England there is a taxonomic complexity of the genus *Ulmus*, which may be of very long standing and perhaps compounded by ancient introductions. In Scotland, however, there is no compelling reason to assume native status for any other species than Wych Elm.

Known simply as the Elm Decline, this dramatic decrease has been dated many times to close to 3800 BC. The causes have been discussed over and over again. Dutch Elm disease is likely to have been a major cause. The ability of the beetle-spread, pathogenic fungus to move swiftly through the country has been recently demonstrated in Britain, with all too drastic results in England and, even if less sweeping in Scotland, still severe there, at least locally. It is also notable that leaves of Elm, of whichever species, make very palatable, nourishing food for animals. Leafy branches have been collected for drying as winter fodder almost up to the present time in Scandinavia and elsewhere. Elms grow on the better soils and it may be that Elm woodlands were cleared preferentially for agriculture. A combination of these two causes, disease and exploitation, may be the best explanation.

The Elm Decline marks the first widespread change in the Scottish woodland composition, that is likely to have been due in part to humans. It represents a suitable marker for early human influence on the vegetation, not just in Scotland but throughout north-western Europe wherever Elms grew. Grass and Ribwort Plantain pollen are frequent accompaniments, sometimes with Bracken spores and pollen of other herbaceous plants. Such pollen grains indicate that openings had been made in the forest canopy which allowed these light-demanding plants to flourish.

Usually, these woodland clearances were associated with pastoralism. Crop growing, however, is indicated by pollen of arable weeds such as Goosefoot, Mugwort and Docks. Unfortunately some of the most common arable weeds, Knotgrass, Black-bindweed, Chickweed and Hemp-nettle are insect-pollinated and their pollen is only sparsely represented in the fossil record because little will have been released into the atmosphere. Very occasional grains of cereal-type pollen may be found in peats or lake muds. Cereal flowers, except for those of Rye, are self-pollinated, and their pollen is usually only recovered from deposits that had formed very close to the cereal fields (or associated with chaff in pits).

Rare occurrences of cereal-type pollen have been identified from levels below that of the Elm Decline in some pollen profiles. This has claimed as an indication of a sparser pioneer agriculture, which may date back to several centuries before the decline in Elm pollen. However, it should be stressed that there may be difficulty in distinguishing cereal pollen grains from those of certain wild Grasses (CD 1988) and it is helpful if these non-cereal species are taken into consideration by the pollen analyst when making a claim of very early cereal cultivation.

The stone village at Skara Brae, Orcadian Mainland

The Neolithic diet at Skara Brae and elsewhere
The evidence for Neolithic arable farming is limited for the whole of the British Isles. In southern Britain, burnt remains of cereals, crop weeds and collected wild plants such as Crab Apple, Wild Cherry, Raspberry, Bramble, Sloe and Hawthorn have been recorded, though mainly as rare finds. As was the case in the Mesolithic, Hazelnut shells have been found at most sites. Finds of gathered fruits has been made in Scotland but the plants producing such edible fruits diminish in frequency in the northernmost areas. Rowans grow on both Orkney and Shetland, Bramble may be native to Orkney but Raspberry is not, and neither occur on Shetland. There are trees which no longer grow on Orkney but did so about 6,000 and more years ago; wood and charcoal of Bird-cherry, Wild Cherry and Sloe suggest that fruits from such trees were formerly available, even if the quantities were small. One very marked exception to the generally limited range of plant remains recovered from Neolithic sites is the best preserved Neolithic village in northern Europe. At Skara Brae on the west coast of the Mainland of Orkney (**15-17**) it is fortunate that the midden/occupation deposits around the stone houses have remained in part waterlogged revealing a rich flora and fauna, which allow many deductions about the environment, exploitation of resources and diet. Superlatives are often and rightly applied to Skara Brae. A few examples are from David Clarke (1998, pp8-10). It is 'the best preserved prehistoric village in northern Europe'; 'No other site in northern Europe provides a comparable insight into the three-dimensional use of domestic space by an early farming community'; and 'It perhaps needs emphasising that villages among early farming communities in Britain outside of Orkney are virtually unknown'.

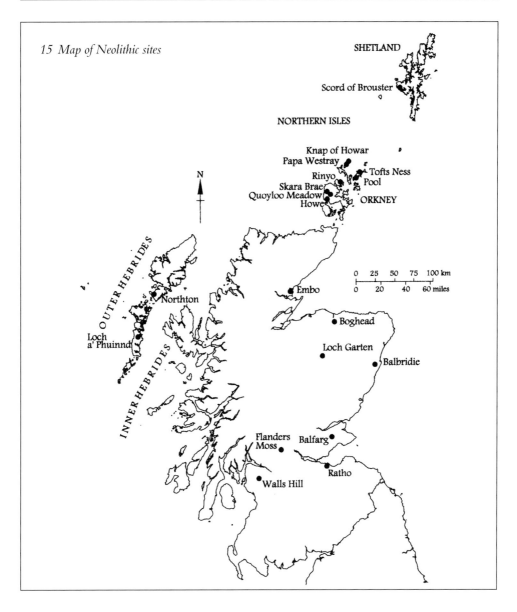

15 Map of Neolithic sites

The bone identifications have yet to be fully published but a summary by David Clarke and Niall Sharples (1985) notes that there were roughly equal numbers of bones of Cattle and Sheep; Cattle include those the size of Aurochs, the wild ancestor, and the Sheep resemble the small modern Soay breed. The hair of Soay Sheep is plucked nowadays for spinning and weaving although there is no archaeological evidence for this. There were a small number of Pig and Deer bones. Sheep require an open environment, whereas Aurochs and Pigs are by nature woodland animals. It will be shown later how this fits in with the evidence from the pollen and larger plant remains. Whales and Seals were hunted, Gannets were being exploited and large quantities of Cod and Saithe, plus freshwater Eel and Trout, suggest that the fishing that took place was coastal and in lochs.

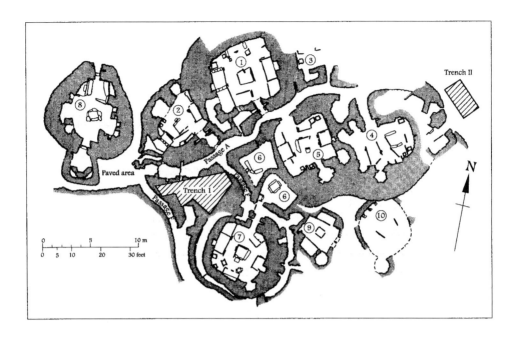

16 Plan of Skara Brae. With permission of Historic Scotland

As at Papa Westray (discussed later), numerous Limpet shells may reflect their use for bait; they were possibly softened in water in clay-sealed, stone slab boxes, which were found in the houses.

More information is available on the animal foods eaten in later Neolithic Orkney from the chambered tombs at Isbister and Quanterness, contemporary with Skara Brae. These also produced animal bones and, among the fish bones, Corkwing Wrasse is an interesting addition, since it lives in warmer waters at the present time. These and other occupation sites in Orkney confirm the importance of Sheep and Aurochs in the diet with Red Deer and Pigs in small numbers. The few finds from Shetland are similar but Pigs are lacking. On Harris, in the Western Isles, Sheep bones predominate with lesser numbers of Aurochs, Red Deer and Pig. Grey and Common Seal were hunted; Crabs, Lobsters and Cockles eaten. Little bone is preserved from other Scottish Neolithic sites where the soils are predominantly acid. Taken together, all these sites suggest that on the Scottish islands, Sheep and Aurochs were the main sources of animal foods with smaller numbers of Red Deer and Pigs. Fish, shellfish and cetaceans seem to have been of lesser importance.

The evidence of plant food in the later Neolithic is chiefly from the Orkney islands. At Skara Brae, organic deposits representing several hundred years from around 3100 to 2450 BC were sieved for larger plant remains. Somewhat surprisingly, cereals were only found in the oldest deposits and these are mainly of Naked Six-row Barley with a very small proportion of Hulled Barley. Twenty of 239 grains are of Emmer Wheat. Grains of both Wheat and Naked Barley from the Neolithic site of Boghead, Moray, on the Scottish mainland, are larger than those of both Skara Brae and Ness of Gruting, a Shetland site to

17 The first excavation of Skara Brae. Professor Gordon Childe can be seen about to climb a ladder, bottom left. With permission of Historic Scotland

be discussed later. It has been suggested that the climate in the more northerly latitudes was then less favourable to the growth of cereals, a situation which has not changed since. Naked Barley is the only cereal present at Barnhouse, a settlement further inland on the Mainland than Skara Brae. Though recovered from many contexts it occurred only in small numbers. Low numbers of grains were recorded from the Neolithic levels at Pool, on Sanday; these are mainly of Naked Barley with a little Hulled grain. At the other end of the Mainland, at Tofts Ness, larger Hulled grains predominate, but the Naked grains are all small.

It may seem strange that such a small range of plants have been found associated with people who from their choice of animal foods had continued the foraging traditions of the Mesolithic. It must be remembered that leafy plants which may have been used as pot-herbs would only be recognisable if their seeds had survived as burnt residues fortuitously preserved on pot fragments. As most pot-herbs are eaten young before flowering, the recovery of seeds seems highly improbable. Pots full of charred weed seeds have been found at Danish Iron Age sites, but as far as the writers are aware not in Britain. The weeds may have sprung up in fallow fields, or among failed crops, and also formed the food of the poor at times of famine in later times.

There are, then, several sites of early and later Neolithic age which have produced both animal and plant foods, the latter consisting overwhelmingly of Barley. The large number of bones recovered from these mainly coastal sites include those of mammals, sea birds, fish, molluscs, cetaceans and seals. A diet dominated by animal foodstuffs is indicated. Of considerable interest is the number of Sheep bones found; these are usually at least as numerous as the Cattle bones. Unlike Cattle, most modern breeds of Sheep do not feed in woodland; they are primarily grazers and avoid coarse vegetation. They will, however, eat young Heather when food is scarce in winter. The well-known flock on the island of North Ronaldsay, are related to the Soay Sheep and to the primitive Sheep of Shetland and Iceland. They subsist almost entirely on seaweed. A plentiful supply is thrown up by storms on the foreshore to which they are largely confined. What do we know of Neolithic vegetation and its suitability for flocks of Sheep?

Flora, vegetation and the origin of the occupation deposits

The midden/occupation deposits surrounding the houses at Skara Brae which yielded quantities of bones also produced seeds and other plant remains, especially from the parts which had remained permanently waterlogged. Over 80 different types of plants were recognised from their fragments. By knowing what type of habitats they grow in now it is possible to reconstruct the vegetation growing around the settlement at about 3000 BC.

Most sites produce charred cereal grains and weeds of arable fields but such grain was only found in the earliest deposits and none of the seeds of arable and waste ground were charred, as would have been the case if they had been processed with the corn. Seeds of Chickweed, Curled Dock, Greater Plantain, Knotgrass, Shepherd's Purse and Wild Turnip are among those identified. All of these could have grown equally well on waste ground as in arable fields and therefore do not necessarily indicate arable farming in the later stages of habitation, when cereal grains are missing from the record. Plants of grassland, heaths and mires form the main group of plants and over 40 different species were recognised in this broad category.

Small Sedges which grow in damp grassland and flushes were present together with Rushes. Other grassland plants include Meadow- and Bent-grasses, Red Fescue, Hawkbit, Ribwort Plantain, Selfheal, Common Mouse-ear, Creeping and Meadow Buttercups. Heathland plants are represented by Heather and Bracken, both in small quantity, as well as Heath-grass, Heath Rush and Tormentil. Occurrences of Crowberry and Cross-leaved Heath were rarely recorded.

Particularly nutritious plants for grazing animals are White Clover and Meadow Vetchling. Many of the above plants, including White Clover, grow in a well-grazed short sward of closely packed plants; this develops over many years of grazing on base-rich soils. Such man-made grassland needs fairly intensive grazing or the Heather and coarser species achieve dominance. Given such continual grazing, the richness of the pasture is maintained.

Other plant remains recognised are those of aquatic and waterside plants. Those particularly well represented are Common Spike-rush, Gypsywort, Lesser Spearwort, Marsh Marigold, Marsh Pennywort, Marsh Violet and Ragged Robin. Gypsywort is of particular interest as it no longer grows in Orkney and is uncommon in northern

Scotland. Seeds of these plants are known to remain floating for days or even months, thus aiding their dispersal. The most likely explanation for their presence is that they were scooped up with domestic water. Where did this water come from? At the present time, the nearest body of fresh water is the Loch of Skaill only about 0.6km from the settlement. But at the time of its early occupation the area of the present bay would have been one of small lochans providing a freshwater supply closer to hand. All except the Marsh Violet grow in the loch, or in the fen which borders one side at the present time.

The presence of such a wide mixture of plant species merits an explanation. Excavation has shown that the later houses were part of a long build-up of midden, construction and occupation debris. How did all the seeds and other plant remains become part of the midden/occupation deposits? This seemed a difficult question to answer until a quantity of hitherto unidentified roots and rhizomes (underground stems), which had been sieved by the excavators, were examined. Some had been preserved because they had been burnt and some of the larger unburnt fragments appeared wrinkled as though dried.

In order to identify the tough perennial structures of roots and rhizomes, a charring experiment was carried out by CD. Fresh roots and rhizomes were collected and dried, then heated in wood ash at about 220°C for an hour or two until thoroughly charred. This method has been found to be most similar in its effect to burning in a fire. Roots will probably then resemble their ancient counterparts but rhizomes, such as those of grasses and sedges, may have leaves and papery scales attached that obscure the tough, durable part of the rhizome. These have to be rubbed off before they can be compared with the sub-fossils. Each of the delicate rhizomes may only measure a few mm in length and less than 3mm across. To confirm the identification, the best-preserved cells of the sub-fossils were examined at magnifications of about x200 and x300, using a microscope with illumination from above. Sedges (*Carex*) have distinctive rhizomes, with characteristic surface cells that are quite different from those of Grasses. A different type of Grass remains are burnt fragments of the basal spikelets of the Heath-grass, some containing Grass seeds. These form at ground level and are diagnostic for the species.

By this charring method it proved possible to identify the rhizomes of small Sedges and those of Grasses, some resembling those of Mat Grass. Woody root fragments of Tormentil were particularly abundant in the midden, some had been burnt and others were wrinkled as though dried but unburnt. It was concluded that the abundance of roots and rhizomes (together with soils of a silty and clayey admixture which make up the bulk of the deposits) must have derived from turves cut from grassy heaths and damp sedgy areas.

These degraded turves must have formed the bulk of the deposits, although they lacked any traces of the original turf lines. They were seemingly not cut for use as insulation but were more likely to have been reused perhaps after partial disintegration. Their original use is unknown; they may have been used for roofing under a sturdy close framework of cleft wood or whalebone. Turf roofs have been used in the recent past in Orkney and Shetland; in Orkney, sometimes in combination with thin flagstones.

The burnt fragments suggest that turves may also have been used to keep the fire in at night. It is unlikely that turf was used as primary fuel, as it would have been difficult to dry and, furthermore, each would have a high inorganic content composed of several cm of soil. Instead of solving the origin of the mass of occupation deposits, we seem to be left with more questions!

Medicinal and other useful plants

There is no knowledge of the illnesses that the Skara Brae folk may have suffered from apart from one hint. A not totally unexpected find on the pollen slides prepared from the Skara Brae midden was of two eggs of the parasitic nematode Whipworm (*Trichuris trichiura*) which lives in the human colon. If the burden of the parasite is light the bearer may not be aware of it but, if heavy, then diarrhoea or even dysentery can result. Such infestations were common from the Iron Age onwards but seldom are suitable samples available from earlier periods. Examination of the colon contents of the 5,300 year old Iceman whose very well preserved body was found high in the Alps in 1991 also revealed these eggs (Dickson *et al.* 2000b). It is becoming very evident that Whipworm has been very widespread both in space and time in Europe. So perhaps some of the Skara Brae folk were weakened by trichuriasis.

Frequent rhizome fragments from 9 to 30mm long with longitudinal wrinkles were recovered (**18**).

They proved to be Yellow Iris, which is not a species of grassy turf. This Iris has a tough rhizome measuring about 15mm across when fresh. If a fresh rhizome is cut and then dried it strongly resembles the Skara Brae material. Slight charring of a very few pieces suggests that the rhizomes may have been left by the fire to dry. The rhizomes contain acrid substances when fresh and were therefore most unlikely to have been collected for food. They also contain a black dye but a mordant (to bind the dye onto the cloth) of a metallic substance such as an iron compound or alum is needed. There is no evidence that such a technique was known to Neolithic peoples. Two carbonised fruits of Yellow Iris were recovered from Early Historic layers at Ratho near Edinburgh (Smith 1995) and one of the fruits was found with loomweights; this led Tim Holden to favour dyeing as the explanation rather than medicinal uses.

To find a plausible use we need to look at the medicinal properties of *Iris*, a genus with many species. The rhizomes of most species contain substances with cathartic and astringent properties, which have resulted in herbal use of the rhizomes for at least the last 2000 years, as recorded in the literature, continuing down to almost the present time. They have been used as purgatives as well as to stop diarrhoea and, in post-Medieval times, to staunch bleeding. Use to ease the pain of toothache has been recorded in the recent past on Orkney by Smith Leaske. For the Highlands and Islands, Mary Beith (1995) mentions the use of Yellow Iris to relieve colds (a snuff was made from the roots) and to cure toothache and sore throats. The chewing of the rhizome of Wild Flag of coastal Alaska is thought by the Tanaina Indians to help colds and sinus problems and the chewed rhizome is placed on sores (Kari 1995). Another possibility comes from vessels from the Greek Bronze Age; organic residue analyses have pointed to oil of Iris; one vessel contained 'a complex preparation for cosmetic use' and 'In addition to iris oil, olive oil is indicated, and pine resin.' (John Evans in Tzedakis and Martlew 1999, p50).

There can be no certainty about the precise use of Yellow Iris some 5,000 years ago at Skara Brae. The diet does seem to have been overwhelmingly of meat and fish and lacking in plant fibre. Is it too frivolous to wonder that perhaps purgatives were required or conversely that anti-diarrhoeal measures were required?

Another possible form of medicine, not from a plant but from a fungus, has been deduced from the presence of a number of mature Puffballs found in the middens (**19**). Identified by Roy Watling, they are too mature to have been collected for food but the internal woolly material has haemostatic qualities and can be used to staunch bleeding. Surgeons in the late nineteenth century used puffball powder in just such a way. Some farmers used to string them up to dry by the kitchen fire in case of emergency. The use of sharp stone knives to clean skins and for many other uses could have called for their frequent use to staunch bleeding. Use as tinder is a less likely possibility. Mary Beith (1995) states that smoke from the burning, mature puffballs has been used to stupefy wild bees.

From the wettest midden an exciting find was several fragments of a Crowberry rope formed by twisting two bundles of slender stems together (**20**). These had been carefully selected to avoid branching stems. The ropes were neatly finished by bending back some of the stems and threading them through the rope. None of the evergreen leaves were preserved; stripping them off initially would have made a tighter rope. The rope fragments measure no more than 2cm wide and it has been suggested that they were used to tether animals. The tradition of rope making in Orkney and Shetland, where such ropes were called simmons, continued almost up to the present time and came to an end only as thatched roofs were replaced with corrugated iron and other materials. A few people still make them for demonstration purposes. Crowberry was used up to the 1900s and when it became scarce it was replaced by Heather or straw rope. Such ropes were thick and a web of simmons was used to secure thatch.

One of the Sedges recognised from rhizome fragments was the Greater Tussock-sedge which inhabits wet woods or swampy areas. Well-grown plants, which can measure up to 1.5m high by 1m across have a remarkable appearance. The dead rhizomes and roots form a pedestal, strong enough to sit on. This is covered by a luxuriant growth of narrow leaves that grow from the top and hang down. In the past these tussocks were cut off at their bases, trimmed and used as fireside seats by poor cottagers and for hassocks in churches in Norfolk, England (Ellis 1965). Such tussocks could have been deliberately collected, perhaps from an area to the north of Skara Brae where the species still grows. Their convenience for seating is clear; large tussocks would have suited adults and smaller ones could have been collected to suit the younger members of the family. When the tussocks began to disintegrate, perhaps they provided a supply of suitable tinder for the fire. Perhaps this is one way in which the burnt rhizomes could have become incorporated in the middens.

Wooden artefacts

Very few wooden artefacts have been identified from the British Neolithic simply because waterlogged deposits have rarely been found. A lakeside dwelling at Ehenside Tarn, Cumberland, was drained last century and wooden artefacts were found and drawn but not conserved. A stone axe with a wooden haft, clubs and fish spears were also recovered. This was clearly a permanent settlement as broken pots and Cattle bones were also found.

18 *Pieces of the underground stem of Yellow Iris. The largest is 31 x 11mm*

The Sweet Track in the Somerset Levels is an early Neolithic trackway with a 'road' of planks, some of which had been radially cut from trunks of about 0.6m diameter. The trackway was built to cross low-lying peaty ground; peat had subsequently grown over it and preserved it and other artefacts such as a spear, bows, arrow shafts, probable paddles, a knife of Hazel wood, an Oak dish and an arrow head in a Hazel wood shaft bound with Nettle fibres. Two longbows made of Yew were found in the Somerset Levels in the 1960s (Clark 1963). A chance find from Scotland in the nineteenth century is a fragment of an arrow shaft, made of Guelder Rose. Much more recently, a longbow of Yew about 1.78m long was found sticking out of the peat at Rotten Bottom, in the Tweedsmuir Hills; the radiocarbon date shows it to have been lost between 4,000 and 3600 BC. Finally, mention must be made of the hafted axe from Shulishader, eastern Lewis; 'the single-piece wooden axe haft had an oval socket into which was fixed a stone axehead, possible of Antrim porcellanite' (Ashmore, 1996, p55).

Although numerous small pieces of wood and charcoal were salvaged from the wettest midden layers at Skara Brae, few of these show definite signs of deliberate shaping. The most outstanding find is a handle, broken where the stone blade was inserted. It is made of Willow and now measures 20cm in length (**21**). The wood was carefully chosen for its broad base and straight shaft, such as would have grown from a coppiced stem. Bark and twigs had been removed but there had been little shaping. There seems to be nothing similar in the few handles from the British Neolithic but a very similar, though longer, handle has been illustrated from the Danish early Neolithic.

Ash wood makes a more resilient handle but that wood was scarce in Neolithic Scotland. Although Willow wood is softer it has been used for a mattock handle in Germany. When we consider that wooden handles have been made for thousands of years, relatively few still survive from prehistoric times. It is only recently that a suitable preservative for wood finds has been developed. Conservation with polyethylene glycol (PEG) can now preserve wood in its original form and sections can still be discretely cut from preserved wood to identify it.

There is a broken spatula measuring 4.6cm across at the wider end and 6-10mm thick. To judge from the curvature of the annual growth rings, it had been cleft from a mature

Scots Pine trunk of about 40cm diameter; cutting in this way would have given the spatula maximum strength and minimum splitting of the wood fibres. There is wear and superficial charring along the working edge. This would seem to be the result of scraping the bottom and sides of a container. The broken end is completely charred, such as would have occurred if the handle of the spatula had been placed on a hot hearth stone. The similarity in shape to that of a modern spatula is striking; the ideal shape had been worked out by some 5000 years ago!

Two long stirring rods, each with a rounded slightly charred end, are of Elm wood; they may have been used to stir the stew pots. Wooden spoons have been recorded from the continent but not as yet from Britain, although two 'spurtles', one of them associated with a pottery vessel, have been found at the Sweet Track in the Somerset Levels.

Four small pieces of barkless Bramble wood, up to 29mm long, were a rather surprising find. Apparently, if the bark and prickles are stripped off, a fibrous core remains which can be used as tying material. This may well have been its use at Skara Brae. Many other pieces of wood appear to have been cleft. This may have been to chop them into smaller billets for firewood. A number of small branch pieces also suggest that much of the wood was collected for firewood.

A

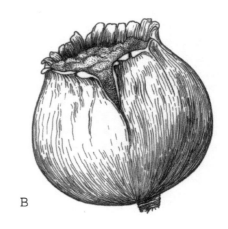

B

*19 A. Looking like a piece of leather, this is the skin of a Puffball fungus (*Bovista nigrescens*) from Skara Brae. It measures 67 x 53mm. B. A drawing to show the appearance of the Puffball when alive. With permission of Historic Scotland*

Firewood from nearby and far afield

Charcoal was found scattered throughout the middens; although wood was absent from the drier deposits. Birch charcoal was slightly more common in the earlier middens (about 3100 BC) otherwise there seemed little change in the different proportions over time. The over 300 wood fragments that have been identified derive from 17 different types of trees and tall shrubs. More than 500 charcoal fragments, from 17 or 18 types of woody plants, were recovered from the wettest midden (about 2450 BC). About 27% of the wood is of driftwood; these pieces are overwhelmingly of Spruce, with a little Weymouth Pine and

20 Crowberry rope from Skara Brae. The pieces are about 10cm long

0   5cm

Larch, probably American Larch. None of these are native to Scotland but all grow on the coasts of North America. Before these coastal forests were chopped down by European settlers, great logs were frequently encountered by sailors sailing near to the Scottish islands. Studies of marine currents have shown that driftwood from eastern North America is the most likely source of that wood. Spruce fragments, in particular, show galleries bored by a marine worm (*Teredo* sp.), thus proving that the wood had been seaborne; such wood could remain afloat for many months at a time. There is no doubt that straight conifer trunks were used by the inhabitants of the Northern Isles and Hebrides, and at all the coastal archaeological sites where wood has been identified, wood or charcoal of these exotic conifers has been found (JHD 1992). The straight logs could be used for internal supporting posts or cleft for roofing timber. Because of the strong winds which are a feature of these islands, the trunks of the native trees were dwarfed and twisted. If rollers were needed to transport standing stones or building stones for the massive tombs that are an outstanding feature of the later Neolithic, the relatively straight driftwood would be the obvious logs to choose.

The earliest brewhouse in Britain?

Arguing from the structural remains and pottery, Merryn and Graham Dineley (2000a and b) have very recently produced a new, exciting interpretation of the purpose of the huts at Skara Brae. They state (2000a) 'In Hut 8, they [the inhabitants] had a well crafted and versatile grain barn for storage, threshing, winnowing and malting as well as a kiln for drying the malt. They had large pots with lids, suitable as fermentation buckets, and a drainage system. Other Neolithic sites on Orkney, such as Barnhouse and Rinyo, are also suitably equipped.' The green deposit that Childe had considered to be excrement '. . . seems more likely to be the decayed residues of sugars from spillage of malt liquors that was either being processed or consumed in Huts 4, 5 and 7'.

Other sites on the Northern Isles and the Outer Hebrides

Two houses at Knap of Howar, Papa Westray, Orkney

The earliest known Scottish houses were oval or straight sided, probably had turf or earth walls and have consequently left little evidence except for post holes. They have been found scattered in the western part of Scotland and date from before 3500 BC. However, the best preserved early Neolithic houses are on Orkney on the coast of the small island Papa Westray (Ritchie 1983). Lived in for several hundred years, from about 3600 to 3100 BC, they were built of the local flagstone, which splits easily to give very durable building stone. There are two houses (**22 & 23**), each with its own entrance, and there is an adjoining passage. The first house has two rooms and the second house has a hearth and stone cupboards and was probably used as a workshop.

Small fragments of wood and conifer charcoal were extracted from a post-hole which probably once contained a roof-supporting post. Other charcoal was of Birch and Alder, as well as of Spruce driftwood which had floated from North America. In the extensive middens, rare grains of Naked Six-row Barley and a Hazelnut fragment were the only plant material found. Used presumably to grind the corn, two large saddle querns were found, but shell fragments used to temper the pots were associated with one of the querns so they may have had grinding functions unconnected with food.

These two houses had been dug into an existing midden so earlier houses must have existed. Midden material were also used as wall core in both the houses to help provide insulation. An extensive midden-rich soil deposit stretched for 20m to the south of the houses. This may indicate that midden was liberally spread to form a rich substrate on which to grow cereals and suggests, at this early stage of farming in Britain, that the value of fertile soil to produce good crops was appreciated.

21 Wooden handle from Skara Brae. The fragment is 19.7cm long and 5.2cm at the widest part

Pottery was recovered from the floors and the occupation deposits into which the houses were set. Petrological analyses by D.F. Williams established that all the pottery and a small polished stone axe were of local materials. Both midden and floors produced a range of artefacts, all also of local materials. Artefacts unique to the Knap of Howar are pitted grinding stones, each a fist-sized cobble with a worn pecked dimple in the centre of the ground surface. These were noted by R.R. Inskeep to be similar to stones in southern Africa, used by hunter gatherers to grind seeds of wild plants. However, they appear not to have been recorded from the Mesolithic or Upper Palaeolithic in Britain. It seems, from the small quantities of cereals found, that plant foods were not the main means of sustenance and, as a comparison with Mesolithic diets, it is of interest to consider the

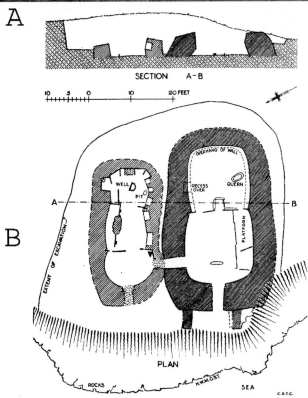

22 Knap of Howar houses — the earliest houses yet found in Scotland. With permission of Historic Scotland

abundant remains of animal foods from this and other sites.

As at most excavations planned from the 1970s onwards, a team of specialists, some of whom have already been mentioned, was assembled to ensure that all artefacts and biological materials were identified and commented upon. Anna Ritchie sought assistance from a dozen such people. The bones, identified by Barbara Noddle, are overwhelmingly of Ox and Sheep; the cattle are primitive forms, probably recently domesticated from the Aurochs known to have lived in Scotland. She comments 'that the animals had a good standard of nutrition, and it is possible that the calves were killed for their skins, other clothing material being in short supply'. Calfskin would have been more suitable than the heavy hide of adults. Sheep must have been brought in with the farmers as there were no wild Sheep in Britain at that or any other time. Noddle suggests that the Sheep might have been Scandinavian or at least North European. There were a few Pig bones, probably of a recently domesticated type. Hunted animals such as Red Deer and Seal were rare. Whalebones may have been derived from beached Whales. A few Dog bones were found.

Forty different species of birds were identified by D. Bramwell. They were predominantly seabirds captured when they came ashore to nest; Bramwell suggests that their oil may have been a useful biproduct for lighting and cooking. The Great Auk seem to have been particularly sought after; four adults and a juvenile were taken. It is ironic that as a flightless bird it managed to survive until 1813 when, as Bramwell reminds us, the last breeding pair in Scotland were exterminated on Papa Westray. Skull and foot bones of birds are absent, suggesting that they were butchered on the shore; the presence of two species of diving bird suggests that boats were used.

Careful sieving of midden samples also produced a quantity of fish bones; Alwyne Wheeler thinks that some of them could only have been caught offshore from boats, and large fish, of at least 10kg, would have been caught using hook and line. Cod, Saithe and Ling were important components of the diet, but Eel, Conger Eel, Turbot, Halibut, Flounder, Ballam Wrasse, Ray and Rockling were also eaten. The shellfish were identified by J.G. Evans and M. Vaughan and were overwhelmingly of Limpets which, though edible, but make good bait, a use this may have accounted for the many thousands of shells. Common Oysters were popular and there were some Winkles, Cockles and Razor Shells. Most of the shellfish could have been collected from the intertidal zone.

Evans and Vaughan also looked at land and freshwater snails from buried soils beneath shell sands. They comment that 'the fauna was characterised by a high species richness . . . at the same time it was similarly devoid of . . . open ground elements . . . It is difficult to avoid the conclusion that this fauna reflects a vegetation of scrub or, more probably, woodland.' When this work was published in 1983 it was not thought that scrub or woodland was ever a part of this now treeless, windswept island of Papa Westray. However, as has already been discussed in the sections on Skara Brae, the Orkney Islands had more tree cover than formerly considered the case. It is remarkable that molluscs should have recorded so sensitively the past vegetation on which they would have fed and sheltered. Commendably, the environmental studies were wide-ranging enough to have dealt with such aspects since in highly calcareous and aerated deposits pollen is usually very poorly preserved or absent. All these reports give an extra dimension to the archaeology but it is only at exceptional sites, such as Knap of Howar, that such a wealth of remains awaits

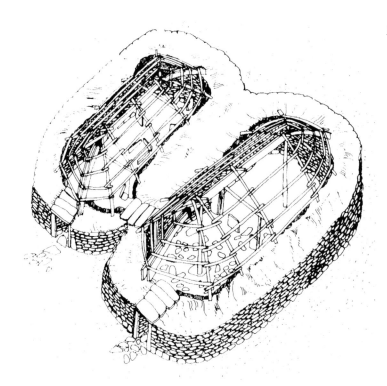

23 Reconstruction of the Knap of Howar houses. With permission of Historic Scotland

investigation and interpretation. The archaeologist must be mindful of all the potential expertise needed before beginning a modern dig.

Tofts Ness, Sanday, Orkney

Another Orcadian site, in part early Neolithic, is Tofts Ness on the island of Sanday (Dockrill *et al.*1994). Excavation yielded bones of a similar range of mammals and marine foods to those at Knap of Howar. Cattle and Sheep/Goat are the main domesticated animals with smaller numbers of Pigs. Fish, bird and marine molluscs are also present. Red Deer, Seal and cetacean bones are occasionally recorded. The early Neolithic cereals were mainly of Hulled Barley.

It seems, then, that the diet of these early Orcadian farmers was not so different from that of the Mesolithic folk. They appear to have eaten a similar range of animal foodstuffs as the hunter-gatherers at Morton, and cereals seem to have formed only a minor part of their diet. The important distinction lies in the presence of domesticated animals and cereals, necessitating a permanent homestead. Self-sufficient not just in foodstuffs, these farmers had a local source of clay for their pots as well as chert or flint for stone implements.

Scord of Brouster, Mainland of Shetland

By about 3400 BC agriculture had spread as far north as the Shetland Islands (Whittle *et al.* 1987). The farmers had travelled, not necessarily from the Orkney Islands, but perhaps directly from Caithness where there are cultural affinities with Shetland. The small farmstead produced small numbers of Hulled Six-row Barley and a few Naked Barley grains, together with cornfield weeds and grass and heathland plants (Milles 1987). The site is of particular interest because it proved possible to pollen analyse soil profiles sealed beneath the archaeological structures as well as blanket peat and a long core from an infilled lake basin with radiocarbon dates for the prehistoric part.

Two Neolithic boundary walls survive, one of them built during the primary clearance and farming phase. From the analyses it was deduced that Birch-Hazel scrub was cleared from the vicinity of the settlement before about 3400 BC. This initial clearance was short-lived with some pasture established before the settlement was built. Two main clearances followed; the first had only small areas of arable land in relation to pasture and the fields may have lain fallow or been grazed. Hazel regenerated, to be followed by a more intensive phase of pasture, but probably less arable farming. It is suggested that the boundary walls probably confined grazing animals to the outfield; but they could also of course have been moved to the infield to manure fallow arable fields. Barbara Noddle identified two Sheep bones, 10 of Cattle (within the range of those from Skara Brae) and one Red Deer antler. The settlement lasted a remarkable 1,500 years before its abandonment.

As in Orkney, it seems that pastoral farming was more important than arable. Because the climate is wet and cloudy at the present time, little grain is grown in Shetland, chiefly a few Bristle Oats for fodder. Even if it was warmer in the Neolithic, Shetland may always have been marginal for cereal growing. It is not known how large or regular these early cereal fields were, but before 3000 BC the tilling of rows left regular ridges in the soil.

Northton, Harris

Little has yet been published on environmental work on the Outer Hebrides relevant to Neolithic sites. One such is at Northton where bones were studied by D.D.A. Simpson as reported in Smith (1981). Sheep and cattle bones were important but there was no Pig. Seal bones were recorded, as were those of seabirds: Gannet, Shag, Guillemot and Puffin. There was a single bone of Conger Eel.

Embo, Sutherland

This chambered cairn is noteworthy archaeobotanically for two reasons (Henshall and Wallace 1965). Firstly, two carbonised berries of Bilberry, or an allied species, were found. This is a very rare discovery in Scottish archaeology; seeds of such species are often found but not carbonised fruits. Secondly, what was probably the first phytolith analysis from Scottish material was carried out by Allard Johnson but there was no substantial result (see Appendix 1). Wood and charcoal identified at Kew Gardens included Hazel, Oak, Willow/Poplar and Birch and Scots Pine, both tentatively recognised, as well as Beech thought to be a by no means a certain identification. If it really were Beech and not intrusive roots then it was a remarkable discovery.

The archaeozoological list prepared by A.S. Clarke was long. The mammalian bones were of Dog, Pig, Red Squirrel, Sheep and tentatively Polecat. Avian bones were of Capercaillie, Duck, Great Auk, Guillemot and perhaps Lapwing and Fulmar. There were also bones of Cod and Gurnard and of amphibians and shells of Dog Welk, Limpet and Winkle and of the land snail, *Helix*.

Twenty trees from Skara Brae: woodland loss from the Northern Isles and the Outer Hebrides

Though there are fairly large trees of the wind-resilient Sycamores in Kirkwall and Stromness and tree plantations at Binscarth, the immediate impression of the Orkney Islands gained by the visitor is one of treelessness. On the archipelago at present there are a mere six types of indigenous woody plants that can reach the stature of trees (or tall shrubs). They are Aspen, Downy Birch, Hazel, Juniper, Rowan and Willow. Sheltered in only one small glen is a woodland; this is Berriedale on Hoy and it is the northernmost woodland in Britain (**24**). This small number of trees and tall shrubs stands in great contrast with the long list of trees represented as wood or charcoal in the Skara Brae middens (Table 1).

British native trees, identified as uncarbonised wood, in descending order of frequency were: Alder, Willow, Hazel, Scots Pine, Birch (perhaps of two types), Elm, Oak, Aspen, Ash, cf Wild Cherry, cf Bird-cherry, Rowan type, Juniper and Guelder Rose/Wayfaring Tree. Small proportions of Heather and Bramble were also noted. Charcoal is present in similar proportions with the addition of small quantities of Sloe type and Hawthorn/Crab Apple. Among the four types of North American coniferous driftwood, Spruce dominates all samples.

To find out where the native trees may have been growing we need to consult local pollen analyses. Were there trees growing around the settlement? Fortunately it proved possible to count pollen preserved in certain of the midden deposits which must, as we have shown, represent very local vegetation. Tree pollen, mainly under 10%, declines to a trace in the youngest samples. Most of this is of Pine pollen. It may be that Pine woodland formed part of the submerged forest which once existed in the Bay of Skaill. There seems little evidence otherwise for trees in the immediate vicinity. The herb pollen confirms the rich flora that was indicated from the identification of the larger plant remains and also suggests that the vegetation was well-grazed, allowing the growth of dwarf ferns such as Moonwort and Adder's Tongue, together with Clubmosses.

The Loch of Skaill, only 0.6km away, had already been pollen analysed by Terry Keatinge and contained, in its lower part, tree pollen Birch, Hazel and Willow in particular, suggesting an open scrub woodland. The upper part shows a sharp decline in trees including that of Elm which, as we have previously seen is an early indicator of woodland disturbance, although Alder and Oak do not decline appreciably from their 5% maximum. Scots Pine is reduced from a maximum of 10% but later shows signs of recovery. Grass and Ribwort Plantain increase as the trees decline. This dramatic change is accompanied by sand and silt, which are present in the pollen cores for the rest of the sequence. This has been interpreted as the beginning of strong south-west winds initiating a sand blow which deposited sand over the area covered by the settlement and for up to 2km inland. Salt spray and sand abrasion very probably had a detrimental effect on tree growth.

Coastal areas of the Outer Hebrides seem to have been similarly affected suggesting that this was more than a local phenomenon. If immediately local woodland became scarcer at Skara Brae, where would the herders go to shelter their animals from the increasingly

24 Berriedale, Isle of Hoy, Orkney, taken in 1973 by JHD. This shows the northernmost woodland in Britain. The trees, many of them Downy Birch, are sheltered in the gully from the fierce winds which frequently blow across Orkney

frequent winter storms? Recent analyses by Jane Bunting from two sites may have provided the answers. At Quoyloo, 3km north-east, and Crudale Moss, 4km to the south-east, long sequences through the post-glacial were pollen analysed. The chief woodland trees were the same as those at the Loch of Skaill but the woodland was denser, with tree pollen at Crudale forming 70-80% of total pollen. At the Elm Decline much of the woodland was cleared and agricultural activity began and continued throughout the subsequent prehistoric period. The effect at Quoyloo where the woodland was less dense was similar.

Juniper and Ash were only reported as rare grains. Insect-pollinated plants are not always represented but Rowan type was and other insect-pollinated trees and shrubs, all found in old woodland on the better soils but which were not recorded by Bunting, are Hawthorn, Wild Cherry, Bird-cherry, Sloe and Guelder Rose. We have, however, a strong case for their presence from the wood or charcoal identified from the middens at Skara Brae.

It has been estimated that the change from woodland to scrub and pasture took place within about 200 years in the Loch of Skaill area. This does not suggest wholesale destruction of the woodland to create more pasture but rather that as trees died they were not replaced by saplings. This was probably due to browsers, such as Cattle and Red Deer, nibbling the succulent young shoots and so preventing regeneration. At Quoyloo, it took

Alder *(Alnus glutinosa)*
Birch *(Betula sp or spp)*
Hazel *(Corylus avellana)*
Ash *(Fraxinus excelsior)*
Juniper *(Juniperus communis)*
Hawthorn/Crab Apple *(Crataegus/Malus sylvestris)*
cf. Scots Pine *(Pinus section sylvestris)*
cf. Aspen *(Populus)*
cf. Wild Cherry *(Prunus cf. avium)*
cf. Bird Cherry *(Prumus cf. padus)*
Sloe *(Prunus spinosa)*
Oak *(Quercus sp or spp)*
Willow *(Salix sp or spp)*
cf. Rowan *(Sorbus cf. aucuparia)*
cf. Wych Elm *(Ulmus cf. glabra)*
cf. Guelder Rose *(Viburnum sp)*
Driftwood
Fir *(Abies sp or spp)*
cf. Tamarack *(Larix cf. laricina)*
Spruce *(Picea sp or spp)*
Weymouth Pine *(Pinus section Strobus)*

Table 1   Wood and charcoal from Skara Brae

several hundred years for the woodland to be reduced and at Crudale, still further away from the settlement, 1000 years. As flocks and herds increased they would move further from the settlement in search of both grass and woodland shelter from winter winds. The herders would return with firewood from dead trees, reflecting the range of trees from the rich woodlands at Quoyloo and Crudale.

Although we do not have such detailed information from the rest of the Orcadian Mainland at this time, pollen analyses from Maes Howe, the magnificent chambered tomb, and from Howe, a tomb that was destroyed for later prehistoric development, both show the presence of a cleared landscape. An early task of the tomb builders would be the removal of woodland so that the imposing mounds over the tombs could be seen from vantage points over the whole area. Thus the local inhabitants could see the final resting place of their ancestors' bones.

This brief survey of Neolithic farming and its effect on the woodland has focused on Orkney as more pollen sites are known and the woodland history can be more confidently interpreted than in many parts of the Scottish mainland and islands. Trees and tall shrubs were by then exceedingly uncommon on Shetland; limited to Downy Birch, Hazel, Rowan and Juniper, mainly in places inaccessible to grazing and browsing. Subfossil wood of Alder has been found in peat on Shetland, even on the small, remote Foula. Pollen analyses by Keith Bennett and his colleagues have indicated the former presence of Oak, which was locally common. It is probable that Wych Elm and Ash also grew there. Scots Pine pollen values are constant, up to 10%, but so far no macroscopic remains have been recovered. In the area of Catta Ness, Nannasting, on Mainland, woodland was cleared by about 1400 BC, probably for rough grazing, and never recovered in that area. Extensive clearance and virtual destruction of the woodland also occurred at Kebister, Dallican Water and Gunnister Water between about 1400 and 1100 BC.

On the Outer Isles, the present trees and shrubs consist of Willows with scattered Downy Birches and Hazel, Aspen, and Rowan; all these are limited to areas unsuitable for grazing. Bramble, also present, was perhaps gathered for food by prehistoric peoples as now. The evidence for past extensive woodland on Lewis is more convincing as subfossil wood remains have been radiocarbon dated from a number of sites and their positions plotted by J. Fossitt, as already considered in chapter 2. Scots Pine has been dated from three sites at around 3600-2700 BC. Alder, Birch and Willow wood have also been dated. Pollen analyses indicate that the onset of a decline in the woodland is correlated with the beginning of the Neolithic period and so seems due to human impact at least in part. The lack of Elm, Ash and Oak as subfossil woods does not imply that these trees were not components of the vegetation but they may not have been present at times or places which were affected by blanket bog development. The demise of Scots Pine in the Outer Hebrides seems linked to a more oceanic climate resulting in the spreading of blanket bog. Such peat development results in increasingly acidic and infertile conditions, more and more unsuitable for tree growth. All these features together with human impact led to the permanent decline of the fragile woodland.

It appears that similar forces were at work in both the Northern and the Outer Isles resulting in the destruction of the remaining woodland. The particularly intensive pastoral farming on Orkney mitigated against the woodland's recovery in spite of the base-rich soils otherwise very suitable for tree growth.

A unique wooden hall at Balbridie, Kincardineshire: Breadwheat and Flax

At about the same time as the Neolithic folk settled in the Orkney Islands, a very different type of house was built just south of the River Dee although the two groups shared a similar style of Unstan ware pottery, named after the site in Orkney where it was first recognised. The ground plan of a very large rectangular wooden house or hall with bowed gable ends has been revealed by aerial photography. The house, which had been burnt down, measured some 24m x 12m (**25**). Although no early house of a similar type has been discovered elsewhere in Britain, there are similar buildings in France and the Netherlands. The excavation revealed over 20,000 charred cereal grains, mainly from post-holes within the building (Fairweather and Ralston 1993).

Archaeobotanical investigations by Alan Fairweather suggest that Emmer Wheat was by far the most abundant grain, with some Naked Six-row Barley, rather rare Hulled Barley and a little Bread Wheat. The site has produced a higher proportion of Emmer Wheat than any other in Scotland; the sunny east side of the country would have suited its growth. Bread Wheat has only been found as occasional grains at other prehistoric sites; it requires a rich soil for its cultivation, but in Germany and Denmark it was the predominant cereal at that period. A burial site at Boghead, in Moray, but not far distant from Balbridie and of similar date, also produced finds of Emmer Wheat with predominantly Naked Barley.

25 A reconstruction of the house at Balbridie. With permission of Historic Scotland

The discovery of a few Flax seeds is of interest, but whether the plant was grown for Linseed, oil or fibre for cloth is not known. Evidence of gathered fruit includes the Crab Apple pips mentioned above, and Hazelnuts were also collected. Unfortunately the soils were not suitable for the preservation of bone. The Dee, a famous salmon river, could have been exploited for fish.

The Bread Wheat gives distinctiveness to this site where, according to Fairweather and Ralston (1993, p321) '. . . the farmers were — in terms of their building and, it would seem, of their strategy with cereals — closer to continental European practice than has normally been identified in the British Isles'.

Although mainland Scotland remained heavily wooded in many parts it is clear from the distribution of megalithic tombs, and later henges and stone circles, that much of lowland Scotland was inhabited by Neolithic peoples. Later monuments, such as ceremonial enclosures and stone circles, seem particularly sited in the fertile eastern part, and rare agricultural ridges remaining in the soil show that arable farming was practised. Settlements have been located but cereals have not yet been commonly found. Metal working began to be practised from about the middle of the third millennium. Grooved ware pottery, which characterised the later Neolithic, was no longer used after 2250 BC. The new pots originated on the continent but were later made in Britain, and are known as beaker pottery. However, beakers are not found at all sites and are rare on Orkney.

4 Bronze Age: funerary flowers, mead or ale?

The Inner Hebrides, Arran and the mainland

Ardnave, Islay

At Ardnave on Islay (**26**), the southernmost island of the Inner Hebrides, Hulled Barley was the main crop (Ritchie and Welfare 1983). Charcoal of Alder, Ash, Birch, Hazel, Rowan type, Sloe, Wild Cherry and Willow show that the island supported a mixed woodland (CD 1983). All these trees still grow on Islay at the present time. There were small numbers of Cattle, Sheep and Pig bones recovered from the floor levels, and midden deposits, identified by Mary Harman. Red Deer and Seal were also represented and a Fox skull is the only record past or present for this animal on the island. John Evans identified Common Limpet as the most numerous of the shells, with the suggestion that it was equally probable that they had been used for food as for bait. The other main marine animal represented was the Edible Crab, which could have been exploited from the low tide zone and not necessarily from deeper water. Winkles, Dog Whelks, Mussels and Razor-shells may also have been collected for food.

Machrie Moor, Arran

The Isle of Arran in the Firth of Clyde has a richness of archaeological monuments that few other places can rival. Machrie Moor, lying in the mid-western part of the island, has a spectacular array of standing stones and hut circles in an extensive peatland. In the late 1970s and early 1980s, excavations were carried out there by John Barber on behalf of Historic Scotland, with David Robinson and JHD as archaeobotanists working on pollen and Alan Fairweather and Sheila Boardman on carbonised remains (Barber 1997; Robinson and Dickson 1988).

At Machrie North, a pit yielded general domestic rubbish 'such as crop processing waste, floor sweepings and debris from cooking accidents' (Barber 1999, p83); the plant remains in small amounts of charred conglomerations were Barley (rachis internodes) and Emmer (glume bases and rachis internodes), and the weeds Broad-leaved Dock, Fathen, Pale Persicaria, Parsley Piert, Ribwort Plantain, Stone Bramble (only tentatively identified; this is a species seldom if ever recorded in Scottish archaeological sites whereas Bramble and Raspberry are commonplace), a Brome (Soft or Rye) and Hazelnut shells. The pit had been used about 2350 BC.

At Tormore, within hut circle 10/1 were three contexts, considered contemporary, rich in carbonised plant remains. Charcoal was of Alder, Birch, Hazel, Oak and Willow. There were fragments of Bracken stems, seeds of Sedge, Chickweed, Fathen, Knotweed,

Redshank and Hemp-nettle. A most unusual find was 'siliquae [long, narrow fruits] of the Brassica family' (p19) but it received no special comment. At least two conflagrations led to the preservation of large quantities of grain, as crop processing material and as discrete clumps of charred grain. The cereals were Barley, Emmer (only one spikelet fork) and 12 grains of Breadwheat, but the latter was only tentatively identified. The cereals had been grown about 1200 BC.

With good radiocarbon control, the pollen analysis was carried out on cores of 4.5m of Moss, Sedge, Reed and Purple Moor-grass peat. A good record of prehistoric agricultural activity was uncovered, well underway at the Elm Decline if not before. From about 1200 BC, very high values of Ribwort Plantain (at up to 49% of total pollen, a value seldom if ever recorded elsewhere) were recorded. The intensity of agriculture was such that '. . . there were periods during the late Neolithic and at the transition between the Bronze and Iron Ages when it could no longer be maintained with the resources available. The latter period coincided with the onset of blanket peat formation.' (Robinson and Dickson 1988, p223).

Lintshie Gutter, Lanarkshire

Dwellings, apart from those in treeless areas, became larger, and the spacious roundhouse which developed at this time has left circular walls of turf and stone as evidence. Sometimes the houses were entirely of wood, apart from the roofing; such dwellings, in time, usually burnt down, and the burnt wood can give clues both to the construction and the local environment. At Lintshie Gutter, near Crawford, in the Clyde Valley (Terry 1995), a large settlement had been terraced into the hillside. The excavated soil was pushed forward to form an apron and thus make a level base, from 8 to 13m in diameter, for a building (**27-29**).

The inconspicuous bases can be overlooked and the platforms may appear to have been cultivation terraces. Such settlements have been recognised along valley sides in Lanarkshire and Peeblesshire; similar examples come from south-west England. The settlements at Lintshie Gutter were discovered because of a rescue operation preceding the construction of the M74/M6 motorway. They lie at 300m on a north-facing hillside with a clear view across the Clyde Valley, and the river Clyde winds 60m below the site. There was a long occupancy with repairs and rebuilding, possibly stretching from the late Neolithic to the middle Bronze Age, based on five radiocarbon dates of wood charcoal. Plant remains from six of the platforms (1, 5, 7, 8, 13 and 14) were identified by CD. Charred wood for identification was obtained by sieving and floating litre samples, or less according to the material available, and came from all available contexts of six of the platforms (most of which proved to have been roundhouses).

Little is known of the woodland history of this part of the Clyde Valley, since it did not prove possible at the time to find long pollen-bearing profiles nearby. The local woodland has long since disappeared. What sort of wood was used for building, and had the trees grown locally?

Much of the charcoal (identified by CD) had been abraded by biological action, probably through earthworm movements. Some was seen to be of roundwood, although its former diameter could not be measured. The identifications were tabulated separately

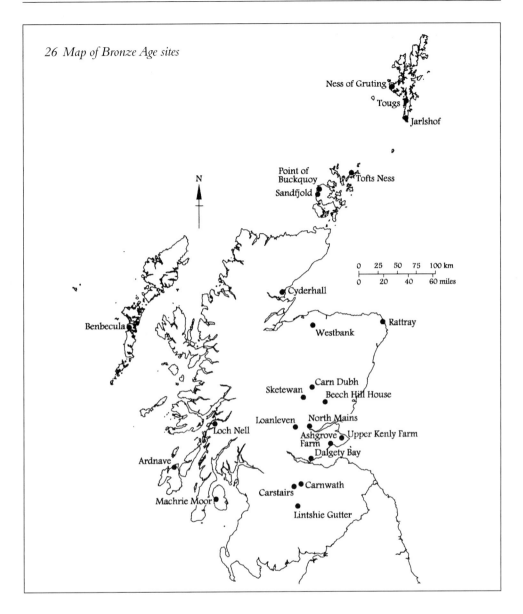

26 *Map of Bronze Age sites*

for the different contexts from each of the six buildings from which evidence was available. Although over 2,000 fragments were identified, there seemed little difference between the types used in each platform, and so the houses are here considered together. The number of contexts in each case is given in brackets. The most abundant wood charcoal came from the ring-grooves (10) and was of Hazel, chiefly of roundwood, as was a little Willow. Alder, Birch and Rowan/Whitebeam were also present; Rowan is the more likely wood on ecological grounds, and hereafter is designated as Rowan type. The Hazel was from burnt wattle, clearly preserved in its original grooves with fragments of clay daub, used to strengthen and weatherproof the wattles. Somewhat unusually, some of the walls appeared to have been double. A post-trench construction (2), forming the front

71

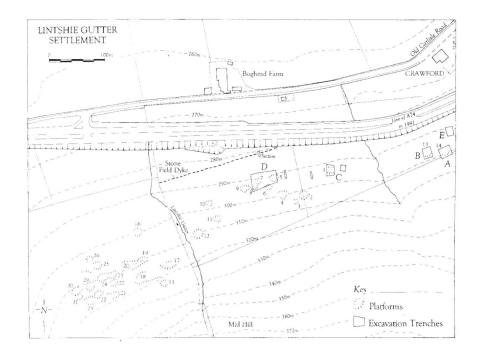

27 Plan of Lintshie Gutter 1. From Terry (1995)

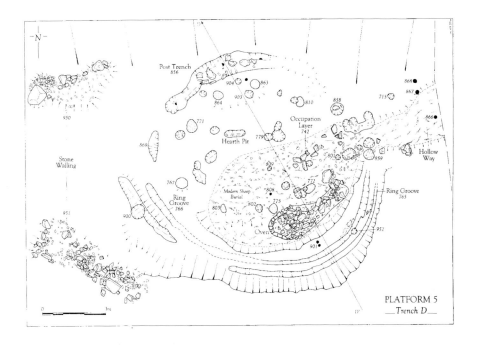

28 Plan of Lintshie Gutter 2. From Terry (1995)

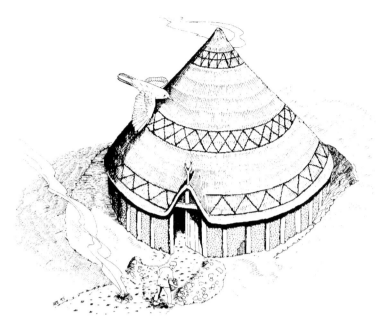

29 Lintshie Gutter. Reconstruction of the house that was built on Platform 13. With permission of Historic Scotland

wall of one of the buildings, was also mainly of Hazel roundwood and similarly must represent burnt wattle. Post-holes (40) contained Birch with some large pieces burnt *in situ*. Hazel, including roundwood, Alder, Rowan type, Oak, and Wild/Bird Cherry, when present as a mixture, probably fell in when posts had rotted and houses burnt down and were abandoned. Hearth pits (4) produced Alder, Birch and Hazel, with smaller quantities of Willow and Rowan type as would be expected if firewood had been gathered without selection. Wood from primary and secondary floors and middens also contained a mixture of species.

One of the buildings contained an oven in a pit with a long stokehole or flue. The oven was full of charcoal, mostly of Birch and Hazel, chiefly roundwood, which dated it to 1500 BC. Unfortunately the superstructure was missing. The rakings of the oven, ashes removed through one of two opposing entrances, contained numerous sherds of pottery, but its function is not clearly understood. A few Barley grains and weed seeds could well have come from weedy straw used as tinder, and a single Raspberry pip was the only one recovered from the site. A saddle quern was found in the rakeout but there had been no industrial activity in the vicinity. The design of the oven, with the deeply cut stokehole, has not been paralleled elsewhere. Had this been the settlement cook-house? A number of contexts produced Barley grains, almost all of Naked Six-row Barley. These were accompanied by a few weed seeds such as Hemp-nettle, Fat Hen, Corn Spurrey and Chickweed. The only wild plant foods, other than the Raspberry pip, were rare fragments of Hazelnut shells. To judge from the small number of Barley grains, cereals were not the main basic foods.

The quantity of Hazel roundwood suggests that Hazel may have been coppiced; see the account of Hazel in Part 2. Silver Birch produces long straight trunks and may have been selected for interior posts, although it rots readily when in contact with damp ground. The posts in one of the ring-grooves were measured by the archaeologist, John Terry, and found to be 0.4m apart and the individual posts 0.04-0.06m diameter. In another house, an inner ring of eight postholes is presumed to have supported the roofing; circular timbers of 0.1-0.14m diameter had been used. Use of even more substantial timbers of 0.15-0.20m has been deduced from two other inner postholes. From the position of the ring-grooves and post-holes it has proved possible to produce a drawing of the outside of a roundhouse with a conical thatched roof, although we have no thatch preserved. An imaginative drawing of the inside of the house with the oven has also been made.

Birch and Hazel charcoal were found in most contexts and their abundance is striking. Oak, which has the most durable timber, was only present in seven contexts. Rowan type was present in 18 contexts and Wild/Bird Cherry was recorded from four contexts. Cherries and Hazel are characteristic of better soils. These trees all grow together in open woodland. Alder was present in many and Willow in a few contexts; they were probably confined to wetter areas around the river.

In order to understand the predominance of Birch and Hazel and the low proportion of Oak wood used, it is necessary to consider the natural woodland of the Southern Uplands at similar altitudes. There are two pollen analysed sites in the Clyde Valley, at Carnwath Moss (Fraser and Godwin 1955) and Carstairs Kames, some 28km to the north at around 220m OD (JHD 1980). Birch, Alder and Hazel pollen predominate and there are smaller proportions of Scots Pine, Wych Elm and Oak. At Carstairs there was evidence of pastoral farming from the Neolithic onwards. Two unpublished pollen diagrams from upland sites, between 40 and 50km to the east of Crawford, have been radiocarbon-dated and record a Birch-Hazel woodland with Elm and Oak restricted, it is thought, to more favourable lowland areas. It would seem that Birch and Hazel woods predominated in these upland locations and Oaks were not common. Such upland woodland is now very rare in Scotland and, where present, intensive grazing by Sheep and/or Red Deer prevents any possible regeneration.

Although there were no suitable waterlogged pollen bearing deposits in the vicinity, a bulk sample from under the front apron of one of the first building phases, darkened from a large content of charcoal, was prepared for pollen analysis and for its larger plant remains. Birch charcoal, together with that of Alder, Hazel, Willow and five grains of Naked Barley were retrieved. This was interpreted as an occupation/destruction level. Pollen from occupation layers is subject to much subsequent biological action, notably earthworm activity, which may move pollen grains both up and down. Rainwater can cause downwash of pollen. Aerated conditions also assist bacterial decomposition, leading to poorly preserved pollen. Geoffrey Dimbleby, who pioneered pollen analyses of deposits from British archaeological sites, considered that 'a cover of 40cm should give adequate protection against contamination from an exposed surface above'. The apron deposit was about 35cm deep at the sampling point and the total depth of the layer about 9cm. It was therefore considered that a pollen analysis was worthwhile. Such a sample may be thought of as a surface sample reflecting very local pollen and so cannot easily be correlated with regional pollen diagrams.

Tree pollen values were under 13% of the total pollen, with Alder 3.7% and Coryloid (probably Hazel) 6.7%. Heather contributed nearly 6%. Grasses were 38.5% and herbs of pasture were represented by Ribwort Plantain, Buttercups, Devil's-bit Scabious and White Clover. Plants of open woodland were Wood Anenome, Enchanter's Nightshade and Greater Stitchwort; fern values were high at 31% and Bracken was present. Pollen of the Barley group reached at least 1.5%; many of the grains were crumpled and the critical diameter of the outside of the pore was not always measurable. This analysis suggests the presence of local Hazel scrub with a little heathland, and Alder in the wetter places. The absence of arable weed pollen suggests that arable farming may have been confined, as at present, to the floor of the valley. The land is now considered to be marginal agricultural land, with rough grazing on the hillsides, although the intensive cultivation that took place in the valley in historic time is now replaced by improved grassland.

To ascertain whether the Bronze Age folk depleted the woodland would require a radiocarbon-dated pollen diagram from a local source. Because the area is rich in archaeological remains of all periods this should prove very rewarding, and such work is already in progress.

Ratho, Edinburgh

Excavation revealed Neolithic, Bronze Age and Early Historic activity (Smith 1995). Investigated by Tim Holden and Dorothy Rankin, charred remains from the Neolithic included Hazel, Hulled Barley, Oat and one grain of Bread Wheat, only tentatively identified. The Bronze Age samples yielded the same cereals. Two upturned cremation urns, apart from human bones, contained soil, charcoal and pottery fragments. Coralie Mills carried out numerous pollen analyses on the urn contents, and impressed by the reasonably large numbers of Bogmoss spores in several samples, argued cautiously that this is best accounted for by the deliberate insertion of Bogmoss stems in the urns before burial.

Wooden objects

A rare hurdle of charred wood dated to about 1400 BC has survived at Rattray, Aberdeenshire (Murray *et al.* 1992). Rowan, Willow and Hazel were used for the verticals and Hazel for the horizontals. No postholes or vertical stumps were seen and so it is just possible that this was a trackway rather than a fence. On the ground underneath the hurdling were traces of former cultivation, consisting of roughly parallel marks with others crossing at right angles. These marks had been made by an ard, a primitive plough. This technique of cross ploughing to prepare the seed bed has been noted at other sites mentioned by Hilary Murray and fellow workers.

Developing bogs have preserved many wooden objects. A yoke dated to about 1700 BC, from Loch Nell, Argyll, is the earliest example from Britain or Ireland. It was suggested that the yoke would have fitted oxen (castrated bulls of four or more years old). In some instances, therefore, animals would have been trained for traction. Slightly later in date is a solid disc wheel of Ash made around 1000 BC, one of three found at Blair Drummond Moss. These wheels are the earliest evidence for wheeled transport in the British Isles (Cowie and Shepherd 1997). Blair Drummond Moss was one of many former large tracts of raised bog in the Upper Forth Valley; in 1794 Rev Christopher Tait reported that a wooden trackway was exposed during the extensive peat removal which turned these wetlands into agricultural ground.

The Outer Hebrides and the Northern Isles

Benebecula

Beaker period cultivation on Benbecula, a small, low island of the Outer Hebrides, has been described by Ian Shepherd and Alexandra Tuckwell (1979). Marks about 70mm wide by 70mm in depth, made by an ard, were revealed on the machair, as were spade marks, which had a slightly rounded, triangular profile. Midden overlying the plough and spade marks contained cereal grains. There were 162 grains of Naked Barley, three of Hulled Barley and five grains of Emmer Wheat. The grain was identified by A.C. Maclean and P.A. Rowley-Conwy, who commented that the Wheat would have been at the limit of its range and poorly adapted to the local climatic conditions; these were similar comments to those made about the Skara Brae wheat.

Point of Buckquoy, Orcadian Mainland

The Orcadian archipelago, so heavily populated in the Neolithic, has, as yet, revealed surprisingly few indications of Bronze Age habitation. On the western side of the Point of Buckquoy, Birsay Bay, at the north-west tip of the Mainland, a midden sample, investigated in 1978, produced over 200 grains of Naked Barley. There is a single radiocarbon date which calibrates to about 1500 BC. The grain was identified by Alison Donaldson who, with co-authors Christopher Morris and James Rackham (1981), noted that an abundance of biological remains awaits publication. The mammalian assemblage was dominated by Red Deer; bones from four or more individuals were present and, of domestic animals, only two Cattle bones were mentioned. The fish assemblage suggests that fishing took place from the shore or close inshore. Bones of wild birds and shells of marine molluscs were also recorded. Apparently a wide range of animals typical of the coastal situation was exploited.

Tofts Ness, Sanday, Orkney

The continuity of Barley growing throughout the Neolithic and Bronze Ages has been recorded from one of the most northern sites at Tofts Ness, Sanday, Orkney. This is one of very few sites with settlement continuing intermittently throughout the prehistoric period. Having replaced the Naked Barley of the Neolithic period, Hulled Barley dominated the Later Bronze Age crops. An interesting feature of the settlement is the evidence from buried soils which contained burnt material, including seaweed with its highest concentration in the Neolithic/Bronze Age levels. The addition of burnt Heather suggests a moorland component, perhaps from heathery turf. Together with burnt bone and flint these all suggest that a former midden had been scattered around the settlement. Midden refuse was probably used to fertilise the infield where the grain, usually Barley, was grown. This was the traditional method of improving the soils in the Northern Isles, as is explained in detail by Fenton in his comprehensive book on past farming practices in Orkney and Shetland (1978).

Ness of Gruting, Shetland

A site which seems to link the Neolithic with pottery sharing Beaker characteristics is a hoard of burnt Barley, dating from around 2000 BC, found at the base of a wall at Ness of Gruting, Shetland. An almost pure cache of burnt corn weighing some 12.7kg was partly identified. It consisted predominantly of Naked Barley with some Hulled grain. Somewhat surprisingly, Two- and Six-rowed Barley was present in both forms. Two-rowed Barley is the type which has replaced Six-rowed Barley at the present time, and is grown for malting. The author, Annie Milles, suggests that archaic crops were much more variable than modern strains and may have been grown together as a single crop. The few accompanying seeds suggest a grassy, heathy vegetation. There are, surprisingly, no weeds of arable crops.

Jarlshof, Shetland

At the southern end of mainland Shetland there is a voe, a broad bay, at Sumburgh, providing safe anchorage in the sheltered waters of the western voe. On the eastern side is a 1.2ha sandy site, with surrounding fertile soils, which has been inhabited for 3,000 years. Jarlshof has been excavated more than once since its discovery in 1897, culminating in complete publication by the most recent excavator, J.R.C. Hamilton, in 1956. The buildings, all of stone, have been preserved where possible. The post-Late Bronze Age buildings, of the Iron Age and Norse period, are discussed in chapters 5 and 8. The reports on the plant material from all periods were by M.Y. Orr and P.S. Green. The animal bones were identified by Marjorie Platt. Unfortunately, because the excavations took place before modern sieving methods were undertaken, much of the evidence from the extensive middens has been lost. However, artefactual evidence regarding crop processing and animal husbandry was carefully recorded giving an extra dimension to this complex site.

The Late Bronze Age village consisted of oval stone houses, of which perhaps two or three were inhabited at any one time. Oak, Willow or Poplar and conifer wood were recorded; we may assume that woodland was sparse in this windswept area. Grain, recorded from the floor of a building, was probably of Barley. Interesting evidence for grinding the corn comes from a trough quern still *in situ*; cereals were placed in the hollow area on the top surface of a large oblong stone and ground by using a rounded stone chosen to fit in the hollow. The quern was contained in a stone setting constructed to slope towards the front where a shallow groove had been cut in the quern. Hamilton states (p20) that the meal was conducted '. . . into a small triangular compartment formed of thin stones set on edge and closed with yellow clay'. Another space was formed alongside the quern for a receptacle to hold the grain ready to be ground. It is only rarely that a quern is found in its original position and this shows one way in which the problem of collecting the ground meal was solved.

Sheep bones were the most numerous and of two breeds; Platt records that some were of the large Soay type and others may have descendants in modern Shetland sheep. Cattle bones were also numerous, with an extensive size range; they included the Celtic shorthorn type. Pig bones were infrequent. A tethering ring of whale bone inserted in a wall indicates that one or more animals were tethered in the settlement. From recent analogues in the Northern Isles this could have been a Cow, perhaps coming into calf, or a Pig fed on scraps. Similar tethering continued in crofts up to the last century, when Pigs were tied by one leg to the kitchen table where they ate up all the scraps.

Horse remains of Shetland pony type were scattered throughout the middens; it is not known if the flesh was eaten. Bones of a terrier type of Dog were found, probably where it had lain and died. Common and Grey Seal were present. Sea birds were particularly plentiful, with a variety of other birds including Stork (no longer native to Britain), Swan and Goose. Fish bone were chiefly of cod with some ling. Marine shells were only found in the earlier deposits and were of Cockles and Limpets.

Burnt mounds

The earliest burnt mounds date from the early Bronze Age. These large mounds of burnt stones with associated stone troughs are often found in areas which, by the Bronze Age, were largely treeless. They are usually interpreted as communal cooking areas. In the Northern Isles they are associated with houses. At Tougs, Burra Isle, Shetland, a burnt mound was adjacent to a cook house containing a hearth and a cooking trough with Cattle bones. There is evidence of cultivation there from the walls of a field system found underneath the peat. A number of ard stones, of which rare examples survive at this and other sites throughout Orkney and Shetland of Bronze and Iron Age date, show that cultivation took place. Stone axes and mattocks were also recognised. Such stone tools were probably used because of a shortage of wood in the Northern Isles and have not been found at other locations. Burnt mounds occur through much of Scotland and field systems, some associated with the mounds, are commonly preserved, often under blanket peat, as at Machrie Moor, Arran, where there is an early burnt mound, with field systems divided by timber fences.

Pollen analysis and burial practices

Some burials of the Scottish Bronze Age have provided highly intriguing pollen analytical evidence with important implications, especially but not only because of the presence of pollen of Meadowsweet, both fully developed and immature (see the account of Meadowsweet and Dropwort in part 2). All the examples are from cists which contained skeletons or cremations or both. As the pollen diagrams in chapter 1 show, pollen of Meadowsweet is frequently recorded in samples of peats and muds in Scotland. Almost always, however, the values are less than 10% and often less than 5% of total land pollen and spores. These are much lower values than have been found in some cists (Table 2).

It is crucially important for correct interpretations of the analyses that there is certainty that the pollen is contemporary with the burial and not, for instance, the result of later intrusion by overlying soil or nest-building Bumble Bees or some other disturbance. Published work from Norway by Knut Faegri (1961) makes it clear that such Bumble Bee nests are a potential source of contamination. Knut Faegri found that Bumble Bee larvae produce faeces that can contain up to nearly 30% Meadowsweet pollen. More recently, Bottema (1975) and Scourse (1991) have drawn attention to the contamination of

TE	ANALYSED MATERIAL	RESIDUE	POLLEN INSIDE	POLLEN OUTSIDE	MACROS	INTERPRETATION
hgrove	beaker		*	*	*	Flowers / mead
rth Mains	food vessel	*	*			Ale / porridge
estbank	"mass of rootlets"				*(but no idents)	Bumble Bee nest / flowers
ech Hill House	"floor material"					Flowers
anleven	"body stain on floor material"					Flowers
etewan	"body stain on floor material"					Flowers
ndfjold	"dust and cremated bone in urn"		*	*	* (but no idents)	Flowers
lgety Bay (2 cists)	"floor material"					Flowers

Table 2   Pollen Analyses from Bronze Age Graves

archaeological layers and Quaternary sediments respectively, by pollen types such as those of Dandelion and Rose families, resulting from the activities of burrowing Bees. Remains of Bees should be sought in any cists examined. Where possible, details of the condition of the cists when opened have been included in the following descriptions.

In 1964, Audrey Henshall reported on three or four cist burials from Ashgrove Farm, Methilhill, Fife, 1.6km inland from the shore of the Firth of Forth, near Kirkcaldy (**26, 30**). Cist 1 had been liberally luted with clay used to seal the side slabs and the cist cover so that the interior had remained dry and free from intrusive soil. Inside was a crouched skeleton of a person, probably a male of some 55 years, laid on his left side. The sealed interior had preserved plant remains as a black crumbly material which formed a deep deposit nearly 30cm across in the region between the forearms and upper arms, and spread over the cist floor. A beaker lay on its side on top of the plant debris, beside the chest. A flat dagger of bronze lay beside the skeleton (**30**).

The plant material consisted of several layers of dicotyledonous leaf fragments, too poorly preserved to separate and identify, a Birch fruit and occasional budscales, a leaf of Cross-leaved Heath, seeds of Compact or Soft Rush, occasional leafy shoots of the moss *Hylocomium splendens*, and abundant leaves of the Bogmoss *Sphagnum palustre*. Inexplicitly, a probable 'fern rhizome', about 30cm long, was identified by Miss Prentice of the Royal Botanic Gardens, Kew [can it be anything other than Bracken?].

In addition to Ashgrove, in the same paper Audrey Henshall also reported on two other cists, at Kirkcaldy, contiguous and almost certainly contemporaneous. One contained a dagger and the other an incised beaker. It is interesting that there were vestiges of leaves in the dagger grave. The scrapings from the inside of the beaker were analysed for pollen but two samples produced only rare pollen grains (JHD, unpublished).

Before the Ashgrove plant material was sent for radiocarbon assay, giving a date of 1250 BC, a sample was taken for pollen analysis by CD. This was the first ever such analysis from inside a Scottish grave and it proved to be most surprising. Of the 350 pollen and spores counted, 54% was of Small-leaved Lime. The herbaceous pollen had 15% Meadowsweet, some of the pollen being immature, 8% Heather, 7% Ribwort Plantain, 5%

30 Ashgrove cist. This shows the beaker on its side and the handle of the dagger surrounded by the black organic matter which is interpreted as the remains of a shroud of plant material

Lamiaceae (or Labiatae, the family of Thyme, Mint, etc, all insect-pollinated) and pollen or spores of some 20 other plants, all in low or very low amounts.

This was an extraordinary count, unprecedented in Britain, for three reasons: the uncertain past status of Lime trees in Scotland, the very high pollen value of Small-leaved Lime, and the high value of Meadowsweet. That any species of Lime has ever occurred in Scotland, indigenously, since the last Ice Age is a matter of doubt. There are no native Limes in Scotland now and the northern British limit of Small-leaved Lime is considered to lie in the southern English Lake District (Pigott and Huntley 1981). Lime trees are primarily insect-pollinated and even in areas where Limes are certainly native, such a high proportion of Lime pollen is seldom, if ever, found by pollen analysts.

Not only was the value of Small-leaved Lime unexpectedly high, so also was that of Meadowsweet. The presence of immature grains of the latter suggested to CD that flowers of both Meadowsweet and Lime had been placed in the grave, although that would have implied that the Small-leaved Lime had been growing in Fife at that time; that explanation was published as an appendix to Audrey Henshall's paper. Subsequently, Peter Moore (1978) thought it possible that Small-leaved Lime could have grown in Fife.

JHD was highly intrigued by the ethnnobotanical and palaeoecological implications of the results from the Ashgrove cist and, when the Dicksons came to live in Scotland, the opportunity arose to investigate the matter further. After discussions with the Danish archaeobotanist Dr J.J. Troels-Smith, JHD investigated the beaker which had been preserved in the Kirkcaldy Museum; permission was obtained to scrape away about 1mm of the inside surface of the beaker for pollen analysis and four such samples were taken with an additional sample from loose material on the bottom of the beaker. A control sample was taken from the clay luting which contained a mere 26 pollen grains, none of which were considered relevant to the problem. All other samples contained Small-leaved Lime pollen from what had been the lowest inside surface; that deduceable by exterior staining from the plant material onto which the beaker had fallen was the most interesting. Five grains of Small-leaved Lime and at least 14 grains of Meadowsweet were identified in a total of 42 pollen and spores.

Pollen of Lime, Meadowsweet, Heather and Mint family are all well-known constituents of honey, which was especially prized in prehistoric times for its sugary sweetness and which could, of course, have been transported readily over long distances without spoiling, if kept dry. JHD's conclusion was that the substance had been basically honey. As explained in part 2, the old name for Meadowsweet refers to mead and not to meadows. If the drink had been fermented honey (mead) with flowers of Meadowsweet added to flavour it and to produce the beneficial effects of aspirin, this would account for the presence of immature grains of Meadowsweet. By a lucky chance, CD's sample for pollen analysis had come from the area in the cist that had been soaked with honey or mead when the beaker had toppled over.

What of the other plant material? Had the vegetable material (fronds of Bracken?) been a covering for the corpse? Had the Bogmoss been used to staunch a wound? The evidence is not good enough to provide a sure answer.

Archaeobotanical results from Denmark have great bearing on this matter, because flowers and leaves are known to have been placed in Bronze Age graves there. For instance, at Egtved, in southern Jutland (Glob 1973), the opening of the well-known Oak coffin revealed a sprig of Yarrow beside a girl's corpse and an accompanying birch bark bucket contained a brown crust. Dr J.J. Troels-Smith pollen analysed this residue, which showed that the major components were Lime, Meadowsweet and White Clover pollen (unpublished). Also from inside the bucket were Wheat grains and leaves of Bog Myrtle, which, together with fruits of Cowberry or Cranberry, were identified by Billie Gram and published by Thomson in 1929. The residue may represent ale with the addition of honey or mead. The contents of a beaker from Nandrup Mors, in Jutland, and another from Bregninge, in Sjealland, have also been pollen analysed. The former contained Lime honey with Meadowsweet and White Clover pollen (a common constituent of honey) also present, while the latter contained mainly Meadowsweet pollen with Lime and White Clover and was thought to be of mead rather than sweetened ale. Small-leaved Lime is a component of Danish woodlands and so there is no possible geographical difficulty, as there is for Scotland. Recently Slavomil Vencl (1994) has reviewed the archaeological evidence for mead and other alcoholic drinks. Apart from Ashgrove and the Danish examples, he mentions discoveries from Egypt, Greece and Germany.

JHD's 1978 paper ended (p112) '. . . a survey of beakers for pollen of honey plants or other honey remants is much to be desired'. Subsequently, the Dicksons examined several containers kept in the National Museum in Edinburgh (EG 7, 24, 30, 32 and 78); all produced negative results, except EG 7 which had some *Filipendula* pollen. A beaker from Balnabraid, kept in the Hunterian Museum of Glasgow University, also proved sterile, as did a food vessel from a cist at Brodick Castle, Isle of Arran. However, a food vessel from North Mains, near Perth, contained both *Filipendula* and cereal pollen, as recognised by CD.

Other investigators have since pollen analysed the contents of Bronze Age cist burials and containers found in Scotland. Soerd Bohncke (1983) examined black, greasy material from inside of the food vessel from the henge monument at North Mains, mentioned just above. Meadowsweet pollen, some of it immature, was found to be present in very high values (up to 82%), but pollen of no other insect-pollinated plants was found in high values. However, cereal pollen was present. Bohncke argued for either a porridge of cereals or a fermented ale that had been flavoured with Meadowsweet flowers. No coarse plant remains were mentioned.

In 1985, a cist at Westbank of Roseisle, Moray, excavated by Ian Shepherd, contained the skeleton of a tall man, probably over 45 years old. There were no grave goods. Sent to JHD, a sample of 'moss', which had lain over the upper chest and over part of the humerus, proved to be a mat-like mass of rootlets, some 15cm long and 7cm wide; perhaps the rootlets were intrusive (**31**). On excavation, the skeleton was found to be completely covered by recent topsoil. Jacqueline Andrews carried out five pollen analyses from the mass. The counts ranged from 175 to 353 and all had Meadowsweet pollen including some clumps; the lowest value was 3.1% and the highest 44.5%, with the others 11.4%, 25.6% and 35.4%. Three of the samples had *Trifolium*-type pollen (Clovers and the like, well-known nectar/honey plants) up to 14.3%, the two others being 8.5% and 11.5%. Faegri had found values of *Trifolium* from 5.1 to 17.4% from the Bumble Bee nest. How can these results from Westbank be interpreted? Are they remains of a Bumble Bee's nest or of funerary flowers? If the latter is accepted, then the flowers must have included Clovers because no such high percentages can be readily accounted for in any other way.

Pollen analyses from four other sites have been published by Richard Tipping (1994, 1995). At Beech Hill House, Coupar Angus, Perthshire, an intact cist was 'devoid of filling material, save for small cones of sand at each corner, presumed to have filtered through cracks between vertical slabs immediately after emplacement of the cover-slab'. Pollen samples were taken: one from a cone of sand in close proximity to a food vessel (251 pollen and spores counted), one from the floor of the cist (323), and one from sand immediately beneath a food vessel (297). All revealed low values for Meadowsweet but higher numbers of cf. Meadowsweet pollen.

At Loanleven, near Crieff, Perthshire, a sealed cist showed a brown-black stain around an adult inhumation. Fairly high levels of cf. Meadowsweet pollen were found in two samples from the stain. Pollen and spore counts were 567 and 726. A human bone gave a date of about 2000 BC.

At Sketewan, near Aberfeldy, Perthshire, a cist containing a cremation revealed a 'body stain', under silts and cobbles which had been rapidly deposited after burial, the stain showed high levels of cf. Meadowsweet (43%); 263 pollen and spores had been counted.

At Sandfjold, near Sandwick, Mainland, Orkney, a free-standing stone-slabbed capped cist was found within a larger rock-cut pit. Two inhumations were present as well as cremated bone on the floor of a large urn probably related to a food vessel. The 157 pollen and spores counted included Meadowsweet (4.5%) and cf. Meadowsweet (41%).

Tipping suggests that the stains represented the remains of decayed plant matter in which flowers of Meadowsweet had been a major component; thus we are back to CD's original explanation — Meadowsweet flowers had been placed in the graves. Why

31 Westbank cist. This clearly shows the mass, initially thought to be moss, which proved to be rootlets; five pollen samples from the mass all had Filipendula pollen, mostly at high values

Meadowsweet should have been chosen is a matter on which Tipping speculates. Without mention of aspirin, he points out that the plant has medicinal properties as an antacid, astringent and antirheumatic. He also notes that the flowers and leaves are aromatic, and it was one of the strewing herbs used in the early modern period and the scent was considered to have an exhilarating effect. No precisely identified, coarse remains of plants are closely identified from in any of Tipping's analyses of cist contents.

Graeme Whittington (1993) published similar results from two Bronze Age burial cists, each containing skeletons, from Dalgety Bay, in Fife. Samples from the clay luting on the corners and top edges of the cist were devoid of pollen. From the floors of the cists, high concentrations of Meadowsweet pollen, with up to 50% of immature grains, were recovered. Whittington concluded that flowers of Meadowsweet were deposited in the grave as a ritual practice. A cist from Upper Kenly Farm, Fife, yielded no Meadowsweet pollen although a food vessel and the floor of the cist were both examined; Whittington suggested that this internment may have taken place outside the long flowering period of Meadowsweet. Again, no coarse remains of plants are mentioned.

None of the above-mentioned samples contained more than a single grain of Lime pollen, and the Ashgrove Farm pollen analysis is, at present, unique in the high value of that pollen. It would appear to be the earliest example of honey to have been found so far in Scotland although it may have originated from England or the continent. However, there are so far positive results from a mere three containers published from Scotland (Table 2).

The latest addition to the story is that Merryn and Graham Dineley (2000b) have experimented with brewing Barley ale with the addition of dried Meadowsweet flowers. They were most impressed, writing '. . . meadowsweet was an excellent preservative as well as being a flavouring of the subsequent ale and it also gave the ale a reddish hue'. Made without Meadowsweet, ale went sour quickly, but that with the Meadowsweet stayed drinkable for several months. These highly interesting observations may mean that the Scottish Bronze Age containers discussed in this section were indeed mugs for drinking alcohol, as first claimed by JHD in 1978 on the basis of pollen counts and then by Soerd Bohncke.

It is clear that beakers particularly, and food vessels too, should be sought, and the general ruling about not cleaning pottery, especially if a stain or crust is present, until examined by a pollen analyst, should be rigorously followed. Floor deposits of cists which have remained sealed should, of course, continue to be examined for pollen. The high values of immature Meadowsweet pollen strongly suggest that flowers were placed in many of the cists, or added to beverages or food in vessels. Peter Moore (1994, p709) accepted cheerfully the floral tribute hypothesis '. . . the Bronze Age people of Scotland do seem to have been early in their expression of grief in floral terms'. Perhaps or perhaps not is the best that can be said as yet, in JHD's opinion.

The funerary flowers and alcohol explanations are not necessarily mutually exclusive. Had Meadowsweet been very important to the prehistoric inhabitants of Scotland, is it then inconceivable that both Meadowsweet-flavoured alcohol and bouquets or shrouds of Meadowsweet were placed in the graves?

Climatic deteriorations

It has been suggested that climatic worsening could have been responsible for the desertion of northern areas during the latter part of the Bronze Age and, at least initially, this could have been due to a volcanic eruption of Mount Hekla, in Iceland, Hekla 3, which took place in 1159 BC, as outlined in chapter 1. Huge dust clouds veiled the atmosphere, bringing increased rainfall and cooler, shorter, growing seasons. Marginal land might have had to be relinquished and the communities forced to move down to the already crowded lowlands.

Climatically induced, unfavourable growing seasons for Oaks have been noted. Such changes, which may have lasted some years, have been seen in a marked narrowing of the tree rings as the trees suffer stress from increasing waterlogging. This is clearly seen in

Oaks dated by dendrochronology, the method of absolute dating of wood outlined in Appendix 3. Series of European Oaks have been dated in this way and, in Ireland, the sequences go back for 7,500 years. Irish bog Oaks have been shown by Mike Baillie to possess these narrow rings from 1159 BC to 1141 BC; the former date has been estimated by radiocarbon dating of ash layers in peat bogs in Iceland to have marked the beginning of the Hekla 3 eruption. Tephra in peat bogs in northern Scotland has been identified by Andrew Dugmore as being from the Hekla 3 eruption.

To link dated Oaks with deserted farmsteads is not an easy task, since Oak was not growing in the most northern marginal areas during the period concerned. The northern woods, which survived into the Late Bronze Age from the depredations of man and his animals, would have been composed of Birch-Hazel copses, with Scots Pine the dominant tree in certain western areas. Anna Ritchie, dealing with Orkney (1995), and Val Turner, dealing with Shetland (1997), treat these volcanically-induced effects on the Bronze Age populations seriously. However, Cowie and Shepherd (1997) view the matter more cautiously.

For many years there have been arguments put forward for a deterioration in climate at around 2,500 years ago in north-west Europe; this is the traditional Sub-boreal/Sub-atlantic transition, coinciding with the Bronze Age/Iron Age transition. In particular, fluctuating precipitation has been deduced by the highly detailed examination of changes in peat composition, for example by Bent Aaby (1978) in Jutland and Keith Barber (1981) in north-west England. Barber has correlated these radiocarbon-dated results. In the mid-Bronze Age there was a pronounced climatic decline, resulting from moist conditions, from 1500-1400 BC. At the Late Bronze Age/Early Iron Age, a marked decline to a cooler and wetter climate followed. Dates vary slightly from different bogs and Barber advises archaeologists 'to look for the nearest available peat-stratigraphic evidence in that peat bogs in a particular area should surely reflect the local conditions of surface wetness which will presumably be more relevant to agricultural conditions of that area'. Baas Van Geel et al (1996) have presented detailed evidence from the Netherlands and compiled evidence from across Europe and elsewhere. They state (p452) that between about 850 and 760 BC '. . . the climate changed from relatively warm and continental to oceanic'.

Whatever the effects of volcanic eruptions and other agents of climatic change, the indications from pollen analysis are that an increase in the population in the early Iron Age led to a substantial deforestation of much of the low-lying parts of Scotland. Where small Bronze Age clearances had already occurred, a much longer more intensive clearance followed. For central and southern Scotland, this is discussed in the section on the pre-Roman vegetation of central Scotland in chapter 6.

5 Late Bronze Age and Iron Age: brochs and crannogs

Crannogs: outstanding sources of waterlogged plant remains

Dwellings constructed in lochs or estuaries, crannogs are one of the distinctive features of Scottish archaeology. Built with solid foundations which can be of timber, brushwood and stones, they can be entirely man-made or used to extend a natural island. Apart from one example from south Wales, crannogs are completely restricted to Scotland and Ireland, where 400 have been recorded. In both countries they are first known from rare examples built in the Neolithic period.

Until the last few decades, not many crannogs had been recorded from the whole of Scotland, but now some 17 are known from Loch Tay alone. The first modern excavation was published by C.M. Piggott in 1953 from the early Iron Age crannog at Milton Loch, in Kirkcudbrightshire; the building was of roundhouse type (**33**). The presence of upright piles and horizontal beams was established and decayed wattling was seen. A wooden plough head and stilt were retrieved from beneath the crannog. Cereal growing was attested by the presence of rotary quern stones, but the only food plant recorded was Hazel, of which there were large numbers of nuts.

It is of interest to consider the disposition of crannogs in the Scottish landscape. Ian Morrison has studied the position of many of these in relation to the adjacent shores. They were often placed near farmland especially where there were no natural defensive places nearby. Morrison concluded that a dwelling in the water may have been the only safe place from attack. Many were sited where shallow water becomes deeper. Both causeways and boats are known to have been used for access. Not all were in arable farming areas, however, they also form links for traditional cattle crossing places on Loch Awe, in Argyll.

Crannogs have been radiocarbon-dated from the Late Bronze Age onwards, some have been inhabited almost continuously, occasionally until as late as the seventeenth century, and in both Scotland and Ireland had reached a high status by the first millennium AD. The great majority have yet to be properly described and radiocarbon-dated. A survey of crannogs in south-west Scotland has been undertaken by John Barber and Anne Crone, on behalf of Historic Scotland, to determine the state of existing crannogs before deciding what measures can be taken to preserve them. The south-west was chosen because in the nineteenth century Robert Munro and others had excavated or surveyed a number of crannogs in that area, and so some knowledge already existed. Some 58 sites were visited and 42 certain or possible crannogs were found. The Scottish Trust for Underwater Archaeology surveyed and sampled some of the sites. Several samples were taken for radiocarbon dating to test the hypothesis that the crannogs were structures extending over more than one period.

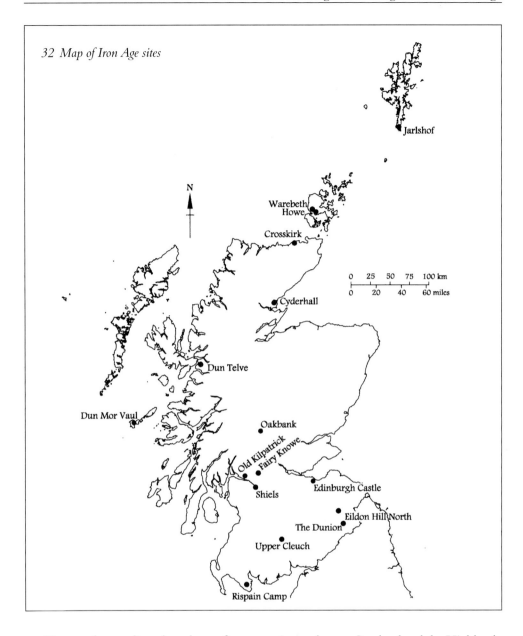

32 Map of Iron Age sites

Twenty-three radiocarbon dates of crannogs in south-west Scotland and the Highlands showed three main periods of crannog construction. Only five dates were available from the Highlands and these all fall within the first millennium BC, but this is probably due to the small number dated since it is known that crannogs were still being constructed in the sixteenth century in parts of the Highlands, at times of unrest.

Barber and Crone found that the crannogs in the south-west of Scotland had a pronounced building phase during the pre-Roman and Roman Iron Age. Dates from three crannogs show extensive use in the Dark Ages, but nineteenth-century excavations had already produced many artefacts of that period from other crannogs. Although only

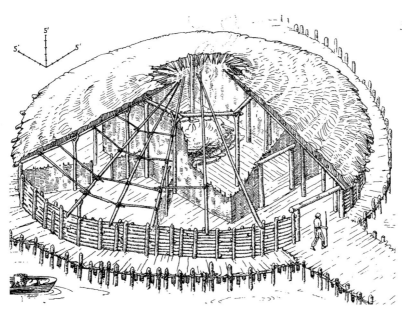

33 Milton Loch Crannog. Reconstruction of crannog 1 from Pigott (1953)

one site has a Medieval date, Medieval pottery has been found in other lake sites. Medieval structures have also been noted on many natural islands, ignored by this survey.

On our present knowledge, the occupancy of crannogs seems to have been intermittent. Anne Crone follows Morrison in suggesting that the sites were defensive. Crone has tentatively correlated the periods of occupancy, based on Buiston crannog, with events further afield in Scotland. Buiston was one of only two sites which appeared to have retained organic deposits to any extent and was therefore the one chosen for excavation to determine the archaeological value and the duration of these settlements. A detailed discussion of Buiston follows in chapter 7.

The potential of crannogs as a source of further information on prehistoric and early historic farming practices is very great because the waterlogged plant material is usually well-preserved. This good preservation contrasts strongly with the sparsity of burnt remains, which are often all that has survived from hillforts and other burnt-down buildings of the late prehistoric and early historic periods. As already stated, crannogs seemed to have reached their highest status in the first millennium AD. This is a little known period of Scottish history, formerly thought of as the Dark Ages. Excavation of crannogs should shed light on domestic life during this period of especial interest, since traded objects from the Mediterranean countries may be expected to be found.

Why should the great labour of driving in hundreds of piles and splitting huge logs to make extensive platforms as bases for buildings in the lochs have been undertaken? There is a marked increase in the construction of defensive buildings at the end of the Bronze Age, which continues throughout the Iron Age, a trend also noticed beyond Britain. Perhaps climatically induced, there was also a move away from marginal land at the end of the Bronze Age in some northern areas, as discussed at the end of the previous chapter. In Caithness, huts and whole villages seem to have become deserted.

Old Kilpatrick, Clyde Estuary

It is fortunate that some of the discoveries made during the few excavations of crannogs in the early twentieth century have been preserved in museums, because some dietary evidence from one of the Clyde Estuary crannogs has survived.

The crannogs of the Clyde Estuary have been largely removed in the course of river deepening operations from the eighteenth century onwards. Six crannogs have been recorded as previously existing in a 10km stretch between West Langbank and Old Kilpatrick. There are radiocarbon dates from two of them. From Erskine crannog, part of which is still visible, an Alder wood pile was dated to about 300 BC and an Oak pile to about 200 BC. Also from Old Kilpatrick, Alder charcoal was dated to about 500 BC. These dates fall into the period of the Early Iron Age.

A few kilometres downstream of Old Kilpatrick, the undated crannog at Dumbuck was excavated at the turn of the twentieth century. The recognised bones were of Domestic Cattle, Horse, Sheep/Goat, Pig, Red and Roe Deer. These were found together with those of a few large birds, and Oyster, Winkle and Mussel shells. The resources of hunting and shellfishing in the estuary were thus being combined with pastoral farming.

Old Kilpatrick crannog was situated some metres offshore, with good farmland nearby. The crannog deposits have had an unusual history, which began in 1906 when Messrs Napier and Miller were building a new dock for their shipyard. Their surveyors recorded a wooden platform of about 10m across. Photographs show huge split timbers but, due to lack of suitable preservation techniques at that time, these were later destroyed. A small fragment of Hazel wood wattle, with burnt daub and a few rough stone and wood implements were retained by the Kelvingrove Museum, Glasgow. Other plant material was collected by Ludovic Mann and exhibited by him in the Palace of History at the 1911 Great Exhibition staged in Glasgow. These remains included a collection of heads of Barley and 92 Cherry stones, the latter recovered from a small area at floor level. Weed seeds and seeds of grassland plants, identified by the eminent palaeobotanist, Clement Reid, were also on display.

Some of the material was later relocated to the Glasgow Museum and CD had the opportunity to re-examine it. Alder was the most abundant of the surviving charcoal pieces; local damp woodland along the estuary would have provided this rot resistant wood, highly suitable for underwater piling. Rare charcoal fragments of Wild/Bird-cherry and Ash suggest that woodland from better soils was also exploited. Rare unburnt, decay-resistant Oak wood survives. Seeds of woodland plants include Dog's Mercury, Pale Sedge and Remote Sedge.

The burnt cereal ear fragments are amazingly well-preserved, with even the awns still surviving (**82**). It is rare indeed to find such highly identifiable grain and chaff. In addition to Barley, which is of the Hulled Six-rowed type, the commonest cereal in the southern part of Scotland in the Early Iron Age, there are ear fragments of Emmer Wheat, a hulled grain grown by earlier prehistoric peoples, and by this time grown mainly by small farmers in northern England. Emmer Wheat is believed to be less weather resistant than Spelt Wheat which replaced it. It may be that the two Wheats were used for different purposes, as is suggested in the section on Roman crops (chapter 6). The Clyde coast comes under the influence of the Gulf Stream, with the consequence of reduced frostiness, and therefore the growing season is longer than even just a few kilometres further inland.

Oat grains were determined by their floret bases (*see* **83**). They are probably all of Wild Oat, which became widespread in this period and is still a common cornfield weed. Seeds of other weeds of arable fields, which were presumably gathered with the crops, include Fat Hen, Black-bindweed, Hemp-nettle, Pale-persicaria, Knotweed, Corn Spurrey and Chickweed. Most of these grow to the same height as the corn and would have been gathered together with the corn by reaping high on the ear. All are still found in cornfields at the present time. A few seeds of species, such as Spike-rush, now restricted to wetter places, perhaps reflecting damp hollows in the cornfield.

The wild fruit component is a rather surprising mixture: Wild Strawberry and Raspberry seeds, which would have ripened in July and August, with Dog Rose, Wild Cherry and Brambles ripening from August to September, and Sloes and Hazelnuts ready in the autumn. To have such a mixture stored in one place suggests that some of them were dried ready for winter use. Although some of these fruits can be considered too astringent for human use, it has been shown by Pat Wiltshire that, after drying and subsequent re-wetting for 12 hours, fruits of Sloes lose their astringency and become more palatable, tasting rather like stewed plums (1995). Brambles, however, do not improve on drying and re-wetting. Wild and cultivated fruits are still dried for winter consumption in Turkey, including such small and unpromising fruits as Wild Strawberries. Warm sun or artificial heat is needed to dry these quickly enough to prevent fungal spoiling of the fruit. This collection suggests that winter stores were moved to a safe haven away from Field Mice who relish such fruit. At one stage a marauder did find the stores, for the gnaw marks of a Bank Vole are visible on Sloe stones where the animal has removed the tasty kernel (*see* **163**).

Burnt and unburnt fragments of Bracken are present in small quantities. Bracken used to be used for animal bedding until recently and the frond stalks make a fairly durable thatch, when the more easily rotted fronds are first stripped off. Little is known of the construction of the dwellings or storehouses on these crannogs, but the strong westerly winds which beat up the Clyde estuary in winter would have necessitated very strong buildings to withstand them. Wattle reinforced with clay daub was used, but even stouter outer walls may have been needed.

Tormentil, Selfheal, Heath-grass, Buttercup, Sheep's Sorrel, Lesser Stitchwort and low-growing Sedges are plants of wet and dry grassy and heathy places. Seeds of all of these were recovered but not grass seeds, most of which need permanent waterlogging to survive. The low close-knit vegetation which this assemblage represents would have been too sparse to gather for litter or fodder. The most likely origin of the seeds is from soil which had disintegrated from turves. Such turf and its binding roots could have been cut and used for the outer walling and even for roofing if the pitch were low. Turf was undoubtedly used a great deal as a building material in treeless parts of Scotland, and much of central Scotland was largely treeless by the Iron Age, as is discussed in the next chapter.

From a knowledge of the Iron Age flora gained from other sites, it is clear that all these plants could have been growing locally and it is not difficult to explain their presence on the crannog. There are, however, seeds which are much more puzzling. Four unburnt Fig pips were identified. This was a potentially exciting find because dried Figs were known to have been imported by the Romans, and indeed pips were found at Bearsden, one of the Antonine Wall forts, some 9km to the east. Had there been an early Roman advance party which had camped on the disused crannog? There was only one way to find out the age of the pips; three of them were sacrificed to provide an AMS date. This refined method of dating can use a single burnt cereal grain or a few small seeds to give a date as accurate as that provided by several grams of carbon by a conventional radiocarbon assay. The dating was kindly provided by Rupert Housley at the Oxford Laboratory. The date was most unexpected; it was recent — in fact from the early twentieth century. We can only assume that one of the excavators had figs as part of his lunch! The alternative explanation is that the Clyde brought modern sewage including fig pips downstream and into the crannog but, surprisingly, no other common sewage constituents such as tomato seeds were found. Neither explanation seems entirely convincing but it was certainly an object lesson in the ever-present possibility of plant material of different ages becoming intermixed in the course of time. Without the benefit of modern dating procedures we could easily have been led to the wrong conclusions.

Oakbank, Loch Tay

Although with their own very considerable interest, both Lochlee and Old Kilpatrick Crannogs are in the lowlands of central Scotland, but the location of Oakbank Crannog in the fertile area of Breadalbane in the central Highlands gives the archaeobotanical studies great force (**34, 35**). The remains of cultivated and otherwise exploited plants have provided a rich detail elsewhere unknown so far from the prehistoric Highlands. Unless the great expense of a coffer dam can be afforded, the excavation of a crannog still underwater requires modern diving equipment and rigorous training in safety procedures before the site, even one in very shallow water, can be excavated. The development of the aqua-lung marked the beginning of serious underwater archaeology. Such work in Scottish lochs will never be as easy as in southern latitudes. Water temperatures in spring can remain low in large bodies of water in Scotland. Suspended, opaque peat particles in many lochs make recording difficult.

The large number of crannogs in Loch Tay, at least 17, have been surveyed by Nick Dixon and one of them, the one at Oakbank, has been excavated by him and numerous helpers. Though other archaeobotanists had already published work on earlier samples, the investigations by Jennifer Miller have revealed even richer assemblages of plant remains, with many implications for the exploitation of wild plants and the growing of crops (Miller *et al* 1998). A variety of timbers were used in the construction of the crannog but by far the most important was Alder; the piles driven into the bed of the Loch were trunks of that tree (**35**), as were some of the horizontal timbers (Sands, 1997).

Oakbank is the oldest of the crannogs so far radiocarbon-dated and dates from the end of the Bronze Age/beginning of the Iron Age at about 650, 500 and 400 BC. It is now is a flat-topped mound measuring 14m x 18m. A platform of parallel planks supported a fill of organic material interpreted as occupation debris. Numerous wooden utensils included a dish, plate, flagon stave, a carved peg and canoe paddle. A core was taken through floor levels, floor covering and dumped organic midden debris. Half the core (split vertically)

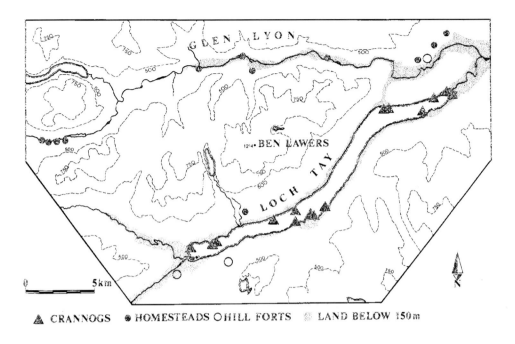

34 Crannogs in Loch Tay. With permission of Historic Scotland

was used for pollen analyses and the other part sieved for larger plant remains. Both pollen and seed diagrams were constructed to enable a comparison between the two types of data and the results published by Alan Clapham and Rob Scaife (1988).

Although a few pollen analyses were published by Elizabeth Knox from the lake mud near Milton Loch crannog, this core from Oakbank is the only core through a Scottish crannog which has so far been published. The sandy sediment of the Loch Tay floor was dominated by spores of Bracken and other Ferns. A number of possible reasons are given by the authors for this. High values for Alder and Coryloid (Hazel/Bog Myrtle) pollen were present throughout but Birch, Pine, Wych Elm and Oak were also present in the pollen catchment area. Two overlying floors were sampled and these, together with the occupation debris between, were dominated by herb pollen such as Grass and Ribwort Plantain with smaller representations of Clovers and Medicks, Docks and the Figwort family. These are plants predominantly associated with pastoral activity which were found together with abundant cereal type pollen. The authors assume that this 'represents plant material brought into the crannog and incorporated into the fabric of the floor'. The very high cereal values of up to 50% of the total pollen need a special explanation. It has been shown that cereal pollen which, with the exception of that of Rye, is not liberated into the air in large quantities, may become trapped in the husks of the cereal ears. Such an abundance of cereal pollen could result from on-site cereal processing. The rare charred and scorched remains of Wheat and Barley chaff which were noted could have resulted from parching the grain to dry it and thus help its preservation, as well as assisting the threshing process of pounding to release the grain.

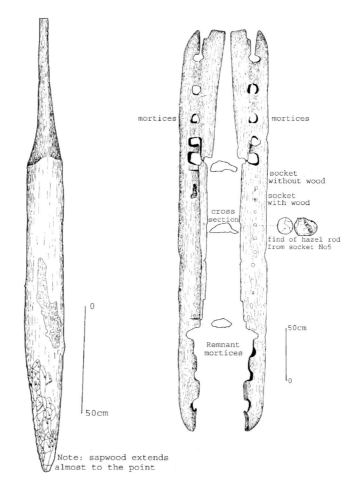

35 Structural timbers made of Alder from Oakbank Crannog. Left, a pile and right, a morticed and socketed horizontal, more than 4m long. Modified from Sands (1997)

The organic debris was seen to include straw and amorphous animal dung. Floor covering, animal foodstuffs or chaff from animal dung, or a combination of these features, could have resulted in the high quantity of cereal pollen. It is pointed out that urban contexts such as in Medieval towns produce similar high cereal and associated weed pollen as the direct result of human activities. The taphonomy, that is the origin of the preserved assemblages, is likely to have been complex in both urban environments and occupation levels of crannogs.

There were high numbers of seeds of Chickweed, Fat Hen, and Stinging Nettle, with smaller quantities of Buttercups, Selfheal, Hemp-nettle and Nipplewort. Abandonment of the site for a season could have resulted in a growth of Nettles and Fat Hen, but contemporaneous low values of pollen of the Fat Hen family could mean that the seeds were deliberately brought to the site. Rush seeds, produced in many thousands by the parent plants, were more common than those of any other types. Rushes were used as thatching material in the past and this could have been their purpose at Oakbank. Present in large quantity, some of it charred, Bracken may have been used in various ways such as thatching and animal bedding.

Several types of fruit were gathered from the wild: Wild Strawberry, Raspberry, Bramble, Sloe and Bird-cherry. All could have grown in the local woodland or at the woodland edge. However, by far the most noteworthy of the wild fruits gathered was Cloudberry, which has been highlighted in part 2.

The crop plants recovered from Oakbank were Flax, Opium Poppy and Wheats. Flax seeds were recorded in small numbers from two levels; Flax has been recorded in Scotland from the Neolithic period onwards. Perhaps the most interesting identifications are the sparse finds of Wheat chaff since these are of Emmer and Spelt. Emmer has been shown to have been present in Scotland in favourable localities from Neolithic and Bronze Age sites. Spelt, however, does not appear in southern Britain until the first millennium BC, but at a similar period has also been recorded from north-east England. About 1000 BC in the Bronze Age, Spelt was grown at Halshill, Northumberland (van der Veen 1992). Spelt seems more tolerant of poor soil conditions and is probably more frost resistant than Emmer. This may have been a rapid response by farmers to the wetter climate that is known to have characterised the Iron Age. Nevertheless, it still seems surprising that Spelt should have penetrated so far into the Highlands so quickly.

At Kenmore, at the eastern end of Loch Tay, an experimental crannog has been constructed by the Scottish Underwater Archaeological Trust (**36**). The general principles employed are based on what is known of the very diverse construction methods of the crannog builders. However, the roofing material used is still a vexed question because prehistoric roofs have disintegrated long since, and the modern crannog builder must use whatever seems to best stand the test of time. Evidence for wattle exists, but unless clay daub is preserved by conflagration as baked clay, the evidence for its use in windproofing and preserving the wattle will have been lost because the tiny particles of clay will have been washed away into the water.

The broch at Howe, Orcadian Mainland: fire produces rare evidence

The environment at Howe and elsewhere

Much of the environmental evidence for Iron Age Scotland comes from brochs. These dry stone, defensive towers, so distinctive and peculiar to Scotland, are particularly common in the far north and on the islands. Only a few are known in central and southern Scotland. All seem to be close to good agricultural land and are thought to have been fortified farmhouses used by high status families. As they are the most durable of the Iron Age buildings, with double walls of up to 5m in thickness, the lower parts of some of them have survived to the present-day. In Glenelg, the wall of the broch called Dun Telve stands almost 11m high (**37, 38**). At the entrance the wall is 4m thick and the courtyard approaches 11m in diameter.

The development of brochs coincided with the spread of the rotary quern, which sped up the grinding of corn compared with the saddle quern, which had been used from the Neolithic onwards. The saddle quern was an oblong stone with a flat upper surface which became concave with use; a flat stone, held above it, was used to grind the grain. The rotary quern consisted of two round stones, resembling miniature mill wheels, but the

36 Reconstructed crannog at the east end of Loch Tay. From Scottish Underwater Trust

upper one was turned by hand. Perhaps this more efficient method of processing cereals, which continued in use in remote areas until the present century, contributed to the expansion in farming. It is not known, however, if cereal products composed the major component of the foods that were consumed by the inhabitants of the brochs.

The evidence for Iron Age farming is chiefly taken from northern Scotland. Pollen analysis sets the scene for us. On Orkney, the open farming landscape with scrub continued to exist throughout the Bronze Age and Iron Age to the present time. On the mainland, at the Loch of Winless, Caithness, a radiocarbon-dated pollen diagram, analysed by Sylvia Peglar (1978), shows a marked decrease in the tree pollen and sharp increase in pollen of grasses and weeds in the late Bronze Age or early Iron Age. Four pollen samples taken from the coastal broch at Crosskirk, 30km north-west of the Loch of Winless, produced less than 7% tree pollen and both pastoral and arable agriculture were indicated (CD and JHD 1984). On the island of Tiree, off the west coast, Jon Pilcher analysed pollen from pre-broch and broch age samples; all showed very low tree pollen; the pre-broch type of agriculture was sustained throughout the broch occupation (Mackie 1974).

Charcoal from Crosskirk consisted of small fragments of Alder, Birch, Hazel, Poplar, Rowan, Scots Pine and Juniper, that from Bu Broch, on the Orcadian Mainland, was of Birch and Willow, with Spruce from driftwood; and at Broch of Burrian, North Ronaldsay, Orkney, Scots Pine were identified. The evidence for local woodland on Tiree was of Alder, Hazel, Oak and Willow.

An important broch site on Orkney at Howe was extensively sampled for charcoal and other plant remains identified by CD (**39, 40** and Table 3). Alder, Birch, Hazel, Ash, Rowan type and Scots Pine were all recovered in small quantities. Spruce driftwood was slightly more commonly found than at Bu broch. Willow, however, was recovered from many contexts, including hearths, collapsed roofing and a furnace. As Willow is not a durable wood and probably grew as stunted bushes, as it does at present on Orkney, its use for construction does suggest a major shortage of more suitable woods. The pollen evidence from these sites is confirmed by the sparse finds of charcoal; wood was obviously not plentiful in these areas by the Iron Age. A further feature of the northern brochs is that the internal divisions and wall cupboards are of stone.

Howe is outstanding in its long, continuous, Iron Age occupation, which lasted for

37 Early illustrations of the broch at Dun Telve, Inverness-shire, drawn in 1772. From Ritchie (1988)

over 1,200 years from the sixth century BC to the eighth century AD. Although finds were sparse from the earlier phases, due to much clearance before rebuilding work, plant and animal remains were preserved throughout that long period. However, they become frequent only in phases 7 and 8 (Table 3). There is no evidence for cultural similarities with the Pictish kingdom and the late period of the occupancy; from the fourth century onwards (Phase 8) is described as the late Iron Age even though at other sites this marks the beginning of the Pictish period. The Iron Age buildings were constructed on top of a major funerary monument of Neolithic age; this and the subsequent long Iron Age are described in the large monograph edited by Beverley Ballin Smith (1994). As was the case at other brochs, a settlement developed outside the broch tower. Several families lived in separate small houses. As the broch was rebuilt following collapse or fires, so too was the settlement, and its use changed to include byres and industrial workshops.

Corn drying and dung
Barley was recorded from the earliest phase, with Naked Six-rowed Barley identified from Phase 5 onwards. Hulled Six-rowed Barley was recovered from Phase 7, the middle Iron

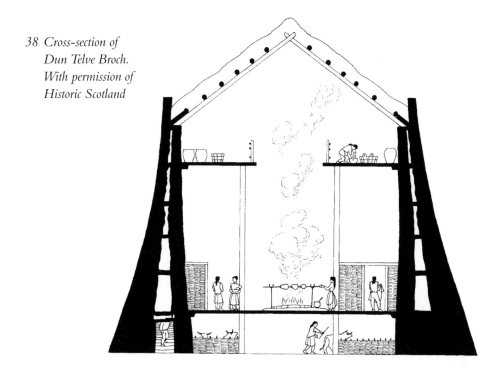

38 Cross-section of Dun Telve Broch. With permission of Historic Scotland

Age, and Phase 8, the late Iron Age. Wild Oat was recorded from Phase 7. The changes in cereals and other crops during that period are discussed later. Oat grains lacking the diagnostic chaff were also recorded from later Phase 8; consequently it is not known if these were wild or cultivated. Five Flax seeds (linseed) from Phase 7 were the earliest found at the site and others were found in Phase 8 contexts. From Phase 5/6 adherent clusters of Naked Barley grains were retrieved from a ditch fill. Several thousand grains in all were found with their sides depressed where they had been squashed against adjacent grains. This suggests that they had been picked at a milk-ripe or nearly dough-ripe stage of ripeness. Pliny records the use of milk-ripe pearl Barley for soups; perhaps a thick Barley broth had burnt dry.

Naked Barley was clearly the major crop, and numerous burnt ears were found on the broch floor where they had been laid out to dry in the heat from the pottery kiln (*see* **81**). Unfortunately for the broch inhabitants, but fortunately for us, the Barley had caught fire; it is rare that such evidence for crop drying survives.

The Barley would normally have been processed before cooking, and querns would have been used to grind the grain for bread making, the flat 'bannocks' that were traditionally cooked on a hot plate by the fire. Fifty-nine saddle querns were found from Phase 5/6 onwards, especially from Phase 7; only twenty-seven rotary querns were found dating from Phase 3 onwards, although none were *in situ*. They have the flat disc-shaped stones which seem to have developed on the Atlantic coastal areas of Scotland. The fact that both types were in use together is puzzling as rotary querns usually replaced saddle querns during the Iron Age as they were so much more efficient to use.

A few seeds of arable weeds were found and they would have been introduced with

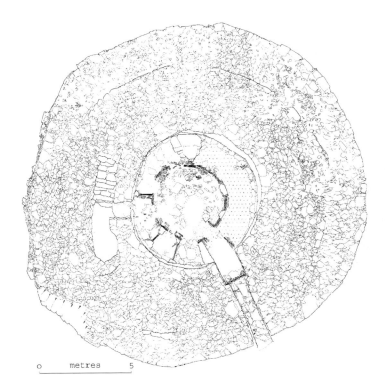

39 Howe. Plan of the Early Phase 7 broch tower: wallhead and floor plan. From Ballin Smoth (1994)

o metres 5

straw and chaff, which were also sometimes preserved. The most common weed, to judge from the number of its seeds, was Chickweed; its presence suggests a richer soil, such as ground which is kept well-manured.

The fire in the broch tower which had burnt the grain had also ignited an Alder wood container and its fragments suggested that it had been a staved bucket, the staves bound together with bands of fibre or metal. A fragment of a Heather basket had also survived the conflagration (*see* **131**). It had been made from double strands of straight Heather stems interwoven with thin Heather shoots passing in front of one pair and behind the next pair of stems. It had been tightly woven and may have been used as a measure for meal. A recent parallel is the traditional Orcadian Heather basket, perhaps the basin-shaped luppie described by Fenton in his book on the Northern Isles (1978).

As at most brochs, the evidence for roofing materials was scanty, but shaped Willow wood appears to have been used for roofing supports in the broch and surrounding settlement. Burnt Larch fragments from driftwood, with very narrow, close rings, probably the outer layers of a substantial trunk, and may have been the remains of a roofing beam.

It is not usually possible to recover evidence for animal housing; it was thus fortunate that one of the settlement buildings had been damaged by fire. Burnt straw littered the floor and this had burnt vesicular material adhering to it. A discrete lump and 'tails', typical of some mammalian dung, were also recovered. The dung-like material was clearly not from weaned animals, since there were no signs of hay or other identifiable remains present. CD was curious to find out what dung of milk-fed animals, including humans,

40 Howe. Early Phase 7. From Ballin Smith (1994)

would look like when burnt. It was not difficult to obtain faeces from an unweaned baby and the Veterinary Department of the University of Glasgow was pleased to supply dung from milk-fed lambs and calves. Not surprisingly a number of substances originally of a thick creamy or viscous consistency, such as honey, look rather similar when burnt. The presence of adherent straw and the tail-like ends strongly suggested that this was animal dung and that the building had been used as a byre before the conflagration. In case the reader is wondering if dried dung, for fuel, could have been stored in the building, rather than the building's use for housing live animals, dry dung does not form vesicles when burnt. Furthermore, it is the dry hay or straw content which provides the firing and this was absent from the milk-fed dung.

Gathered from the wild: Hazel, soft fruit and heathy turf

Seeds from berries were only found in the hearth deposits from the later Phase 8 house. Black Bearberry, Crowberry, and Bog Bilberry or Cowberry may have been brought indoors to dry for winter use. Berries would have been sought after, but some would usually have been eaten where collected and so are not usually recorded. Only a few fragments of Hazelnuts were found, also from later Phase 8. Could this be an indication that even then, some 1,200 years ago, Hazel bushes were already few and far between on Orkney? Cowberry and Black Bearberry are only found locally now on Orkney and would have been restricted to the summits of hills and, indeed, the latter is not known

Howe: Iron Age phases			
PHASES	**CALIBRATED C14 DATES**	**BUILDINGS**	**MAIN EVENTS**
Phase 3-4	?6th-4th century BC	Enclosed settlement	Barley
Phase 5	Probably 4th & 3rd century BC	Roundhouse 4m thick walls	
	(500-400 BC)	Earthhouse (souterrain)	In use for several centuries, perhaps for storage.
		Enclosed settlement	
Phase 6	est. 2nd & 1st century BC (?400-200 BC)	Broch 1	Central hearth suggests single household Naked Barley
		Outside settlement rebuilt	Settlement i.e. dwelling house Both broch and settlement destroyed after collapse of broch
Phase 7 early	1st-4th century AD (200 BC-AD 100)	Broch 2	Single household Fire in broch passage Cupboard with charred seeds of medicinal plants
		Enclosed settlement	Six or more households in settlement
Phase 7 later		Broch 2	Used as workshop pottery and stone tools Charred Naked Barley drying on floor Basket
		Settlement	NE rebuilding of settlement — partial reoccupation Much Heather charcoal Iron working in west building Fire preceded 2nd collapse of broch tower Hulled and Naked Barley
Phase 7 / 8	4th century AD	Broch 2	Iron smelting furnace fired with Willow twigs in partly collapsed broch
Phase 8 early	4th-7th century AD	Broch abandonment	
		Settlement	Single farmstead with iron working Linseed/Flax Heathy turf used as fuel
Phase 8 later	7th-8th century AD	Settlement	Single farmstead; no iron working

Table 3   Howe: Iron Age Phases

from the Orcadian Mainland; here would seem to be evidence of foraging well away from the low-lying Howe farmland.

Before much of the Mainland of Orkney was converted to improved pasture in recent years, dwarf shrub heathland covered much of the better drained land. Now much reduced in area, these heaths, in addition to Heather, support Crowberry, Bell Heather, Cross-leaved Heath, dwarf Sedges, Tormentil, Heath Rush, Louseworts and Woodrushes. The Heather binds the acid humus-rich soil together and can be stripped off with the uppermost peaty layer and then dried. This results in a turf some 30-50mm thick. Remains of turf-forming plants were found in quantity from late Phase 7 onwards. The numerous hearth deposits sampled from the early and later Phase 8 contained remains of both turf plants and peat. Turf was used up to modern times in Orkney to eke out peat when it was scarce and also to increase the amount of ashes produced for manure. Turf may have been used in just such a way at Howe.

A medicine cupboard?

From early Phase 7, a stone cupboard in the broch produced a charred seed of each of Skull-cap, Dead-nettle and Sheep's Sorrel. Seeds of these wild plants were not found in any other context. According to habitat, this is an odd mixture. Skull-cap is a plant of stream-sides and fens; such a habitat is not represented by any other plant finds of that period. At present on Orkney, Skull-cap is restricted to the storm beaches (Bullard 1995). Dead-nettles are weeds of fertile, cultivated and disturbed ground, and Sheep's Sorrel is a plant of blanket bog, species-poor heath and acid cultivated ground. A Barley grain and a little charcoal were the only other contents of the cupboard.

Skull-cap

The active ingredient is scutellarin. A related species from China has been extensively researched and found to have anti-inflammatory and anti-allergic properties. The flowering shoots of the European species, have been used as an anti-inflammatory and to alleviate fever. As a herbal remedy it is still in use for its nervine and antispasmodic qualities, although derived from the American species, Blue Skullcap. It is thought that the European Skull-cap possesses similar nervine properties.

Dead-nettle

The active ingredients include tannins, amines, flavonoids and saponin. The plant has astringent properties and controls bleeding. It has been used for bathing burns and septic cuts. An infusion is made from the petals and flowering shoots.

Sheep's Sorrel

The active ingredients, similar to those found in Common Sorrel, are anthraquinones, chrysophanol, emodin and physcion. Both Sheep's Sorrel and Common Sorrel are used as diuretics for urinary conditions.

Lesser Celandine

This plant has been highlighted in part 2, and its medicinal uses were stressed. Tubers were found in the early Phase 7 broch tower in an intra-mural cell, and were also present on the paving of one of the settlements and in ash under a hearth from a Late Iron Age phase. The tubers are unlikely to have arrived accidentally at the site because they grow just below ground and the plant is pulled up to recover them. Lesser Celandine has also been found by European archaeobotanists. At Neolithic Hekelingen in the Netherlands, Corrie Bakels (1988) noted that the tubers were among the more common finds from the site and she presumed that they were eaten. From middle Bronze Age Gotland in Sweden, the tubers were found in hearths, cooking pits and cultural layers. The authors, Roger Engelmark and Karin Viklund (1988), considered that the tubers had been roasted and eaten like popcorn.

Juniper

Single seeds were recorded from a hearth deposit in the early Phase 7 settlement and later Phase 8 farmstead. The plant has many complex chemical constituents including volatile oils, tannin and resin. Its powerful properties were known to Theophrastus and classical authors recognised its antiseptic and emmenagogic properties. It is strongly diuretic, antiseptic and anti-inflammatory and is used to treat chronic cystitis and rheumatism in herbal medicine.

No doubt other plants were used, but only ripe seed would have lasted through the centuries and most plants would have been collected at the flowering stage. Assuming that these plants had been used medicinally, do any of these finds shed light on the health of the broch inhabitants? As most plants have several properties, this cannot be readily determined. However, as mentioned above, certain of the plants found contain tannins with astringent properties, as do some species of *Vaccinium* (collected as berried fruits). Astringents cause tissues to contract and so reduce discharges; some of the plants may therefore have been used to cure diarrhoea and dysentery. Tannins also have an antibiotic effect by precipitating protein in mucus membranes so depriving bacteria of nutrition and may help with slow-healing wounds. Scurvy may have been a problem then as it was in historic Scotland; Sheep's Sorrel and Lesser Celandine have vitamin C in the leaves, as do *Vaccinium* species and Crowberry in the fruits. Plants with anti-inflammatory properties could have been used for treating rheumatism. Bladder problems and illnesses peculiar to women may have been treated with Juniper. Savin (*Juniperus sabina*, a shrub of central Europe but not Britain) has been well-known till now as an abortifacient (Dickson and Gauld 1986). Herbs with antiseptic properties would always have been sought after, as tumbling masonry, knife cuts and gores from unpolled animals left their mark in cuts which became infected. In order to survive we may assume that the broch peoples had a good knowledge of herbal medicine.

Animal remains

The faunal remains, according to Catherine Smith and George Hodgson, whose work is described here, were unsurpassed by any other Iron Age excavation in the Northern Isles. Animal bones were found throughout the long occupation, but the very small numbers surviving from the earlier phases do not allow comparison with those from the later occupation. From the earliest Iron Age, mixed farming was practised and Domestic Cattle, Sheep and Pigs were kept. Red Deer were hunted and beached Whale carcasses exploited. Phase 4 saw the first bones of Dogs and Horses, the latter showed signs of butchering, so that although Horses were no doubt introduced for traction, when their useful life was over they were slaughtered for food. From Phase 4/5 came evidence for Domestic Cats, probably introduced to control the Orkney Vole population. A well, dated to Phases 4-6, produced six young Deer skeletons; they had been cooked as whole carcasses.

The number of preserved bones increased considerably in Phases 7 and 8. In both phases the number of individual sheep exceeded those of Domestic Cattle, with smaller numbers of Pigs. Red Deer numbers were high in Phase 7 but low in 8. Whether this was due to an increase in domestic stock removing the need for hunting or to a decline of suitable food for Deer in competition with Sheep and Pigs, or simply due to over exploitation, is not known. In Phase 7, Seals were probably caught for their oil and skin. Foxes and Otters may have been hunted for food, as well as for their skins. Throughout, the Cattle were of shorthorn type, the Sheep resembled modern Soay in many respects and the Pigs were probably all domesticated; Horses were of the Shetland pony type.

Don Bramwell identified an amazing 113 species of birds, representing one of the largest stratified bird bone assemblages in the north of Scotland. Only one species, the Great Auk, is now extinct, the others still occur in the islands as either breeding or visiting birds. Bramwell lists a number of habitats; these include sea cliffs for Gannet, Cormorant, Guillemot, Razorbill and Shag, estuaries for Duck and wading birds, and moorland for Golden Plover, Red Grouse and some Gulls. Marshes and lochs would have supported Ducks, Geese and Swans, and farmland, wintering birds and foragers which would have included Greylag Goose, Rock Dove, Golden Plover and Starling. Smaller birds, such as Thrushes and Buntings, may have been brought as prey to the settlement by Cats and birds of prey. Larger birds would have been caught for food. Howe is near to the shore and inland lochs, with moorland and marsh and high sea cliffs within 6km. Seabird eggs would have been collected early in the season, a tradition which continued until recent times. The flightless Great Auk, which bred in colonies, provided more bones than any other seabird. It appears to have been very easy to catch. Domestic Fowl and Geese were recorded from Phase 7 with Domestic Duck present in phase 7/8. In spite of the large number of items recorded in terms of available flesh, the birds would only have provided a subsidiary part of the diet.

Fish remains, identified by Alison Locker, were recovered from all phases, especially 7 and 8. They were mainly of the Cod group with a preponderance of Saithe. Over 30 types were recorded and other prime food fish were Roker, Eel, Conger Eel, salmonids, Ling and flatfish. The Saithe were immature and the young fish would have been abundant in inshore waters; all the fish could have been caught with nets or lines from small boats or from the shoreline. The record of Corkwing Wrasse, a shoreline species, is of interest as it is scarce in the region at present. As for other foods, the later phases provided the most evidence for shellfish. Common Limpets were the most numerous but there were also substantial numbers of Common Periwinkles, Common Mussels and some Common Cockles which, A. Kimble Howard states, were the shellfish of greatest dietary importance. As has been remarked several times, at this and other Scottish sites including Mesolithic ones, it is not known if the Limpets were collected for food or bait or both.

103

Other brochs on the Northern Isles: immersion preserves human coprolites

Warebeth, Orcadian Mainland

What did an Iron Age meal consist of and how was it cooked? It might be surmised that because querns have been found on most Iron Age sites that Barley was ground for unleavened bannocks. In Scottish native sites, however, there has yet to be found evidence for bread of any types in these early periods. Pot boilers indicate use to heat water and perhaps the liquid for meat and fish dishes. To answer our question we need human gut contents, a rare commodity, faeces dispersed in cess pits, or, even rarer, faeces preserved as coprolites by mineralisation or dessication (**41**). One of the rare instances of human coprolites being preserved occurred at Warebeth Broch, near Stromness, Orcadian Mainland (Bell and Dickson 1989).

A disused well, partly filled with water, was used as a midden, and bones, shells, pot sherds and faeces were tipped down the well steps and remained partly waterlogged. The faeces became coprolites by penetration by the very hard water resulting from contact with the highly calciferous sandstone with which the well had been built. The mineralised faeces had thus been preserved for some 1,800 years. Occasional fragments of Bracken fronds and Heather leaves were noted adhering to the outside; the faeces had probably been voided on to Bracken and Heather before being transferred to the well.

In the laboratory several coprolites were decalcified with dilute acid and the sparse contents identified. Remains of 33 types of flowering plants and mosses were recovered together with tiny pieces of bone, hair and feather fragments. Fragments of Barley grain bran consisted of little more than the thickened long hilum with much degraded adherent tissues. In order to elucidate the preparation and cooking which could have resulted in the degraded grains, Hulled Barley was processed in the traditional Scots manner for broth making. Deep stone mortars known as knocking stones producing 'knockit Barley' were used until recently and are still seen occasionally standing by cottage doors. In the experiment a ceramic mortar was used with a wooden pounder, and a handful of Hulled Six-row Barley first had the long awns removed and was then gently pounded in water. The husks floated to the top and were removed; the grain coats had rubbed away leaving the hilum and adjacent tissues protected by the deep hilar groove. The grain was then cooked and cell degradation watched for. After about three to four hours the cells had become degraded in a similar manner to those from the coprolites. The conclusion was that the Barley had been cooked in broth as the equivalent of modern machine-processed pearl Barley.

A fragment of Linseed and its capsule fragments were also recognised; linseed can be used as a laxative although this effect can be removed by boiling or soaking the seeds and disposing of the water. Small weed seeds, such as fragments of Chickweed, were probably inadvertently included from weeds reaped with the crop and ground with the grain. Heath and bog plants were well represented as both burnt and unburnt fragments; they are common components of peat, and tiny peat fragments were also found. These all suggest that at least some of the meat was cooked in the embers of a peat fire.

Degraded mammalian hairs were recovered from all coprolites; these were tentatively

41 Warebeth coprolite; this is a rare example of ancient human excrement retaining its original shape

identified by H.M. Appleyard. Deer hair was the most common with several Sheep or Goat hairs preserved. Coarse, very degraded hair could have come from Cattle and Pigs. Confirmation was obtained from the bones identified by Timothy Sellars who recorded Sheep especially, with Cattle and Red Deer as the next most numerous and Pig bones were also present. Bones from large Cods indicate that the fish were caught from boats offshore. Limpets may have been obtained for bait.

Pollen analyses from three of the coprolites included Barley type pollen, probably from the Barley in the broth. Remarkably, a Cat or Dog coprolite also contained Barley type pollen. Can it have been that the creature had been fed the remains of the broth? Numerous parasite eggs were identified but none found in the human coprolites. This was a little surprising as there are now so many records spatially and temporally across Europe that such infections were evidently commonplace.

The coprolite contents have given a substantial insight into some of the meals taken by the broch dwellers. Barley broth with Linseed, as well as venison, mutton and other meats were consumed. Until more investigations can take place it will remain unclear if this was typical of the Iron Age Orcadian diet, but the large number of bones recovered, over 2,000 fragments, perhaps suggests that there was no shortage of meat.

Jarlshof, Shetland

When brochs were excavated in the nineteenth and earlier twentieth centuries, the floor and midden deposits were usually discarded without detailed, microscopic examination. Recent experience has shown that the greater the number of contexts examined carefully, the longer the list of species recognised and consequently the more can be deduced about the environment.

A single sample of Naked Barley was kept from the excavations at Lingro. At Bu, Orcadian Mainland, an early building, originally thought to be a broch but reinterpreted as a roundhouse, produced Naked Barley and perhaps Emmer. There were also seeds of small grassland sedges, together with Heather and Heaths, similar to the assemblage at Howe, and also interpreted as heathy turf used for fuel. This suggested that wood or peat for fuel was in short supply; this is rather surprising at this very early Iron Age site (CD 1987).

The settlement at Jarlshof was very long and complex. It began in the Bronze Age and continued through to the Medieval period. A brief summary of the site has already been given in chapter 4; Norse and Medieval periods are described in the appropriate later chapters.

The Iron Age habitation was of long duration. Hamilton's sequence begins with circular houses and souterrains, followed by a period of abandonment. The building of a broch tower was followed by an aisled roundhouse built within a walled courtyard attached to the broch; unfortunately part of the broch has eroded into the sea. A probable byre, evinced by a roughly cobbled floor and a drain, was part of the complex. Wheelhouses were the next to be built within the courtyard and outside it; this increased accommodation suggests a rise in population. Wheelhouses, distinctive stone-built houses, were built in the Outer Hebrides and the Northern isles in the Late Iron Age. They were like a wheel in plan with the inside divided by radial piers of stone-work and a central hearth. An aisled roundhouse had spaces between the piers and the wall but was otherwise similar in construction. Further domestic buildings, huts, pits and byres were added later. Some of these were still occupied when Viking settlers arrived in the early ninth century. Unfortunately no material was sieved from the extensive middens which accompanied these dwellings, with the subsequent loss of information on plant resources used, and on fish bone in particular.

Charcoal from a camp fire in the broch courtyard was mainly of Spruce with a little Willow. Spruce and Birch charcoal was recovered from a secondary wheelhouse within the remains of the broch. Peat ash from the primary wheelhouse and other contexts shows that peat, abundant in Shetland, was probably the main source of fuel. The plant report records Bere Barley from the steps of the broch well and from a secondary wheelhouse built within the broch tower.

A particularly interesting find was of a long slate stick, notched along one side with a partly unnotched end serving as a handle and illustrated by Hamilton (plate 17b). It was found in a wall-cupboard within a large wheelhouse. Hamilton notes that a similar implement made of wood was used in Norway until comparatively recently to detach ears of grain from the stalks. A possible earlier version was recovered from the Late Bronze Age settlement (12.5). If it were used to cut ears in the harvest field, the straw could have been collected later for thatching or animal bedding. If few ears had been cut at a time, the incidence of weeds harvested with the corn would have been small.

From the earliest buildings both saddle and rotary querns were recorded, but by the later Iron Age only rotary querns were used. Storage pits, thought to have been used for grain, and a system of field walls, all dating from the Late Iron Age, all point to an expansion of arable farming. This was presumably in response to what seems, from the greater numbers of dwellings, to have been an increase in population.

Bones from the aisled roundhouse were identified by Marjorie Platt; no numbers were given but Cattle, Sheep and Pig bones were recorded. Grey Seal bones were equally numerous but Common Seal and Whale bones were less plentiful. Dog bones were also present, presumably from one or more working animals. A few fish bones were noted by the excavator. Later deposits, contemporary with the wheelhouses, contained bones of domestic animals. Two Red Deer bones are of interest as indications of hunting, and these particular beasts had been of particularly large size. A Wild Cat bone, the only one from Jarlshof, is noteworthy as such shy creatures are difficult to see and even more difficult to capture. Both types of Seal were again present. The only bird bones mentioned are those of the Great Auk now extinct, of larger size than those in the museum collection, and of Shags and Cormorants, larger than those of the present day.

Also on Shetland, the broch of Burland produced Hulled Six-rowed Barley and a little tentatively identified Emmer. Heather stems predominated but charcoal of Alder, Ash, Birch, Hazel and Scots Pine with Larch driftwood were also identified. The broch at East Shore (Carter et al 1995) produced Emmer (tentative), Hulled Barley (but no Naked Barley), Heather and wood charcoal of Alder, Ash, Birch, Hazel, Larch and Scots Pine. Andrew Jones recognised eggs of human Whipworm. At Clikhimin, an early Iron Age hut beneath a broch floor revealed rare charcoal of Willow, Pine and Spruce (Hamilton 1968).

Brochs on the Inner Hebrides and the mainland

Dun Mor Vaul, Tiree

From Dun Mor Vaul, on the Inner Hebridean island of Tiree (Mackie 1974), Jane Renfrew recorded Barley from all stages of the occupation. Both as charred remains and impressions on chaff-tempered pottery, she found chiefly Hulled Barley with a little Naked Barley. Jon Pilcher recognised the non-native Spruce among the charcoal which also included Alder, Hazel, Oak and Willow, and he also tentatively identified Reed 'laid in a wetter part of the wall gallery' (p204). From 30 pollen samples taken from different parts of the site by Pilcher, the deductions were that the vicinity of the broch was not wooded at the time of the construction and that there had been a high level of agricultural activity on Iron Age Tiree. The bones from this site are of particular interest as the proportion of Sheep exceeded those of Cattle for most periods. The Sheep resembled the primitive Soay type, which Barbara Noddle notes are the type still found on North Ronaldsay, one of the Orkney islands. The recovery of Roe Deer with possible Aurochs and Wild Pig may indicate that there were considerable areas of woodland on the island. A single Goat horn perhaps implies that some of the bones may be of Goat rather than

Sheep. Seal bones were also present. Noddle also writes that the 'very high proportion of juvenile animals . . . indicates that the herds were kept mainly to supply meat'. Don Bramwell's report on the bird bones notes that Shag bones were the most numerous; Puffin and Little Auk were also represented.

Crosskirk, Caithness

At Crosskirk Broch on the north coast of Caithness, Naked Barley and a few Wild Oats were found, and also a single seed of Flax (Dickson 1979, Dickson and Dickson 1984). Seeds of plants of heath, mire, grassland and pasture are represented, along with mosses preserved under paving and in the broch well. A stone tank contained ash from cereal chaff. The ash resulted from chaff which had been burnt leaving the heavily silicified walls intact. A sealed stone cist from the broch at Burrian, North Ronaldsay, Orkney, also contained ash and it was there suggested that the ash-filled tank was used to preserve seafood. Such a use continued until modern times on St Kilda and the Faroe Islands. A similar use is suggested for Crosskirk. A pollen analysis of mud from the bottom of the broch well produced a single grain of Cornflower as well as 4.7% cereal pollen. Among the wood and/or charcoal were Aspen, Alder, Birch, Hazel, Juniper, Pine, Rowan and Willow. Four radiocarbon dates place the occupation of the broch around 100 BC.

Fairy Knowe, Stirlingshire

One of the few southern brochs to have been sampled extensively for plant remains is just east of Buchlyvie, in Stirlingshire, a little north of the Campsie Fells and close to the flat carselands of the upper Forth Valley. It was occupied during the first and second centuries AD. Hulled Barley with very small quantities of other cereals including Emmer, Bread Wheat and Bristle Oat were identified by Bill Boyd (1985); Bristle Oat was grown extensively in the past as it survived poor soils and windy conditions better than the Common Oat. This seems to be the earliest record in Scotland. A limited number of weed seeds was recovered from a Barley-rich sample: Fat Hen, Black Bindweed, Goosegrass, Knotgrass, Pale Persicaria, Wild Radish, Sheep's Sorrel, Bloody Dock, Chickweed, and Stinging Nettle. All these discoveries add to our knowledge of Iron Age agriculture but the unparalled find was, of course, the several carbonised bulbs of Ramsons from an occupation layer (*see* **157**); this species is highlighted in part 2. The other edible plant found was Hazel.

Other sites on the mainland

Cyderhall, Sutherland

Gravel quarrying operations revealed a roundhouse and souterrain (underground store) at Cyderhall, west of Dornoch in north-east Scotland. This necessitated excavations in midwinter 1987-8 by Robert Pollock (1992) and members of the Dornoch Heritage Society. The first phase of a wooden roundhouse which had burnt down showed that posts of 20cm diameter were used to carry the roof and a piece of charred Oak post was still *in situ*; charcoal of roundwood Oak, 8-12cm diameter, was also recognised. Four radiocarbon dates fall within the early Iron Age. The reconstructed roundhouse again burnt down; in the destruction layer there was an open pattern of charred Oak beams which Pollock says gave 'the impression of connected roof members which had collapsed together . . . most of the timbers radiated to the edge of the house, with one longer timber, probably a tie-beam, interlaced at right angles'. It is rare that such evidence for the construction of roundhouse roofs is preserved. The quantity of Oak wood used suggests that primary Oak woodland may still have been present in the area and so the inhabitants were able to choose the most durable wood for roofing. The outer layer would have been thatch of some sort; such thatch would be quickly consumed in the flames.

Associated with the roundhouse was a sub-rectangular storage pit, measuring 0.9 x 1.3m, with traces of a clayey sand lining and burnt boards lying within it. The pit was filled to a depth of 0.1m with burnt grain; this was subsampled and part was identified by Sheila Boardman. Over 2500 grains of Hulled Six-rowed Barley and 282 of Naked Barley were identified. Over 500 Barley rachis segments (chaff) were recorded. Thirty Emmer grains and glume bases (chaff) were definitely identified, and three Spelt grains with glume bases tentatively identified. A few grains of Oat, including Common Oat, were also recorded with some weed seeds including 104 of Wormwood, which is rarely found as a subfossil. This is a very noteworthy assemblage and may represent a mixed crop or Hulled Barley with residual Naked Barley and Emmer. The quantity of chaff suggests that the grain was not winnowed thoroughly or had not been finally sieved before it caught fire. The very small quantity of Common Oat suggests contamination of seed corn from the south where it was established early in the Iron Age.

Much further to the south on the Mainland, at Balloch hillfort, Kintyre, Hulled Barley was identified and at Leckie dun just north of the Campsie Hills, Hulled Barley was recognised.

Several other sites in the more southern parts of Scotland are worth detailed discussion concerning the crops that were grown in the pre-Roman Iron Age.

Carn Dubh, Perthshire

This site, some 6km north-east of Pitlochry, covers the later Bronze Age and Iron Ages (Rideout 1995). Forty-six contexts produced charred plant material. According to Sheila Boardman all the productive samples came from the houses. Hulled Six-rowed Barley, Oat, and Flax were the cultivated plants. There was a good range of arable weeds such as Wild Radish, Black-bindweed, Corn Spurrey, Chickweed and Redshank. A variety of other habitats are indicated by, amongst others, Wood Sage, Gypsywort, Fairy Flax and Pale Sedge.

Sheils, Glasgow

On the flood plain of the River Clyde just west of Govan, the site was a ring-ditch enclosure within which were traces of hut circles (Scott 1996). A column of ditch infill, some 80cm in depth, from one point in the ditch near the northern terminal was analysed by David Robinson (1983), who counted pollen and plant macroscopic fossils including mosses. Charred Barley, both grain and rachis fragments, and Hazelnut fragments were found in only one sample. There was a considerable diversity of arable weeds, heath, bog and waterside plants in many of the samples. Pollen of trees and shrubs was low but that of Grasses and Ribwort Plantain high and uniformly so. Wood from deep in the ditch (possibly stakes) had grown about 2,000 years ago.

Rispain Camp, Wigtonshire

This later Iron Age site was excavated by Alison and George Haggerty (1983). A circular building was at least partially plank built; a single date from a substantial piece of Oak calibrates to about 2,000 years ago. Charcoal, identified by Carole Keepax, was of Oak, Birch, Wild Cherry, Ash, Hazel/Alder, Hawthorn type, conifer and Heaths. These indicate woodland on better soils and heathland. The seeds were identified by Alan Fairweather; burnt grain was found in pits and other features and it is suggested that the pits may have been originally for storage. His results were surprising; 80 grains of Bread Wheat and 40 of Hulled Barley were present, accompanied by weeds of arable land. This high proportion of Bread Wheat is unexpected, especially at this early period. Rispain is on boulder clay; Bread Wheat grows best on land with a high proportion of silt and clay and needs fertilising and weeding to achieve its high yield potential. As Rispain is not far from the sea it is possible that it represents an early import although most of the grain in England at this time is of Spelt Wheat and Hulled Barley. This site must remain somewhat anomalous at present. Perhaps future Iron Age sites will confirm this early record for Bread Wheat, and it must be recalled that Bread Wheat was found much earlier in prehistory at Balbridie (see chapter 3). Mammal bones, identified by Lin Barnetson, were of mature Sheep, Pig and Cattle. An antler of Red Deer was recovered from the main ditch.

Upper Cleuch, Dumfriesshire

A farmstead enclosure in the valley of the Annan was excavated ahead of the upgrading of the A74 road to a motorway (Terry 1993). Pollen analyses by D. Hale from two sections of deposits in the enclosure ditch gave broadly similar results. Tree pollen values are low and average 30% in one profile and 10% in the other. Hazel, Heather and grasses predominate throughout with smaller values for Birch and Alder. A little cereal pollen and that of a few arable weeds were noted. Dry and wet pasture and heathland are in evidence. Hale concludes that the Iron Age inhabitants were primarily concerned with pastoral farming. Woodland had been extensively cleared at an earlier unknown period and secondary light woodland established.

Extensive sampling for carbonised plant remains by Rob Scaife and Alan Clapham produced only meagre results both quantitatively and qualitatively: Barley, a Bent-grass, *Brassica*, *Chenopodium*, Corn Marigold, Emmer, False Oat, Hazel, Oat, Lesser Spearwort, Sedge and Vetch/Vetchling. The interest centres on the predominance of Emmer. Charcoal included Alder, Hazel, Oak and Aspen/Willow. The results of pollen analyses from two ditch sections agree with the seeds in pointing to a mainly pastoral economy.

Eildon Hill North and The Dunion, Roxburgh

With the exception of crannogs, the paucity of sites with environmental information from southern Scotland is, at first sight, puzzling. The few brochs, however, were mainly excavated in the nineteenth or earlier twentieth century before sieving techniques were used. The few hillforts excavated by modern methods have yielded mainly just a few burnt grains and, although the intensively farmed south-eastern side of the country is not lacking in later prehistoric settlements, most have not been excavated. Two recent rescue excavations in Roxburghshire have helped to fill this gap, as has Edinburgh Castle. To set the scene it is pertinent to consider pollen diagrams to the south of the present city of Edinburgh. Regional landscape conditions have been inferred from a pollen core from Blackpool Moss, a few kilometres from the two sites in Roxburghshire described below. Together with three earlier undated pollen diagrams from Midlothian and Peeblesshire, they indicate progressive deforestation from about 4000 BC onwards. At Blackpool Moss Neolithic clearance was followed by the later growth of secondary woodland which was gradually re-cleared, probably from about the third millennium BC.

Eildon Hill has a commanding position overlooking the valleys of the Tweed and Leader Water and can be seen from over 40km away. It thus formed an ideal situation for a hillfort. Furthermore the soils around the Eildon Hills are very fertile and yield very good crops of cereals and moderate yields of vegetables including root crops. A small excavation at Eildon Hill North by Olwyn Owen (Rideout *et al.* 1992) has revealed occupation dating to the Late Bronze Age and Roman Iron Age. Charcoal analysis by Rod McCullagh from a number of samples, mainly from hearth contexts, produced in particular Alder and Hazel, with some Oak, Birch, Elm, Ash and Wild Cherry; this indicates oak woodland with some better soils. The presence of Heather shows the development of heathland and Willow, perhaps wetter ground. The type of woodland does not seem to have changed during the lifetime of the fort. A few Barley grains were identified from two contexts.

At the present time the lower slopes of The Dunion range from land producing moderate crops of cereals, vegetables and root crops to pasture with forage crops. The Dunion, excavated by Jim Rideout (Rideout et al 1992), was fast disappearing under quarrying and most of the formerly large hillfort had already vanished. However, seven Late Iron Age roundhouses on scooped platforms were excavated. The dates probably range from the second century BC to first century AD with possible occupation into the Roman Iron Age. Charcoal from six of the houses was identified by Rod McCullagh and found to be chiefly Hazel, Birch, Oak, Wild Cherry, Willow and Alder. Only one house produced any quantity of cereals including 19 grains of Barley and six of Wild or Common Oats; there were only a very few weed seeds. Neither site produced sufficient bone to analyse due to the acid soils at the sites.

There is no indication of great wealth in the artefacts from either fort, but the first and second century AD inhabitants of Eildon Hill had access to Roman goods. There is evidence for metal working at both sites. Both forts can be considered as small oppida (minor towns), probably functioning as local or regional centres. Although Eildon may have co-existed with the Roman fort of Newstead, occupied from AD 80 to probably the early third century, few Roman remains have so far been recovered and most are not in secure contexts. The next site, Edinburgh Castle, shows unmistakable Roman contacts.

Edinburgh Castle

From 1984-91, rescue excavations in advance of improvements to the visitor facilities to the present castle were carried out by Stephen Driscoll and Peter Yeoman (1997). The castle stands on a volcanic crag and dominates the present city. The regional vegetation is discussed in the section on the pre-Roman vegetation of central Scotland, and extensive clearance has been indicated prior to the Roman occupations. The environmental samples were taken from the Mills Mount area and span a long period from *c*.900 BC to AD 1745. The results from each period have been discussed in the appropriate chapters.

Phase 1

The features sampled from the period 900 to 200 BC are assumed to have been related to one or more timber buildings, probably part of an enclosed hilltop settlement. The plant material, identified by Sheila Boardman, came from a variety of contexts. Of the total 224 cereal grains, most were of Hulled Barley with a small admixture of Naked Barley, Emmer Wheat, Bread Wheat and Wild or Common Oats. Cereal chaff, in this and the other Iron Age samples, was rare or absent. Weeds of cultivated ground and grassland species were also present. A single Flax seed was found and fragments of Hazel shells were present in most samples.

Phase 2

Deriving from the period 200 BC to 100 AD, hearths and occupation debris were sampled from three stone-floored round houses, part of a hill fort abandoned at the start of, or during, the second century AD. A total of 362 cereal grains were recognised and the types and proportions of these and other plant remains were very similar to those from the earlier period although Naked Barley was absent.

Phase 3

The period 100 to 300 AD is represented by deep midden deposits with short-term use of hearths on the midden surface; traces of slag connected with the hearths point to some industrial use. The occupation is assumed to have been nearby, presumably at the summit. A range of first to third century Roman pottery, particularly numerous from the second century, two sherds of Roman glass and Romano-British bronze work were recovered from the midden which was clearly the settlement's rubbish dump. Evidently there was sufficient wealth to import fine quality goods and the high status of the native settlement seems to have been maintained throughout the Roman presence in the area.

Samples from hearth and burnt soil layers yielded 686 cereal grains, dominated by Hulled Barley with rare Bread Wheat and Wild or Common Oat grains. Most samples contained seeds of weeds associated with arable crops. This period spans the Antonine occupation and this part of eastern Scotland is a Wheat growing area at the present time. It might therefore be expected that if Emmer and Spelt Wheats, the Roman army's staple grains, were being grown for the troops in this part of Scotland, such grain would also be used by a high status native site. However, these species are notably not represented at this period. Twenty-one Flax seeds were found in one of the hearths and, from another sample from the same hearth, 22 seeds of Henbane were discovered. Henbane grows in the

Lothians at the present time but may have been introduced for its medicinal properties from southern England. It may have been growing on disturbed ground and brought in accidentally with other weed seeds. Alternatively, it may have been deliberately collected (see the highlighted account in Part 2). A fragment of a Plum or Bullace type stone was also found.

A layer of almost pure plant material, principally of decayed grass stems or leaves, seemed to be partly of cereal straw. Two bulk samples produced a few Hulled Barley grains and numerous seeds of wild plants representing a variety of habitats. These included arable fields and disturbed ground, grassland and heath. Boardman considers that much of the material such as straw and grassy debris is typical of byres, but she pointed out that it might also have derived from thatch or bedding from human habitation. Only a small fraction of the widespread layer had become charred and may represent clearance from different types of buildings and deposits.

Anne Crone has identified charcoal of predominately Oak and Hazel from these three phases, with Alder, Birch and Ash also present. Together with Wild Cherry (in phase 1 only), these would have grown in Oak woodland, as could have Willow, from phase 3. Heather twigs from a late Iron Age context could have been brought in for a number of purposes including thatching, bedding and broom making.

The bones were identified by Finbar McCormick. Unfortunately small quantities have precluded useful comparison between all the different phases. From the late Iron Age two samples, based on minimum numbers of individuals, showed cattle to predominate with Sheep or Goat and Pigs in roughly equal numbers. Few definite Goat remains were recorded from the site. Of the wild animals, Red Deer, and both a Wild Pig and Badger were eaten; Wild Pig implies nearby woodland. Horse and Dog were also represented but not thought to have been used as food. The bone report does not distinguish between Roman, Iron Age and Dark Age assemblages, although McCormick mentions that there is a general similarity between them.

6 Roman invasions: foreign foodstuffs, weeds and medicines

The landscape of lowland Scotland about 2,000 years ago

The Romans occupied central Scotland mainly in two brief episodes: from 79 to 86 AD, under the governor Agricola, and then the more intensive Antonine period, marked by the building of the great turf wall which stretched across central Scotland from the Firth of Clyde to Bowness on the Firth of Forth. The building of the Antonine Wall and main occupation of its forts took place between 142 and 158 AD (**42, 43**).

A Roman soldier looking northwards from the western part of the Antonine Wall as it followed the high ground would have seen undulating terrain stretching to the Campsie Fells in the north and the Kilpatrick Hills in the west. Ground level and aerial survey by archaeologists has suggested that Iron Age farms were few and widely scattered to the north of this part of the Wall although they were more numerous beyond the eastern part of the Wall where the land would have been less rocky and marshy. Nevertheless, as will be subsequently deduced, intensive pastoral farming must have been carried out just in the last few centuries BC all along the route to be taken by the Wall. The farms between the Wall and the hills to the north would probably have continued to function during the brief Roman occupation, although the forts strategically placed along the Wall controlled the frontier in much the same way that customs posts operate. Those farmers with surplus cattle would have sold them to the Romans who needed a continuous supply of animals for sacrifice, for food on feast days, for hides for tents, for shoes and clothing. Barley, the staple Iron Age crop in Scotland, would have been needed for the horses of the cavalry units known to have been stationed along the Wall and perhaps also malted to provide beer for the troops.

There is no reason to believe that, in this part of Scotland, coexistence was anything other than peaceful. Civilian traders may have set up booths beside the forts, although we have little firm archaeological evidence for this in Scotland. At Inveresk there is evidence for timber and stone buildings and possibly an amphitheatre, and there were field systems at Carriden, Croy and Rough Castle.

What was the nature of the countryside that the Romans marched into? In particular what changes to the woodland had the native Iron Age peoples made in the area? Several pollen diagrams from the vicinity of the Forth-Clyde valleys have been radiocarbon-dated. All show a dramatic increase in pre-Roman woodland clearance. In a review article, Susan Ramsay and JHD (1997) have assessed the data from that area, partly from unpublished work by Susan Ramsay. Both mature trees and understorey vegetation were cleared to

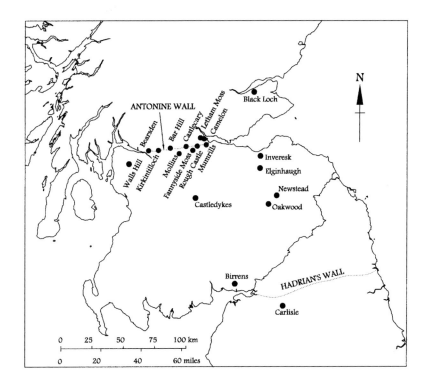

42 Map of Roman sites

produce land for agriculture, and mainly pastoralism is indicated from all sites. This cleared landscape extended from the most westerly bog, that at Walls Hill analysed by Susan Ramsay (1996), to the easterly ones at Fannyside Muir and Letham Moss both less than 5km from the Wall and analysed by Lisa Dumayne (1993a, b; Dumayne-Peaty 1998). These analyses depict the regional vegetation. Tipping's exploration (1994) of the pollen analytical data for southern Scotland and other regions reveals an intensification of farming activity after 500 BC.

It is fortunate that very local analyses have been possible from the forts themselves. At Mollins, just to the south of the Antonine Wall, the ditches of an Agricolan fort were infilled with turf fragments from acid soils. The strong acidity had proved unfavourable to earthworms, which otherwise would have mixed the pollen of different years, and well stratified pollen spectra were able to be counted from the Mollins turves and also from others from the Antonine fort at Bar Hill, 4km to the north (Boyd 1984a and b). By counting contiguous pollen samples, each 5mm in thickness, through the mossy turves, distinct changes in the pollen spectra were revealed from level to level. The closed woodland, dominated by Oak and Birch, had been removed by Iron Age peoples and replaced by pasture. The turves from Bar Hill, probably mainly of later date, revealed a gradual change to an open landscape but with more Heather suggesting a decline in grazing just before the main occupation of the Antonine Wall. It is striking that Oak, the most durable building wood, was selected for removal and therefore may have been scarce in the area by the time the Romans came to build their forts.

A first century fort at Elginhaugh, just south of Dalkeith, was excavated in the 1980s

43 The Antonine Wall, as it may have looked when under construction. With permission of Historic Scotland

by Bill Hanson. The whole of the fort and its annexe were revealed. Extensive sampling of charred and waterlogged material was carried out. Pollen analyses from Roman and immediately post-Roman ditch samples showed that Alder woodland with Willow predominated in wet areas and Hazel scrub on drier ground. It is notable that Oak and Birch showed exceptionally low values and had been largely removed before the Roman presence in the area. Elginhaugh soils are sandy and therefore suitable for Heather, but heathland had not developed and herb pollen values such as those for Ribwort Plantain and the Asteraceae (Daisy) family are low. This perhaps indicates that the grazing pressure was great enough to prevent herbs from flowering and Heather from becoming established, both during and after the occupation. There is a little evidence for arable cultivation and pollen of Barley group type suggests that Barley may have been cultivated locally after the Roman withdrawal.

Radiocarbon-dated pollen diagrams by Graeme Whittington and Kevin Edwards (1993) from sites to the north-east of the Antonine Wall tell a different story. Within a few kilometres of Black Loch, in northern Fife, are two marching camps of the Severan period and, also from the third century, there is the military station at Carpow, on the south side of the Firth of Tay. The pollen from the lake muds shows woodland clearance and farming continuing from the Bronze Age until about AD 60 when tree pollen shows a marked increase and plants of pastoral and arable agriculture declined. At about AD 630 the trees receded and the farming indicators resurged. The woodlands had recolonised during the Roman period. This is interpreted as the Roman army having been antagonistic to the local natives who had re-located or starved as a result of confiscation of crops and livestock. A similar massive abandonment of farmland is also reflected in two pollen diagrams from east Aberdeenshire with Roman camps in the vicinity.

At Bearsden and Kirkintilloch, two of the Antonine Wall forts, pollen from ditches which had remained open during the occupation told a similar story of a sparsely wooded landscape with a little pastoral farming, unchanged during the forts' brief occupations.

It seems probable that local farming continued during the occupation as the radiocarbon-dated brochs at Buchlyvie and Leckie, just to the north of the Campsie Fells, were in use during the first and second centuries AD. Roman objects have been found in both of these high status farms which grew Barley and, certainly for Leckie, also had domestic animals. The Romans would have required a continuous supply of Barley for their horses. Did a barter system operate with high status Roman glass and pottery being exchanged for these commodities? Or were these perhaps personal gifts given to the chiefs of these imposing broch towers in exchange for their co-operation? We only know that the Romans preferred to exploit local resources whenever this was feasible.

What did the Romans use for building materials for the Wall and its numerous forts? If we accept that the pre-Roman woodland had been turned into pasture, as both local and regional analyses would indicate, it becomes clear that an expanse of well-grazed turf could be readily cut to make the turf wall and the fort ramparts. The area of turf needed for the wall has been calculated by Bill Hanson at about 325-385ha (800-900 acres). In addition each auxiliary fort would be stripped of about 2ha (5 acres) to form its protective ramparts. At Bearsden, turves were recovered by David Breeze during his excavations of the 1970s and found to measure about 45x30x10cm, close to the regulation size. It proved possible to extract pollen and larger plant remains from the decayed turves. The pollen, though poorly preserved, depicted an open pastoral landscape. The larger plant remains, Rush seeds, Heather and Bogmoss leaves in particular, suggested that the turves were cut from damp, rushy, boggy ground with drier heathy areas.

The general absence of cereal pollen and arable weeds is notable from these analyses. It has been estimated that around 20,000 Roman soldiers were serving in Scotland during both the Agricolan and Antonine periods. What did these soldiers eat and where were the sources of the food? The question of diet was solved by a combination of botanical and chemical analyses and a degree of good fortune!

The sewage-filled ditch at the Bearsden fort

The initial investigation
When David Breeze was excavating the fort at Bearsden in the 1970s (**44-46**, Table 4), JHD went along to investigate. The outer east annexe ditch was in the process of excavation with a cut vertical section exposing the silty contents; the excavation was quite dry. JHD jumped down into the ditch, took out his hand lens and peered at moss fragments and charred wood protruding from the cut face. These remains looked as

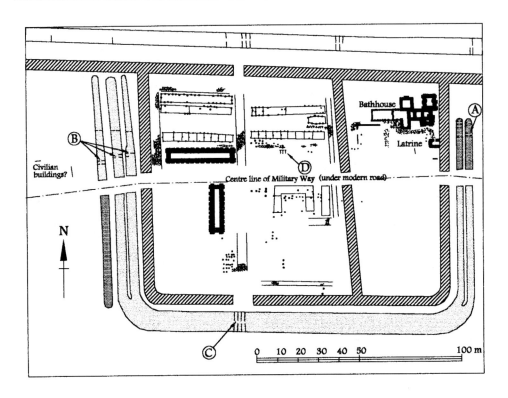

44 Plan of Bearsden Fort. Plant remains were extracted from samples taken at points A to D. From the east annexe ditch, the in-fill impregnated with sewage was particularly important (sample A)

though they could represent the Roman occupation. He soon returned to the site with metal boxes, and columns were taken through the ditch and subsequently through the other ditches surrounding the fort. Samples were broken down with dilute alkali in the laboratory and sieved. The first discoveries were of great interest; they were Fig pips. It seemed clear that they represented some of the food issued to the soldiers. Other unusual seeds were found: Coriander, Dill and Wild Celery. The Coriander in particular was mainly in fragments (**101**), much as is produced at present when the seeds are ground in a mortar to release the aromatic oils. Large mortars, pieces of which were found at the fort, would have been used to grind these and other seeds which are used as spices and also have medicinal uses. Coriander and Dill are not native to Britain but they all grow well in Mediterranean countries and were also probably imported. Fragments of Linseed may have been used in a poultice; Pliny, writing in the first century AD records such a use. In the twentieth century Linseed has been used similarly in Europe for the heat retaining properties of the oily seeds. Rare Opium Poppy seeds were recognised; these could have been sprinkled on bread, a Roman custom which we have adopted, or they could have been used medicinally. Minute remains of the seed coats of Lentils and Field Beans (the forerunner of the Broad Bean; **77**) were also noted; Beans and Lentils are included in a list of food provided by Egyptian villages for the Roman army in AD 199. A number of other

45 *The outer east annexe ditch showing the Roman and later in-fills. The darker material at the bottom is the sewage-rich silty clay, with abundant plant remains. The ranging pole divisions are 0.5m. With permission of Historic Scotland*

seeds representing the vegetation which must have existed before the ditch was dug were also recovered.

Bran: a largely plant-based diet?

Interesting as the remains of these food or medicinal plants were, the bulk of the organic material, however, was composed of bran fragments, each measuring about 3mm in diameter but there were no whole grains (**47**). Because of poor preservation the bran was identifiable only as Wheat or Rye type (Dickson 1987). However, chaff fragments established the presence of two primitive hulled wheats, Emmer and Spelt. The bran fragments resembled those in wholemeal flour, minus the floury particles. Fragments of grain weevils were also found; was this the remains of contaminated flour or bread (CD et al 1979)? The bran-rich silty sediments were about 1m deep — a considerable depth. Eventually CD made a small experiment to try to solve the mystery. Making sure that her diet included wholemeal bread, a day or so later she kept a sample of the expelled product. Sieving left only the inodorous plant fragments from the faeces; these consisted to a large extent of bran. CD had not told JHD of the experiment but placed some beside the Bearsden bran under the microscope — the mystery appeared solved. Next, everyone else had to be convinced, not least the archaeologists who were most reluctant to believe that the Romans, renowned for their cleanliness, should have tolerated what was an open septic tank in a boundary ditch (*see* **111, 112**).

Corroboration was sought by enlisting the help of a chemist colleague, Brian Knights, who examined samples through the ditch deposits using thin layer and gas chromatography. His results showed that coprosterols and bile acids were present, thus

46 The Bearsden fort after the excavation and open to the public. In the foreground is the latrine and in the background the bathhouse. The channel that carried the used water from the bathhouse into the latrine can be seen. The east annexe ditches are to the right, outside the photograph. With permission of Historic Scotland

proving that the foodstuffs had passed through the mammalian gut (Knights et al 1983). The surprising part was that cholesterol levels were low, consistent with a largely plant-based diet. This certainly fitted in with the large quantity of wheat products, probably eaten as bread. Rare tiny bone fragments in the ditch suggested that some meat was eaten. We were fortunate in that the pollen slides, which had been taken at intervals through the ditch, contained eggs of the human Whipworm with those of the roundworm; this identification was confirmed by Andrew Jones. This finally convinced the sceptics that the ditch was full of human sewage. Although the Romans usually used sponges for toilet purposes, there are no suitable ones in northern waters and the presence of weft-forming mosses in the ditch strongly suggested that these had been gathered as a substitute.

Could anything be deduced about the type of bread that was made? It was known that the Romans used rotary querns, a type of hand mill, which they brought with them, to grind their corn. These querns were capable of adjustment; the upper stone could be raised to allow a 2-3mm clearance between the stones. This method of loose querning would have been used to remove the husks from cereals with persistent glumes such as Emmer and Spelt. Using a rather inferior native quern, CD ground up both Emmer and Spelt grains, winnowed, sieved and reground whole spikelets and then sieved the resultant groats and meals through a standard colander. Occasional chaff fragments were noted in the sieved meal similar to those in the ditch. The two types of coarse flour were rather different; Ground up Emmer grains consisted of groats with a glassy appearance, very little meal was produced due to the hard, flinty nature of the grain. The sieved Spelt had a larger

SOURCES	BUILDING OF FORT	USED IN FORT	FUEL FOR HYOPOCAUST	GRAIN	FRUIT/NUTS	CULINARY SPICES/ MEDICINAL PLANTS
LOCAL	Chiefly Alder, some Birch and Oak Rush roofing Willow and Hazel wattle fence on top of ramparts Turf cut from pasture for ramparts	Heather and Bracken Local meadow hay for fodder	Wood Peat	Barley	Wild Fruit Hazel Nuts	Common Mallow Pearl Barley
IMPORTED				Emmer & Spelt for bread and porridge Pulses: Lentil, Broad Bean	Fig Walnut	Coriander Dill Wild Celery Opium Poppy Linseed

Table 4   Roman army use of local plant resources and imported foods at Bearsden and other Antonine forts

meal component similar to that of present day Bread Wheat which was also processed. The meal from each was divided into two parts, one portion was made into porridge and one, with the addition of yeast, was made into bread. Bread Wheat was similarly prepared (Dickson 1990).

The Spelt bread rose more than the Bread Wheat loaf and a panel of tasters agreed that it had the better flavour. The Emmer bread rose the least and was heavy in texture. Spelt contains a higher proportion of gluten forming proteins than Bread Wheat. Its flour is once again available in Britain and considered to have a superior flavour and texture to that of Bread Wheat.

Porridge was made in the traditional Scots manner and compared with that made from Oatmeal. The tasters agreed that both Spelt and Bread Wheats made flavourless, slightly gritty porridge. In contrast the Emmer porridge was enthusiastically sampled and its flavour and texture appreciated. It was not quite as smooth as the Oatmeal porridge, the bran coats are thicker, but the groats were well-swollen and tender as in the best Oatmeal porridge. It is well documented that the Roman army ate both bread and porridge, and clay-topped ovens have been found in Roman forts, notably in Scotland, at Elginhaugh, the Agricloan fort. Emmer Wheat was made into a type of porridge, called *alica* in ancient Rome. The Emmer was sieved and, according to Pliny, the largest groats made the best *alica*. CD heated small samples of the cooked products in dilute hydrochloric acid for a few minutes in order to soften and remove the starchy portion. The bran fragments were then compared with the sewage bran; they were remarkably similar in size range. This suggests that the Romans also used a sieve of 3mm aperture, the size of holes in a colander, which

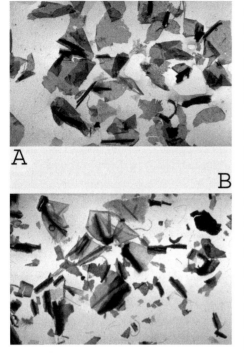

47 *A Fragments of Wheat/Rye bran (up to about 4mm long) from the sewage produced in Bearsden about AD 145.*
B Fragments of Bread Wheat bran (among other food debris) from faeces produced in Milngavie in AD 1978

ensured that no whole grains passed through the sieve. Unfortunately it is not known if the two Wheats were kept separate to be used for bread and porridge, and it does not seem possible to distinguish porridge from bread in the ancient sewage on physical appearance.

Fragments of amphorae imported from southern Spain were found at the fort. It is probable that the plant foods, Wheats, spices, pulses and Figs all came from the Mediterranean area. Antonine forts at Castlecary and Rough Castle have produced charred grain of Emmer and Spelt Wheats, and presumably the cargoes of ships berthed in the Forth and Clyde estuaries were unloaded onto wagons which lumbered along the cobble road linking the forts. According to Tacitus, granaries were built to house a year's grain and the spice seeds, dried pulses and Figs could all have been stored for protracted periods in a similar manner. Barley was also recovered from the forts and would also have been stored in the granary.

Nuts and soft fruits

In addition to Figs, seeds of wild fruits were found sparsely in the sewage; Raspberry, Bramble, Bilberry and Wild Strawberry were noted. Occasional Hazelnut shells were also seen but not Walnuts. From the Antonine fort at Bar Hill, small Walnuts had been found by Sir George Macdonald almost 100 years ago. A drain in the Bearsden bathhouse *sudatorium*, the hot, dry room similar to a sauna, produced Hazelnut fragments, representing perhaps half a dozen nuts. Clay from the *tepidarium*, the first warm room, yielded three Wild Strawberry seeds. It is tempting to imagine the soldiers taking refuge from the elements and enjoying a snack, while sitting on one of the benches in the second *tepidarium*; these benches still remain with other parts of the well-preserved bathhouse (**46**).

The diet elsewhere including Germany and the Netherlands

Although the Bearsden Romans seemed to have existed on a mainly plant-based diet, bones have survived the acid soils at Rough Castle and Mumrills; these and records for the Hadrian's Wall forts have been summarised by Roy Davies (1971). He has listed beef, lamb, pork and venison from the Antonine forts. Chicken was eaten at Mumrills, and a hen-size egg was found in the well at Bar Hill. Oysters and Mussels were recorded rather surprisingly at Bar Hill and Mumrills, both well away from the coasts; this suggests speedy distribution to ensure their freshness. Davies has studied the archaeological sources for food and alcoholic beverages and concluded that in peace time the basic army diet would have consisted of corn, bacon, cheese and probably vegetables to eat, and sour wine to drink. At Bar Hill and Castlecary were found portions of shallow perforated containers thought to be cheese-making vessels.

How typical was the diet revealed at Bearsden to that at other forts? The examination of the larger plant remains from many samples by Gill Campbell and Alan Clapham from the first century fort and its annexe at Elginhaugh has produced a rich flora, soon to be published in detail. Charred Spelt and Emmer Wheats with chiefly Hulled Barley was found together with seeds of arable weeds. In waterlogged samples Clapham found a large quantity of Figs (from an officer's latrine) and other Mediterranean foods, Coriander, Wild Celery, Dill and possibly Opium Poppy. Fragments of Linseed were also present. Bran fragments of Barley and Wheat or Rye type represented part of the diet, but the evidence for their being of faecal origin is not conclusive, though highly probable. Raspberry or Bramble as well as Sloes and Hazelnuts were collected.

Unfortunately the sandy soils were not conducive to the preservation of bone. This is the only other waterlogged Roman fort in Scotland which has been extensively sampled.

Just over the border in England, Goodwin and Huntley (1991) have analysed waterlogged deposits in Carlisle, adjacent to the Roman fort and probably from its annexe. These suggest that a similar diet was enjoyed by the soldiers stationed there, and presumably also at the Hadrian's Wall forts just to the north. Coriander, Celery, Fig and Opium Poppy are recorded. In addition Henbane and Hog's Fennel, a rare plant restricted to south-east England, were probably brought to the site for medicinal purposes. Wild fruit, such as Bramble and Bilberry, were recorded in quantity, together with Sloes. Animal bones are similar to those recorded from Antonine sites with the addition of Goat, Roe Deer and Goose.

Other Roman army sites in England with waterlogged deposits include York where a sewer, probably leading from a legionary bathhouse, yielded tentatively identified Wild Celery and Opium Poppy (Hall and Kenward 1990). The soldiers were also gathering Wild Strawberries, Brambles and Raspberries. A timber warehouse, just south of the legionary fortress, produced burnt grain, chiefly of Spelt but with some Barley and Rye. Three Fig seeds were also recognised.

In the Netherlands, a centurion's latrine produced a wealth of seeds in addition to cereal bran and chaff of both Emmer and Spelt Wheats (Kuijper and Turner 1992). Also identified were all the imported seeds found at Bearsden excepting Lentils, with the addition of Olive, Grape and Peach. Fruit which would have been gathered locally included Apple, Pear, Dewberry, Wild Cherry and fruit of Danewort and Midland Hawthorn, neither of which would not usually be eaten at present, as well as many Sloes.

At the military fort at Welzheim in south-east Germany, a well, filled with midden material and stable refuse, produced a very similar list of seeds to that at Bearsden (CD 1989). It is a remarkable tribute to Roman military planning that wherever a soldier was stationed, be it on the far western part of the Antonine Wall or the south-eastern frontier in Germany, the basic diet was essentially similar.

48 Latrine in use. No remains of sponges were recovered during the excavation but there were numerous large mosses which could well have served as wiping material. With permission of Historic Scotland

These imported foods were also enjoyed by the citizens of the towns which sprung up in England. As well as the discovery of Figs, Allan Hall's researches at the York *colonia* revealed spices, Lentils and Field Bean with wild fruit such as Brambles, Raspberries, Sloes, Elderberries and Hazelnuts. There were Olive, Grape, Stone Pine, Black Mulberry and Walnut as exotic additions to the diet. Some must have been imported from the Mediterranean regions as the British climate is not suitable for the cultivation of Olives and Stone Pines. Apples and Peas may have grown locally, and the herb Summer Savory, which is used as a green plant, was certainly grown from imported seed. Animal bones included cattle marrow bones, bones of young lamb and frequent bones of hare. Shellfish were well-represented, and edible crabs, oysters and mussels were all identified by Terry O'Connor. Fresh water and marine fish were also recorded. A traveller from the Mediterranean area who visited York could have had much of the type of food he would have enjoyed at home.

Medicine

Barley was not used entirely for animal feed as tiny bran fragments from the Bearsden sewage testify. A few are much degraded and resemble pearl Barley rubbed with a pestle in a mortar, as has been described from the native site at Warebeth, Orkney. Pliny writes of the many medicinal uses the Romans had for pearl Barley. There were also the spices already mentioned as having medicinal properties. The evidence for medicinal plants does not only stem from seeds. The pollen of Common Mallow was recovered from occupation levels of the Bearsden ditches but not from later levels, suggesting that it was deliberately introduced and grown at the fort (*see* **98**). Pollen clusters were also found in the sievings from the pollen samples; these would not result from natural dispersal. No fruits were found. Common Mallow is highlighted in part 2.

The earliest written plant name in Scottish history consists of five Greek letters inscribed on a fragment of a buff amphora found at the Roman fortress of Carpow on the south side of the Firth of Tay (Collingwood and Wright 1994). They are 'PACI [OV]'. This is the name for White Horehound. Dioscorides gives the recipe for a wine flavoured with Horehound which was deemed to be beneficial for complaints of the chest. The plant is still used for such medicinal purposes at present.

Buildings and Fuel

Wood, charcoal and their associated plant remains were collected from the remains of the Bearsden buildings which had been burnt down before the fort was abandoned. Alder, with some Oak and Ash, were used for structural timbers. As long-lasting Oak was the Roman army's preferred building timber, it seems probable, as has been suggested from the pollen analyses, that Oak had been largely removed from the vicinity. Hanson (1997) has estimated that a typical auxiliary fort would have required clear felling of between 6.9-12.1ha (17-30 acres). If the woods had already been depleted of their best timber by the Iron Age tribes, this area would have been considerably increased.

Alder wood, as suggested by the pollen analyses, would have been plentiful in damper areas. Wattles from the timber buildings were chiefly of Hazel and Willow with some Alder; Hazel and Willow would have been preferred for their flexibility. A strip of burnt branches of Alder, Hazel and Willow was found in front of the east rampart of the fort; this may have been a wattle breastwork from the top of the fort rampart. The Romans were concerned that nothing of use should be left; wooden barrack blocks were burnt but charred wood was preserved, in spite of Victorian building on top of the fort, to enable a surprisingly thorough analysis of the woods used. In addition to those already mentioned, woods used were Birch, Wild Cherry and Rowan. Fragments of Spruce wood must have originated from an imported container. Rushes were used to temper clay daub and probably for roofing thatch although little evidence remains for such a use. The hypocaust system was chiefly wood-fired, but rare peat and turf fragments were present. All these materials could have been obtained locally.

The natural environment around the fort

From the many large plant remains found, not only in the sewage-filled ditch but also in the other ditches which surrounded the Bearsden fort, it is possible to build up a picture of the local environment (**44**). Together with the pollen identifications, over 200 plant taxa were recorded. Those plants thought to be imported and ground-up weed seeds which probably came in with the imported wheat have been omitted from consideration in this section.

Local plants included weeds of cultivated and waste ground such as Annual Meadow-grass, Knotgrass, Broad-leaved Dock and Chickweed. Stinging Nettles sprang up as soon as the fort was abandoned leaving evidence as both pollen and seeds. Heath and mire plants included Heather, Bell Heather and Cross-leaved Heath which would have coloured the ground in late summer. Heath Rush and the bright yellow flowers of Tormentil would have grown among the Heather. Sandy ground supported the ground-covering Creeping Willow and in damp areas and in peat bogs Bogmosses grew.

Plants of deciduous woodland were well-represented; we can envisage an open woodland of Birch and some Oak with Hazel on the better soils. Less common trees would have been Ash, Rowan, Wild Cherry and Holly with Ivy and Honeysuckle climbing among them. These trees are characteristic of ancient woodland, which had grown for thousands of years and was gradually cut down, extensively first by the Iron Age peoples and then continued by the Romans. As the woodland was opened up, more light-demanding plants would have colonised felled areas such as Bittersweet, Bracken, Pignut, Greater Stitchwort, Bracken and various mosses. Colourful Bluebell and Red Campion would have carpeted the ground in early summer. Woodland margins would have been invaded by Raspberry and Bramble. Wet woodland, common on the undrained ground around the fort, was represented by Alder and Willow with Wood Forget-me-not and mosses.

Areas of grassland, developed for pasture by Iron Age farmers, would have had a rich flora: Harebell, Cat's Ear, Ribwort Plantain, Self-heal, Meadow and Creeping Buttercups, Common Sorrel, Lesser Stitchwort and mosses. Purging Flax would have been restricted to richer soils. Grasses found were Yorkshire Fog, Bent-grasses and Smooth and Rough Meadow-grasses. Leaves of Meadow Vetchling, petals of White Clover and pollen of Greater Bird's-foot-trefoil in the ditches suggest that meadow hay had been collected to be dried for winter fodder for the horses. Rushes of wet pasture and damp woods were identified as the Sharp-flowered or Jointed Rush and Soft or Compact Rush. Damp meadows would have graded into places liable to winter flooding, fens and marshes. These would be colourful with bright yellow Marsh Marigold and Lesser Spearwort and the pinks and reds of Ragged Robin, Willow-herbs and Marsh Cinquefoil. Common and Greater Tussock Sedges, Common Spike-rush, Gypsywort, and the grasses, Tufted Hair-grass, Flote-grass and Reed Canary-grass were all present.

Ancient woodland, undrained fens and marshes, pasture, grassland and wasteland in which these plants grow can all be found within a few kilometres of the fort at the present time. Before suburbia spread from Glasgow in the nineteenth and twentieth centuries, the semi-natural landscape would have borne a strong resemblance to that of 2,000 years ago.

Other Roman forts in Scotland

In chapter 1 there were brief summaries of the archaeobiological discoveries from Roman forts excavated in Scotland before 1970. At least two more, investigated since then, are worthy of mention.

Inveresk, near Edinburgh
In 1976-7 excavations by Graham Thomas (1988) of the Roman civil settlement at Inveresk, on the southern side of the Firth of Forth, east of Edinburgh, revealed two occupations in Antonine times. The local making of pottery, and even a possible potter's workshop, were indicated by a clay furnace or kiln. Outside the present village, aerial

49 The stone base of the Wall under excavation at Bearsden. The black material in the trench is interpreted as the burnt remains of the wooden rampart. With permission of Historic Scotland

photography showed patterns which had the appearance of garden plots and cereal fields. Identified by Alan Hayes, substantial quantities of charcoal consisted of Alder, Birch, Hazel, Oak, Poplar and Cherry/Thorn. 'Certainly the main floor of structure 3 was poplar while the overlying floor boards comprised hazel, birch and alder as well as oak', according to Thomas (p159). No species of *Populus* other than Aspen is native in Scotland and Hayes does not give reasons for his separation from Willow and so we are left in a state of uncertainty about this tricky distinction. Lin Barnetson identified bones of Domestic Cattle and Sheep, which had been slaughtered when fully grown. There were also Pig bones and some of small Horses, perhaps native ponies. Oysters and Mussels predominated among the molluscs, studied by Anne Howard.

Elginhaugh, near Edinburgh
With nine infantry and two cavalry barracks (Hanson and Yeoman 1988), this fort has already been mentioned with regard to pollen analysis and food plants. However there are other macroscopic fossils of interest, notably seeds of Henbane and Hemlock, both plants used as painkillers or sedatives, recovered from a cess pit. Corn-drying kilns were found in an annexe, presumably used for locally grown Barley. There were clay-domed ovens which would have been used by groups of troops to bake their own bread from imported Wheats, as was customary. Fortunately the water table had remained high and the shallow wells had in part retained their linings of wattle, which suggests that coppicing was being practised in order to produce the flexible straight stems.

7 Early Historic Scotland: Roman spices still used

Diversity of people and religion

The period from the fifth to the ninth centuries AD covers what is still sometimes called 'the Dark Ages', but more recently the Early Historic Period. In Scotland, as in the rest of the British Isles, archaeologists are dispelling the darkness and the understanding of the period is increasing, in spite of the lack of written records. Knowledge of diets is also growing as many samples from recent excavations have been investigated by archaeobiological methods.

The descendants of former Iron Age tribes received new names, and during this period invaders settled in the east and west of the country as is shown in **50**. North of the Clyde-Forth isthmus became known as Pictland, recognisable as such from the sixth-century; whilst to the south the descendants of the Iron Age farmers became known as the Britons. By about AD 500 a new kingdom of Gaels of the Del Riata tribe from Northern Ireland became established in Argyll. From the seventh to the tenth centuries the Angles, the Germanic people who invaded England in the early fifth century, had gained territory in eastern Scotland, and they brought Roman Catholicism with them. There is a tradition that monasticism was first brought by Ninian to Whithorn in Wigtonshire and by the fifth century sub-Roman beliefs had probably become established in southern Scotland. The Celtic church, centred on Iona, was established by Columba from Ireland in the sixth century.

Orkney has been termed 'peripheral Pictish'. Howe, a radiocarbon-dated site of this period in Orkney, lacks Pictish artefacts and seems continuous with the preceding Iron Age culture; it is termed Late Iron Age by the site's author. Sites around Birsay Bay on the Orcadian Mainland differ only in their buildings from the following Norse cultures and some types of artefacts of the earlier period remained in use in the Norse period; they have been termed pre-Norse by their investigators.

Christianity developed slowly but was well-established by the eighth century in Orkney, as in Pictland, and Roman Catholicism won the power struggle against the Celtic church. Ecclesiastical establishments prospered as the Church gained in wealth and power and the international movements of missionaries and other incomers stimulated trade from abroad.

Dundurn, Perthshire: a Pictish stronghold

One of the best known Pictish forts is at Dundurn near St Fillans in Perthshire (**51**). The fort is on top of a craggy hill and protected the Pictish heartland against the Dalriadic Scots

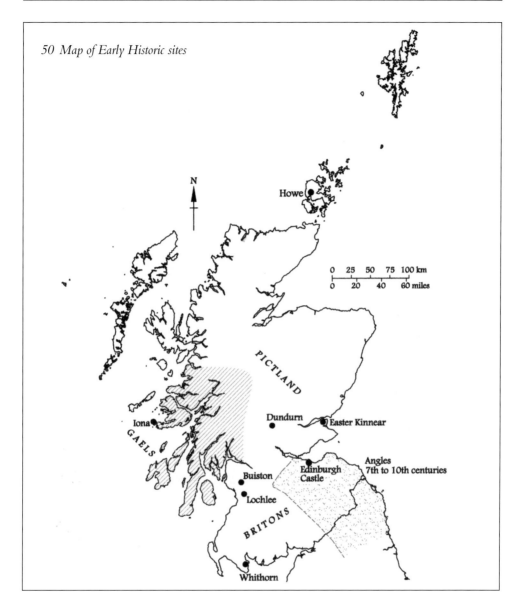

50 Map of Early Historic sites

in the west of Scotland. The fort was excavated in 1976-7 by Leslie Alcock (Alcock et al 1984). The earliest known occupation has been calibrated from radiocarbon-dated Cattle bones at AD 600. The earliest citadel is dated, on structural timber, to between AD 780 and 850. Dundurn is recorded in the *Iona Annals* as being under siege in 683, which is consistent with a seventh-century building date. This early fortification was of dry stone walling with Oak beams and Hazel wattles, fastened with iron nails, and was destroyed by fire. The debris was dragged down hill and overlay a midden layer dated to 550 and 650. This layer was analysed for pollen and larger plant remains by Douglas Brough and published by JHD and Brough (1989). The pollen percentages have been recalculated to conform to the other analyses in this book.

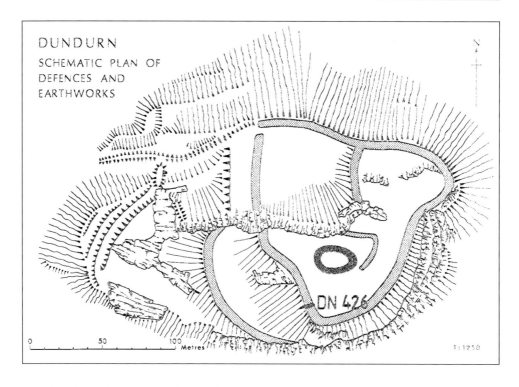

51 Plan of Dundurn From Dickson and Brough (1989). DN426 indicates the plant-rich sample

Pollen from the midden showed trees and tall shrubs to be 50% of the total pollen. Alder, Oak, Hazel and Hazel-type (Coryloid) pollen were the main tree types, with Birch of lesser importance. A moss sample from the midden gave a similar pollen spectrum, but with more Birch and less Oak. Grass pollen dominated the non-tree pollen with small proportions of Heather, Ribwort Plantain and Bracken. Analyses from recent pollen samples collected from mosses growing under a Birch-Oak canopy on the north side of the hill showed trees and tall shrubs to represent a slightly higher proportion at 68%. The main component was Oak with Birch the only other major contributor. Interestingly, Bracken provided only 0.3%, although large swards grew on all sides of the prominence. Grass and other non-tree pollen are similar in proportion to the fossil assemblage. Trees growing in the vicinity at present are Ash, Beech, Downy Birch, Hazel, Oak, Rowan and Wych Elm encircling the base of the knoll, Grass covers the upper slopes, and the flat ground by the River Earn, which runs close to the hill, is used for pasture. Signs of former cultivation were noted by Alcock on this flat ground and on the eastern side of the hill. Though with somewhat more tree cover, the local vegetation at the present time is thus broadly similar to that of the times of the Pictish stronghold.

Fourteen flowering plants and ferns were represented in the midden; the commonest of these was Bracken, which may have been collected for thatch, bedding or flooring. A similar occurrence of Bracken, though inside buildings, has been recorded by Mark Seaward from the Roman fort of Vindolanda south of Hadrian's Wall (1976).

Of particular note is the evidence for diet. Dundurn and Easter Kinnear, in Fife, are the only Pictish sites so far investigated with remains of both food plants and animal foods. Cereal grains were few; one grain of Naked and two of Hulled Barley with a single grain of Wild or Cultivated Oat were all that were recovered. Hazelnut fragments representing up to 50 nuts were found and five Raspberry seeds. An elongated clump of Wild Cherry stones resembled a coprolite in shape, and sterol analysis proved that excrement had been present, although other samples taken through the midden showed very low levels of coprosterols. No cereal bran fragments or other plant fragments indicating cess were seen and so the midden was not thought to have been intended for use as a cess-pit. The rich assemblage of 15 species of mosses is of interest as the majority are of robust species suitable for wiping and packing and indeed have been found at other sites in contexts which suggested they had been used for toilet purposes. The midden deposits also produced bones scattered throughout the layer, identified by Ian Hodgson; they were from mature Cattle, Sheep or Goat and young Pig.

Buiston Crannog, Ayrshire: foreign spices

As previously stated in chapter 5, crannogs can form an invaluable source of waterlogged deposits recording the day-to-day life of their occupants. Oakbank showed that very well and so did Lochlee, investigated by Bayley Balfour well over 100 years ago (see chapter 1).

As a result of their survey of crannogs, mentioned in chapter 5, Barber and Crone considered that Buiston was one of only two crannogs which appeared to have retained organic deposits to any extent and so it was the one chosen for excavation to determine the archaeological value and the duration of these settlements (**52**).

The first settlement at Buiston took place in the first century, as shown by calibrated radiocarbon dates; Crone suggests that this is probably at about the same time as the first Roman invasion of Scotland in AD 79. The second occupation lasted for about a century from the end of the fourth to the late fifth century, corresponding to the final withdrawal of the Romans from Britain after a period of unrest. A later stage of habitation in the seventh century AD is contemporary with the Anglian invasion of south-east Scotland from Northumbria. These are interesting possible correlations and need confirmation from other crannogs. It is worth noting that 13 radiocarbon dates were obtained from Buiston. Although it may not be possible for financial reasons to have so many dates from other sites (Buiston is particularly complex stratigraphically), clearly a single date is not going to answer many questions, especially from an unexcavated site. Barber and Crone (1993) have noted that 'without excavation, we cannot know which dates relate to primary construction, subsequent refurbishments or later phases of occupation; they simply indicate that there was activity on the crannog at that time'.

What remained of Buiston, after Munro's work, was excavated in 1989 and 1990. The complex story is soon to appear as a monograph. In work already published, the stratigraphy has been outlined by Tim Holden (as well as by Barber and Crone), who also identified the waterlogged plant remains. The foundation was of large boulders and massive Oak beams beneath alternate layers of clay turves and Hazel, Willow and Birch

52 Buiston Crannog. From Munro (1882), showing stockades and part of the log platform

brushwood; Heather was also present. Pollen and plant remains, including mosses, from the turf suggested that they were cut from open or lightly wooded vegetation. The earliest date for the brushwood was about AD 80, the later Iron Age. The mound, some 11.6m across, was then abandoned, and lake deposits accumulated. Two charred Hulled Barley grains and a quantity of Hazelnut shells were the only finds to record this early occupation. The crannog was reoccupied in the mid- and late sixth century AD and further activity recorded. In the later period concentric walkways and a palisade of Oak and Alder were connected by slotted planks forming a ring-beam round the crannog. Dendrochronological dating of these timbers by Crone showed that, with repairs and consolidation, this occupation lasted for 80 or more years.

At least one large building, a roundhouse *c*.7m across, was built and rebuilt within the palisade. Its hearth was remade three times, certainly once after flooding; the waterlogging left its mark in the form of unburnt seeds of Pondweeds, Yellow Water Lily, Mare's-tail, Bur-reed and Spike-rush among the charred debris of one of the hearths. Part of the palisade collapsed after AD 609 and semi-aquatic plants grew in the debris. One of the houses was destroyed after 613 when the archaeological story ends; perhaps the uppermost layers had been removed by Munro's excavation. There was no causeway to link the crannog to the shore, but two dugout canoes have been found in the mud.

The occupation periods *in toto* produced much evidence of the economy of the inhabitants and the environment of the surrounding loch. Wood litter seems to have been used for flooring. Charred plant remains, identified by Sheila Boardman, are of Hulled Six-rowed Barley with some Oats and there were tentative identifications of rare Bread

Wheat grains. Flax seed was found in quantity with small numbers of waterlogged seeds. They may have been grown for fibre or oil seed although there is evidence for spinning and probably weaving. Waterlogged grains were found in smaller concentrations, but very little chaff. Holden equates this with crop cleaning away from the site, but corn was ground for flour on the crannog as is evinced by the presence of rotary querns. The grain was probably grown locally, because two crook ards were found in the mud around the sunken palisade.

Evidence for collected food comes from remains of Bird Cherry, Rowan, Raspberry, Bramble, Rose-hips and quantities of Hazelnut shells. Among mosses identified by Andy McMullen was a quantity of *Rhytidiadelphus squarrosus* packed beneath a hearth complex, perhaps to help prevent the wooden floor from burning. The plank walkways were caulked with Bogmoss, and a rope made of the tough long stems of Hairmoss was retrieved (**53**).

Especially interesting additions were seeds of imported plants; these were Dill and Coriander both native to the Mediterranean region. The green parts are used for culinary purposes as well as the seeds; seeds of both are also used medicinally. These seeds have been closely dated as they were found in sediments between wood which has been dendrochronologically dated to AD 594 and 620. The seeds of these plants have also been found at Whithorn, an early monastic site described below, from sixth-century deposits. Both sites are of high status and both have imported pottery. At other early historic sites wine was imported in amphorae from the Mediterranean or in wooden barrels from France. Doubtless other goods such as seeds for medicinal and culinary uses and, by monastic foundations, dyes to colour the illuminated manuscripts would also have been imported, perhaps in exchange for hides and furs.

T. O'Sullivan identified bones of Domestic Cattle, Pig and Sheep; Red and Roe Deer and Geese were also part of the diet. The inhabitants seem to have been to a large degree self-supporting, as leather-working and shoe-making, metal-working and lathe-turning were also carried out on the site.

The only other crannog of a similar age to have yielded a quantity of organic material is that at Loch Glashan in Mid Argyll. It was excavated by Jack Scott (1960) in advance of hydroelectric developments. Situated on a shelf in the loch at the edge of deeper water, the crannog had a substructure of brushwood and Bracken beneath a rectangular timber building. Pottery from the foundation layer and the surface was dated to the sixth to eighth centuries AD; some had been imported. A quantity of worked wood and leather was also recovered. Examined by Caroline Earwood (1990), the wood had been crafted into dishes and troughs, a carved tub or barrel, spatulas, pegs, pins and handles. This crannog was not excavated below the water table.

Ecclesiastical communities: Iona and Whithorn, Wigtonshire

Iona

The economy of early ecclesiastical communities is of considerable interest. To what extent were the inhabitants self-sufficient? In Iona we have the earliest example of an

53 Hairmoss from Buiston Crannog. With permission of Historic Scotland

CM 2 4 6 8 10

excavated site which also has historical records to illuminate aspects of the economy. Only about 5km long by just over 2km wide, Iona is a low-lying island off the south-west coast of the large island of Mull. There is evidence for Mesolithic, Neolithic, Bronze and Iron Age occupation of this fertile island.

The most recent excavation was carried out in 1979 by John Barber (1981). The buildings of the original monastery, founded by Columba, the first Abbot, in AD 563 have still to be located. They are thought to have been in the vicinity of the present Abbey which dates from the tenth or eleventh century and built on a raised beach on the lee side of the island. The only indication on the ground of the original site is a slight bank, a small part of the vallum, which defined the original monastic area. The interpretation of a geophysical survey has added to the presumed line of the vallum. A ditch accompanied the vallum on the inside and a small part of it was excavated and the deposits examined for pollen, larger plant remains and occupation debris.

The radiocarbon date for the lowest organic deposit in the ditch is of the sixth to seventh century AD. The remains described below are from the lower part of the ditch and probably cover the period up to the eighth and ninth century. It is suggested by Barber that the ditch was dug when the community was well-established. Fortunately the ditch was used continuously for the disposal of monastic rubbish and has remained waterlogged since then, so that bones, which would normally have perished in the acid soil, have survived. Pollen analysis of the organic infill of the ditch proved informative. The lowermost pollen is of Oak and Ash, which probably grew on the sheltered eastern side and Birch, Hazel and Willow, which could have survived on the exposed west. The trees soon declined sharply and cereal type pollen with weeds of arable land appeared. This clearance of the island produced land for arable and pastoral farming and perhaps also good timber for building. As cereal pollen is, in general, not wind-dispersed it may well be that the crops were growing just outside the vallum and close to that part of the ditch.

Identified by Alan Fairweather, the larger plant fragments included 'keys' (the fruits) of Ash sandwiched between Holly and Sallow leaves, with seeds of Rowan, Bramble and Elder. Hazelnuts were present as whole nuts and fragments. Other plants such as Cow

Parsley, Hogweed, Red Campion and Nettle indicate enriched soils. Fairweather concluded that 'the ditch was close to an established hedge or wood edge (confirmed by the number of woody species represented) and that the bank was nutrient-rich especially in phosphate'. The pollen from this part of the ditch is local in origin, with Grasses, Elder, Nettle, Sorrel and Sedges predominating. Ferns, including Bracken, flourished for a while. Trees retained small values, with Holly, Rowan and Hawthorn as well as the woody climbers, Honeysuckle and Ivy. The upper levels of the ditch fill became dominated by Birch with increasing Grasses, Heather and Heaths. Cereal farming continued and so these changes are thought to have been local ones. The upper part of the ditch section shows a sudden decline in Birch with an increase in Grasses and cereals. Bohncke suggested that this might reflect the settlement of Benedictine monks in the twelfth century. The departure of the monks to Ireland following Viking raids in the ninth century does not seem to be reflected in the pollen analyses.

Finbar McCormick examined the animal bones and identified a minimum number of 27 individuals. There was a high predominance of Domestic Cattle, of a small type, with small numbers of Sheep of the Soay type, and Pigs. Butchering marks on the pony-sized Horse bones showed that they were occasionally eaten. Wild animals were unusually important, especially Red Deer, but with Roe Deer and Grey Seal also represented. McCormick comments that the needs of arable crops may have limited the land available for livestock on the small island. As in Ireland, the Domestic Cattle may have been kept primarily for milk. It was forbidden by the Early Church to eat horse flesh, but McCormick suggests that this ban may not have come into force until the reforms introduced by the Catholic Church at the end of the seventh century. The deer may well have been caught on the neighbouring island of Mull. Otter bones may relate to animals trapped for their skins rather than their flesh. Fowling is represented by Raven and Goose bones. R. Reece identified bones of Cod and Hake and also shells of Limpets, Winkles, Whelks and Oysters.

Fragments of shoes and the side of a purse were examined by Willy Groenman van Waateringe, who reported that the quality of the tanning was not good. Skins of cow, calf, Goat or Sheep, Horse, Red Deer and Seal were used, probably from animals slaughtered locally and, as they relate to the bones from the ditch, the rest of the animals were apparently used for food. From their position in the ditch, the shoes appear to date from the late sixth to early seventh century AD; shoes of this period are, not surprisingly, very rarely preserved.

Numerous pieces of worked wood were recovered and 31 of these were of turning wasters, mostly of Alder, produced when a bowl or similar object is turned on a lathe. This was probably a pole lathe, a tool still in use in parts of Britain until the first half of the twentieth century. Fragments of three bowls of Alder wood were all that remained of the turned receptacles. Little pottery was found at the site and it seems that wood may have replaced ceramics. Timber off-cuts, worked wood fragments, pegs and stakes were found in quantity. The wood was identified and described by Anne Crone and Rod McCullagh. Stakes and pegs of Alder, Hazel, Birch, Willow, Pine, Oak, Poplar and Ash were identified, with pins of Oak, Pine and Yew. The authors note that the bulk of the material is very small, 'perhaps the type of distribution which might be expected from the use of sill-beams with wattle walls'. Several pins are of Pine which does not appear to have grown on the island. From higher in the ditch six spatula-like objects of Pine with three spoon fragments, a small bung or stopper of Ash wood, and a staff or walking stick were also found.

It is unlikely that trees would have developed the large straight timbers needed to build the principal buildings on such a small wind-swept island. Documentary evidence for the source of the wood comes from Adomnan's *Life of Columba* written between AD 658 and 692. Adomnan, who was Abbot from 679-704, records that dressed timbers of Pine and Oak were brought to the island by land and sea; further Oak timbers were brought in twelve curraghs (skin-covered boats). Bundles of wattles, perhaps from Mull, were also imported for the construction of a guest-house.

The excavation of pits and post-holes, a few metres from the ditch and still within the enclosure, produced pieces of slag, iron and charcoal from a pit dated to the early seventh century. A glass bar and bronze fragments from the same pit all indicate local industrial processes.

Whithorn: an early herb garden?

From 1984-91 excavations were carried out in Whithorn, Wigtownshire, in south-west Scotland by Peter Hill (1996). The excavation to the south-west of the twelfth century Cathedral Priory soon revealed that the site was a rich one (*see* **116**). Habitation extended from *c*.AD 500 almost to the present time. Only those samples spanning the Early Historic period, which for this purpose extends to AD 1000 or later, are here considered. Later episodes are discussed in the chapter covering the Medieval period. Traditionally it has been thought that Nynia (St Ninian) became bishop of a Christian community which had developed from a late Roman period trading settlement and which became a monastic town from about AD 500 under Ninian's guidance.

c.AD 500-730

The early monastic establishment had trade links with Europe. Fragments of amphorae, originally containing wine and olive oil from the Mediterranean region, pottery from North Africa and the eastern Mediterranean, and glassware from the continent were recovered. Industrial processing is shown by smelting and smithying using imported haematite ore. Imported lime from the Solway coast showed that coastal trade was established for iron and lime.

An exciting discovery was of plough pebbles from a mouldboard plough, which allowed cultivation of heavy clay soils not previously possible with a simple ard plough. These pebbles were found in deposits dating from the late fifth or early sixth century to the middle of the ninth century. Such ploughs would require a large team of Horses or Oxen and indicate a community effort by a wealthy institution. Expansion of arable farming would thus be possible on hitherto uncultivated ground. This monastery was clearly well-to-do and had far ranging contacts, perhaps partly as a result of well-organised farming and industry, enabling it to have surplus products to sell.

Investigation of possible stores of charcoal, that would have been used for the extensive iron-working, showed mainly roundwood of Oak, Alder, Ash, Hazel, Birch, Willow,

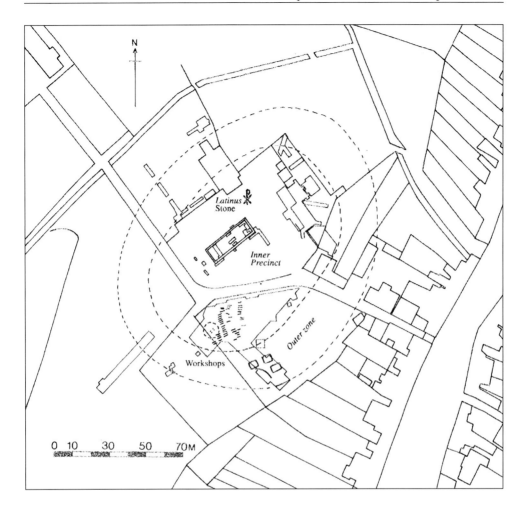

54 Plan of Whithorn 1. From Hill (1996)

Rowan and Pomoidae (Wild Cherries and Hawthorn type). This is the only indication of the composition of the local mixed woodland.

In a residential zone, outside the inner precinct of the monastery, two pits are tentatively dated to the earlier part of this period. Pit 1 contained abundant cereal bran, seeds, mosses and fly puparia, which showed that the pits contained human faeces. The seeds include 18 Coriander, five Dill, one Black Mustard, two Bramble, three Fat Hen and one Dog Rose. The Coriander and Dill must have been introduced from the Mediterranean area. The pit also contained a sherd of an amphora, probably originally containing wine, and dated to the late fifth or early sixth centuries. It seems probable that the seeds were imported with the amphorae or other pottery or glass. Although Coriander and Dill both have culinary uses, both could also have been used medicinally, as for instance, for flatulence. Black Mustard was formerly cultivated as a condiment, but was originally used medicinally. The seeds have diuretic and emetic properties and have been used for mustard poultices. The Romans used it to enhance the flavour of their food and Black Mustard seeds have been recovered from Roman sites in England and from seventh to ninth century AD deposits in Southampton, as well as later finds. The plant is rare in Scotland and does not grow in the south-west. CD considered that Coriander, Dill and Black Mustard could have been grown in the monastery's herb garden. If this were so, then Whithorn had the earliest herb garden so far recorded in Britain.

Another pit contained over 3,000 Bramble, 450 Small Nettle, over 60 Field Woundwort, 50 Elder and two Hemlock seeds; Heather, wood and bark fragments were also present. There was no indication of excrement. Two interpretations have been put forward; the first that the seeds are dyers' waste and the second that they represent a collection of medicinal plants. Both leaves and berries of Bramble and Elder yield dyes, although, as with all berry dyes, these tend to be fugitive. Flowering tops of Marsh Woundwort and Nettle tops have also been used for dyeing. Bramble leaves also have medicinal properties. Elder fruits are diuretic and sudorific (stimulate sweating). The Woundworts have been used as a vulnerary, both externally and internally, and have antiseptic and antispasmodic qualities. They have also been used for gout and cramp. Hemlock is a very powerful drug plant; it has been used to ease swollen joints and pain since classical times and, with care, as a sedative. The Stinging Nettles have mildly diuretic, anti-rheumatic and tonic qualities. All these plants could have been gathered in the wild, some from cultivated ground. It is possible that both dyeing waste and medicinal plants are represented. From the pit, Ewan Campbell identified two vessel glass sherds of continental origin, one of them probably from western France. These, together with the stratigraphy, suggest a seventh-century date. A spindle whorl was a rare find.

The animal bones were identified by Finbar McCormick and Eileen Murphy; they state that small samples and differential survival have limited the number of samples considered to those with over 100 fragments. The period 1 bones date from the seventh century and are of mature or older animals. Cattle are dominant, Pig next in importance and there are very few Sheep; Roe Deer was also eaten. A single Salmon vertebra was the only fish bone identified.

c.AD 730-845

South-west Scotland came under Northumbrian control in the seventh century, following the Anglian expansion northwards which covered the huge territory from the Humber to the Forth. The Anglians became Christian in the early seventh century. A Northumbrian bishopric was established at Whithorn to rule over their western territory, so Whithorn remained an important ecclesiastical centre. A timber church was built, only to burn down between AD 840 and 845. Charred planks sealed in a deposit of burnt grain on the floor of the nave. The plant material for this period was examined by Jacqui Huntley who identified a remarkably pure assemblage of about 200 Barley and 10 Oat grains. This must represent fully processed grain ready for use. A second sample, from under an earth floor in the chancel, contained a mixture of 30 Barley and 6 Oat grains with arable weed seeds and grassland species. More than one habitat is suggested from the plant species with Stinking Mayweed, a plant of heavier soils, indicating that clay soils were still being worked. Little closely dated grain has hitherto been recorded from this period. The only other plant remains so far published from Whithorn are of wild plants, from a wide range of habitats, of later twelfth- and thirteenth-century date.

A Northumbrian midden, which had rapidly accumulated, consisted mainly of kitchen refuse. Cattle again provided the most bones, with a high proportion of young animals. Sheep or Goat bones were much more numerous than in the preceding period; most are thought to have been of Sheep, although Goat horn cores were found elsewhere on the site. It has been suggested that the increase in Sheep was due to the growing importance of wool. It is notable that spindle whorls and combs increase at this time. The proportion of Pig bones remained unchanged. All the deer bones are of Roe Deer, which apparently produces the best venison. Goose and Domestic Fowl bones were plentiful; Duck and Gull were also present. Fish bones were few, probably mainly of Cod, with rare Herring and Salmon bones.

c.AD 845-1000

Although the ecclesiastical buildings were rebuilt after the fire the Northumbrian influence had diminished. A few artefacts suggest Scandinavian influence in the tenth century but there is no definite evidence of marauding Vikings at Whithorn. The relatively few animal bones from this period show little difference in their proportions to those from the previous period with Cattle still clearly dominating. The very few fish and bird bones were not tabulated separately from those belonging to the next period (1000-1250).

Other bones found in all the chief contexts in the periods we have been considering so far included Horse, Domestic Cat and Dog. Horse bones were represented by small quantities of mature or old animals. It is not known if they were eaten at the end of their useful lives. The Cats were young when slaughtered and the authors suggested they were deliberately bred for their skins.

As from other sites which span a long period, the interest lies in the changes from period to period. Although bones were recorded from *c*.AD 500 to 1500, from none of those periods, excepting the Northumbrian midden, were there sufficiently large numbers to produce confidently detailed analyses of changes through time. The period of Northumbrian dominance seems to have been the most affluent period, with prime beef and lamb joints, the best venison, and Geese and Domestic Fowl popular.

Edinburgh Castle and Easter Kinnear, Fife

High Status Castle
The earlier phases at Edinburgh Castle have been described in chapter 5 and later periods are covered in chapter 9. Midden accumulation began in the Roman period and continued throughout the Early Historic period, as evinced by rare artefacts from the seventh to tenth centuries. Inferences from the bone assemblages are that it was initially a royal British stronghold. It can be assumed from the known Anglian advances to beyond the river Forth in the seventh century that the site must have been held by the Angles, perhaps up to the tenth century. The sparse charcoal remains, identified by Anne Crone, show that Oak woodland with Hazel still grew in the vicinity. The other charred plant remains,

identified by Sheila Boardman, produced 1,352 cereal grains, 82% of which were of Hulled Barley, some of them had germinated, and Boardman suggests that part of the crop may have been deliberately destroyed. Both Common and Bristle Oat were present but only a trace of Bread Wheat. There is also one of the earliest records for Peas in Scotland; legumes are normally under-represented in the fossil record because their preparation does not include drying by heat, so they are seldom accidentally burnt. Flax seeds were present in three samples. Black Mustard, with over 300 seeds in one sample, is an interesting addition. Its seeds were also recorded at Whithorn and the plant's culinary and medicinal uses have been described in that section. The introduction of Oats, Peas and Black Mustard to the eastern side of the country poses the question 'Were they the result of trade or was a wider range of crop plants introduced by the Anglians?'

Bones of Cattle, Sheep/Goat and Pig, identified by Finbar McCormick, were present in roughly equal amounts; the relatively high numbers of Pigs could be accounted for by the availability of acorns in the Oak woodland which had persisted in the area. There is a slight increase in Red Deer numbers from the Roman Iron Age; Roe Deer, Fox and Beaver were also hunted. McCormick noted that Beaver remains are very rare on Scottish archaeological sites. Hunting was a favourite past-time of the Medieval aristocracy and it may be that the site had become the seat of the nobility.

Low Status Easter Kinnear

The contribution to our understanding of past landscapes by aerial photography of crop marks is well-known. The Royal Commission on the Ancient and Historical Monuments of Scotland has systematically recorded parts of Scotland, and north-east Fife has proved to have one of the densest concentrations of surviving crop marks in Scotland. This potentially rich archaeological heritage is due to the sunny climate and light sandy and silty soils, which have attracted settlers as far back as the long-lasting Mesolithic habitation at Morton.

The excavation of two crop mark sites in 1989 and 1990 by Stephen Driscoll and Trevor Watkins was preceded by studies of the history of the area (Driscoll 1997). They found that Pictish place-name elements are associated with the richest land, and deduced that many farms in Fife, Angus and Perthshire were already successful in Pictish times. As the main farmhouses have probably been built on the same sites for hundreds of years and are still flourishing agricultural centres (Easter Kinnear was first recorded in the thirteenth century), the opportunities for excavation of these potentially wealthy sites will be very few, if any. Examination of solid, sub-rectangular crop marks suggested, however, where the peasant farms servicing these major centres might lie. The marks are not easy to interpret since the absence of good building stone, later robbing and truncation by Medieval and later cultivation have left little more than these dark areas on the ground.

The main feature found in 1989 was a large sub-rectangular structure scooped out of the sand and gravel, with coarse dry stone walls built with boulders from the glacial sub-soil. The scoop covered an area of 12m x 10.5m and was later infilled, followed by a sequence of wattle and daub walls. Fragments of round wood from the latter were identified as Hazel and Oak with occasional Alder, Birch and Willow. Charred Heather fragments are likely to have been derived from thatch or bedding. Other woods found in a hearth and other contexts were Ash, Wild Cherry, Rowan type and Elm. Most was of

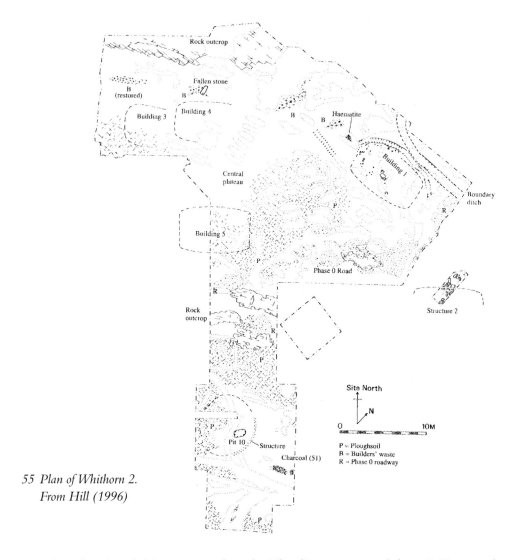

55 Plan of Whithorn 2. From Hill (1996)

roundwood and probably remains of wattle. The diameters ranged from 5-25mm and probably included the narrow ends of the rods. The ages of these pieces of roundwood are not consistent with the trees having been cut on a deliberate coppice cycle. The calibrated radiocarbon dates for the hearth charcoal and probable wattle all fall within the mid-sixth to mid-seventh century AD.

The analysis of the roundwood indicates an open woodland with Hazel, Ash, Wild Cherry and Wych Elm on the better soils and Alder and Willow in the wetter areas. The continuance of a woodland so rich in species is surprising in a long settled area and so a wider view of the regional vegetation was sought from two nearby pollen diagrams. Pitbladdo, about 8km to the south-west, analysed by A.P. Donald (1981) has not been radiocarbon-dated, but from the Neolithic to the top of the diagram tree pollen values gradually decline to very low values. Grasses increase concomitantly and there is some Ribwort Plantain indicating gradual removal of woodland with, until recently Alder,

Hazel and Oak with a little Birch, Wych Elm and Scots Pine remaining. Graeme Whittington and colleagues (1991) have pollen analysed cores from the Black Loch, Fife, some 15km to the south-west. Radiocarbon-dated diagrams show a similar overall picture, with the addition of Ash and rare Rowan type pollen, from the middle of the first millennium AD. Extensive farming is indicated, but there must have been sufficient wood both for building and fuel to meet the needs of the Pictish inhabitants.

At Easter Kinnear over 2000 grains of Barley, probably all of lax-eared Six-row Hulled type, were recorded by CD, many of them from around the hearth. Four seeds of Flax, including two from a hearth, were recovered. Oat grains were present in all contexts yielding Barley and, from their size range (28 grains measured 4.4-7.7mm in length), some at least appear to be of a cultivated species. Arable weed seeds were rather sparse, apart from the hearth sample which had the greatest number and variety; these may have originated with straw for kindling. The grain appears then to have been carefully cleaned of weed seeds, or else the ears were gathered individually.

The hearth also produced seeds of grass and heathland plants and many Heather stems. Similar plant remains would be expected if organic turf from dry heath had been stripped off to eke out the other fuel, as is suggested for Howe, in Orkney, from a similar period. A much more noteworthy discovery from the hearth was a very fragile, small bulbil, tentatively identified as Sand Leek, also known as Spanish Garlic. These bulbils grow at the top of the stem and the larger bulbs develop at the base of the plant. The Sand Leek was formerly cultivated in England for flavouring. The bulbs are smaller and milder than those of Garlic and the medicinal properties are similar but less powerful. A single Raspberry pip came from the same context and Bramble from another context. Rare seeds of plants of watersides and mires, confined to the hearth, may have been brought in with domestic water supplies.

No doubt these represent only a small proportion of the foodstuffs used. Only the excavation of other small farms in these rich agricultural lands and equally thorough environmental sampling will give a more comprehensive view of the diet at this time in eastern Pictland. The acidic soils did not preserve bone well; a few fragments of Cattle bone, one Pig tooth and Horse teeth fragments were all that were identifiable. Driscoll thought the artefacts suggest people of modest status. Perhaps the excavated areas were the remains of peasant dwellings. Elite settlements would have produced imported goods, metal work and weapons, none of which were recovered.

An intriguing feature is the scooped surface of the earliest house and of similar structures about 1km to the north-east. These are reminiscent of the souterrains of an earlier period, also found in this area, which are widely thought to have served as underground storage pits. The scoops are situated above the water table and could have been used for cereal storage. As the cereals would have been stored in sacks, and there were no hearths that may have accidentally set fire to the grain and so preserved it, such storage spaces could well have left no indication of their uses. Driscoll believed that the scoops were deliberately filled in and other types of storage may have subsequently been employed. He suggested a change of policy, perhaps the creation of an estate, with the control of agricultural produce moving to a smaller elite group. Clearly, new research designs will be needed to investigate these rural settlements further.

8 The Norse versus the Northern Picts

Caithness and the Northern Isles

Norse versus Picts

The Pictish (pre-Norse) period overlaps substantially in time with the sites for the Early Historic period discussed in the previous chapter. For the purpose of these chapters, both date from the fourth and fifth centuries AD. The Norse period marks the settlement of the Scandinavians as farmers from the beginning of the ninth century and lasts until about AD 1100. Norse political influence continued to dominate large areas of northern Scotland until about AD 1300, and this Late Norse period extended until AD 1500 in the Northern Isles. Sites which continued in use from the Norse to the Medieval or later periods are considered here; such sites retained their Norse character. The term Viking is, on the whole, not used here since a Viking, strictly speaking, was a sea-faring raider. Such raids took place from about AD 780 in England, and continued in Ireland until the mid-tenth century.

A glance at figure **56** shows that the Norse influence is confined to the north and west of Scotland, which is geographically distinct from the more southern and eastern areas of the Early Historic sites. As will be shown these last two areas are culturally distinct, although some Norse influence has inevitably been noted also at those Early Historic sites which are near to the western sea routes taken by the Viking marauders on their way to pillage Ireland.

How did the Norse influence change the way of life of the indigenous peoples? Was their culture suddenly obliterated? Did they introduce new crops and animals? Did their farming methods differ? There is as yet too little evidence to give definitive answers, but we now know the type of questions that environmental evidence will be expected to answer in the future.

In the north of Scotland and the Northern Isles, the later settlement sites are usually those of the indigenous pre-Norse population, with Norse buildings or middens either on top of or closely associated with them. So far destruction by Vikings has not been conclusively proved, and in one instance at Pool, Orkney, the two cultures seem to have existed side by side. Pictish-style artefacts continued to be used on Norse house sites and the conclusion must be that the Norse incomers settled down to farm alongside the indigenous farmers or were given recently vacated farms. Because these combined Pictish and Norse sites have been dug and published together, and as their economies are strongly related, they are here considered together.

It has been pointed out by Anna Ritchie, in her book *Viking Scotland,* that no trading towns developed in Scotland, such as in England at York, or in Ireland at Dublin. Goods seem to have been imported directly by wealthy Norse farmers, who may have been descended from the Norwegian nobility, or received land for their services. Although the Vikings came from Sweden and Denmark as well as Norway, only the Norse (from Norway) seem to have settled in Scotland. In England, the Danes were the chief settlers, with rather different cultural traditions as has been demonstrated, for instance, at the extensively excavated Viking town of York, presented to the public as 'Jorvik'.

Norse farms were established, or re-established, in the ninth and tenth centuries and were chiefly composed of rectangular buildings, the minimum being a house, byre and barn. The hearth was central and peat was the main fuel used. Low benches, running along the two long sides, served both for sitting and sleeping. Walls were usually of stone, with an inner core of turf or rubble. In Orkney and Caithness, the local flagstones provided an excellent building material, as it had for the previous cultures. The roof construction probably varied according to the materials available, but native woodland was not plentiful in northern Scotland or its islands. Old farms were converted into outhouses and new farm buildings built alongside. This was seen, for instance, in the earliest Norse farmhouse at Jarlshof on Shetland and remained a common practice right into the twentieth century in the Northern Isles.

The culture of the Orkney and Shetland islands differs from that of the rest of Scotland, for it was there that the Norse influence was most widespread and lasted the longest. From the ninth century to AD 1472, when the Scottish crown took over the islands, they belonged to Norway, although Scottish influence was felt from the thirteenth century onwards. The Norse language was retained as a local development known as Old Norn until the eighteenth century and so it is possible to trace back farming terminology to its presumed use in the Early Norse settlements. Using the knowledge gained from environmental archaeology we may thus attempt to reconstruct a coherent picture of aspects of the Norse way of life.

It is fortunate that traditional patterns of settlement, farming and fishing were recorded in great detail by Alexander Fenton in *The Northern Isles: Orkney and Shetland* before the changes of the late twentieth century took place. His evidence is particularly valuable for its insights into early farming practices through the persistence of Old Norn, as very few reliable documents referring to the Northern Isles exist before the late twelfth century.

The larger number of excavated sites on Orkney, compared to those on Shetland, reflect, in part, the differing agricultural potential of the two groups of islands. In 1931, 37.3% of Orkney land was under arable, but only 3.4% of Shetland land was used for growing crops. This has changed in recent times on Orkney, where much of the former arable is now under pasture. A great deal of Shetland has for long been covered by peat-bogs and moorland. There is a well-known saying in the Northern Isles that an Orkney man is a farmer who fishes, whereas a Shetlander is a fisherman who farms. This is clearly based on the differing agricultural potential of the two sets of islands. In Orkney especially, as farmers have required more land, rescue excavations have dug sites before they were destroyed by the plough. Erosion of coastal cliffs has also necessitated rescue archaeology.

56 Plan of Norse Sites. The shaded areas are those occupied by the invaders

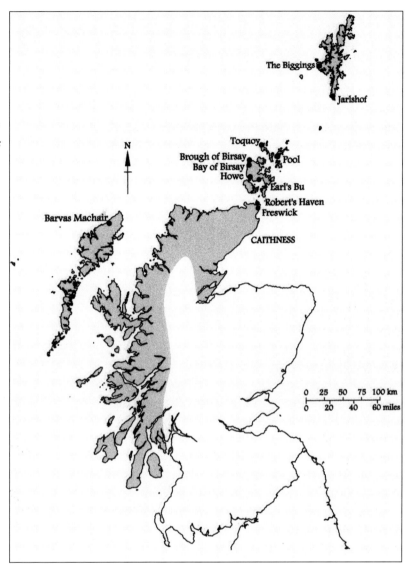

Land of good quality was recognised early on in prehistory and some sites, such as Pool on the Orcadian island of Sanday, have lengthy multi-period occupations culminating in the Norse period. This gives us an excellent opportunity to investigate continuity as well as innovation in farming practices. Caithness was also an important centre for Norse settlements, but the Norse language and laws were not adopted there. Settlement sites there are less easy to find, as much of the evidence so far is from middens being eroded from underneath sand dunes by wave action, and the structures lie elusively under the sand or have already succumbed to the encroaching sea. Pre-Norse middens can only be distinguished by radiocarbon dating, which for financial reasons may not be possible for each horizon of the many middens which have been extensively researched for environmental evidence. The Norse settled firstly in the Northern Isles, only a few days'

sail from Norway, in the later ninth century and they extended into more fertile areas, such as parts of Caithness and Easter Ross. We will begin by considering sites in Caithness which, from their environmental richness, give us hypotheses to test in other parts of Norse Scotland.

Freswick, Caithness

The existence of Freswick is known from the sagas, which tell of the exploits of the Earls who ruled Caithness and Orkney under the Norwegian kings. Freswick was the first Norse settlement to have been discovered on mainland Scotland and was first excavated early in the twentieth century when the remains of a major Norse farm was discovered (**57** & Table 5). Chris Morris and Colleen Batey (1995), the husband and wife team, excavated 500m² during 1980-5 and a comprehensive programme of environmental analysis was instigated. The sites are in Freswick Bay and consist mainly of middens, partially buried in extensive sand dunes. There is severe, active erosion on the seaward edge of the dunes, with consequent loss of part of the Norse middens and so much of the excavation was of a rescue nature. The dunes face east across the cold North Sea, towards the not-too-distant Norway. The low-lying windswept hinterland is largely bare of trees. Blanket peat covers about two thirds of Caithness and may formerly have been more extensive. Peat has been the chief fuel in this part of Scotland for many centuries and much of the peat near Freswick has been cut over. Pastoral farming is carried out at the present time and extends for several kilometres inland.

The gently undulating land with areas suitable for pasture and arable farming must have seemed inviting to the land-hungry Norse farmers, leaving behind them rocky, mountainous Norway with its limited stone-free, level areas suitable for farming. Travelling with skilled seamanship across the North Sea they must have been impressed by the broad, sandy beaches and rock-free hinterland. The relatively short growing season was similar to that in their homeland. What was the nature of the vegetation in the ninth century when the Norse first arrived?

It was partly to answer this question that pollen analysis was undertaken by Jacqueline Huntley. The nearest peat of any depth is at the Hill of Harley, 1.5km to the west of Freswick. This proved to be a good choice because peat accumulation had begun several thousand years ago. Tree pollen is low throughout, seldom exceeding 20% of total land pollen. The exceptionally low tree values are probably due to the windswept situation, preventing tree establishment. Birch, Alder and Hazel predominate and it is thought that these, with Rowan (Rowan type pollen), could have grown nearby in sheltered valleys. There are high values for Scots Pine, around 10%, before a slight Neolithic clearance when values decrease together with those of local trees. Did Scots Pine formerly grow in the neighbourhood or does this represent long distance transport of its pollen? The identification of wood, from the lower part of peat cuttings or in peat banks revealed in drainage ditches, might resolve this question. Willows show low values throughout and Heather is very well represented, though its values fluctuate. Barley type and Ribwort Plantain pollen first appear at about 5,000 years ago with other farming indicators. During the Iron Age, pollen types of cereal and pastoral farming increase, corresponding to the period when the brochs dominated the Caithness countryside. Farming indicators

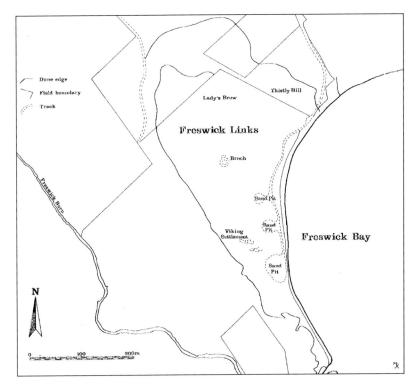

57 Plan of Freswick. From Morris et al. (1995)

continue up to the present time. There is no suggestion of an increase in an arable or pastoral economy during the period covering the Norse occupation. This could be because this activity was too far from the pollen site to reflect the poorly distributed pollen of the largely self- or insect-pollinated plants, which characterise arable farming. Huntley summarises the pollen of the Norse period as follows:

> The landscape probably looked rather similar to that of today with Heather moorland and blanket-peat communities on the higher ground, more species-rich sedge swamps and grassland in the valleys and mixed farming on the low, flat land nearer the coast.

The coarse plant remains came from middens exposed in the calcareous shell sand along the seaward side of the dunes; 14 areas were chosen for excavation. Charred wood was recovered from all these areas and in descending frequency of areas in which they were found are: Heather, Birch, Pine, Oak, Willow and lastly Hazel. Heather would have been a common plant of the blanket bogs and drier areas, as the pollen analysis shows. All these wood types excepting Scots Pine can be found in Caithness at the present time in sheltered ravines which is the only habitat free from grazing. The small sizes of the charcoal pieces gave no inkling as to whether the wood had been artefactual. Sandra Nye noted that the local trees would have been very stunted and gnarled, due to their exposed position, and suggested that some wood may have been imported from further south or gathered as driftwood. Peat was noted from all the areas and would have been the main

	FRESWICK			BROUGH OF BIRSAY			BUCKQUOY		BROUGH ROAD		SAEVAR HOWE		POOL	
	Pictish	Norse	Late Norse	Pictish	Norse	Late Norse	Pictish	Norse	Pictish	Norse	Pictish	Norse	Pictish	Norse
Hulled Barley	*	*	*		*	*				*		*	*	*
Naked Barley													*	*
Bristle Oat					*								*	*
Common Oat	*	*	*							*		*		*
Cultivated Oats (undiff.)		*	*							*				
Wild Oat										*			*	
Wild/cultivated Oat	*	*	*	*	*	*				*		*	*	*
Broad Bean		*												
Flax	*		*											
Henbane										*				
Juniper														
Lesser Celandine														
Cat	*		*				*~	*~		*			*	*
Cattle	*	*	*	*	*	*+	*	*		*	*	*+	*+	*+
Dog	*						*	*						
Domestic Duck														
Domestic Fowl	*	*	*		*	*	*	*		*	*	*		
Domestic Goose	*		*		*			*		*				
Egg collecting	*	*	*											
Goat							*	*						
Hare			*	*		*								
Horse	*	*	*				*	*		*		*	*+	*+
Otter					*		*			*			*	*
Pig	*+	*		*	*	*	*	*		*	*	*+	*	*
Red Deer	*	*	*	*	*	*	*	*		*			*	*
Roe Deer						*								
Sheep	*	*		*	*	*	*	*		*	*+	*+	*	*
Wild Fowl	*	*	*	*	*	*	*	*	*	*	*	*	*	*
Cetacean							*	*		*				
Crab		*			*	*	*	*		*				
Deepwater fishing	*	*	*		*	*		*	*	*	*	*		*
Inshore fishing	*	*	*				*	*	*	*			*	
Seal					*		*	*						*
Shellfish	*	*	*				*	*	*	*	*	*	*	*

KEY: ★ = present / ★+ = high proportion of young animals / ★~ = Wild Cat

Table 5 Resources used at Pictish (pre-Norse), Norse and Late Norse sites in Caithness and Orkney

fuel. Present in ten areas, Seaweed, including Bladderwrack, could have had several uses including that of fertiliser.

The deposits from areas 2 to 14 were sieved for seeds and analysed by Jacqueline Huntley and Judith Turner. Large numbers of samples were examined, often several within each phase from each area. It became obvious from the radiocarbon dates that both Pictish and Norse occupations were present and it was not feasible to date every phase. Many of the results of the environmental analyses, both plant and animal, showed no distinctive differences between either phases or areas. The results summarised here cover the Pictish, Norse and Late Norse periods unless otherwise stated. In all areas the two Scottish staples, Barley and Oats, were identified in approximately equal numbers. The Barley was all Hulled Six-rowed and the Oats considered to be mainly a cultivated species. A few chaff fragments of both Common and Wild Oat were recorded. Seventeen grains of Bread Wheat were recovered from an undated phase and Wheat chaff from the Late Norse deposits. Whether this was an attempt to grow Wheat in this marginal area, or simply represented contaminants in the seed corn, is not known.

Flax is of interest; a few seeds were present in possibly late Pictish as well as Late Norse levels. For simplicity, Flax is used throughout this chapter although the plant may also have been used as Linseed. Flax may have been grown for its fibre, the Norse people having appreciated fine linen, or for its oil-rich seeds. Bone and antler artefacts testify to domestic weaving, but whether this was for linen or wool is not known. Just two seeds of Broad Bean were recorded and are of considerable importance as pulses are so rarely preserved; see part 2. They may be of Late Norse age; there is a Medieval record from Edinburgh Castle. There were relatively low numbers of arable weed seeds and these represent both light sandy soils and heavier clayey ones. Chickweed, characteristic of nitrogen-rich, well-manured soils, was present in five areas.

Cultivation furrows were clearly distinguished by light bands of sand which had blown into the furrows; a later phase was distinguished above a deposit of sand. There was a consistent inclusion of cultural debris in the furrows, presumably spread from the midden heap to enrich the light sandy soil. These furrows have been tentatively correlated with similar horizons in three nearby areas. Radiocarbon dating showed that all three of the areas tested were Pictish. Although these areas are now at the front of the cliff, erosion is such that it is thought that Pictish habitation sites and further middens may formerly have existed on the seaward side, perhaps 100m or more from the present seaward edge of the dunes.

Louisa Gidding reported on the relatively few mammal bones; they were heavily fragmented and many of them burnt. They were predominantly of Cattle with smaller quantities of Sheep and Pig. Many were of neo-natal or juvenile animals which suggested a very high infant mortality and perhaps casualties rather than deliberate slaughtering for food. Wild animals were generally not exploited and there were few Red Deer. Red Deer are, of course, forest animals and the bare peatlands would have had little to attract or shelter them. Horse and Dog bones were rarely found; there were no visible butchering marks to suggest that the Horses had been used for food. A number of Cat bones from a Late Norse area may have been from Domestic Cats, perhaps deliberately kept for their skins. A very few Whale bones were present in one area. There were proportionally lower numbers of mammal bone in the later period, with a higher proportion of fish bones. This would suggest that fish provided the bulk of the protein but it is also possible that the majority of animal bone was deposited elsewhere on the site. Bone numbers were too small to determine any changes in proportion between Pictish and Viking periods.

Over 1,100 fragments of bird bone were recovered from all areas, spanning all periods, and of this number about half were identifiable. These were mainly of seabirds such as Gulls, Guillemots, Shags and Puffins. Enid Allison noted that the bones of a few Domestic Fowl, both cocks and hens, had butchering marks and some were still in a laying condition. A few Goose bones were either of Greylag or its domesticated form. Nineteen species of birds were recorded from eggshells by Elizabeth Sidell and these were present in all areas; this is exceptional as eggshell is rarely recorded to species level from archaeological deposits. Two or three domestic species were represented: Fowl and Goose, with Duck which could have been wild or domesticated. The other eggshells were mainly of seabirds, with most of the seabirds also present as bones. The cliffs which rise at either end of the dunes and the moorland beyond the dunes would have provided a wide range of nesting habitats. Sidell points out that eggs from certain wild birds would have been available from March to September. They could have been preserved in peat ash as was recorded from the once inhabited island of Hirta, part of the St Kilda group. Seabird eggs are larger than hens' eggs and would have added to the protein available as well as providing dietary variety. They were particularly collected in the Late Norse period; not surprisingly, hens' eggs were found in most areas.

Over 40 tonnes of archaeological material was wet-sieved on a 1mm mesh sieve by Andrew Jones in his search for fish bones and otoliths (present in the heads and highly resistant to decay). As a result 34 species were identified and the vast majority of the remains were of Cod, Ling and Saithe; the larger fish were probably caught on lines from boats.

It was striking that Late Norse middens were the most numerous, some consisting of very little else but fish bone. It may be that shell sand rapidly overwhelmed these later middens and so preserved more of them. It does seem, however, that fishing had become an important part of the economy. Why this should have been so is discussed by James Barrett, who investigated the Late Norse site at Robert's Haven on the Caithness coast. He found such quantities and types of fish bone with knife marks indicative of processing that he argued that the communities had been sea fishing not just for local consumption but for foreign trade (with the Hanseatic League).

Earl's Bu, Orcadian Mainland

A most interesting find by a farmer, Mr Stevenson, at Orphir, Orkney Mainland, was a drystone tunnel-like construction discovered when he was preparing foundations for a barn. He brought the discovery to the attention of the archaeologists Colleen Batey and Chris Morris and the site was excavated from the late 1970s onwards and the results published in 1992. It was soon realised that an attached structure was the underhouse of a water mill, with walls surviving up to a metre in height. The waterwheel which it housed had long since gone. The stone passage with a slab covering which led from it, and which was the original structure found, represented the leat or tail race leading the water out of the mill, presumably to rejoin a stream. The lade or headrace, which provided the head of water from a diverted stream to drive the mill, consisted of 'a narrow chute-like feature with substantial slabs lying on end and with a slight gradient towards the underhouse'.

This is the earliest example of a horizontal water-mill, sometimes called a Norse mill, in Scotland. Such mills, though less efficient than the usual vertical mill wheel, continued in use in the Northern Isles until the present century. The mill formed part of the buildings associated with the 'Earl's Hall', dating from the eleventh to fifteenth centuries and not excavated, and indicated that the high status Norse settlement had sufficient grain to merit building a mill. For some reason the mill had ceased to be used by a century or two later.

Of equal interest are the Late Norse middens, of eleventh to twelfth century date, which gradually covered the site. From only a small proportion of the sieved material, burnt plant remains were examined by Jacqueline Huntley and a preliminary assessment has revealed large quantities of Heather wood, leaves and flowers, representing branches probably used for bedding or roofing. Oat grains were dominant with some evidence for Common Oat and there were some Hulled Six-rowed Barley grains and arable weed seeds. Flax seeds were found in several contexts. The high proportion of Oats is interesting and Huntley points out that in that respect the material is more similar to that at Freswick than at other Orcadian sites.

Considerable quantities of animal bones were largely of Cattle, Sheep and Pig with a small number of Seal and the usual Cat and Dog bones. Earlier middens under the mill, of Norse date, have still to be analysed. For James Barrett, Earl's Bu provides an interesting comparison with Robert's Haven, as it is about 200m from the shore of Scapa Flow and not right on the coast as are the other sites, which also have more extensive fish middens. About 87% of the bones were from mammals, and marine shells were virtually absent. Fish of the Cod and Hake families made up over 99% of the identified bone. Cod and Haddock predominated with smaller numbers of Saithe and Ling; Saithe were much less common than at Robert's Haven. Barrett noted that Haddock are a deep water fish which at the present time are not found in Scapa Flow but only in deeper waters to the west and in the Pentland Firth. The different bone types and butchering marks were analysed, as at Robert's Haven, and these suggested that both whole and decapitated fish were brought to the site. It is probable that some Cod with a little Saithe were cured and could have come from a fish processing site such as Robert's Haven. This was then a community wealthy enough to buy some of their fish ready cured for winter use. Following this glimpse of the middens of a wealthy community, we move on to other sites in Orkney which were not seats of earls.

Westness, Rousay, Orkney

The western side of Rousay has been more or less continuously settled since the Neolithic. At Westness, a Pictish cemetery was used by the Norse living in a nearby settlement, but the Pictish graves were not violated by them. Two parallel longhouses housed family and stock. Excavation by a team from Bergen University revealed artefacts and environmental material present in the houses. The preliminary results, by Sigrid Kaland, have been published (1993). She considered that the smaller of the two houses consisted of two byres, one would have held about 18 Cows, a smaller byre for Sheep measured 5 x 5m.

Carbonised grain was of Barley, Rye and Oats with Flax seed also found, and pollen analysis showed that the three cereals had been grown locally. This is the earliest record for Rye for the Northern Isles, although it was being grown in southern Norway at that time. Seal, Deer and Otters were hunted and beached whales will have provided more meat. Seabirds were caught, probably while nesting on the cliffs at Scabra Head and Red Grouse would have been snared on the Heather moorlands.

Line sinkers and bones of many fish varieties, especially Cod and Ling, showed fishing to have been an important occupation. The remains of a boat house showed where the boats had been beached; Kaland thought that there was room for two small boats, or one larger one. By good fortune there was enough evidence to reconstruct the type of these boats. Graves were excavated and two Norse boat graves found. The boats had decayed away but sufficient wood had been preserved, adhering by corrosion to the iron rivets, to identify the wood used as Oak; clearly these were imported vessels. Kaland found that the shape remained as an impression in the soil which showed that they were clinker built, with three or four strakes. One of the boats had a deer antler rowlock on one gunwhale and a *vadbein* of antler on the other. The *vadbein* or *vadhorn* is described by Fenton as an upright piece of horn with a notch cut in the top to allow a fishing line to run when it was being cast out or hauled in. Among the grave goods a weaving baton and an iron ploughshare were found; it is unfortunate that so few Norse graves have so far been found to illuminate what the Norse considered as necessities in the afterlife.

Pool, Sanday, Orkney

Sanday is a low-lying island with fertile sandy soils; it lies to the north-east of Orkney Mainland. Pool is situated on the coast in a sheltered bay and its archaeological layers are now suffering greatly from erosion. It is a multi-period site situated on prime land; remains of structures and middens are more than 3m deep and 65m in extent. Excavation began in 1983 and continued until 1988, led by John Hunter with a team from Bradford University, excavating on behalf of Historic Scotland. Many samples were analysed by environmental archaeologists but the site awaits full publication.

Pool was first inhabited in the Neolithic and then deserted until Iron Age buildings were constructed, including a roundhouse, probably of fourth-century AD date, which remained in use until the eleventh century. A nucleated settlement had developed by the sixth century and occupation continued throughout the Norse period up to the eleventh century AD. One of the more interesting aspects of the site is what Hunter terms the 'cultural interface' between the Late Iron Age (Pictish) and Norse habitation levels. The indigenous culture reached its peak in the sixth century AD. This was later followed by a contraction in the number of buildings in use, but with the addition of two sub-rectangular buildings with both Iron Age and Norse cultures represented and a more advanced type of iron-working.

The remains of crop plants were identified by Julie Bond. Bristle Oat was first identified from a probable fourth- to fifth-century level and Wild Oat, always a minor contaminant at the site, dates from Pictish levels. A peak of cereals was noted during the Pictish period with Hulled Barley, some Naked Barley, and Bristle Oat. This was followed by a slight decrease in the number of samples containing Oats and the first appearance of

Flax seeds, both occurring at the beginning of the Pictish/Norse interface. This is particularly interesting as it suggests that Flax seed may have been brought in by the Norse incomers although Flax was already present on Orkney Mainland. Oats then increased during the Norse period to become a more important crop than Hulled Barley with an increase in Flax and decrease in Naked Barley.

The decrease in the number of samples containing cereals is substantiated by the fact that the samples taken throughout the settlement showed similar results. Context types are similar for each phase. Bond noted that the number of seeds per litre for the interface samples was also low. Her conclusion was that either there was less agricultural activity at the interface, or the lower numbers were due to destruction and rebuilding. This interpretation can be compared with results from other interfaces of this period. Also at the interface, the associated arable weeds of lighter, sandy soils, Corn Spurrey and Small Nettle appeared and increased during the Norse period as did those of particularly well-cultivated soils, characterised by Chickweed and Wild Radish. Bond suggested that this may reflect the bringing into cultivation of dry sandy soils and the more intensive use of manure on the original cultivated soils to increase yields of Barley. Such cultivation practices could represent the beginning of the infield and outfield system traditionally used in the Scottish Highlands and islands. If this is so, its introduction by the Norse would be in keeping with an Old Norse phrase for 'a strip of the infield' which became 'tounmal' in Orkney and is mentioned by Fenton (p24). The infield was well-manured and used for Barley, part of which was used for the payment of rents. The outfield was not always manured and Oats, which tolerate poor sandy soils, were grown on it.

Bond noted that the number of samples in which Oat grains were more numerous than those of Barley increased during the Norse period, which further suggests that more land was being brought into cultivation. It appears that there are differences between Pictish and Norse agriculture which may be distinguished by multiple sampling of similar contexts from each period.

Although the mammal bone report is not yet published in full, Julie Bond has published a summary of her results. She notes that there was no real change in the proportions of the main domestic animals between the Pictish and Norse periods. Minimum numbers of individuals were calculated and these indicated that a high proportion of beef was eaten with a relatively high proportion of pork, as at other Orkney sites. Sheep or Goats contributed about a third of the individuals from each phase. There was a high proportion of very young Cattle which intensified during the Norse period. Bond suggested that one reason for culling such young beasts would be to milk the cows for dairy products. A similar presumed increase in dairying has been noted at other sites. Bond also stated that, from the interface onwards, the bones of the older Cattle showed wear and infection of joints, possibly the result of an increased use of the beasts for ploughing. The Horses apparently suffered no pathological conditions. The presence of bones of very young Horses in the Norse period shows that they were being bred at the site; there also appeared to be a slight increase in numbers. Whatever the use of the Horses, for prestige or hunting, at the end of their lives they were eaten, as butchery marks testify. Cat bones were present in small numbers throughout. Otters, presumably caught for their pelts, may have become gradually scarcer. Red Deer were present in small numbers, with all parts of the body represented and most ages present. These, together with naturally shed antlers, suggest that they were caught on the islands rather than being jointed for the long journey back from the Scottish mainland. Bond considers that Sanday would have had insufficient uncultivated land to have maintained a breeding herd, so time would have been spent travelling to other islands, perhaps to adjacent Eday, to hunt them there. Since the dietary contribution of venison was not great, these may have been expeditions for the thrill of the hunt rather than for necessary food. The number of Deer bones seems to decline further at the end of the habitation period.

Analyses by Dale Serjeantson indicate that Cormorant or Shag were important at the interface whereas Gannet became the commonest bird caught during the Norse period proper. Fish bones were examined by Rebecca Nicholson who noted a change in fishing strategy at the interface, with increasing numbers of medium to large numbers of the Cod family. The exploitation of shellfish was a minor activity with Iceland Mussel, Limpet and Periwinkle shells present.

Howe, Orcadian Mainland

The long occupation at Howe, described in chapter 5, lasted until the seventh or eighth centuries AD. Woodland was even sparser than in the earlier Iron Age, consisting of little more than Willow scrub. Heather and other heathland plants increased. An increase of rank weeds, such as Broad-leaved Dock, suggest that either the arable fields became more weedy or the extent of waste ground increased. This could mean that fewer people were available to weed the crops, or that less ground was being cultivated.

From dwellings for several families in the earlier Iron Age, settlement size had declined to one farmstead by the first to fourth centuries AD (Phase 7) and continued so from the fourth until at least the seventh century AD (Phase 8), the period dealt with in this section (*see* **39** & **40**). Pictish artefacts are few and are thought to have been obtained by trade. It has been suggested that the site went into decline and was not part of the fully developed Pictish state. Nevertheless, the inhabitants did not live isolated lives and items continued to be traded. Composite combs of Reindeer antler, identified by Birthe Weber, are dated to before the seventh century; they came from Norway well before the Viking invasions began and were distributed widely in the Northern Isles. There are hints of a Scandinavian presence in the form of rare artefacts at the site, including a glass linen smoother, but unlike the other sites described in this chapter, no Norse settlement has been found in the immediate vicinity.

As in the earlier part of the Iron Age, Naked Barley continued to be the most important cereal, with Hulled Barley less frequently found. Oats were recorded in more contexts than previously, but usually as a very few grains together with Barley. The richest grain context had only 36 grains of Naked Barley and 13 of Oats. There are, unfortunately, no flowering bases to separate the Oats into wild or cultivated. Wild Oat has been used for food in historic times and may have been eaten in former periods. Flax is first recorded from a stalled building, probably dating from the fifth to sixth centuries AD. This is a particularly interesting record because, unlike Pool on the island of Sanday, Flax seems to have been introduced here well before the Norse presence, but whether for fibre or the oily seeds is not known. Plants of heathy turf, including Heather, from hearth and floor deposits became more numerous during Phase 8. The description of how a heathy turf develops has been given in chapter 5. Burnt peat was found in the same samples. The heathy turf, unsuitable for building or roofing, could have been used as back peats for the fire. In historic time, Fenton (p207, 212) describes how turf and peat were used together when peat was scarce; by this means the quantity of ashes for distribution from the midden onto the arable fields was increased. It is notable that the number of contexts containing wood had decreased considerably from the previous Phase 7 and that most of the wood from both phases was of Willow, suggesting that much of the local wood had been used up and that even peat may have been locally in short supply.

Over 10,000 mammal bones were identified from Phase 8 by Catherine Smith and George Hodgson, and these show different proportions to those from the preceding Phase. Minimum numbers of individuals are given. There were twice as many Sheep (63) as Cattle (34) and, surprisingly, even more Pigs (41) than Cattle. Sheep were killed at a later stage than previously after producing five crops of lambs rather than four in the earlier Iron Age. Horse bones were referable to two small pony-sized animals, a decrease from the earlier Iron Age. Bones of three Domestic Cats were noted and those of a single Dog. Red Deer became a less important part of the diet, or perhaps simply became less numerous as the woodland decreased. Foxes seem to have been on the decrease, as only one individual was caught; butchering marks on its bones and those of Otter and Cat suggest that their skins were used. A few bones of Seal pups and Whales remind us that the coast was only about a kilometre away at that time.

The bird bones, identified by Don Bramwell, were essentially the same numerous species described from the earlier Iron Age in chapter 5. The bones from both phases are listed by McCormick and Buckland. Domestic Fowl was recorded in this and the previous phase. Domestic Duck came from Phase 7/8. Neither have been found commonly at the later Iron Age sites of northern Scotland. All the local habitats would have been exploited as previously. Howe is near to the open sea with accessible seashore and nearby inland lochs. Marsh and moorland habitats are now about 3km distant; modern drainage, essential before land could be brought into cultivation, has now limited the extent of such areas in Orkney. High sea cliffs, with nesting seabirds, ideal for wild fowling, are about 6km distant. Their eggs would have been collected, although egg shells were infrequently found and not further identified. Evidence for extinct or very rare birds is an interesting addition. Bones of a very young Common Crane constitute good evidence for local breeding although the bird no longer nests in the British Isles. The White-tailed Eagle and Red Kite have been recently reintroduced to Scotland and Goshawk is a rare visitor. Great Auk, with bones found throughout the site, is now extinct.

A total of 1148 fish bones were identified by Alison Locker: those of the Cod group were, as in the earlier Iron Age, the most numerous. Of the prime food fish, Saithe as before, was the most numerous and netting or catching by line from the shore is again indicated. A wide variety of species, although their bones were not very numerous, suggested to Locker that fishing was opportunistic, exploiting many marine habitats. A very similar selection of shellfish to that recorded from the previous phase has been listed from the later Iron Age. The most common were Limpets, Common Periwinkle, Common Mussel and Common Cockle. From both Phases 7 and 8, small numbers of Sea

Urchins, claws of Edible and Common Shore Crabs and with remains of Norway Lobster were identified. They are all to be found around Orkney coasts at the present time.

Birsay Bay, Orcadian Mainland

On the largest of the Orkney islands the focus of pre-Norse (Pictish), Norse and later habitation seems to have been Birsay Bay (Morris 1989, 1996). Situated at the north-western tip of the island, Birsay appears to have been favoured above most other areas to judge from the number of farmsteads which have been discovered. Sites have been particularly sampled for environmental material by several excavators, and a summary of this extensive work is discussed here (**58**). The soils around the bay, derived from shell sand, are very fertile. Alison Donaldson and Sandra Nye set the scene by describing the area as follows: 'The rocky shore of the bay with low cliffs in places is bounded by extensive areas of machair (links) ie. dune grassland with a soil derived from calcareous shellsand. Further inland is fenced pasture-land and arable fields where Barley and Oats are grown. To the south is the valley of the Burn of Boardhouse which drains Boardhouse loch'. They point out that 'Since the period of occupation of the sites, one would expect changes in coastal morphology, sand-blow and the effects of settlement and agricultural practices to have altered the local environment'.

The Brough of Birsay is a small tidal island just off Birsay mainland. Both formed a focus for ecclesiastical power in the Pictish and Norse periods. The important Pictish sites were taken over by the Norse farmers early in the ninth century. According to the *Orkneyinga Saga*, Birsay became the permanent residence of Earl Thorfinn who, when the Vikings had become Christian, established the first Bishop's seat and also built a minster there. Anna Ritchie, in *Viking Scotland*, notes that 'In virtually every case, Viking settlements were built literally on top of earlier native farms'. It appears that on the Brough of Birsay the individual house plots were kept. Ritchie points out that the Norse took over and retained the existing patterns of landholding and their administration. How this was achieved is not known, since there must have been a gulf between the Christian Picts and the illiterate pagan Scandinavians. If the Norse used the native small farmers as labourers, they would have continued farming in their own traditions. The problems would have arisen over the best farms owned by the ruling Picts, including those with church holdings. We may suppose that considerable resistance would be offered by those who had no wish to become servants of the Norse. However there were instances where there seems to have been a peaceful transition, at least concerning occupation of farmsteads.

A good example is that of Buckquoy, which is immediately opposite the Brough of Birsay and was discovered as a low mound on the cliff edge eroding into the sea. When it was excavated as a rescue dig by Anna Ritchie in the summers of 1970 and 1971, a Pictish farm of distinctive 'figure of eight' houses was found in ruins beneath three phases of Norse buildings. These consisted of a byre, which was followed by a small threshing barn and then a dwelling house. The settlement probably dates from about AD 800. At the top of the mound a tenth-century grave contained the remains of a tenth century Norseman dated by an Anglo-Saxon coin of AD 940-4. Each phase must have had other farm buildings, however, which have since disappeared into the sea.

58 Plan of the sites at Birsay Bay. From Morris (1996)

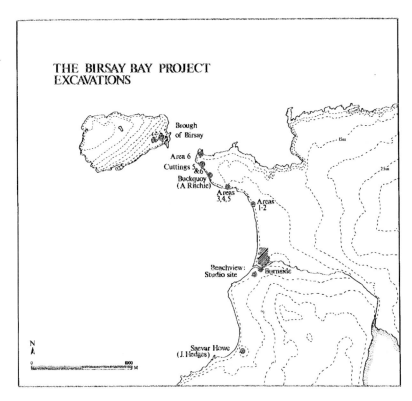

THE BIRSAY BAY PROJECT
EXCAVATIONS

The most interesting disclosure came when the finds were cleaned and identified; the Norse house levels did not contain Viking artefacts, but Pictish bone pins and combs. This implied a continuing tradition of Picts working in the area and suggests that the artisans, at least, continued their trades, making items which the Norse farmers bought or bartered for. At Saevar Howe, about 1.5km to the south, Norse dwellings overlay previous Pictish settlement and Pictish artefacts also remained in use in the Norse houses.

It has been suggested that at the peasant level, such as that of the small farms at Buckquoy and Saevar Howe, there was a gradual transition between native and incomer. At high status sites we would expect an abrupt change as the powerful Norse, with their superior sea power, were prepared to ruthlessly usurp the Pictish nobility in order to control the administration.

Wood charcoal and seeds have been identified from the Brough of Birsay and the sites around Birsay Bay (Beachview, Saevar Howe, Brough Road and Buckquoy), chiefly by Alison Donaldson and Sandra Nye. The sites show similar assemblages through time and space and are considered together. Willow is the commonest charcoal and often of small round wood. Alder, Birch, Hazel and Juniper were all, with Willow, probably growing locally. There is a record for Ivy from the Bay of Birsay which may equally have grown on a cliff face as on a tree. Donaldson and Nye suggest that some of these at least probably grew in the valley of the Burn of Boardhouse, but they may also have contributed to coastal scrub woodland. All such woodland has now been cleared from the area which is virtually treeless. Ash, Oak and Scots Pine were probably brought in as timber, and parts of boat, and other Spruce would have been collected as driftwood and its long straight logs could have been used for building timbers; it has been found in archaeological sites throughout prehistory in Orkney and other islands.

It is unclear what the native woods were used for but they are unlikely to have been suitable for major building purposes as the windswept situation in which they would have grown would not have produced straight timbers. Donaldson and Nye mention that a large volume of carbonised wood fragments were recovered, although this is not quantified, particularly from hearth and midden samples. Wood must have formed only part of the fuel because burnt peat was recovered from all contexts.

The richest site for plant remains proved to be Beachview, a late Norse site, spanning the period AD 1000-1300, dug by Chris Morris and published in 1996. The richness is due to the fact that many large samples from hearths and middens were wet-sieved; identifications were by Sandra Nye. Both Common and Bristle Oat, from 30 contexts, were recovered with Hulled Barley from a similar number of contexts. Flax seeds were identified from 15 contexts. Both linen and woollen clothes were worn by the Vikings and it seems probable that the Flax was grown for its fibre, although the seeds may also have been consumed as linseed.

At Beachview, a rectangular slab-lined hearth was found in the corner of a sub-rectangular building; the kiln itself was circular. It has been interpreted as the remains of a corn-drying kiln. A higher proportion of both Common and Bristle Oats with Barley was found around the hearth than in surrounding samples. Weed seeds were also numerous and it may be that grain was laid out to dry on weedy straw. Cereal grain needs to be dried before grinding, so that the kernels become granular and thus speed up the grinding process.

Seeds of plants of arable and waste ground, such as Knotgrass, Wild Radish, Corn Spurrey, Chickweed and Dock, were present in most samples. Nye points out that the coast provides a range of habitats, including shingle beaches, dunes and cliffs, often with enriched places suitable for Orache, Fat Hen, Scentless Mayweed and other members of the Daisy family. Greater Woodrush, tentatively identified, could have grown on cliffs; Ribwort Plantain and Meadow Buttercup are characteristic of pastures. Evidence for heathland comes from Heather, Crowberry, Tormentil and Sheep's Sorrel. Spikerush and Lesser Spearwort grow in marshy places and their seeds may have come from damp areas in the corn fields, or were perhaps brought in with water supplies along with seeds of Blinks, Marsh Marigold, Shoreweed and Cinquefoil.

Edible wild plants which may have been gathered are Rowan, Wild Strawberry and Crowberry. Wild Strawberry is a rare plant in Orkney at present, only growing on the island of Rousay.

A few seeds of the toxic Henbane are an interesting discovery (see the account in Part 2). One from a hearth deposit may well have resulted from deliberate introduction for medicinal use. Burnt seaweed was recovered from all contexts. Nye sums up the results of the plant analyses as follows: 'The habitats indicated are heathland, grassland, marsh and coastal habitats and waste or cultivated land'. All these habitats would have existed nearby around the farmstead.

The Brough of Birsay is a small island less than 250m off the coast. It was formerly reached by a natural rock causeway at low tide, but now there is a concrete causeway. Two to three kilograms of midden samples were treated by paraffin flotation on site. From the pre-Norse levels sparse wild or cultivated Oat grains and a few arable weed seeds were recognised by Alison Donaldson. These are thought to have been grown on the mainland, because the very windswept Brough is not suitable for cereal cultivation. From Norse levels there, Donaldson recorded Bristle Oat grains, which were more numerous in all contexts than those of Hulled Barley. Both seeds of arable weeds and plants of heaths and moorland were also recorded. A single floret base of Common Oat, with slightly larger Oat grains present than in the pre-Norse period, was recorded from Brough Road, together with Flax seeds from two contexts. Seeds of weeds of cultivation included Corn Spurrey, Chickweed, Scentless Mayweed and Wild Radish. Pasture was suggested by the presence of Ribwort Plantain, Speedwell and Tormentil. Heather and Crowberry were also represented. Again, notably, Henbane was found. From Saevar Howe some Oats and Barley and over 100 Flax seeds were identified. Seeds of a few arable weeds, including those of Corn Spurrey and a species of Poppy, were recognised. There were also four seeds of Crowberry and two seeds tentatively identified as Rowan; these could have come from fruits collected for food.

From later Norse samples, the Brough of Birsay produced 18 Oat and a single Barley grain. Some crop evidence can be gleaned from the four sites yielding grain in the Birsay area. There are unfortunately very few contexts which were undoubtedly Pictish. The Oats from Brough of Birsay was probably grown on the Mainland. In the Norse and later Norse periods, Common and Bristle Oats and Hulled Barley were grown. Single samples did not produce many grains and it is not possible to estimate the relative importance of the different cereal crops. Flax was grown in the Norse and later phases, primarily for the use of its fibre. Sheep were kept for their wool, as well as for their meat, and loom weights and spindle whorls were found, as for instance at Saevar Howe. Henbane may have been used medicinally. The rather slight evidence of wild plants from the Brough, Brough Road and Saevar Howe confirm the mixture of available habitats indicated for Beachview.

From the Brough of Birsay, Hunter recorded shallow circular or sub-circular pits bordered with coursed stonework, but none with prepared floor surfaces; their diameters were between 0.8 and 1.8m. A small number of seaweed fragments of Bladderwrack type was found in each. Hunter notes that they all post-date the destruction of the final Norse buildings after AD 1150, but some may belong to the end of the Norse period. A commercial kelp burning industry, for soap and glass production in England, took place in Orkney and Shetland mainly from the mid-eighteenth to the first part of the nineteenth century. The kelp was burnt in more carefully made pits with flat stones at the base to avoid contamination from the soil. The Birsay pits suggest a more primitive industry. Similar pits were found at The Biggins on Papa Stour, one of the Shetland Islands, and possible uses for the seaweed are discussed further in that section.

Bones have also been recovered from the Brough and from other sites in the Bay; different sampling and sieving methods and widely differing numbers of identified bones do not permit direct comparisons between these sites. As these span only about 1.5km of the coast, conditions for farming and exploiting coastal resources seem, from the plant evidence, not to have been widely different. Difference in status would perhaps show different patterns of consumption, but high status buildings from both the Pictish and Norse periods have yet to be definitely located. Small farms seem to have been the general pattern of settlement. Generally speaking there seems to have been little difference between the proportions of domestic animals consumed from Pictish, Norse and Late Norse periods, and they are here considered together. Differences lie chiefly in the proportion of Sheep to Cattle bones and since these vary between different areas of the same site and period at Beachview, the overall pattern is given until more detailed work in the future clarifies the picture.

From Buckquoy, Barbara Noddle estimated that, from a total of over 7,000 bones, 50% of the bones were from Cattle, 30% from Sheep and 20% from Pig. A few Goat bones were recovered, mostly from the Norse horizons. A preponderance of Cattle bones was noted from most sites together with high numbers for Sheep. In all instances there would have been more beef available than lamb due to the much larger carcasses. Horse, Dog and Cat bones were all infrequent, the Cats perhaps having earned their keep as mousers! A few Deer bones were recovered from most sites, but hunting does not seem to have been a major pursuit by either Picts or Norsemen. Seals were present as small numbers of bones, and Whale bones were even less frequent.

Bird bones have been recorded from all sites and long lists have been compiled from Buckquoy and Beachview. Bones of domestic birds are scarce, especially in the Pictish, with only Domestic Fowl recorded from Saevar Howe. Domestic Geese and Fowl were recorded from both Norse and Late Norse contexts at various sites. Don Bramwell identified the bones from Buckquoy and arranged the wild bird list according to habitat. These fall into four main groups and the examples given here for each group are of species also present at Beachview, identified by Enid Allison:

Moorland, cliff and scrubland	Kestrel, Red Grouse, Starling, Rook or Crow and Raven
Meadow, marsh and freshwater	Mallard, Goldeneye and Corncrake
Sea shore and mud flats	Great and Lesser Black-backed Gulls, Knot, Jack Snipe and Turnstone
The open sea	Gannet, Great Northern Diver, Manx Shearwater, Cormorant, Shag, Guillemot, Puffin and Eider

Wild fowling must have taken place in all the habitats around the bay. Sea birds would only have been available in the summer months, whilst nesting on the cliffs. Bramwell points out that the presence of Knot, Jack Snipe and Turnstone, autumn and winter visitors, show that wild fowling was spread over the whole year. Gannets were the most numerous and Bramwell notes that Gannet, Guillemot, Cormorant and Razorbill are very easily taken when nesting. The Great Auk, a now extinct bird, has also been recorded from earlier Orkney sites. Although the number of species is high, over 50 at Buckquoy, the actual number of bones from any one sample is very small. The contribution to the diet is likely to have been minimal, and the excitement of the capture was probably the main reason for taking them, although oil and feathers would have been useful by-products.

All the sites produced fish bones, but there are only small numbers recorded from the Pictish horizons. These do not seem to differ in type from those in the succeeding Norse layers. Cod, Saithe and Ling are the commonest fish throughout the Pictish and Norse layers, and chiefly medium to large fish were caught. Fishing must have been from boats in deeper water, where occasional Hake and Torsk were also caught. Fishing from the shore and even from rock pools at low tide would account for small Saithe and other young fish of the Cod family. At Brough Road site there was a possible increased intensity of fishing during the Later Norse period.

Larger numbers of fish bones from Beachview were identified by Sarah Colley. Most samples were wet-sieved to collect the smaller bones. Radiocarbon dates suggest that the deposits span the three centuries from AD 1000 to 1300, the later Viking and Late Norse periods, but precise dating of individual samples was not possible. Cod were the most numerous, with over 2,000 bones from the Norse and Late Norse levels, with a similar number of other members of the Cod family identified. Saithe may have been caught seasonally in late autumn and early winter, but a larger sample would be needed to confirm this. James Rackham's examination of the evidence has led him to suggest '. . . that most of the fish bone at Beachview derives from the final processing and disposal at, during or after cooking and consumption'. There is, as yet, no evidence to suggest that the fish were caught for other than local consumption.

It is exceptional to have material from all aspects of the diet from the five excavated settlements on the Brough of Birsay and around the Bay. The local vegetation does not seem to have changed between the eighth to the thirteenth centuries, the period covered by the excavations. It is not known if the proportion of arable land increased with the Norse incomers, since there are no immediately local pollen diagrams to record such changes. As has already been shown, full use was made of the local environment. Peat was cut and dried for fuel. Scrub woodland was perhaps coppiced; Willow responds particularly quickly to this management, and was used for firewood. As elsewhere and at different periods on the Northern Isles, driftwood would have been collected and the larger timbers may have been used for building. Seaweed was gathered and, in the late Norse period, was burnt in shallow pits, perhaps for an industrial purpose. Meat from domestic animals and a little from hunting seems to have been the main food according to Rackham, particularly the Beachview results (Table 5). Fish were quite an important supplement, but wild fowl provided only a small proportion of the diet. Commercial wild fowling continued in that area on Orkney until the end of the last century and, for dietary variety, up to and including the Second World War. It is still carried out in the Faroe Islands. Oil for lamps could have been obtained from fish, Seals and Whales as well as sea birds.

Tuquoy, Westray, Orkney

A Norse site of particular interest for its wealth of environmental archaeology is the Later Norse site of Tuquoy. This is another coastal settlement now eroding into the sea. The results of preliminary excavations of the structures and rich midden deposits have been published by Olwyn Owen, who dug the site for Historic Scotland. Both twelfth- and fourteenth- or fifteenth-century habitation is indicated. There is a large present-day farm to the north; it was usual to rebuild farms adjacent to old buildings on Orkney. Owen notes that most late Norse farms were not abandoned, but the farmhouses were successively rebuilt and are still occupied at the present time. As the Norse buildings became abandoned at Tuquoy they were filled with midden rubbish, rich in fish bones. Some pottery from the middens was locally made and some imported, the latter has been traced to the Low Countries and other north European sources of thirteenth to fifteenth century date.

On examining the eroding cliff face, a substantial waterlogged pit was seen; such waterlogged deposits are very rare on Orkney. The pit was at least 7m long, about 3.5m wide and 1.65m deep. Compacted organic material within the pit accumulated about AD 1100. The material at different levels varied, with admixtures of animal dung, straw, grasses, ash, peat, wood, insects and other material. Byre manure would normally have been transferred to a dunghill and then spread onto the land, so its presence in a pit is rather puzzling. Other material may have originally come from animal bedding or human habitation, mixed up with the ashes of peat fires. Insect remains were identified in an attempt to shed more light on the origin of the material. Jon Sadler analysed the fauna and found insects from a wide range of sources. Aquatic, waterside and peatland habitats were represented and so were insects which lived in stored hay and rotting organic material. Together with Fleas, Lice and Sheep Keds, these insects suggest that a good proportion of the material accumulated within a building. The outdoor species could have arrived through doors and windows while some others could have been brought in with hay. Owen points out that a similar range of species was recorded from floor deposits in Viking sites of York and in other northern countries. The presence of the parasites, from both humans and animals, suggest a fairly low level of hygiene, which seems to have been common at that time.

Richard Tipping analysed the organic layers, which were rich in pollen of cereals and arable weeds with pastoral indicators also present. Pollen of Oats and Barley in varying proportions may have derived from mixed straw. Such straw may have been used to soak up liquid in the byre, but was perhaps too valuable for that and was fed to the Horses. Anne Crone examined a large assemblage of wood fragments, many of them worked. There were Willow withies, the peeled bark used as twine, and domestic items of Willow. Birch consisted of only three pieces, one of which was a carved handle. Larch and Spruce would have been collected as driftwood, and the presence of boreholes made by marine molluscs confirmed this. These were offcuts indicating that the wood had been used for constructional purposes. As has already been shown, the woodland in Orkney Mainland had already been reduced to scrub and only Willow seems to have been plentiful on the island. A small quantity of Oak and Ash was presumably imported, as was a Maple wood handle. Maples belong to the genus *Acer* which is not indigenous in Scotland, but Field Maple grows naturally in England and Norway Maple lives up to its name. A range of tools included axes, adzes, knives and spoon-bits. Unfinished objects showed that this was a local domestic industry. Off-cuts of Pine probably came from radially split planks which are thought to have originated in Norway. The planks were probably debarked and squared before they were imported. Similar Pine planks, used as flooring and also of Norse age, will be described from Papa Stour, Shetland. The wooden flooring and imported goods, including pottery, all point to a prosperous farmstead. Owen suggests that such productive farms may have been typical of those set-up by the early Norse settlers. Later re-use of the pit is shown by deposits of burnt stones and peat ash, to 1.4m in depth; these would have been used for domestic water heating. Such material is typical of farm mounds, which are a particular feature of the Norse and later periods in Orkney.

Jarlshof, Shetland

The proportion of land suitable for settlement has always been less in Shetland than in Orkney, since there is a smaller area of fertile soil; most good farming land is on the coastal shell sand. Much of the interior is of acid rock, now covered by blanket bog and partly used for grazing. The deep peats still provide domestic fuel. The islands are now seemingly treeless, although stunted trees still grow on cliffs and islands inaccessible to Sheep. Modern plantations are protected by walls; the strong, salt-laden winds limit tree growth. Arable farming has been precarious in historic time because the summers are short and cool. Only a little Bristle Oat is now grown for fodder. There are large populations of seabirds and good fishing all round the coast. It is not surprising that the few Norse sites excavated so far are coastal or not away from the sea, and are close to good arable, grazing land and to shores suitable for beaching boats above the high tide mark.

Being only 340km or two days sailing from Norway, the islands would have been colonised early on by the Vikings. Linguistic evidence points to the Norse farmers having come from south-west Norway. The largest settlements so far excavated are at Jarlshof and Old Scatness, both in the fertile southern tip of Shetland. This area would have formed a natural staging post to the Orkney Islands and Caithness. Many Norse sites, especially in Shetland, remain to be excavated, and this is being actively pursued at the present time with the emphasis on environmental archaeology.

This complex site at the southern tip of mainland Shetland was inhabited from the Bronze Age through to the post-Medieval period. It was most recently excavated by Hamilton who published the site in 1956. Neither plant material nor bones were recorded after the Late Norse occupation. The background has been briefly described in chapters 4 and 5. Unfortunately the extensive middens were not sieved and no cereals were recorded from the Norse and later phases. Hamilton estimated that the Norse habitation began early in the ninth century. He recorded a mixture of late Iron Age and Norse artefacts on part of the site, suggesting an initial peaceful coexistence before the Norse culture became dominant. Seven phases of Viking and Late Norse habitation have been described, with several rebuilding stages. The second farmhouse, perhaps of eleventh century date, a traditional Scandinavian longhouse, had provided evidence for Cattle housing at the lower end of the building, a custom still to be seen in the rural parts of Scandinavia. The farm seems to have been the home of a single extended family.

Willow, Oak, Hazel and Pine charcoal date from the ninth and tenth centuries. Later charcoal, of thirteenth and fourteenth century date, was of Birch and Oak; Pine was tentatively identified. It is unlikely that Oak was still growing on Shetland, and Pine may have never grown there. It seems more likely that these woods were either brought in or obtained by trade. The first settlers brought steatite (soapstone) bowls and spindle whorls from Norway, and no doubt also brought tools with wooden handles and other wooden kitchen equipment.

No numbers of bone fragments are given in the report by Marjorie Platt, who noted that the bones from ninth-, tenth- to eleventh- and eleventh- to thirteenth-century middens are all essentially similar. Those from the ninth century she described in detail. The Cattle were all of small animals, mostly of young individuals and, to judge from variation in the horns, of more than one type. Sheep were also of mixed breeds and there were quite frequent bones of very immature lambs. Pigs were less numerous, with young and old animals represented. Rare Red Deer bones show that occasional hunting took place. A few adult Horse bones were slightly larger than those of the very small ponies found in the Shetlands at the present time. The remains of a Dog of terrier type was identified; it may be assumed that both ponies and Dogs were kept for work rather than food. Bones of Grey Seals were particularly common, with only rare bones of Common Seals. A few bones of a Sperm Whale and those of a very large Whale were also identified.

Bones of domesticated birds were of Duck, Goose and Domestic Fowl. Sea birds were frequent especially Black-backed Gull, Shag and Cormorant; Herring Gull, Gannet, Eider and other species were also noted. Species from inland habitats were less common. Cod, Saithe and Ling were identified as bones from very large fish, which suggests deep water fishing. As the material was not sieved, bones from smaller fish were doubtless overlooked. Indirect evidence, from an increase in line sinkers, identified from the eleventh to thirteenth century, suggests that fishing became more important in the late Norse period. Miss Platt noted that on the whole the fauna is the same as that at present.

Several fragments of iron sickle blades were recorded by Hamilton; if, as seems likely, these were used to harvest crops and to separate the ears from the straw, they may have replaced the slate blades found in later Iron Age contexts. Iron heckle teeth are likely to have been used to comb fibres before spinning. Because no Flax seeds were recovered from the Norse middens, there is as yet no corroborative evidence to support linen production. Hay was collected and stored in a walled yard of about tenth-century date. Evidence for this comes from a rectangular stone setting, illustrated by Hamilton (plate 28b). This is remarkably similar to the stone bases still in use on Shetland crofts.

Evidence for tethering Cattle is provided by steatite tethering rope blocks. Tethered Cattle would have been confined to grazing strips between arable rows. A similar method was presumably in use wherever mixed farming was practised. An advantage of examining the artefacts from a rural area where farming methods have changed little until recently is that the purposes of the archaeological material can be recognised from its modern counterpart. Small bone bits known as kevls, with a hole at either end, used to be widely used in western Europe to prevent lambs sucking all their mother's milk. The finds of kevls in eleventh-century deposits suggests that the Sheep were kept as a source of milk and dairy foods.

Sandwick, Unst, Shetland

The northernmost site for this or any period is of a Late Norse farmstead at Sandwick, on Unst, the furthest north island of Shetland. In 1978 and 1979, Gerry Bigelow (1985) excavated this eroding site, sponsored mainly by Historic Scotland. Situated in a bay of shell sand, the calcareous soils preserved a quantity of bone and plant material and preliminary results have been published. Radiocarbon dates show that a longhouse was occupied from the twelfth to fourteenth centuries. This dating was confirmed by the presence of artefacts similar to some of twelfth-to fourteenth-century date found in Norway, including a small quantity of imported wheel-thrown pottery.

Hulled Barley and Oats were recognised by Glynis Jones; full-size and miniature rotary querns were recovered — the small versions were presumably children's toys. Bigelow considered that the grain was locally grown. Cattle were important, as the numerous bones testify, and one end of the longhouse used as a byre had a cow-shaped doorway (broader in the middle than at the base). Sheep were also a significant part of the economy, shown by bones, loom weights and spindle whorls. There were very few Pig bones and Bigelow considered that there would have been only small quantities of suitable forage in this northern treeless island. A few bones of Horse and Dog were found and traces of Seal bones. Seafowl bones were present, but far fewer than those of fish. Bones of small and large Saithe were recovered; Saithe is still one of the main fish eaten in Shetland. Large Cod and Saithe would have been caught at sea from boats. Limpets and Whelks were thought by Bigelow to have been food at times of scarcity. Until the full analyses are published, direct comparison with other sites will not be possible. The preliminary results are similar to those from the Late Norse Jarlshof, except that Pig bones were more plentiful there; Bigelow suggested, however, that the large farm at Jarlshof may have had greater resources for Pig rearing, whereas pork was probably a luxury food at Sandwick.

Old Scatness, Shetland

A multi-period site at Old Scatness, just over a kilometre to the north-west of Jarlshof, is being excavated by a Bradford University team led by Steve Dockrill and Julie Bond. An interim report shows that the Bronze Age, Early and Late Iron Age (Pictish), Norse and post-Medieval settlements are similar to those at Jarlshof. With the emphasis on environmental archaeology, it is thus hoped to be able to amplify the results from Jarlshof. A Pictish multi-cellular structure, provisionally dated from the sixth to ninth century, contained middens and rubble, with evidence of smithying and Norse artefacts. This suggests a Pictish/Norse transition phase which should provide an interesting comparison with that at Pool, Orkney. A soil sample produced a quantity of Hulled Barley and Common Oat grains, with seeds of Flax and arable weeds. This is the first find of Flax in Shetland; in the eighteenth century Flax was grown in Shetland but the industry collapsed for lack of support.

The Biggins, Papa Stour, Shetland

Medieval historians, especially in Scotland, have sometimes to rely on their detective powers because of the general lack of early documents. Barbara Crawford discovered the remarkable Norse and post-Norse site of the Biggings by patient sleuthing (Crawford and Ballin Smith 1998). The earliest document from Shetland to have survived is dated AD 1299 and records a disagreement between a woman on the island of Papa Stour and an official collecting rents and taxes on behalf of Duke Håkon of Norway who later that year acceded to the Norwegian throne. The disputed property was the sitting room, the Norse *stofa*, in the Duke's house or farm, part of the royal Norwegian estates. These estates on Papa Stour, an island just off the west coast of Mainland Shetland, the eastern half of which is prized for its exceptionally fertile soils, continued in the possession of the Norwegian aristocracy until the later Middle Ages. Furthermore, Crawford discovered that Papa Stour continued in the ownership of Norwegian families after Shetland was pledged to the Scottish crown in 1469 and remained so until the seventeenth century.

Buildings of the Late Norse period are hardly known from Shetland. The Late Norse farmhouse at Sandwick, already described, was a simple farmstead. The Medieval farm at Jarlshof was partly destroyed before it was adequately recorded. If the Duke's house could be located, an insight into the lifestyle of the Norse nobility might be obtained. Barbara Crawford, therefore, narrowed down the possible area for the farm, which had to be close to good land, beaches and the island's church. Farm names were also studied and these suggested that the probable Royal farm had been in the settlement of North Biggings. The core of the settlement was found to lie under an abandoned croft-house, probably built in the mid-nineteenth century and deserted in the 1930s. Subsequent excavation between 1977 and 1990 revealed a house site (partly under the croft-house) which had been occupied continuously from at least the Norse period to the twentieth century and known as the Biggings (**59**). Remains of at least five other buildings were also excavated. This long occupancy has, as yet, no parallel in Norse and post-Norse Scotland.

In the nineteenth century there were 36 households in the township (farming community). Rebuilding over the centuries had destroyed some of the Norse house walls, including all of those above present ground level. Disturbed and compressed occupation layers have been painstakingly separated by Barbara Crawford and Beverley Ballin Smith and a chronology established. The best preserved part was a large room 5m wide, where only the substantial basal stone of an outer protective wall survived. The double wall had a core of compacted earth; there were two benches and a corner hearth and near to it the remains of a floor of Scots Pine overlying transverse sill beams. Partial burning of the wood, from the destruction of the building, had helped in its preservation and in contrast most of the uncharred wood had the consistency of peat with microbial activity in evidence. The floor ended 55cm from the side wall, where it was replaced with a band of hard-packed earth about 15cm high. In two places, fragments of upright Oak wood extended in front of the earth bank; this would appear to be the remains of the front panelling to a wall bench which encased the earth bank. In Medieval houses Crawford noted that the '*moldbenke*' was usually half a metre wide, which would accord with the width of the earth bank. This narrow bench was for sitting, wider benches would have been used for sleeping. This must have been the best room and, in all probability, the '*stofa*' referred to in the document. A radiocarbon date from the wooden floor calibrates to AD 1013-56, a remarkably early floor and surprisingly preserved by persistent dampness. A clay sealing layer covered part of it, as well as flagstones which patched it; all of these conditions had preserved artefacts and enabled some aspects of domestic life in the Late Norse period onwards to be investigated.

Pollen analyses were carried out by Graeme Whittington and Kevin Edwards on two sequences of very thin sandy soils, less than one metre apart, within the excavated area and by CD on four samples from occupation layers which were also studied for macroscopic debris. The results are all very similar and point to no immediately local tree growth, but much heath and grassland of some considerable species-richness. The

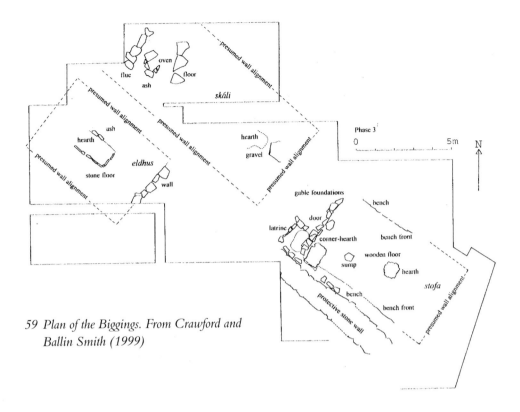

59 Plan of the Biggings. From Crawford and Ballin Smith (1999)

occupation layers contained coarse remains of cereals and seeds of cornfield weeds, with, as was to have been expected, large amounts of grass pollen, taken to be that of cereals.

In her detailed studies of many samples for macroscopic remains, CD found that burnt cereal grains were surprisingly sparse and found only in Late Norse contexts onwards; Six-rowed Hulled Barley and Oats were noted. A late Medieval record of Naked Six-row Barley is one of the latest finds from Scotland. A Late Norse sample from the main dwelling consisted of a 25mm thick layer of plant tissues interspersed with fine sand; each layer was less than 0.5mm in thickness. After three days soaking in water it proved possible to tease apart layers of highly degraded plant tissue, tentatively identified from a few remaining cells viewed under a high power microscope as Oat straw. Sixty flattened empty Oat grains and nine Barley grains were recognised from their shape and cell patterns. Seeds of Common Spike-rush and Floating Sweet-grass and frequent embryos, probably of cornfield weeds, were also found. The just specified plants can grow in marshes and shallow water and may have been collected from a winter-wet field margin along with the straw. The layers of straw and sand suggest a problem of recurring damp. This was later improved by laying a clay floor on top, which effectively sealed in and preserved the underlying damp layers. A Medieval layer from another building contained better-preserved material, which yielded a rich assembly of unburnt cornfield weeds with occasional Oat grains. Parsley Piert, Annual Dead-nettle, Forget-me-not, Knotgrass, Corn Spurrey, Chickweed, Scentless and Sea May-weed and Spiny Sow-thistle were identified. Plants not so readily associated with cornfields, such as Toad

Rush, Meadow and Creeping Buttercup and Northern Dock, all of which were present in the layer, have been noted by Pat Hinton as growing in present day fields of Bristle Oat in Shetland. Common Spike-rush, Floating Sweet-grass and Lesser Spearwort were also present in these cultivated fields. Pollen analyses from both samples at the Biggings produced a very similar pollen spectrum with Oat and Barley type and pollen of arable weeds present. Substantial quantities of Mugwort pollen, a weed preferring sandy soils in Shetland, were also noted.

Although straw was not found in this context it could well have decayed away or this deposit could have resulted from sieving grain to remove weed seeds. In either case the results give us a good picture of the very weedy late Norse and Medieval cornfields on Shetland. The presence of low-growing plants like Parsley Piert, Forget-me-not and Toad Rush suggests that the corn was reaped low on the stalk or even uprooted.

Fragments of steatite girdles, or griddles as they are sometimes called, were recovered from Late Norse to fifteenth-century levels; they had a circular margin. They would have been used for cooking flat Barley bannocks or Oatcakes over an open fire. Neither Oat nor Barley grain produces leavened bread and so flat breads would have been cooked on these thin soapstone plates by the side of a glowing peat fire. Their disappearance in the fifteenth century suggests that they may have been replaced by the circular iron girdles, with a hoop to hang over the fire, which date from that time. Iron was poorly preserved in the acid peat and such utensils were not found. The bakestones described from Howe in Orkney would have had a similar function.

The earliest Norse occupation was marked by shallow unlined pits, 20-30cm deep, dug into rock and clean sand; such were also found in Medieval contexts above the early wooden floor. Two of the pits contained a high proportion of burnt seaweed, often of Knotted and Flat Wracks, commonly found on sheltered seashores. Other pits contained rare seaweed fragments and burnt and unburnt peat; the peat was probably used to help burn the seaweed. Remains of plants of damp habitats, such as Rush seeds and megaspores of Lesser Clubmoss, were found, as were Heather shoots and seeds of Bell Heather and Crowberry in one pit. These have been interpreted as the remains of turves from heathy land and sods from damp areas used to stop burning until the seaweed was needed for industrial processes. Similar unlined pits containing burnt seaweed, recovered by John Hunter on the Brough of Birsay from the end of the Norse period, have already been described.

Seaweed was collected for its salts, which were used in glass making in the Northern Isles in the eighteenth and nineteenth centuries, but it was necessarily burnt in deeper stone-lined pits to avoid soil contamination. The most likely explanation is that the seaweed was burnt for its ashes; ashes were widely used in Europe to make lye, detergent, soap and glass. Wood ashes were generally used, but wood was very scarce on Shetland and so it would appear that seaweed was used instead. Water percolating through the burnt seaweed would have released sodium and potassium salts to produce a lye used for cleansing and scouring, necessary processes before dying wool. However, in Scotland, stale urine was traditionally used for such a purpose. If lime was burnt (obtainable from the Mainland of Shetland), added to the caustic solution and boiled or stirred with oil or fat, soap could be made to cleanse and thicken, or full, the cloth. Woven and knitted dyed cloth found in Norse and Medieval layers suggests that such cleansing of the wool and cloth was undertaken. It is worth noting that lyes are still used in Norway and Sweden for preserving fish. This is called '*lute fisk*' and is an acquired taste. Unfortunately only a few fish scales were preserved although to judge from other Late Norse sites fish must have provided a major resource.

Except on crannogs, wooden vessels and utensils have rarely been found in Scottish archaeology. Where damp conditions have preserved a quantity of wooden domestic items, this allowed Carole Morris to discuss their uses and draw parallels from elsewhere in Britain and Scandinavia too. Although some of the items are from post-Medieval layers, they are included in this account because they show the continuity of use of the Biggings dwelling house which remained in the hands of Norwegian families until the early seventeenth century. Spoons and spatulas were found in contexts which were dated from pottery evidence from the thirteenth to the early seventeenth century. Two spoons were of Scots Pine and spatulas were of Hazel and Oak. The spoon would have been the main utensil after the knife, and wear on the spoon bowls suggested that either the user was left-handed or the knife was used in the right hand and spoon in the left, taking the place of a fork. A variety of bowl shapes were carved, but these cannot be determined chronologically.

Spoons were made from split roundwood and Morris explains that an axe would have been used to make a roughout, a knife used for the final shaping, and the bowl hollowed out with a gouge or chisel. Those from the Biggings show a degree of skill that suggests that all were imported. From the Medieval contexts, vessels were recovered as stave fragments; most are of Scots Pine although there are Oak fragments from a later context. Morris considers that the vessels were probably imported from Scandinavia or mainland Britain. All were fragments of probably open-topped pails, tubs and casks, and would have been fashioned from seasoned timber. A hinged Oak lid, made from a radially split section, bears an incised cross with inverted triangular ends. Morris notes that it was the lid of a stave-built container, perhaps for milk. The saltire-like cross is likely to have been a symbolic mark to keep away the evil eye; similar examples exist from other excavations, including a Medieval lid from Oslo. A Pine bodkin, or similar textile tool tapered to a point, could have been used in the hand on a loom; Morris explains that they were used to push up the weft threads and rearrange displaced warp threads. Wooden examples have also been found at Haithabu in Germany. A Pine wedge was recovered from Medieval layers; a tough wood such as seasoned Oak, or an iron wedge, is normally used. An axe would have been used to drive the wedges in along the length of the trunk, splitting the wood along the radial planes of weakness. These are the medullary rays, which can be clearly seen on a cross section of Oak wood. Wood can also be split tangentially across the grain. Most iron tools had disappeared due to the acid nature of the ground, but axe marks were seen on a plank fragment and on various wooden objects. Morris identified radially split Pine plank fragments, slightly wedge-shaped in cross section; pieces of staves were found to have been split tangentially.

The Late Norse wooden floor was too degraded to lift and examine, but flat-faced Pine planks, laid in parallel rows, were recorded. Late Medieval Oak planks, imported as trunks or already split into planks, were examined by Morris. The planks were heavily worn but could originally have been 20-30mm thick. Morris noted that excavated wooden floors are rarely recorded from early buildings in the British Isles. Similar planks were found in a tenth century Anglo-Scandinavian building in York, and three buildings in Viking Dublin also had planks over part of the floors.

A late Medieval iron twist-bit in a transverse cow horn handle (a boring tool) was an interesting rare find, identified by Morris. Such augurs were used to make starting cuts for spoon-bits to enlarge into holes in wood. Similar implements have been found in Viking York and Dublin. Carole Morris has identified various types of pegging devices of Hazel and Pine wood; both roundwood and radially split sections were used. All were headless and had been used to fasten planks and smaller wooden objects. Fragments of Beech and Ash probably arrived as traded artefacts.

Birch bark was found scattered over much of the site, from Medieval to post-Medieval contexts. Pieces ranged from large flat pieces measuring up to 110 x 80mm, with two edges deliberately cut at right angles, to small bark rolls. The bark resembles that of Silver Birch, which produces a readily peeling white bark similar to these pieces but which does not grow in the far north of Scotland. The rare Birch trees which still grow in Shetland are the Downy Birch. This bark would thus seem to have been imported. The cut pieces and other large pieces were probably laid under turf roofing to form a waterproof layer, used traditionally in Scandinavia. Similar roofing was used until recently in the Faroe Islands, which were settled by Norse farmers. Bark is known to have been used to make containers since the Mesolithic period. However, Morris considers that most of the bark fragments and rolls had other uses, perhaps for tanning hides, sails, netting and cordage. These are uses which continued into the nineteenth century in Scotland. Birch bark also contains pitch, and rolled pieces can be used as tapers since they burn well with a clear flame. The pitch can also be extracted and used as glue, another use which Mesolithic people had discovered and put to good effect.

The late Norse period at the Biggings was dated by the presence of imported goods, including late thirteenth- to fourteenth-century pottery from Yorkshire and German wares. Continental redwares from northern Germany and southern Scandinavia were also recorded. Such glazed and brightly decorated wares would have been status symbols. From the wooden floor of the *stofa* (mid-thirteenth to beginning of the fifteenth century), an irregularly shaped piece of cork was found. The Cork Oak is a native of the western Mediterranean and Portugal, and was first imported into England in the fourteenth century. A lump of wood tar, found in a Medieval context and identified by Andrew Crawshaw, would have been invaluable for caulking boat seams; there was so little wood available locally that this too must have been imported, probably from Scandinavia.

Textile production, in the form of tabby weave woollen cloth, dates from the thirteenth, fifteenth and later centuries; this and late Medieval twill textiles and knitting were examined by Penelope Walton Rogers. She found that Madder dyes had been used on the tabby textiles in the early to mid-seventeenth century. This dye plant would have been imported in the form of the dried roots. It was grown in the early Middle Ages in the south of England, but the demand was such that it was imported throughout the Medieval period from Flanders. We may assume that the wool came from local Sheep and that it was cleaned with lye, probably made at the farm, spun and woven on an upright loom (loom weights were found). Dyeing could have been carried out at any stage, depending on the size of the cloth or knitted garment and that of the iron cauldron traditionally used for dyeing. The material would have been first treated with a mordant, a metal salt, to enable the fibres to take up the dye permanently. Alum gave the brightest red shades with Madder. The cloth would then have been boiled with the Madder until the desired shade of red was attained. The colour contained in Madder roots has been found to be still present after 1000 years in the middens of Viking York at Coppergate. The Madder was identified by Allan Hall, who asked Sue Grierson, a specialist in natural dyes, to see if any more dye could be extracted from the still reddish roots. Wool yarn was mordanted with tin and alum and Sue Grierson was able to extract several paler colours. At York, alum was obtained from an imported Clubmoss which was also found by Hall in the middens. It may be that alum salt was also used at the Biggings; it was known to have been imported into Scotland in the fourteenth century.

Few bones were found; Cattle, Sheep or Goat and Pig bones were recorded, as were pads of hair of Cattle, and Sheep or Goat. A few bones of birds and fish scales were present; occasional feather fragments could have originated from plucking birds for the table in the house. Evidence for Horse Mussel survived as the periostracum (the noncalcareous outer part of the shell), and there were operculae of Iceland Whelk and Periwinkle. All were identified by Fred Woodward.

Paul Buckland reported on the insects from two small samples; one from above the planked floor in trench J in the main farmhouse produced 26 species and the other from trench K in another building yielded 21 beetle taxa from a 1.3kg sample above the wooden floor. Research on similar sites has shown that samples of this size are not necessarily big enough to produce the most detail; nevertheless interesting data were obtained. Although wool processing would seem, from associated artefacts, to have been an important occupation, no sheep ectoparasites were found. The beetles identified included species which feed on mouldy hay, and another beetle, blind and flightless, also feeds on the fungi which grow on decaying plant debris. Buckland notes that the latter was particularly common in Scandinavian deposits in Dublin and York. A beetle from trench K feeds on the fungi which cause dry rot, and was found in quantity along with the Spider Beetle; these suggest that rotting timber was present, although neither wooden flooring nor wooden roofing were noted in that structure. Specimens from trench J included wetland species living on sedges, and another which feeds on heaths and Heather. These may have been associated with roofing or other plant material brought in for domestic use. Beetles identified as feeding on other plant species could have come in with the weedy straw which has already been discussed.

Most of the organic material at the Biggings will have completely disappeared due to the acidity of the soil and later disturbance. What remains shows that far from living isolated lives on the periphery of Europe, the Norse and their descendants had access to goods available from all around the North Sea. These goods would have been available to all who had money or goods to exchange. It is the waterlogged sites which have yielded the most information, such as these remarkably preserved floor levels at the Biggings, and the waterlogged pit at Tuquoy on Orkney. Pine, Oak and Ash woods were imported to both places, with the addition of Maple at Tuquoy and Beech at the Biggings. Imported wooden articles such as staved buckets and wooden utensils and a Pine floor proclaim the high status of the Biggings, maintained throughout the Middle Ages. Imported decorated pottery, found at this and other sites, was another conspicuous sign of local wealth.

Norse sites in the Hebrides

Barvas Machair, Lewis

The Norse trading routes to Ireland ran between the Inner and Outer Hebrides. The western side of some of the islands is a fertile machair or dune pasture, built up from wind-blown sands rich in shell fragments. The topography of the relevant islands of the Outer Hebrides has been briefly described in the chapter 5. Few Norse sites have at present been excavated and some will be hidden under the machair soils and shifting dunes. The site at Barvas Machair was found during a 1978 survey of eroding sites by Trevor Cowie, on behalf of Historic Scotland, and excavated before further destruction by wind erosion occurred. A substantial midden up to 1.5m thick was sampled; it was associated with two sub-rectangular, double-walled structures, each reminiscent of a 'black house', the traditional Hebridean home. The bulk of the midden was sieved and a very large assemblage of bones, including Cattle, Sheep, Red Deer and Dog, was retrieved, along with massive quantities of fish bone. A rich pottery assemblage revealed this to be a single period Norse site, tentatively dated to the tenth to eleventh centuries AD. The site has not yet been published.

A few small fragments of Birch charcoal were found. Woodland on the west coast, exposed to westerly gales, only developed Birch and Hazel scrub, and much of the hinterland became peat covered already in the Mesolithic period. Spruce charcoal, from two of the contexts, represents driftwood. The long west-facing, largely sandy, coastline would have accumulated much stranded driftwood, brought over with the prevailing currents from the North American Spruce forests. Long straight timbers for roofing and peat for fuel would have been readily available and the machair would have provided good pasture and arable ground. The Hulled Barley was of the lax-eared type and was the main cereal in eight of the nine contexts, with a total of over 1,200 grains. Oats, presumably of cultivated type, totalled 458 grains. Thirty-three Flax seeds were recovered. Only a very few arable weed seeds were found; Chickweed, a weed of good soils, was present in most contexts. These are similar to Norse results from Orkney, where Barley predominated on the fertile soils.

Drimore Machair, South Uist

The prospective construction of a guided missile range prompted a fortnight's dig in 1956 by A. MacLaren on behalf of the Royal Commission on the Ancient and Historical Monuments of Scotland. Drimore machair lies at an altitude of about 5m above O.D. and the site, partly buried in sand, is within 300m of the west coast. The ground plan of an early Norse long house, or hall house, was uncovered, with bones and artefacts found within the house. Small domestic items had been made from bone, ivory and antler. The bones were identified by various specialists and included Cattle, Sheep and Pig; Horse and

Dog would have been kept as working animals. Red Deer bone and antler derived from small beasts of poor quality, similar to those at present in the Outer Isles. Whale bone was found in some quantity and included one used as a socket for the entrance. Bird bones included Great Black-backed Gull, Razorbill and species of Duck. Fish bones consisted of only a few Cod bones. Shellfish were Cockle, Limpet, Mussel, Oyster, Scallop, Whelk and Winkle. A few scraps of Birch charcoal were the only remains of wood. The environmental work was carried out before sieving for seeds and bones became standard procedure. Steatite vessel fragments had adherent burnt matter and this could be further explored with modern methods of analysis.

Machrins, Colonsay

Although just as exposed as the Outer Hebrides, the Inner Hebridean island of Colonsay has good soils, with low hills providing shelter for a well-grown woodland. A machair stretches along the west coast and Iron Age habitation flourished there and on similar fertile sites on other Inner Hebridean islands. The site at Machrins was discovered through field walking during the preparation of the RCAHMS inventory for Argyll. It was excavated in 1977 and 1978 by Graham Ritchie. The remains of four small buildings of native Iron Age type were uncovered from the sand and animal bone from a secure context within one of the houses was radiocarbon-dated about AD 850.

Plant material from one of the hearths contained burnt peat. Wet-sieving of a midden overlying the fourth house produced Heather and possible Ash charcoal. Sixty Barley grains, probably all of Hulled Barley, were recognised. It is not known if the four Oat grains were of wild or cultivated grain. No weed seeds were found and this small collection would therefore seem to represent cleaned grain, charred whilst being dried or processed for food.

Much bone came from the same midden as the plant remains; the rest, from house 2, included the radiocarbon-dated sample. Mary Harman identified mainly Cattle with some Sheep and a little Pig bone from these two small collections of mainly poorly preserved bone. Harman noted that most were from fully grown animals of small breeds. A Roe Deer antler had a portion of the skull still attached; this suggests hunting rather than the chance find of a shed antler.

Alwyn Wheeler identified fish bone, most of it from the house 4 midden. Numbers are not given but most of the remains were of small Saithe of about 300mm in length, which would have been caught in shallow inshore waters. A single bone was of Ling. Sea shells were very rare and only a single spine of a Sea Urchin proved identifiable.

A burial, some 14m from the settlement, revealed a Norse inhumation of similar date. A Dog, cause of death unknown, had been laid on the knees of the corpse. Although the Dog bones were friable, Juliet Clutton-Brock was able to identify the animal as being very similar to a Welsh Corgi; these were bred as cattle dogs in the west of Britain. It was also almost identical to a Västgöta Spets, the Swedish cattle dog. It is not known if these cattle dogs were first bred in Scandinavia or in Britain, but Clutton-Brock noted that this was the earliest to have been excavated in Britain.

In spite of the probable Norse date, Ritchie points out that the plan and building techniques of the houses followed the native styles. A saddle quern was found on a stone work-bench at the entrance to one of the houses; it is a very late survival as these were generally superseded by the rotary quern by the later Iron Age.

Other occurrences on Colonsay of Norse burials and small finds of a similar date suggest that this was not an isolated farmstead. Had it for some reason failed to be taken over by the Norse and did they build their own, as yet undiscovered, houses nearby? As these islands were on the well-travelled route to Ireland we may expect more habitations to be discovered. Just how much the native Iron Age population was absorbed, or displaced, in the Inner Hebrides and to what extent Norse agricultural practices, such as the intensive cultivation of Oats and Flax, were introduced remains for future research to discover.

Landscape and farming

Especially in the Northern Isles, the Norse farmers left their imprint in language, place names and the way of life, and we can attempt to trace some agricultural and fishing practices from their Norse origins to the present time, beginnimg with a summary of the Norse environment, reconstructed from pollen analysis and larger plant remains. The broad picture of the Caithness landscape in the region of Freswick and Robert's Haven from nearby pollen analyses, did not differ greatly from the present, largely treeless vegetation. Heather moorland covered the higher parts and grassland with undrained swampy ground occupied the lower-lying areas. Mixed farming took place on the coastal land, with its fertile shell sands. The Birsay Bay area of Orkney supported a little scrub woodland in sheltered valleys. Heather, grassland and marshland with cultivated land and attendant wasteland are indicated by the larger plant remains. The pre-Norse vegetation seems to have been little different. The larger plant remains from Howe, only 17km to the south of Birsay, indicate that the Willow scrub was sparser than in the earlier Iron Age. Heather and heathland plants increased. A greater number of seeds of arable and waste ground suggest that rank, uncared for land existed at the end of the thousand-year-long habitation period, which has already been discussed.

There is very little evidence from larger plant remains of Norse date from the Outer Isles. The islands have been shown from pollen analyses to have been largely treeless from the Neolithic period onwards; the trees having been mainly replaced by blanket bog. The Inner Hebrides, with securely dated Norse sites still to be revealed, seem from pollen analyses from Iron Age and later sites to have retained mixed woodland in sheltered areas. The generally sparse woodland of the Shetland Isles seems to have suffered a similar fate to the Outer Hebrides in that it was replaced by bog from the Neolithic onwards. With much environmental work in progress there, it is hoped soon to enlarge the picture. The Norse sites with relevance to farming so far excavated are coastal, predominantly on fertile shell-sands and in areas earlier cleared of woodland. Scrub woodland survived probably, as at the present time, only in sheltered valleys away from the strong winds which are a feature of these northern areas of Scotland.

There is sufficient dietary evidence to suggest ways in which the plant and animal husbandry may have changed with the advent of the Norse farmer. There is also evidence of the importance of wild resources: mammals, birds, fish and shellfish. Table 5 shows published records for Freswick, Caithness, and the Orkney Islands for all of these resources. The numbers vary widely within and between species and the relative proportions of each species or group has been given, where available, in the text. Actual numbers are given in the specialists' published accounts.

Naked Barley, the early staple cereal which was already being replaced by Hulled Barley in the Iron Age, had been reduced to such a small proportion of the grain recovered by the Norse period that it was probably no longer being grown as a separate crop. Hulled Barley was accompanied by Common Oat in the pre-Norse period, but remained the predominant cereal, except at Freswick, where both Barley and Oats attained equal importance. Analyses from more pre-Norse sites are needed to clarify this as the data base is very small. However, there are a number of Norse, including Late Norse, sites from which data are plentiful. A good number of contexts were analysed from each of the following sites and the proportions are internally consistent.

Sites with a higher proportion of Hulled Barley than Common Oats:
Barvas Machair, Lewis, and Brough Road, Birsay, Orkney.

Sites with a higher proportion of Common Oats:
Pool, Sanday and Beachview, Birsay (1000-1300) and Earl's Bu, Orkney (Late Norse).

At Freswick, similar numbers of Barley and Oat grains occur throughout the pre-Norse, Norse and Late Norse contexts.

The proportion of land growing Oats had clearly increased since the pre-Norse period and this was maintained throughout the Late Norse times. New land seems to have been brought into cultivation. Oats will grow on poorer soil than Barley and freshly dug or ploughed land would not necessarily need extra dung to fertilise it, at least initially. The data from Pool suggests that unfertilised sandy soils may have been brought newly into cultivation to grow Oats while Barley was, as previously, grown in manured ground and this could have been the beginning of the infield — outfield system which has already been described. It is unfortunate that it does not seem possible to separate the two cultivated Oat species known to have been grown in Scotland on the basis of their grain, although at the present time the improved varieties of the Common Oat produce the larger grain. Flax fields would have been similarly manured as the crop requires fertile soils.

The introduction of the Common Oat onto these predominantly coastal shell-sands at Freswick and two sites in the Bay of Birsay is puzzling. Only one to a few floret bases were identified from each site, but at Freswick this was the only cultivated Oat that was represented. The seed corn may have come from Norway, where shell sand is not a feature of the mainly inland farms and where it is the only cultivated Oat grown. At Pool, Bristle Oat is thought to have been the cultivated species (Julie Bond, personal communication), probably going back to the fourth or fifth centuries AD when it vastly outnumbered the Wild Oat. An intriguing question is: why were cultivated Oats grown in addition to Barley in the Pictish period at Pool and Freswick (and possibly Howe) at a time when there seems to have been a contraction, rather than an expansion of population at both Pool and Howe?

Where did the pre-Norse Oat seed corn come from? Bristle Oat is not a Norwegian crop and has not been recorded from there in the past. Evidence from sites of the Early Historic period further south suggests that it was also becoming important at sites not under the influence of Norse settlers. Coastal sites in particular are where we might expect innovative cereals to be first imported and grown.

There is the possibility of earlier, pre-settlement contact with the Norse, as combs of Reindeer antler were traded before the seventh century at Howe, and other pre-Norse sites in Orkney. Did the pre-Norse Flax at Howe come from these traders? The complex processing of Flax, described below, suggests that the Pictish peoples would have needed assistance to learn it. Perhaps Linseed was reintroduced for medicinal purposes.

Rectangular kilns, have been found on Shetland, Orkney and the Viking settlement at Freswick, Caithness, where a similar kiln was still in use until the late thirteenth century. Fenton relates that circular or semi-circular kilns, one of which was excavated at Beachview, replaced most of the early kilns and these survive on Orkney and on the more fertile parts of south Shetland. Another early circular kiln is from Medieval Jarlshof and is of fourteenth- or fifteenth-century date. The Barley or Oat grain was dried on a bed of straw and great care was needed to prevent it catching alight from the glowing peat fire below. The practice of drying malted Barley (after the grain had been germinated by wetting it to turn the starch to sugar), continued after the kiln had ceased to be used for corn drying. It would be interesting to know when drying malt first took place in these kilns and the archaeobotanist is constantly looking for such evidence in the form of germinated grain. As the Vikings were well known for their drinking bouts, it may be that the kilns were primarily built for drying malt for Barley ale!

We may wonder how corn was dried before kilns were built. Fenton has described the method of pot drying, whereby grain was dried in a round-bottomed pot placed over the fire. The drying grain was turned with the hand, or a flat piece of wood. As this was described by a Norwegian word *lum,* meaning warm, we may assume that this was the Norse method used before kilns were introduced. Another method of drying grain was to put it in a container and roll heated stones into it; in Orkney a flat stone with a rim of clay, called a *hellio* in old Norse, was used for the purpose. Although the larger farms would have adopted a kiln, probably sometime in the Late Norse period, the continued use of the Norse words suggests that, for small quantities, these simple grain drying methods continued in use.

Medicinal and spice plants

With regard to native pre-Norse plants, Juniper is still present throughout Orkney in suitable habitats, and single seeds were recovered from hearth deposits from Howe dating from the fourth to seventh centuries AD. The medicinal uses of the plant were known to Theophrastus, the Greek botanist (370-285 BC). Juniper has powerful properties, the fruits are antiseptic, anti-inflammatory, diuretic and emmenagogic. From the uses given by Dioscorides (fl AD 64), the antiseptic and emmenagogue properties were also known by him. The Savin, not a native of Britain but of Central Europe, is even better known as an emmenagogue and has been cultivated in Scotland since at least the mid-sixteenth century (Dickson and Gauld 1986) . The culinary use of Juniper with meat seems to be of recent origin.

Tubers of Lesser Celandine indicate the continuation of its use at Howe from the first to the fourth and from the fourth to seventh centuries AD, where they were associated with hearth deposits. Astringent properties, found throughout the plant, were also known to the ancient herbalists at which time it was used for catarrh and sore throats. Henbane is an intriguing plant in that it has not been found in pre-Norse contexts in these northern areas. It was found in Edinburgh Castle deposits dated to AD 100-300. Had it been traded north from Edinburgh or was it a Viking import? Henbane was introduced into Scandinavia by the Vikings and its seeds have been found in deposits of that age in Denmark, Sweden and Finland. The earliest record from Norway is from deposits of AD 1200-50 in Oslo.

These three plants, Henbane, Juniper and Lesser Celandine represent only a very small proportion of the many plants known from classical sources to have been used medicinally and which were presumably used in both pre-Norse and Norse times. Many plants would have been gathered before they fruited and used in infusions or poultices, thus leaving no trace in the archaeological record. The above-mentioned seeds and tubers were recorded in general from hearth deposits; perhaps the fireplace formed the focus of preparation of medicines as well as of food. Anglo-Saxon leech (medical) books date from this period but these herbals describe plants used for spells and charms, with few medicinal recipes. These finds of seeds are therefore invaluable as a source material if we are to learn which plants were used by our ancestors before the late Medieval period when printing made such herbals more readily available.

Although no spice plants have so far been recorded in Norse Scotland, plant remains from Viking and later deposits in Norway give some indication as to which plants were gathered from their native flora, or acquired by trade. At Bryggen, Bergen, Krzywinski records Caraway seeds from a latrine dated to AD 1250. Caraway is doubtfully native in some south-eastern counties of England and has been introduced to scattered habitats throughout the British Isles with several sites in north-eastern Scotland, Orkney and Shetland, where it is particularly concentrated. From Oslo, Kirstin Griffin records Fennel and probably Chives from AD 1275-1300, with the Chives type also recorded earlier from AD 1025-75. Fennel was introduced into Norway, though it is possibly native in southern England. Although Fennel is very rare in Scotland at present and found no further north than the Moray Firth, there is a former record from Orkney! Chives are only present in Scotland as rare, established introductions, originally thrown out from gardens.

The Faroe Islands have retained their Norse culture to a much larger extent than Scotland, perhaps because of their greater remoteness, lying to the north-west of Shetland. Jóhannes Jóhansen, a Faroese botanist, recorded two interesting plants from these largely treeless islands. Tormentil was used for tanning, in place of Oak bark, until the 1950s. Jóhansen recounts that the women would crush the rhizomes in round hollows in rocks, with a pebble. The crushed underground stems were then mixed with water and smeared on Sheep fleeces to preserve them. Does such a use go back to Norse times?

Kvann is Norse for Garden Angelica, the stems of which are candied and chewed or used as culinary decorations. Jóhansen reported that it was highly prized by the Vikings for its numerous medicinal properties. They exported it, mainly to France. The plant was specially grown in *kvann* gardens in Norway and the Faroes, although it also grows wild in both countries. It has persisted in cultivation until recent times and has been grown for hundreds of years in one walled garden, to protect it from the Sheep, on one of the Faroe Islands. Jóhansen considered that it was brought to the Faroes by the Vikings. By the sixteenth century, the sweet aromatic stems were peeled and eaten as a sweetmeat on the Faroes, its medicinal uses by then largely forgotten. Garden Angelica's complex active ingredients have recently been isolated. It has proven anti-inflammatory properties and the root oil has been shown to inhibit bacterial and fungal growth. Its uses, largely in herbal medicine, are for colds, as an expectorant, for pleurisy and rheumatism. The plant was introduced into Britain and is very local in Scotland though it is abundant on the banks of the Clyde and the Kelvin (Dickson *et al.* 2000a). Interestingly enough it was grown in gardens in Shetland until 1973; it still grows near to the harbours on three of the Orkney islands.

These aromatic plants, Caraway, Fennel and Garden Angelica, have their medicinal properties concentrated in the seeds. Norse deposits should be searched for these seeds. That they have all recently been recorded in the Northern Isles, away from their main centres of distribution, may indicate their deliberate introduction. Another plant which should be looked for in high status sites is the Walnut; shell fragments have been found in Norse Trondheim and Dublin and must have been imported.

9 The Medieval period: productive cess-pits and drains

Three ancient burghs

Urban growth

The development of Medieval towns in Scotland is a fascinating subject and one which is largely lacking in documentation and this gives archaeology great importance to our understanding of the development of urban Scotland, especially before the fourteenth century. In the past 25 years redevelopments of the old parts of Perth, Aberdeen and Elgin, for instance, have revealed that much of the waterlogged, Medieval hearts still remain under later buildings (**60-62**). As fire frequently destroyed the wooden buildings and further building took place on top of the levelled debris, up to 3m of deposits developed in less than 250 years. These deposits have been excavated before being re-interred beneath new commercial buildings. Pits and middens have also been found and their contents passed on to environmental archaeologists. The essential difference between town and rural communities was that the towns were trading establishments with a new immigrant merchant class from England and mainland Europe, whereas in the country people generally supplied raw materials for the towns or existed on a subsistence economy. A cash economy did not develop in Scotland until the twelfth century. Castles and rural settlements have also been examined so that it is becoming possible to compare the differing life styles from these diverse habitations, although for the twelfth century, this is difficult because the wealthy burgher may have lived on the same plot of land as the peasant fresh from the rural hinterland.

Scotland had been united as a country since AD 842 but the Norse domination of the far north did not lead to town growth there until the twelfth century. The development of towns was in response to the European expansion of trade from the eleventh century onwards. David I (1124-53) created many royal burghs with monopolies of trades, crafts and markets; charters record their privileges as existing before the 1160s. Religious houses were established and those in the southern lowlands soon became wealthy from sheep farming and the tithes which they exacted from the parish churches. Those who found favour with royalty gained titles and land through services to the King. Increasingly a wealthy land-owning and merchant class developed, serviced by a peasant class dependent on their land and the vagaries of the weather for the harvest. What can be deduced about the different lifestyles of the rich and poor?

Excavations have shown that town planning existed from the twelfth century with relatively straight roads and regular sized lots. Stalls, both temporary and permanent, were usually owned by burgesses, the more important citizens. These fronted the street, the foreland; to the rear were the backlands with boundaries of shallow drainage ditches or wattle fences. Insubstantial homes and workshops were built in these areas, sometimes a byre would be built at one end of a house, distinguished by the presence of a stony floor and a drain. Burghers would have their animals driven out to pasture by day onto croft lands which they owned and which were divided between arable and pasture. If there was a nearby woodland the Pigs would go there for pannage, the owner permitting. The pathways used to herd the animals through the town became established and 'Cowgate' still exists in the city of Edinburgh with a rather cleaner surface now than formerly! Some yards served as gardens and others became filled with pits and middens and latrines. Homes and workshops would each last for about 20 years before they caught fire or collapsed. Larger industrial processes would be sited in the suburbs, especially if a source of water were needed from the town ditch.

In order to find out something of the lives of the inhabitants of these backlands, we will investigate two ports, Perth and Aberdeen, which should record traces of imported goods and exports in their midden deposits, and Elgin with the nearby port of Lossiemouth (Table 6). The pioneer archaeobotanical work at all three burghs was carried out by Mary Fraser (1981).

Perth

As a river crossing and port on the River Tay in a region of fertile soils, Perth was well placed for development. The town was granted a charter by David I and, after Berwick, became the most important town for overseas trade. Royalty, in their frequent visits to nearby Scone Palace, brought wealth to the town. Records show that woolfells (sheepskins), fleece and hides were the main exports, although salted Salmon, rabbit skins and woollen cloth were also mentioned. Wine and luxury goods were imported.

Numerous excavations have taken place in Perth, as different parts of the town have been rebuilt and this hive of archaeological activity attracted the Scottish Urban Archaeological Trust to base itself in Perth. Work has been chiefly funded by Historic Scotland and the government financed Manpower Services Commission. The most notable publications for environmental archaeology were in 1987, 1995 and 1996 and these may be expected to continue. The excavations have been chiefly of undisturbed backlands belonging to Medieval properties, thus enabling comparison with Medieval Aberdeen.

Mary Fraser's analyses of plant material were followed by those by David Robinson, with later samples investigated by Alan Fairweather (Coleman 1996). Waterlogged material was collected by the excavators and wet sieved through fine meshes by the botanists. The variety of deposits and general species richness of the plant and bone material has resulted in much environmental information of the early town. Samples dated from 1150-1300 included floor levels, latrines, middens, yards, hearths, pits and ditches. Oats, Barley, Wheat and Rye grains were found scattered throughout the site as both burnt and unburnt grain. Common Oat was the most abundant grain. By contrast cess-pits were rich in Wheat and Rye bran fragments from the consumption of bread. Barley and Oats were present as minor components; chaff showed that Barley was of the lax-eared Bere type. As at Aberdeen, eggs of internal parasites were found adhering to the

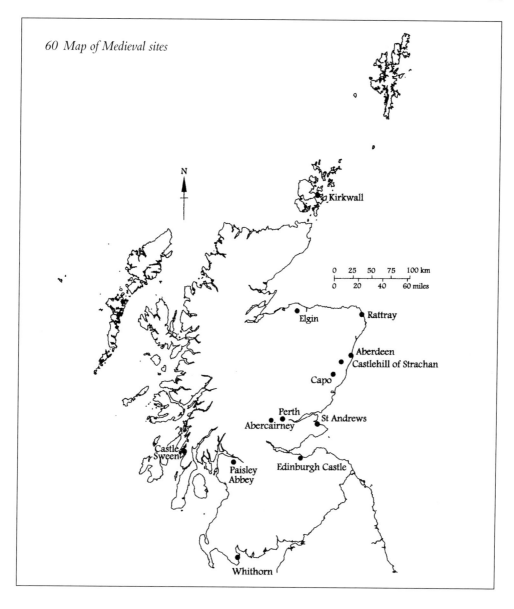

60 Map of Medieval sites

bran fragments thus confirming its faecal origin. *Brassica* seeds may have been used as a spice as the green vegetable would have been eaten before fruiting took place. Wild Radish may have been a crop contaminant although its seeds used to be eaten as 'Durham mustard'. Two certain contaminants were Corncockle and Cornflower, both major weeds of Rye and other cereals. The presence of Flax seeds suggests medicinal use as Linseed. Fruit of Wild Cherry, Raspberry and Bilberry were eaten. Layers of tufted mosses suggested their use as toilet paper. Unlike Aberdeen, Fig seeds were absent, so wealthy people are not thought to have used that particular latrine. However, the presence of Wheat could mean a degree of affluence but Robinson suggests that the contamination of grain by Corncockle may have resulted in its having been sold off cheaply to the poor. The

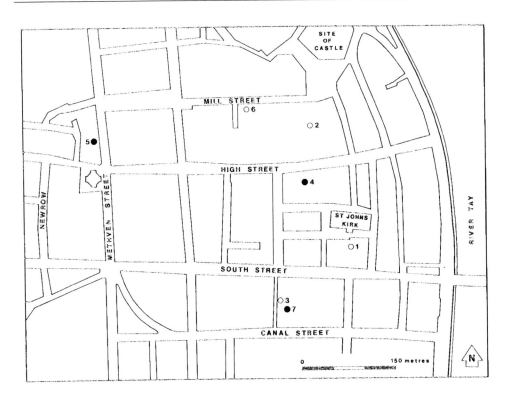

61 Locations of the excavations at Perth. 1. St Annes Lane. 2. High Street. 3. Canal Street 1. 4. Kirk Close. 5. South Methven Street. From Holdsworth (1987)

contents of the latrine included meat, shellfish, eggs and fish, some of which are to be discussed later.

Flooring from nine contexts suggests that Bracken, Heather, cereal straw and chaff with weed seeds seem to have accumulated over an extended period until they reached a considerable thickness, probably to combat continuing damp. Other admixtures were Flax and *Brassica* remains with wood shavings and wood chips. Samples from floor levels at Kirk Close included significant numbers of seeds and pod fragments of a species of *Brassica*; these most resemble the Turnip Rape which was grown in thirteenth-century Europe for the oil content of the seeds. Domestic hearths contained abundant charcoal, occasional Oats and a few Barley grains. Industrial hearths, in contrast, produced charcoal and occasional slag. Two contexts from yards were similar in content to the floor levels, as were those of middens which also had a dung component. Remains of wetland plants suggested that they may have been collected, perhaps with grasses, for hay. Pit contents suggested that flooring may have been tipped into them as well as dung.

Town ditch deposits showed that they had initially had an aquatic flora with Water Starwort, Rushes, Bog Pondweed, Lesser Spearwort and Water Crowfoot. The ditch was obviously not particularly polluted, but was soon used for rubbish such as flooring, cereal waste, roofing, heathland plants and faecal material. The stench, especially in warm

182

	Aberdeen	Perth	Elgin	St. Andrews	Kirkwall	Whithorn 1000-1250	Whithorn 1250-1600	Edinburgh Castle	Castle Sween	Paisley Abbey	Castlehill of Strachan	Rattay
Barley	*	*	*	*				*	*	*		
Bristle Oat		*						*	*	*	*	
Common Oat	*	*	*									
Rye		*								*		
Wheat	*	*	*	*				*	*	*		
Bog Myrtle	*											
Broad Bean								*				
Caper Spurge			*									
Coriander	*											
Deadly Nightshade		*	*									
Dye Plants	*	*	*									
Figs	*	*	*		*					*		
Flax	*	*	*		*			*		*		
Greater Celandine										*		
Hemlock	*											
Hemp	*		*								*	
Henbane		*										
Kale		*?								*?		
Mace												
Mosses	*	*	*									
Onion family	*											
Opium Poppy	*	*										
Orchard fruit			*							*		
Peas				*				*				
Raisins	*		*									
Wild fruit			*							*		
Alder		*			*				*	*	*	
Ash		*			*				*	*	*	
Birch	*	*	*	*	*				*	*	*	
Bracken												
Gorse		*			*					*		
Hawthorn/Apple		*			*						*	
Hazel		*		*	*				*			
Heather	*	*	*	*							*	*
Hornbeam											*	*
Oak		*	*	*	*				*		*	*
Peat	*	*	*		*					*	*	
Rowan					*							
Scots Pine		*			*							
Sloe				*						*		
Spruce					*							
Wild Cherry										*		
Willow	*	*			*							
Wych Elm		*										
Cat	*	*	*	*								
Cattle	*	*	*	*	*	*	*	*	*	*	*	*
Dog	*	*	*						*			
Domestic Duck		*?					*?	*?				
Domestic Fowl		*		*		*	*					*
Domestic Goose		*		*		*	*					*?
Fallow Deer												*
Goat	*~	*	*~		*~		*~		*~	*~		
Hare												*
Horse	*	*	*		*			*				*
Peafowl												*
Pig	*	*	*	*	*	*	*	*	*	*	*	*
Rabbit								*				*
Red Deer	*	*	*					*	*			*
Roe Deer		*						*	*			*
Sheep	*~	*	*~	*	*~	*	*~	*	*~	*~	*	*
Wild Birds								*				*
Cetaceans				*								*
Deep Water Fish												*
Other Fish	*	*	*			*	*	*		*	*	*
Seal		*								*		*
Shellfish		*								*		*

KEY: ★ = present / ★~ = sheep/goat present / ★? = tentative record

Table 6   Resources used at Medieval towns and other places

183

weather, must have been considerable from all the wet, open dumps.

There is evidence to suggest the use of the Flax plant for both Linseed and linen; the latrine seed suggests medicinal use. One of the ditches produced a ball of hard silty clay containing a linen thread; Robinson considers that the encapsulation had led to its preservation which so rarely occurs.

Occasional finds of Elderberry and Rowan add to the list of fruits and Walnut shell fragments from one sample may well represent imports; see the Part 2 account. As at Aberdeen, seeds of Dyer's Rocket, often called Weld, imported for the yellow dye obtained from the flowering tops, were occasionally found. Four seeds of the two poisonous plants with similar narcotic properties, Henbane and Deadly Nightshade, were identified; see the Part 2 accounts. A number of plaits and moss fragments of Common Hairmoss were recovered from a fourteenth-century context. Long, tough pliable stems can be plaited and would have made tough ropes suitable to hold down roofing. This was traditional in both highland and lowland Scotland where use was made of whatever was readily available; straw and Heather were also used for roofing ropes and long flat stones were employed to hold down the ends. Hairmoss was also found in cess-pits where it would have been abandoned after use for wiping purposes.

Industry may have been concentrated in the suburbs bounded by the town ditch. Dating from the thirteenth century, kilns were used for both grain drying and malting; they had been built close to the ditch, no doubt to ensure a source of water in case of fire! David Robinson investigated the contents of two of them and found charred Oat and Barley grains in the base. He commented that Corncockle seeds were absent and suggested that this weed may have been confined to Wheat fields or perhaps Rye crops with which it has been particularly associated. Alan Fairweather continued the investigation and from three kilns in Meal Vennel found Bristle Oat to have been the most plentiful cereal with a little Wild Oat. A kiln from Canal Street contained Barley, Bristle and Common Oat grains. From a fourteenth-century context, Fairweather tentatively identified a seed of Field Bean; see the Part 2 account of Broad Bean.

Many wild plants have been used for dyeing and so it is not always easy to distinguish them in archaeological deposits. David Robinson, however, investigating an industrial quarter in twelfth-century King Edward Street, has found fragments of two plants particularly connected with dyeing. These are the Alpine Clubmoss and Stag's-horn Clubmoss which are both notable for their high alum content; in the nineteenth century they were used as mordants to fix the colours. Recent experimental work by Su Grierson has shown that Clubmosses can produce as brilliant a yellow with Dyer's Rocket as the mineral form of alum. Other plants associated with the Clubmosses were Heather shoot tips and flowers, Dyer's Rocket seeds, slivers of Birch bark, Bracken fronds and Tormentil seeds. All could have been used for dyeing, although the roots of Tormentil would have been pulled up and used rather than the seed. It is interesting that Alan Hall working on Viking deposits at Coppergate, York, produced another species of Clubmoss, Issler's Clubmoss, accompanied by dye plant remains. As this Clubmoss is very rare in England it seems probable that the Danes brought it with them specially for dyeing. Alpine Clubmoss is a mountain plant, which does not grow close to Perth; it is just possible that it was obtained from abroad in trade. The mineral alum was imported into Scotland in about the twelfth century.

A wooden stave-built cask was found at Scott Street and described by Adrian Cox; the hoops were of Hazel withies. It had been reused as a well lining. Kirk Close in Perth produced large numbers of well-preserved timbers which were identified by Anne Crone and John Barber. All the timber had been reused; almost all was of Oak representing large trees of about 0.4m in diameter. Lesser quantities of Alder, Birch, Ash, Elm, Willow and Hawthorn/Apple woods were also used. Wattle screens gave no evidence of a coppicing cycle; withies, mostly of Hazel and Alder with a little Birch, Willow, Elm and Hawthorn/Apple were identified. Crone and Barber suggested that riverside trees from the Tay valley were used. The Oak, however, was derived from forest-grown trees which would, by the Medieval period, have belonged to either the crown or a private landowner. The Oak was probably scavanged from superior buildings which would have fronted onto the street. A burnt wattle fence from Mill Street examined by Robinson was of Hazel and Heather, plastered with clay daub which had been tempered with straw and chaff. Buildings were described by Linda Blandford as being of stake and wattle either free-standing or, from the thirteenth century, with ground sills; clay cladding survived on some of them. Roofing material, to judge from what was found in the middens, was of straw, Heather or Bracken; doors did not survive. Hearths were simple, of a clay-lined hollow or a stone slab. A probable bakery contained a commercial sized oven of 2.0 x 0.7m; peasants would not have been able to afford their own ovens.

Lathe-turned wooden bowls were commonly used and four of these of Ash wood were recovered. Another bowl was stave-built of Scots Pine with a base plate of Alder and bindings of Hazel withies. An Oak toilet seat was found *in situ* over a cess-pit of late thirteenth- to early fourteenth-century date. The cess-pit appeared to have been surrounded by a wattle screen. Such seats remained in use on outside 'privies' until the twentieth century. A barrel lid was dated to the late fourteenth to early fifteenth century. Wooden items, especially bowls were commonly used in the Medieval period and it is somewhat surprising that not more of these have so far been published, although wood from Perth High Street, awaiting publication, should help to redress the balance in this respect.

Bones, reported on by Catherine Smith and Ian Hodgson, were from Kirk Close, Methven Street and Canal Street 11; almost 6,000 bones in total were identified to the species level. Ian Hodgson (1983) reported on the 21,655 bones from High Street, Perth (twelfth-fourteenth century) and Catherine Smith identified 15,982 bones from a long sequence from the mid-fourteenth to beginning of the eighteenth century from Meal Vennel. At each site Cattle bones were the most numerous. A few of these showed pathology suggesting heavy use as draught animals. Sheep increased throughout this time and as animals had to come to market 'on the hoof' this probably represents an increase in wool-fells (sheepskins) for export. Cuts on skulls and lower limbs of Cattle, Sheep or Goats and Horses were noted by Smith for Meal Vennel. This indicates that their primary use was for hides and wool-fells rather than a deliberate increase in meat consumption. Pig, Red and Roe Deer, Hare and Domestic Fowl appear to have been much less exploited but small bones may have been missed because of the lack of flotation during the excavation. Dogs and Cats were present and knife cuts on a Cat skull suggested that the animal had been skinned. Furs of small animals were traded and Smith noted that Cat skins were mentioned in a list from Perth in 1551. Dogs, Cats and Horses were noticeably more numerous in late and post-Medieval contexts. Smith noted that domestic animals remained small in size throughout the period from 1250 to 1700 in Perth, which is not surprising as stock-rearing improvements did not take place until the eighteenth century.

Bird bones from Meal Vennel produced evidence for Domestic Fowl and Domestic or Greylag Goose with lesser numbers of Mallard or Domestic Duck, Barnacle Goose, Widgeon and Cormorant. These would have contributed to the diet to a small extent. Domestic Fowl may have been kept in the backlands by the servants providing protein from flesh and eggs. Fowl and Goose bones were also recorded from Scott Street. Fish remains were very limited probably due to the general lack of sieving; only Cod, Salmon and Thorn-backed Ray were identified from Perth. P.G. Vasey identified 2,400 shells from Kirk Close; most were of Oysters with some marine Mussels.

Aberdeen

The town of Aberdeen probably developed from fishermen's huts; it is still a fishing port at the present time. It stands at the mouth of the River Dee and was well-placed for exporting wool, oxhides and also Salmon for which the River Dee is still famed. Town excavation needs many hands with trowels and between 1973 and 1981 professional and part-time archaeologists worked in the damp, often malodorous bowels of the old town (**62, 63**). Historic Scotland initially financed the dig by J.C. Murray (1982) and sponsored all the post-excavation work. Aberdeen City Council later employed a full-time Archaeology Unit thus ensuring that a watching brief was kept on all future redevelopment.

Aberdeen was a Royal burgh and this gave the town the right to overseas trade; a weekly market was established by Royal assent from 1222. Aberdeen also had a monopoly for cloth making. The most visible result of the imports in the excavations was pottery from Yorkshire, France, the Low Countries and the Rhineland. Wooden objects from the excavation were few; a Birch-wood bowl was found and barrel staves conserved. In the backlands several small lightweight post and wattle buildings were recorded of Birch and Willow; no roofing was found and no evidence for daub survived. The best-preserved of these buildings contained a hearth with burnt chaff of the Common Oat. The Oat chaff may have been the remains of 'graddaning', an ancient method of separating Oat grain from chaff, in which the heads of Oats were set on fire. When the grain dropped out the remaining chaff was extinguished or the chaff thrown on the fire. The backlands, which date from about 1200, were partly filled with animals and wooden dwellings, probably of wattle. Unfortunately, the buildings which fronted the street were not within the excavated area. It has been suggested that the simple huts were the homes of the poorer inhabitants who would have kept Pigs and Fowl in wattle-fenced yards. Also in the backlands was a probable domestic oven which may have been shared among the burgesses, the merchant classes, and provided them with wheaten bread.

By about 1300 more pits and middens developed with less buildings in these squalid, smelly yards. The contents of the pits were welcomed by the environmental archaeologists and botanical samples were analysed, dating from the late twelfth to late fourteenth century, by Mary Fraser. Wet sieving with mesh widths down to 250μ ensured that all

62 Plans of Aberdeen:
A. Main features
and topography.
B. Excavated sites in
relation to Medieval
street pattern.
From Murray
(1982)

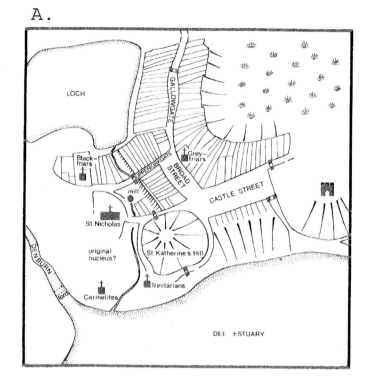

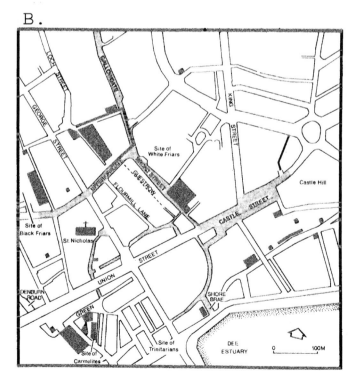

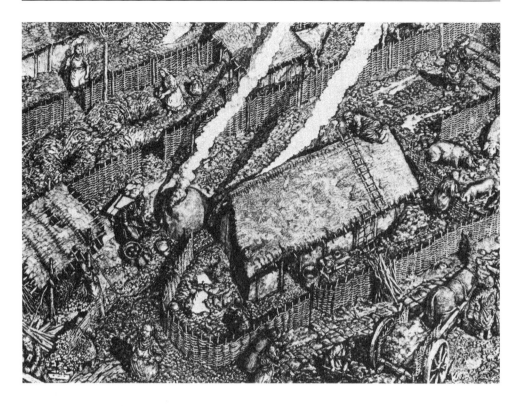

63 Reconstruction of Aberdeen. From Murray (1982)

identifiable plant material was retrieved. Most contexts produced Common Oat whereas Barley was only recorded from a few; some of the grains had been ground for flour. Bread Wheat was only present as grain fragments and was abundant in cess-pits; this was particularly interesting as these are the earliest Medieval records for Bread Wheat in any quantity. Wheat was only grown on well-manured ground and wheaten bread was a status symbol, enjoyed by the wealthy. Among the arable weeds was Corncockle, also in fragments, as would be expected if it had been ground with the corn. Confirmation that this was human sewage came from the eggs of internal parasites, Whipworm and Roundworm, which were recognised using a high power microscope. Mosses of the large weft-making types were particularly abundant and were presumed to have been used for wiping purposes as has been shown at other Medieval sites. A number of other weeds of arable land were recovered; these could have equally well grown in waste places which must have been common in these unkempt backlands. The presence of seeds of Fat Hen, Charlock and Nettle reminds us that the young green leaves of these plants may have been eaten in times of scarcity. Flax or Linseed was recovered. By the eighteenth century Flax was grown domestically and linen made as a family concern although it is not known if this was so in the Medieval period. No linen was found but linen is rarely preserved in archaeological sites.

Documents inform us that a number of dyes were imported; some wild plants were used also, especially by the poorer people. One of the imports was Dyer's Rocket which produces what was then the staple yellow. Its seeds were recovered from several contexts as well as in Perth and Medieval towns elsewhere. The plant has since spread and is quite common in suitable habitats. The cloth would first need to be mordanted in order for the dye to adhere to the fibres, and alum, which was also imported, was usually used for this, although as plants from Perth have shown, a plant mordant could have been used.

Bog Myrtle was found as leaf fragments, flowers and a burnt seed. The plant was formerly used in beer making before Hops became popular. Wild fruit was gathered; the small size of the Medieval town meant that heath and scrubland would still have existed nearby and Bilberry, Rowan, Bramble and Raspberry were collected. Hazelnuts would have been popular and a few shell fragments were found. Figs and grapes would both have been imported as dried fruit. They would have been bought by the wealthy and may have accompanied wine imports. Figs have many pips and were particularly common in cess-pits whereas pips of the few-seeded grape were very rare. Opium Poppy was a rare but interesting find as its use as an opiate and sedative continues to the present time; it too was imported.

Excavation has continued in advance of redevelopment and Allan Hall has extended the botanical work and kindly given access to his forthcoming list before publication. His main results are from the thirteenth and fourteenth centuries and have added several species of interest. Coriander was found as fruit fragments as would be expected if the fruits had been crushed in a mortar with a pestle to release the aromatic oils. A single Hemp seed may relate to the plant fibre's use for making coarse sacking and as is likely at this port, also for cordage or sails. The plant was grown in Scotland in Medieval times, as highlighted in Part 2.

By high power examination of their cell pattern, tiny translucent epidermal fragments have been shown to be of the Onion genus. Similar fragments identified by Philippa Tomlinson from Viking York were further identified as Leek. These Onion type fragments came from a former tanning pit which seems to have been reused as a cess and rubbish pit at about 1400; Wheat bran fragments and parasite eggs were also found.

Bones have been identified by Ian Hodgson and Angela Jones from the same two late twelfth- to fourteenth-century sites. Over 2,400 bones were identified in total and the minimum number of individuals estimated at both sites. Cattle were the most numerous and most were five years old when slaughtered to provide hides in their best condition, and so it seems that beef was a by-product of the hide industry. The discovery of tanning pits suggests that after the animals were slaughtered in the town and the meat sold, the hides were tanned before export. Sheep and Goats exceeded Pigs; prime lamb and young mutton joints were evident at the St Paul Street site with older mutton at Queen Street. Similarly piglets and young Pigs had been eaten preferentially at St Paul Street; this may be taken to suggest a greater degree of affluence there in the fourteenth century. There was a relatively high number of Goat horn cores which may relate to horn production. Red Deer were present in small numbers. Horses, with rare bones present, were probably used as pack animals. Dogs and Cats were presumed to be domestic and kept as scavengers as well as to keep down rodent pests. Bones of large birds were found but not identified and nor were fish bones.

Elgin

Elgin is near to the mild Moray coast with good free-draining soils. It was a royal burgh and by 1383 had its own trading vessel. The plant material identified by Mary Fraser has yet to be published, and the following account is taken, with kind permission, from her thesis. In the redevelopment of backlands to the north of High Street, a small area was excavated and deposits of thirteenth- to fifteenth-century date were examined from seven pits, a barrel and a soakaway. The pits were holes dug into fine sand, some with the remains of wattled walls. All contained a mixture of midden and sewage. The sewage was recognised from Wheat bran fragments with some Oat and Barley. Quantities of Raspberry and Bramble pips and a single Grape pip were found. Small numbers of Fig pips were also recovered. Weeds of arable and waste places included Corncockle, Fat Hen, Red Dead-nettle, Nipplewort, Knotgrass, Chickweed, Black Bindweed and Nettle with pods and seeds of Wild Radish noted. Carbonised grain of Common Oat, Barley and a few Bread Wheat were found in some of the pits.

A reused, mid-fourteenth-century barrel had been set into the ground and used for sewage and midden material. Much was of bran fragments, especially Wheat, with parasite eggs seen adhering to the bran. Numerous fruitstones, especially of Wild Cherry, with some Bullace, Bird-cherry, Sloe and a few Apple pips were also part of the mixture. Mary Fraser suggested that the fruit may have been made into a drink and a Dutch pottery vessel, in fragments, could have contained it. Seeds of Dog Rose, Elder, Rowan, Bilberry and Wild Strawberry were also recovered. Although orchards existed in the sixteenth century in Elgin, all of these could well have been collected from the wild. Burnt pips of Grapevine show that grapes had been imported.

A fifteenth-century soakaway had been dug into the natural sand and lined with Oak timber. The primary fill contained Wheat and Barley bran. The remainder was a mixture of Common Oat, Barley and Wheat with a wide range of fruit and including Hazel and Walnut shells. Seeds of a *Brassica*, probably Wild Turnip, may have been used for flavouring. Flax seeds probably taken medicinally as Linseed, were found and Hemp seed was an interesting addition. Dyer's Rocket seeds were present in small numbers. Deadly Nightshade, with 160 seeds, mostly in the soakaway, was originally imported as a medicinal plant. A hospital was founded in the first half of the thirteenth century, which may have had a small herb garden where it was originally grown, although the King's garden was even closer to the site. Only a single seed was found of the unmistakable Caper Spurge, a powerful purgative and a plant of doubtful British status and certainly an archaeophyte in Scotland.

Heathland plants and those of wet habitats were found scattered throughout the samples. Mosses of the weft-forming type were particularly abundant in the samples containing sewage and were doubtless used for wiping purposes. With the exception of the imported Figs and raisins, all the other plants could have grown around Elgin. Some of the best fertile land was owned by the monks of Kinloss, near Elgin, and was known to have grown Wheat. Monks had a daily allowance of white flour. Wheat was, however, also imported from England in the twelfth and thirteenth centuries but, presumably by the fourteenth century, locally grown Wheat was sufficient to fulfil local demands.

Only 510 bones were retrieved from thirteenth- to sixteenth-century deposits near the

High Street; they were sieved and floated and described in Ian Hodgson's 1983 paper. In terms of meat available, beef was once more the most common, with Sheep or Goat numbers slightly higher than those of Pig. Horse, Red Deer, Dog and Cat were also present in small numbers. Most Cattle had not been slaughtered until about five years of age.

Four more burghs

Edinburgh

Described here is the Medieval part (*c*.AD 1000-1400) of the series of deposits from Edinburgh Castle which began to accumulate about 900 BC and continued almost continuously until AD 1745. The earlier phases have been described in chapters 5 and 6. The deposits of this phase were notable for intensive industrial activity. Hearths were used intensively for iron smithing with coal used as part of the fuel. Middens had been mixed and redeposited. Of the 365 cereal grains identified by Sheila Boardman from *c*.AD 1000-1325, 62% were of Hulled Barley and Oats, including Bristle Oat, made up 22% of the grain. Bread Wheat was probably more important than in previous periods. Flax was found in at least two samples and several seeds of Broad Bean were recovered. This crop has only been certainly found in Norse Freswick in Caithness, as is discussed in chapter 8. Arable weeds included Scarlet Pimpernel, Field Madder and Smooth Tare; the latter is a very uncommon plant in Scotland, largely confined to the Edinburgh area although it is recorded as an introduction, mainly in east-central Scotland. Later Medieval deposits may be largely reworked and are therefore not discussed here.

Although the Castle rock had been of high status from the Iron Age onwards, by the end of the fourteenth century when the wars against the English had receded, the Castle was rebuilt and became a royal palace. Unfortunately the excavation did not discover the 'royal middens'; had it done so a far richer and more varied diet would have been revealed. Sheila Boardman quotes Malcolm's *The Gardens of the Castle,* which describes the Castle gardens and orchards that extended along the Grassmarket and King's Stables just below the Castle rock. These were replaced by housing in the Grassmarket in the fourteenth century and other gardens had ceased to be by the fifteenth century. The kitchen gardens grew Onions, Leeks, Cabbages, Garlic, Peas and Beans. It therefore seems probable that the pulses recorded from the eleventh- to early fourteenth-century deposits were grown in the Castle gardens. The orchards produced Apples, Pears, Cherries, Strawberries and Plums; none of these have been recognised from samples taken during the recent excavation. The particular value of this environmental information is that a continuous record of diet and its changes through time is depicted from a site which had retained a high status from the Iron Age to the Medieval period.

Only two samples from the later Medieval periods, from AD 1325 onwards, contained sufficient bones to make reliable estimates as to the proportion of meat eaten. Sheep form a higher proportion than Cattle and were slaughtered at on or two years old to give prime meat. Polled sheep of about fifteenth-century date were noted. By the early twelfth century McCormick notes that there was a great expansion in numbers of flocks of Sheep. Monasteries in southern Scotland reared Sheep to profit from the flourishing wool trade, mutton being sold to urban areas. Sheep manure was sought after to fertilise ground for cereal crops. Pigs contributed smaller numbers of bones which included neonatal bones so they must have been breeding locally and McCormick states that they were a menace in the fifteenth century, roaming the town. Hunting was less important than formerly and only one Red and two Roe Deer were recorded; these could have come from the royal parks at Seton or Dalkeith. Butchered Horse bones, one of them split open to extract the marrow, testify to their use for food. McCormick suggested that they were eaten at times of food shortage caused when the town was under siege. In the Medieval period the town developed beneath the Castle walls and Castle and town were constantly besieged by the English until the late fourteenth century.

Jenny Coy and Sheila Hamilton-Dyer examined bird and fish bones. Domestic Fowl was present throughout the Medieval period with rare finds of possibly Domestic Goose and Duck and Common Crane. Fish bones from AD 1325-1550 consisted of a wide variety of sea and perhaps river fish. This included Ray, Herring, flat fish, large Cod, Haddock and Conger Eel, Salmon or Trout and Common Eel. The authors suggest that large members of the Cod family may have been traded as preserved fish.

St Andrews, Fife

An excavation immediately to the west of St Andrews Castle on the north-east side of the town was carried out from 1988-90 before a new visitors' centre for the Castle was built by Historic Scotland, which also financed the excavation (Lewis 1996). Occupation from about AD 1200 to at least the sixteenth century was found associated with the Medieval burgh. Plant remains were identified by Sheila Boardman who found charred small roundwood of only 3-4mm in diameter. Most of it was of Rowan-type with a little Hazel, Oak, Birch and Sloe type. This suggests casual gleaning of firewood in woodland or scrub. From the same sample came frequent cereal grains of Hulled Six-row Barley and Oats, some Wheat and rare possible Rye together with chaff and possible weeds of cultivation. An interesting find is of Peas, infrequently found in Scottish archaeology. The presence of wood, burnt peat or turf and Heather shoots and the cereal assemblage suggested to Boardman that it was a hearth deposit.

Nearly 500 mammal bones, identified by Finbar McCormick, are of particular interest in that Sheep bones were more common than Cttle bones, unlike most of the other Medieval sites which have been discussed. Pig bones were less important. The bones from a pit consisted almost entirely of Cat; these were immature individuals of between eight months and a year old and appear to have been reared for their skins. Dog bones from another pit seem also to have been skinned. Sheila Hamilton-Dyer identified 25 bird bones, chiefly of Domestic Fowl and Goose; the few remaining bones were of Gull, Guillemot and Curlew. The absence of butchery marks, except on one Fowl, means that it cannot be certainly ascertained that the wild birds were caught for food. Fish bones were of Cod and Ling with a few Haddock and Pollack; a single bone from a Conger Eel weighing no more than 3kg was recognised. The Haddock would have been 0.5-0.7m in length and the other members of the Cod family, 1.0m long. Hamilton-Dyer comments that these are very similar to those found at Rattray Castle. Head bones were present indicating that the fish were fresh or processed on the site.

Rattray, Aberdeenshire

Field walking can be a very rewarding occupation and the discovery of Medieval pottery at what is now a single farmstead at Rattray, alerted archaeologists to a possibly rich site. Aerial photography confirmed presence of a former settlement and it was excavated between 1985 and 1990 as intensive agricultural activity threatened to erode away part of the site. Excavation, funded by Historic Scotland, revealed a late twelfth- or early thirteenth-century motte with adjacent thirteenth- to fifteenth-century settlement. Thirty-seven plots were found and although Rattray was given royal burgh status from the mid-sixteenth century it was no larger than a village. There is very little evidence for such rural settlement in Medieval Scotland and so the site is of particular interest. Settlement buildings from the thirteenth century were examined and the sill and timber framing showed the former presence of a wooden building. In the fourteenth century a rectangular building with thick clay walls burnt down leaving charred Heather thatch over two Oak timbers. It is rarely that roofing survives as most buildings were of wood, which burns rapidly, and the roof is the first to burn away.

The community seems to have supported itself by making good wheel-thrown glazed pottery, using peat-fuelled kilns. However, there was also some imported pottery. Metal-working and wood-working tools were also identified, horseshoes and spurs were present. Bog iron could have come from the same area as the peat, to the south and west of the settlement. Copper-alloy cooking pots were found, chiefly at the castle site whereas sooty, coarse pottery vessels were recovered from the settlement. Aerial photographs showed widely spaced rig marks, and excavating indicated Medieval manuring near to the settlement. Unfortunately domestic rubbish dumps were not fine-sieved for plant material so it is not known what grain was grown.

Most of the bone was retrieved from the castle site and identified by Sheila Hamilton-Dyer and Finbar McCormick, who estimated that 86% of the meat eaten was beef, 9.2% was pork and 4% lamb and mutton. Most of the Cattle had been killed at over three years of age, similar to the slaughter pattern of Aberdeen and Perth. Bone pathology suggested that some may have been used as draught oxen. Sheep were usually over two years old when killed; at least two female Goats were represented and would have been kept for dairying, as probably would the Sheep. Evidence for dairy Cattle was equivocal. Pigs were slaughtered at a young age, at their best for flavour but less economically than when larger. Horses were present as singletons throughout the habitation, only one bone had butchering marks suggesting that it had been eaten. Pony-sized animals are indicated. Cat and Dog bones appeared be from skinned animals. Hunting took place throughout the life of the settlement with Red, Roe and Fallow Deer taken; Fallow Deer are thought to have been a Medieval introduction into Scotland for hunting. It is known that a hunting reserve lay to the west of Rattray; the presence of Wild Pig from a fourteenth-century deposit suggests a forested reserve. Hare and Rabbit were also caught.

Domestic Fowl were kept and hens still in lay were killed. Geese may have been of the domestic type and Mallard or Domestic Duck were less common. Peafowl are an interesting addition, dating from the period when a stone manor house existed on the site in the fourteenth or fifteenth century and Peacocks would have impressed visitors to this high-status site by their appearance but not by their calls! Seals and both large and small cetaceans would have come from the nearby shore. Wild seabirds eaten were Fulmar, Cormorant, Shag, Brent or Barnacle Goose. Others were Rock Dove or Domestic Pigeon and Raven. Fish bones were poorly preserved though some contexts were sieved and large Cod, over 1m in length, with Haddock and Ling were recorded. Shellfish provided little protein with a few fragments mainly of Oyster and Winkle identified.

Rattray appears, then, to have been one of the few high-status communities from which we have environmental information. It typifies the popular conception of Medieval noblemen hunting on horseback in the forest for Deer and Wild Boar. They imported some pottery and Peafowl to add status. It is unfortunate that we have no evidence for any imported foodstuffs though it is hard to believe there were none.

Kirkwall, Orcadian Mainland

The furthest north town to have been excavated is Kirkwall, the principal town of Orkney, which flourished as a Norse market town until it was colonised by the Scots and in 1468 was ceded to Scotland. A small excavation by N. McGavin in 1978 revealed dumped ground of mixed origin of mainly fifteenth- or sixteenth-century date. Imported pottery showed evidence of wealth as did Fig seeds, identified by Allan Hall. He also recorded occasional deeds and capsules of Flax and a few charred cereal grains. Wood identified by Rod McCullagh was predominantly of imported Scots Pine and Oak with lesser quantities of Birch, Hazel and Willow, likely to have been of local origin. Worked wood of Alder, Spruce and Ash and a bowl of Hawthorn wood were also found in middens. The few animal bones, identified by Ian Hodgson and Angela Jones, were of Cattle and Sheep or Goat with smaller numbers of Pig and Horse.

Paisley Abbey: a neglected drain reveals monastic life

The drain and contents

The Abbey church in the centre of Paisley now stands alone with traffic surrounding it. Founded in the late twelfth century, the Abbey was a Cluniac house with never more than a mere 25 monks but it housed numerous pilgrims, venerating Saint Mirren, the local saint, and many were en route via Crossraguel Abbey to the shrine of St Ninian at Whithorn (see next section). Founded in *c*.1165, the monastery was raised to the status of an abbey in 1219 becoming the fourth richest foundation in Scotland. There is no sign of the other Abbey buildings which were burnt down three times, rebuilt and survived up to the Reformation in the mid-sixteenth century. They degenerated into slums and were then pulled down and forgotten.

In 1990 easy access to the Medieval drain was drawn to the attention of John Malden of Paisley Museum by Frank Snow of West Scotland Water (**65**). The drain formed an extensive system, lined and arched with dressed stone in the fourteenth century. The accumulated silt and Medieval rubbish was cleared from one stretch and when pumped out, it proved possible to walk dry shod along the drains. The rubbish included artefacts of high status, with lead seals indicated that fine cloth had been imported from France, Germany, the Low Countries and London. These and many other artefacts of value dated

64 Medieval herbalist.
Sitting in his herb
garden, John Arden has
an opened cabinet of
medicaments and holds a
large dispensing spoon.
The drawing shows
perhaps six different
plants, none of which can
be identified with
confidence. From
Glasgow University
Library MS Hunter 112

from the first half of the fifteenth century. The records suggest that the silt from the river, which had been diverted to flush the drain, had accumulated at a period when two rival Abbots had been quarrelling and had neglected to clean out the drain, according to John Malden (1995) who has just edited a volume which includes two botanical articles (CD 2000 and JHD 2000).

Members of Glasgow University Archaeological Research Division collected a preliminary sample for fine sieving for plant material. Other samples were rich in bone. There was a mixture of habitats represented in the plant remains; some were from natural vegetation which had been swept along the river and some were from the Abbey's kitchen and latrines. An intact chamber pot was rescued from the silts. A second sample from another part of the waterlogged drain and consisting of a column through the sediments was also sampled and the two plant assemblages were compared. They were very similar and over 140 different plants were represented in all. Riverside and aquatic plants, plants of damp and dry grassland, heathland and bog showed the semi-natural habitats that the river had passed through. Arable and ruderal weeds suggested that cornfields also existed by the river.

Charcoal of Alder, Ash, Birch, Oak, Wild Cherry and Sloe type indicated that firewood had been collected from a species-rich woodland. Peat and coal were also found in the drain; the Abbey owned a peat moss to the north and their Ayrshire estates would have supplied coal. Gorse charcoal, from spiny branches gathered from heathland must have been collected for a special purpose; Gorse was particularly used in bread ovens as it gives out a fierce heat.

Monks had an allowance of wheaten and oaten bread and tiny fragments of Wheat type bran suggested that their flour had been sifted so that it was almost white. A few Barley grains remind us that the monks also had an allowance of Barley, sufficient to make two gallons of Barley ale daily! Ale was the chief beverage drunk in Medieval times, due to the lack of clean water, and any surplus food and drink would be readily consumed by the monks' dependants and pilgrims. Wheat, Oats and Barley were grown locally and paid as rents from Kilpatrick, a nearby parish. The Abbey also owned a mill in Paisley where the tenants ground their corn, and paid for the privilege! Abbeys were always ready to acquire more wealth and in 1451 the king granted the Abbot of Paisley 'full power of holding tavern, and of selling wines within the gates of the monastery, at the will and pleasure of the Abbot, without any hindrance or disturbance from any of the lieges whatsoever'. Paisley Abbey was by no means alone in enjoying a brewing monopoly on its lands.

A burnt mass of Bristle Oat chaff and straw may have been fodder and bedding for Horses, or thatch. Burnt weed seeds, which probably accompanied the Oat crop, included Hemp-nettle, Nipplewort, Scentless Mayweed and Pale Persicaria. Corn Spurrey and Annual Knawel are low-growing arable weeds of sandy soils and they suggest that Oats were deliberately cut low to give long lengths of straw. Local edible fruit were Elder berries, Bramble and Raspberry, Bilberry and Rowan. Bramble were eaten in nearby Glasgow in the fourteenth century as was shown by about 2,000 pips which Bill Boyd identified from a cess-pit sample. Hazelnuts were found as occasional shell fragments. One of these was adhering to burnt peat and gives a brief glimpse into the Abbey's social life as the monks sat round a glowing peat fire enjoying the nuts and no doubt quaffing their Barley ale. A few Apple pips and tiny core fragments and Damson stones were recognised. The Abbey had its own orchard of over two hectares just across the river. A fragment of Walnut shell and a tiny piece of a wooden artefact could represent local trees growing in a sheltered position. It is also known that Walnuts were imported into Scotland from France in the sixteenth century. Almost all Medieval urban and religious sites in Britain have produced Fig pips and Paisley Abbey was no exception. They undoubtedly represent imported fruit. It is not surprising to have found them, as dried Figs were given to monks after blood-letting, a regular feature of monastic life. No doubt the fruit's high sugar content helped to revive the brothers.

Vegetables and pottage

The evidence for vegetables is tantalizingly inexact. Two tiny fragments of the formerly green leaves of the Onion genus were recognised. Onions, Leeks and Garlic are all known to have been imported into Berwick from the thirteenth century. It is also known that Onions and Garlic were grown in Edinburgh Castle gardens before the fourteenth century. Leek seed was brought up to Scotland from Huntingdonshire, now part of

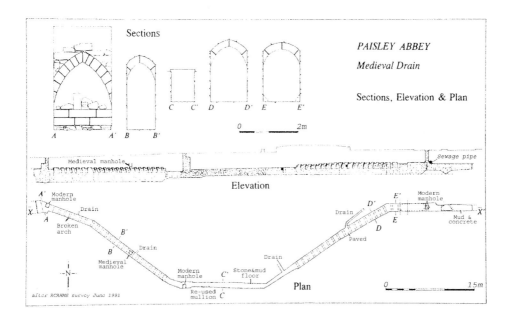

65 *The Paisley Abbey drain. The drain lies to the south of the Abbey and joins the river White Cart flowing northwards into the Clyde. From Malden (2000)*

Cambridgeshire, by horseback in 1296. This was obviously a successful venture as two further trips were made before the two entrepreneurs responsible fell out over the division of the profits!

The vegetable most commonly grown in Scotland in former times was Kale, sometimes known as coleworts, and plantiecuries; small enclosures for raising the young plants, used to be a familiar sight and can still be seen in parts of the Northern Isles. Kale could be sown at any time of the year almost anywhere in Scotland and, by successive plantings, would provide a year-long supply of vegetables. Kale also has the advantage of being a loose-headed *Brassica* and consequently a few leaves could be pulled at a time. A single Kale seed was tentatively identified but we know that the Abbey had its own kaleyard and pottage would be available, especially for any sick monks. Stock could be fed on Kale too. Poor people would subsist mainly on pottage with pearl Barley to thicken it and Kale and Leeks added in season. Sometimes a little salted meat or fish was added. In England, Peas and Beans would be added with Parsley for flavouring but these were less likely to have been available in Scotland. Another plant used as a potherb or salad herb was Monk's-rhubarb; see the account in Part 2. Wild Cresses of various species would be eaten and seeds of Winter-cress were found. Gerard, the sixteenth-century herbalist, considered that this was equal to Garden-cress and gave medical uses for both seeds and the entire plant. Gerard also noted that it was of use for scurvy if boiled up with Scurvy Grass. This observation is an interesting early recognition that green vegetables could correct vitamin C deficiency.

Medicinal plants

Elder, Greater Plantain, Nettle, Yarrow, Water Pepper, Wood Avens and Woundwort may have been used medicinally; all were found as seeds in the silt and all still grow in the Paisley area. Woundwort has antiseptic properties and the leafy plant would have been used as wound dressings as would the highly absorbent Bogmosses, also found in the silts. Bogmosses were used to staunch wounds on the Scottish battlefields over 1000 years ago. Weft-forming mosses were also used, as in the town cess-pits which have been discussed, for toilet purposes. Rare Flax seeds are likely to have been used medicinally as wealthy institutions such as Abbeys would buy manufactured linen. Greater Celandine seeds were an interesting discovery as the plant has been used medicinally since classical times and this is the first record of subfossil seeds from Scotland. The plant was formerly cultivated and grows along roadsides and near habitations in Britain. Its acrid juice contains alkaloids and in Medieval times was chiefly used to remove film from the cornea of the eye. James Robertson recorded its use in Scotland in 1767 when a 90-year-old gardener used to anoint his sore eyes with the juice (Henderson and Dickson 1994). On the continent the seeds have been found in a fifteenth-century monastic deposit in Denmark and in Germany in a thirteenth-century level close to a monastery. It does seem to have been deliberately planted in monastery gardens where it was used for a wide range of ailments.

A single seed of a Caper Spurge was recognised. The seeds contain an irritant oil which was formerly used as a violent purgative. Another plant with monastic connections, at fifteenth-century Elgin, it grew near the site of a Medieval monastery. In England it was recognised from twelfth- to fourteenth-century deposits at Reading Abbey and in a Danish monastery. Chaucer, the fourteenth-century English author wrote in *The Canterbury Tales* '. . . then your laxative . . . Caper Spurge . . . will make a splendid purge . . .'. other plants with a less powerful action were also mentioned by Chaucer giving an insight into what was collected from the wild for the do-it-yourself medicine used by the poor. Hemlock is a plant now widespread in Britain and is probably an archaeophyte in Scotland, introduced for its medicinal properties. It is the plant reported to have killed Socrates and there is no doubt about its lethal properties, again due to alkaloids, as reported by Cooper and Johnson (1998), whose characterised the occurrence and habitats as 'damp places, open woods and waste ground throughout Britain'(p220). Of these habitats, only waste ground applies to Scotland. North of the border Hemlock is strongly connected with waste places and roadsides often near the sea. JHD has never seen it in a wood. Used carefully, Hemlock has sedative and pain-relieving properties. An anaesthetic mixture in a fifteenth-century herbal (recipe no. 832) uses the juice of Hemlock root mixed with pig's gall and vinegar and taken in wine or alcohol. This was drunk before surgery, such as amputation, as it had a long-lasting effect. There are no records as to its success or otherwise. Apart from Paisley Abbey, seeds were found in twelfth- or thirteenth-century Perth.

As has been commented on previously, knowledge of the soporific qualities of the Opium Poppy go back to classical times. It has been used as an anaesthetic draught as well as for its analgesic qualities in some Medieval recipes and as a cough medicine. Seeds of this plant, imported from the Mediterranean region, have also been found in Medieval Perth and Aberdeen. William Schevez (*c*.1428-97) who was a cleric and the best known

SPICES	OTHER FOODS	DYES	OTHER ITEMS
Galangal	Saffron	Brazilwood	Drugs
Cinnamon	Figs	Woad	Claret Wine
Mace & Nutmeg	Olives		Rhenish Vinegar
Pepper	Rice		
Cloves	Almonds		
Ginger	Sugar		
	Raisins		

Table 7   Andrew Haliburton's purchase of plant products at Bruges, Antwerp and Berry 1493-1503

medical practitioner in fifteenth-century Scotland, described the uses of the drug. Two of the hand-written medical works which he used are preserved in Edinburgh University Library and the British Museum in London. Doubtless the Abbey had its own herbals but these would have been dispersed at the time of the Reformation. Similar mixtures of medicinal herbs were recorded for the fifteenth-century Dominican Priory at Oxford with Greater Celandine, Hemlock, and Opium Poppy present. From the strong connections with monasteries both in Britain and abroad, it seems likely that these plants were growing in physic gardens attached to the monasteries. This is particularly valuable information as lists of medicinal and other plants grown by the monks seldom survive in British written sources (**64**).

Spicy foodstuffs

We know something of the tastes of wealthy people of the Medieval period from their cookery books. Spicy food was popular and spices were added to meat dishes, particularly useful if salted meat had lost some of its flavour. This knowledge gave a clue to the identification of plant fragments of irregular shape and a woody appearance. They proved to be fragments of the arils known as Mace, highlighted in Part 2. Although used as a condiment both Nutmeg and Mace can also be used medicinally in small quantities. In larger amounts their narcotic properties can have harmful effects. The question is how did the seeds of drug and spice plants get to the Abbey? Rich Abbeys, such as Scone near Perth had their own ships but even so they would have bought from fairs such as those at Bruges and Antwerp. Some wealthy people such as the Prior of St Andrews employed a Scottish merchant, Andrew Haliburton who lived in Middleburg, to purchase goods on their behalf (Table 7). Haliburton kept a ledger from 1493-1503, which has survived, and information from part of it is given below. The goods were detailed by Innes (1860).

Haliburton's lists also included fine cloths, fur, clothing, books and feather beds. Monumental brasses, altar pieces and pictures, gold and silverware were also featured in his lists; no doubt for clerical customers. By the fifteenth century, Leith, now part of Edinburgh, had become the country's chief port, trading in particular with Bruges, then an international trading centre. Goods would be loaded onto packhorses for the west of

Scotland to be sold at fairs at Glasgow and Dumbarton. We do not know if this is the way that the Abbot of Paisley bought some of his luxury goods but it is already clear that goods from all over the known world were enjoyed by the wealthy, nobles, royalty and clerics.

It is known from the large number of animal bones found in the silts that the diet was a meat-rich one with joints of beef, pork, lamb or kid. Preliminary identification of fish bone by James Barrett included Eel and the Cod fish family. Cockles, Mussels and Oysters were also found; these could have been acquired locally in the Clyde estuary. The monks were in theory vegetarian but there is no way of knowing if the meat and fish were eaten by the monks or the pilgrims or both.

Other Medieval sites

Whithorn, Wigtonshire
c.AD 1000-1250

The early monastic town of Whithorn described in the chapter 7 continued to thrive both as a church and a developing commercial centre. A cathedral was built in the mid-twelfth century replacing the Northumbrian church. The monastic community supplemented their income from the pilgrims who continued to venerate St Ninian's remains and a market developed to fulfil their material needs. There was an extensive marine trade network around the Irish Sea and a strong Irish influence is seen in the artefacts although Britons, Northumbrians and Gaels co-existed in the area. From these and other characters it is clear that Whithorn was attaining an urban status which had been gradually developing since the early sixth century. Unfortunately no plant remains have been published from this period but some bones have been identified. Cattle predominate as they had throughout the earlier period; Sheep and Pig bones were present in similar numbers and Goats became possibly more important than in preceding periods. A ditch produced very high numbers of young Pigs; as Finbar McCormick and Eileen Murphy point out these were more succulent but were less economic to slaughter than larger animals. The same ditch produced a number of Domestic Fowl bones which, with the sucking pigs, suggested the food remains of an affluent group of people. A high proportion of Cat bones, also from the same ditch, were small and immature. McCormick and Murphy suggest that they were bred for their skins. This may have been a lucrative business resulting in a high standard of living. Fish bones were identified by Sheila Hamilton-Dyer who found three bones of Ballan Wrasse. This suggested that, as at an earlier period, fish was not very popular.

c.AD 1250-c.1600

This period extends to just beyond the Reformation. The cathedral was expanded and a graveyard developed. Early in the period the population moved away to the new town. A few pottery sherds from northern France and the Low Countries showed expanding trade contacts. Cultivation terraces, spade dug, were recognised but no plants were recorded. Bones were recorded from two intersections, dated to about AD 1500. For one of these the proportion of meat available from the bones was: Domestic Cattle 86%, Sheep or Goat

11%, Pig 3.8%. Red Deer bones had disappeared from the record and Pigs had declined in numbers. McCormick and Murphy suggested that this may have been associated with declining woodland; they note that acorns can play an important role in the Pigs' diet. Bones of Domestic Fowl and Goose were recovered with two bones of Mallard or Domestic Duck. Small numbers of a wide range of fish included Herring, Cod, Ballan Wrasse and flatfish, probably Plaice. Hamilton-Dyer noted that the numbers were still extremely low compared with many urban assemblages, which may contain thousands of fish bones. The excavator also recorded thousands of shells: Oyster, Periwinkle and Cockle. These may have been food waste or they could have been collected for shell mortar. A chunk of a glassy cylinder containing partly fused shell fragments suggests another possibility, as a metal-working flux.

Castlehill of Strachan, Aberdeenshire

When the mottes of Aberdeenshire were occupied, these palisaded wooden halls raised on low natural or artificial mounds, must have appeared superior to the owners of the dispersed small houses in the rural hinterland. Peter Yeoman noted in preliminary investigations in 1979 that Strachan, one of these mottes, was being seriously eroded by Rabbits and a weathered quarry face and in 1981 Historic Scotland funded an excavation. Yeoman discovered from a charter that it had been a hunting lodge, and coins and pottery testified to occupation from about AD 1250 for less than a century when it was destroyed, either deliberately or accidentally. The single-storied hall had been circular, apparently built of wattles, finished with clay daub and surrounded with a palisade. Three ovens or furnaces each with a broken circular millstone as its base were obviously rescued from the noble's watermill on the nearby River Freoch. Middens surrounded these ovens and they were subsequently searched for bones. Metal-working debris was examined by Michael Spearman who concluded that iron working took place during the construction of the motte and continued throughout the life of the hall. It may be thought strange that iron-working took place in a hunting lodge but as Yeoman points out in *Medieval Scotland* these earthwork castles, built from the twelfth century, were multi-functional. They operated as manor houses, forts and seats of local government where tenants would pay rents in crops and livestock. Many were destroyed during the fourteenth-century wars of independence between England and Scotland. They were the predecessors of the defensive stone castles of the thirteenth century onwards.

What can we learn of the countryside which supported these early castles? Fortunately it proved possible for Peter Hulme and J Shirriffs to analyse six pollen samples from the motte soil. Pre-occupation soil was dominated by Birch and Alder pollen with a little Hazel, Grasses and Heather and low values for ruderal plants. Seemingly there had been some woodland clearance involving Oak but little agricultural activity. Three samples from the primary occupation showed a distinct reduction in Birch and increase in Heather with increased agricultural activity probably of a mainly pastoral nature. Bill Boyd reported on the larger plant fragments; in the midden he found a few charred grains of probable Hulled Barley, Bristle Oat and weeds of disturbed ground with a few Hazelnut fragments. It is somewhat surprising to find that the low-yielding Bristle Oat had been grown but this may have been due to its tolerance of wet fields; the motte was surrounded by rivers and draining was not generally undertaken. Analysis of 41 samples taken for charcoal analysis, showed Alder to be the most abundant wood with some Oak and Hawthorn, Rowan type, and Poplar, some of this probably from the palisade. Possible large timbers were of Oak, with one piece squared off, and Alder. It would appear that lack of good Oak timber necessitated the use of Alder, which is not a durable wood but would have been plentiful along the watercourses surrounding the motte. A surprising find was that of Hornbeam wood; its timber is the hardest and strongest of all the European trees and one of the heaviest. Before it was replaced by cast iron, it was used for cogwheels in mills, pulley blocks, roller bearings and for many other uses where a dense hard wood was needed. Hornbeam is native in south-east England but not in Scotland where nevertheless it grows well. The wood may have been brought from the south as an artefact; it will be interesting to see if any other records occur of this useful wood. Unfortunately few bones survived; only 36 in total. These were identified by Catherine Smith and Ian Hodgson; most were of Cattle with some Sheep and one each of Pig and a fish.

Castle Sween, Argyll

Castle Sween is a well-known and picturesque ruin; it dominates the entrance to Loch Sween on the west coast of Argyll. It is thought to have formed part of a network of fortresses controlling the important sea lanes from Kintyre to the mainland. The excavation was carried out in relation to Historic Scotland's programme of landscaping the inside of the castle's courtyard for the benefit of visitors (Ewart and Triscott 1996). It was constructed in about AD 1200 with additions built up to the sixteenth or seventeenth century but no evidence exists for a contemporary township until 1693. A mill was in existence in the fourteenth century, presumably for the use of tenant farmers as well as the Castle's inmates.

Eighteen bulk samples from the thirteenth to sixteenth centuries were floated and wet-sieved by Tim Holden. Most samples were surprisingly consistent in content and some reworking is possible. They were generally dominated by Oats, most of which had been dehusked. The quantity of grain suggested that this was a cultivated crop although Wild Oat was present. The generally small size of the grain suggested Bristle Oat. A little Bread Wheat type grain was also recovered with that of Hulled Six-rowed Barley. Two grains of Rye were positively identified. Weeds of cultivated ground were few and point to the grain having been cleaned. Hazelnut shell was present in seven of the samples. Charcoal identified by Coralie Mills, from a probable stokehole to an industrial kiln, and dated to mid-sixteenth to the early seventeenth century, was predominantly of Birch and Alder with Hazel, Ash and Oak were also present; most of the wood was from reasonably mature trees. Such woodland is still to be found in the area at the present time.

The sample of bones, identified by Finbar McCormick, was very small although it does extend from the twelfth to the twentieth century. The bulk of the meat eaten was beef with Sheep or Goat generally next in importance. Pigs were of less importance although there should have been plenty of acorns for them to have fed on. Dogs were only found in a sixteenth to mid-seventeenth century context; they were of small and medium size. Both Red and Roe Deer were hunted. McCormick notes the absence of Hare but presence of Rabbit which he suggests may have been kept in warrens and semi-domesticated. Domestic Fowl was the only bird recorded in the Medieval period. Medium to large Cod were present, suggesting offshore fishing but shellfish were scarcely present until the post-Medieval periods.

Kilns at Abercairney, Perthshire and Capo, Kincardineshire

These kilns were formerly thought to be post-Medieval and generally not excavated. In Scotland where grain often had to be harvested in damp weather, it was essential to dry the grain, both to stop it going mouldy and to facilitate grinding as well as to stop the malting process in the making of Barley ale. Annemarie Gibson describes the process. 'A fire was lit at the mouth of a covered flue and the heat produced was drawn along the passage to enter the kiln bowl below a raised floor, usually of wooden or iron struts. The grain was dried on this floor on a bedding of straw or such like.' On mainland Scotland almost every farm had its own kiln before the eighteenth-century agricultural improvements although in the Northern Isles they continued in use up to twentieth century.

A kiln from Abercairny, Perthshire, and two kilns from Capo, Kincardineshire, were excavated and radiocarbon-dated. Owned by individual farmers, they were typically sunk into hillsides well away from buildings as they were liable to catch fire. The Abercairny kiln was found in advance of levelling a natural gravel mound. The upper part of the kiln was constructed of turf and further turves were found in the kiln fill. The floor of the kiln passage was covered with layers of charcoal-rich deposits with carbonised grain, the accumulated debris from a succession of kiln firings. Alan Fairweather identified cereals and arable weed seeds. The cereals comprised about half the sample with 60% of the grain of Hulled Barley and 40% of Bristle Oat, and Wild Oat also present in significant quantity. Most of the weed seeds were of Hemp-nettle, Red Shank, Sheep's Sorrel and Corn Spurrey.

The two kilns at Capo were revealed by quarrying into a gravel terrace. Roofing structures were present as a thick-layer of smoke-blackened turf which had fallen into one of the kilns. The turf may have been supported by a network of branches, now collapsed and burnt. The second kiln had deposits of carbonised grain up to several centimetres thick with burnt stems and fragments of burnt slats of wood. The corn had been spread out to dry on straw on top of the wooden structure. Most of the grain was of Bristle and Wild Oat with some lax-eared Hulled Barley. The most frequent seeds of the associated weeds were the same species as at Abercairny. As was noted for the kilns found in Perth, no Corncockle seeds were found. The radiocarbon dating for Abercairny was of eleventh-century date, that for one of the Capo kilns was of thirteenth-century to fourteenth-century date; the construction and close proximity of the two Capo kilns suggests that they were both of similar dates.

10 The present achievement and the future

Advances in the Last Thirty Years

In 1973 Jane Renfrew could write (p134) 'Figs [meaning whole fruits] are rarely found in palaeoethnobotanical material — when they survive, however, they are often remarkably well preserved'. She made no particular mention of dispersed pips and at that time few such pips had, indeed, been recovered from British or foreign contexts, even though about 100 years ago Clement Reid had identified pips from Silchester, the Roman settlement in southernmost England. Now the recovery of Fig pips from Roman and Medieval layers is utterly commonplace in Scotland, no less than elsewhere (Dickson and Dickson 1996). When pips were extracted from the Bearsden sewage in the late 1970s the Dicksons were delighted. Such has been the progress in environmental archaeology in the last few decades in Britain and other European countries that now the surprise would be not to find Fig pips in suitably preservative, usually waterlogged, or rarely burnt, contexts in Roman or Medieval layers. Fig pips recovered from archaeological contexts are in themselves a strong indication of the former presence of sewage. That is merely one example of how much information has accrued in the last few decades.

Mesolithic

Other than Hazelnuts, which are so easy to recognise, whole or in fragments, even by the non-botanist, the hard evidence for Mesolithic food plants from Scotland and even elsewhere is scanty. It is of course very probable that Mesolithic folk would have used a considerable diversity of edible plants, even if only seasonally and in small quantities. Referring to the Inuit and other indigenous peoples of Alaska and/or adjacent Russia, Eric Hulten (1968) has listed among many others the use as food of leaves, other green parts or underground organs of Bottle Sedge, Common Bistort, Common Scurvygrass, Fathen, Rosebay Willowherb, Roseroot and Scots Lovage. All of these are mentioned here because they also grow in Scotland, mostly or entirely as native populations now and very probably also in Mesolithic times, even if confirmatory fossils are lacking in some cases.

This list of plants which grow both in Scotland and America and are known to have been used as food by native North Americans is a long one, as consulting the recent volume on ethnobotany by Moerman (1998) shows. Apart from the plants just listed, Hulten states (p66) that the young stems and spikes (the dense inflorescences) of Bulrush can be eaten. In California the Indians used the pollen of this tall plant of fens and other watery habitats to make a kind of bread, the rhizomes were roasted or dried raw and ground into meal and the young shoots eaten (Balls 1962). A small group of Northern Paiutes were known as Cat-tail [i.e. Bulrush] Eaters (Law 1998) and, according to Taylor and Sturtevant (1992), the Northern Paiutes used 150 different wild plants. Far from North America, in New Zealand, the Maoris also made bread from the pollen of Lesser Bulrush (Cranwell 1953). Bulrush was present in Britain, though perhaps not in Scotland, since before the end of the last glacial period and was potentially exploitable by Mesolithic people. The deliberate gathering and eating of pollen as food has no history whatsoever in ancient Europe (Linkens and Jorde 1997, Dickson *et al.* 2000b).

Marsh Marigold is another common Scottish plant which grows in North America. According to Yanovsky, writing in 1936 (p25), its leaves and stems were boiled for greens and 'used by Iroquois Indians and in Minnesota, Wisconsin and Eastern States'. Like the Bulrushes, the Common Reed is a tall marsh plant, commonly forming large stands, and it may have been eaten in Mesolithic times (Law 1998). The grains were eaten by North American Natives and the Japanese eat the young shoots. Common Reed has a wide ecological tolerance but the set of good grains is very variable (Haslam 1972). About this grass, Yanovsky (1936, p8) states 'stems containing sweet gum used for food: Utah, Nevada, and Oregon'. Another possible wild grass used as an ancient foodstuff is Lyme-grass, a species of coastal dunes in Britain and in many other places including the coasts of the Arctic Ocean. Though the processing was complex, its grains were harvested until the early twentieth century in Iceland (Godmunsson 1996). There appear to be no British records indicative of Mesolithic utilisation of the Bulrushes, Common Reed or Lyme-grass.

Field Horsetail is common in Scotland and in north-western North America, as are Bracken, Lady Fern and Broad Buckler-fern. All are, or were, eaten by Native Americans (Gunther 1973, Kari 1995) and, if there, why not in Mesolithic Scotland? Perhaps the most likely plants, common along the coasts of both North America and Europe, that may have been eaten by Mesolithic Scots, are Sea Plantain and Silverweed. In Alaska, the Dena'ina Indians and Chugach Inuit eat the leaves of Sea Plantain raw or boiled (Kari 1995) and according to Heller (1953, page 45) 'This plant is gathered in quantity by many Southeastern Alaskans. It is eaten fresh, cooked and canned for winter use'. The Mesolithic Scots had no knowledge of cans but they must have encountered lots of Sea Plantain as they camped along the shores. Sandy shores often support Silverweed both in Scotland and the Pacific Northwest of North America. In Alaska, according to Heller (1953), Natives and Oldtimers eat the roots raw, boiled or roasted. According to Nancy Turner (in Pojar and Mackinnon 1994) the coastal Indians further south attached great importance to Silverweed as a food which when cooked tasted somewhat like Sweet Potatoes. She gives precise details on how to cook the roots. CD and Jennifer Miller tried eating some and found them not very palatable, though reminiscent of Parnsips which is just what John Lightfoot (1777) stated in his *Flora Scotica* as regards taste. He goes on (p269) that the roots '. . . are frequently eaten by the common people in Scotland . . . In the islands of *Tirey* and *Col* they are much esteemed, answering in some measure the purposes of bread . . .'.

One last item which should be looked for in Mesolithic and later layers is a chewing gum made from Birch tar. Clearly marked by young teeth, this substance has been found in Sweden dated to 4500 BC, and also in other European sites but not yet in Scotland or elsewhere in Britain. Birch 'gum' has been made in the laboratory and judged not entirely unpleasant (Aveling 1997). Was it used medicinally for sore throats or, as now, as primarily a habit of the young?

If such plants as have just been considered were indeed used by Mesolithic folk in Scotland traces may have been left, at least in some or even many cases. However, as more excavations take place, especially of waterlogged sites if such can be found, there is the hope that some sharp-eyed investigator will add to the disappointingly short list of food plants so that it becomes more of a reflection of what must have been the reality. Another hope is that evidence for coppicing may one day be recovered. If the Mesolithic folk in Denmark were coppicing Hazel why not the inhabitants of Scotland too?

The possible permanency of occupation at any one place is often considered by archaeologists studying Mesolithic sites The measurement of stable isotopes of carbon and nitrogen has been used very recently to bear on this matter for six shell heaps on Oronsay (Richards and Mellars 1998), the site discussed at length in chapter 2. The isotopes from human bones showed that marine resources had provided the majority of the consumed protein; this supports the year-round occupation theory. Neveretheless, one individual had a mixed diet of marine and terrestrial protein which suggests that there had been seasonal visits and different patterns of site occupation. For the whole important topic of ancient diets, not only in the Mesolithic, the use of such stable isotopes is a promising development. Combining the traditonal investigations of plant and animal remains with these new methods may prove to be the best way forward (Dickson et al 2000b).

Neolithic and Bronze Ages

Although mainland Scotland remained heavily wooded in many parts it is clear from the distribution of megalithic tombs and later henges and stone circles that much of lowland Scotland was inhabited by Neolithic peoples, if only sparsely. Later monuments, such as ceremonial enclosures and stone circles, seem particularly common in the fertile east of the country and rare traces of agricultural ridges remaining in the soil show that arable farming was practised. Settlements have been located but cereals have not yet been commonly found.

Even discounting the four types of driftwood from North America, the diversity of the woody plants recovered from the Skara Brae middens stands in great contrast with the sparseness now. This treelessness of the Northern Isles and the Hebrides has long been noted — for almost 500 years — and various explanations advanced, as these comments about Orkney alone show.

Jo Ben, 1529: 'Birch trees grow on this island [Hoy] and not in others, for the other islands are without trees'. (Hunter 1996).

James Wallace 1693: 'This [saltwater], with the violent Winds that oft blow in this Country, I think, may be one reason why Trees do not prosper so well; but if they have the same Breaches in Norway, I do not know what to say to it. Whether Trees have grown here of old; or, what is more probable, if it be the remains of the Flood, but commonly in their Mosses they find Trees of twenty or thirty foot long'. (Small 1883, p182)

James Robertson 1769: 'To what must we impute this want of wood? Not surely to the climate, for in Norway & Sweden which are several degrees further North, trees thrive extremely well; nor to the soil, for in one exactly similar, throughout Scotland, Trees are planted with success. Is the spray which falls on the Islands pernicious to the Trees? Probably it is, but then how shall we account for the large pieces of Oak and Fir which are frequently dug out of the Mosses? They undoubtedly grew in these Islands, which shows, that whatever causes may now prevent the propagation of trees here, these causes did not always operate.' (Henderson and Dickson 1994, p118).

Though climatic change, the great frequency of salt-laden gales, and the spread of infertile peaty soils over the last few thousand years will have played some part, the true explanation is now somewhat clearer; humankind must bear the biggest share of the responsibility by greatly altering the environment, directly by woodland clearance and indirectly by the husbandry of large herds of grazers: Cattle, Goats, Sheep and Red Deer.

The sites on the Northern Isles at Knap of Howar, Tofts Ness and Scord of Brouster are of considerable archaeobotanical interest but Skara Brae is outstanding in the long list of both macroscopic fossils and pollen that has allowed very detailed deductions about the environment and ethnobotany, including the use for fuel of driftwood from far, distant parts. There is no other Neolithic site in Britain that has been so productive. Though much remains to be discovered, the interactions of people and plants on the Northern Isles is well known and, indeed, very well known compared to the Scottish mainland where, while not quite alone, Balbridie has the greatest interest, with its distinctive long house and the discovery of Breadwheat.

The British tree and tall shrub flora is very limited and the Scottish woody flora is even more impoverished than that of England. North of the border there is no evidence that Beech, Black Poplar, Box, Buckthorn, Elms other than Wych Elm, Field Maple, Hornbeam, Midland Hawthorn, Sea-buckthorn, some of the taller Willows, Wayfaring Tree and Wild Service-tree have been native within last 11,000 years. That assessment probably also applies to all the Limes, but it is a neat point with regard to pollen values and the matter needs more investigation. Nor may Yew be native in Scotland. Given this very low diversity it is all too easy to think that the identification of wood and charcoal is not difficult but there are many pitfalls and charcoal in particular is troublesome. However, that is not to say that wood and charcoal analyses should be thought mostly too difficult to be worthwhile. The results from Skara Brae make that point abundantly clear, as do those from Lintshie Gutter in Lanarkshire. At that latter site, of the Bronze Age and well inland, seven types of charcoal were identified: Alder, Birch, Hazel, Oak, Rowan/Whitebeam, Wild/Bird Cherry and Willow. These are almost all that could have been reasonably expected to have turned up according to our knowledge of the local woodland history from pollen analysis. The total lack of non-native trees is very noticeable and the contrast with the long list from coastal Skara Brae is very striking. That no driftwood was recognised causes no surprise. Nor was there exotic wood of southern origin, in contrast with Roman sites which often yield non-Scottish woods.

CD's pioneering pollen and macro work on the grave at Ashgrove, extended and re-interpreted by JHD, and then taken up by others from various Scottish sites, has produced a fascinating imbroglio concerning the significance of pollen analyses of the contents of containers in Bronze Age cist graves. So far, it is a controversy that is almost uniquely Scottish. No such work has been published from England and, regrettably, the Danish work has been published only obscurely and incompletely. The great interest of

Meadowsweet and Lime is by no means just Scottish/Danish as the following quotation makes clear: 'A pilot study of a human coprolite from Birka, central Sweden, shows the use of lime-honey (Tilia) as a sweetener in food . . . Perhaps the honey was used in the local mead? The origin of the lime-honey is still an open question, it may have been imported from South Sweden, or more likely from Poland of the Baltic republics' (Moe 1998, p105). Furthermore, very high values of Meadowsweet pollen have been found in coprolites produced by ancient saltminers in Salzburg, Austria (Klaus Oeggl, personal communication).

More work may resolve the problem. What is very badly needed is a Scottish cist, or one elsewhere, which became waterlogged immediately after burial and remained in such a condition thereafter, like the Oak coffin with the beautifully preserved girl, possibly a dancing girl, at Egtved in Jutland, Denmark (Glob 1973). If such a coffin can be found in Denmark why not a flooded cist in Scotland? Unexpected archaeological discoveries are made over and over again. Who would ever have thought that melting ice, very high in the Alps, would expose a 5,300-year-old mummy complete with clothes and gear or that, as this book was nearing completion, a 5,000- to 6,000-year-old mummy (the local First People have called the site Kwaday Dän Sinchí = Long Ago Person Found) would be found in an icy waste at 1980m a.s.l. in British Columbia, again complete with some clothes and much gear (Nichols 1999).

If a cist is ever found in Scotland, or England for that matter, with superb organic preservation then, before any disturbance, the contents should be examined minutely in Holmesian fashion and numerous samples taken for pollen and macroscopic analyses. That may help resolve the issues. Beakers or food vessels should be tested for organic residues, as outlined by Curt Beck, John Evans and Patrick McGovern in *Minoans and Myceneans Flavours of their Time* (Tzedakis and Martlew 2000). Containers from Bronze Age Greece have been examined and traces of olive oil, beeswax (a good indication of honey), Chick Peas, Barley, Wheat, wine, with or without resination from Pine, as well as Terebinth, Rue and other aromatic plants were found. Conical cups revealed 'The possibility of a mixed fermented beverage comprised of wine, barley beer and honey mead'(p167). From organic residue analyses, McGovern *et al.* (1992) claimed the recognition of the earliest wine from the Neolithic of Iran; a stoppered jar had contained wine resinated with Terebinth. Some of these results are tentative or concern only very broad groups of plants. Nonetheless, such analyses are an important way forward and should be tried out on Scottish material. Again this may help to resolve the issues.

Engaging as they undoubtedly are, the ideas about Icelandic volcanic eruptions in the Bronze Age and Asian eruptions in Early Historic times, or large objects colliding with the Earth need more testing before the full impact on vegetational and social changes can be assessed.

Iron Age and Roman
Study of the organic remains from the Buiston and Oakbank Crannogs have revealed just what an abundance of information awaits the excavators of more of these water-logged dwellings which are such an outstanding feature of Scottish archaeology. The archaeobotany of Oakbank Crannog has added greatly to our knowledge of the economy

and ethnobotany of the inhabitants of the Highlands in the mid- and late first millennium BC. Spelt Wheat, Opium Poppy and Cloudberry were particularly notable discoveries.

No Roman fort in Scotland or England has produced more botanical information than that at Bearsden. The sewage-filled ditch contained a richness of plant remains from a single column of sediment unparalleled in Britain and perhaps in Europe. It is a richness that bears on imported foodstuffs, on crops, locally grown or not, and on the environment of some 2000 years ago, particularly the extent of woodland. What the Romans found when they invaded Scotland and precisely what their impact on the environment was are old questions. As written by JHD (1992, p157), 'Certainly as early as Sibbald (1684, 1711), 300 years ago, followed one hundred years later by Tait (1794) in very explicit terms, authors have assumed that the Roman army was confronted with a Scotland densely covered with woodland. In efficiently setting about clearing it, the invaders denied hiding places to the natives. Nineteenth-century historians repeated and embellished the story, though the geologist Geikie (1866), not so in awe of the Romans, presented a better balanced appraisal. In 1891 the story appeared again in Nairne (1891) though with some caveats. In 1913 Caddell restated the case in excessive terms and much more recently the credulous compiler Anderson (1967) credited the Romans with the accomplishment though he knew about the doubting Geikie (1897). Even in 1991, Scott tersely but uncritically gave this out-of-date tale of the Romans marching into a densely tree-covered Scotland.' In the last ten years or so, pollen analysts, notably Susan Ramsay and Lisa Dumayne, in producing well-dated diagrams from peats across central Scotland, have recomposed this auld sang which should never be sung again in its original version.

In southern and central Scotland, the late prehistoric peoples had made big inroads into the woodlands before the Romans marched and sailed up from the south. On Orkney, Roman sailors would have seen a landscape which had, for long, been as windswept and bare of trees as now. Peter Marren has already sung the new version, perhaps too forcefully (1990, p53) 'When General Agricola marched into Scotland, he found already largely treeless northern pastures, with scattered scrubby woods of hazel and alder in hollows and burns. The natives were already learning to live without oak. Only in the remote interior, among trackless glens and mountainsides were there still substantial remnants of the legendary Wildwood of Caledonia.' The Romans certainly carried out some woodland clearance but in Fife and points further north, if the arguments of Whittington and Edwards are correct, their activities allowed trees to re-invade, the very opposite of the old song.

As can be seen from Table 4, our knowledge of the environment gained from pollen and larger plant remains suggests that the Romans would have found most of the resources to build and maintain the Bearsden fort locally. Presumably this also applies to the other Antonine forts. Local stone would have provided the cobbles for the military way and the base of the turf Wall. Stone would have been dressed to build the bathhouse and two granaries. Well-grazed turf would have been dug up from local pastures to build the wall and the fort ramparts. Building timber and wattle would have been cut from nearest woodland, although suitable Oak for planks or boards would need to have been specially sought. Clay to coat wattle walls would have been dug from boulder clay sub-soils and, for thatching and tempering the clay daub, there would have been no shortage of Rushes growing in an undrained countryside much wetter than now.

Heather makes a springy mattress and Bracken has been used for animal bedding until recent times. Its use as absorbent flooring at Roman Vindolanda near Hadrian's Wall has been recorded. Firewood, trimmed from timber or collected from deadwood, fuelled the hypocaust and sparse finds of peat suggest that the local peat bogs were also exploited for fuel. There seems to have been a detachment of cavalry along the Wall, if not at Bearsden, and meadow hay would have supplemented Barley for fodder. Pearl Barley made into a soothing gruel may have been taken medicinally and Common Mallow seems to have been grown at the fort for its mucilaginous properties. Fragments of amphorae show that wine was imported. Barley ale is mentioned on the wooden tablets recording the accounts from the Hadrianic forts and no doubt was also available in the Antonine forts.

Of the food consumed, only wild fruits and nuts may have been obtained locally. All the foodstuffs listed in Table 4 were probably imported from the Mediterranean area. As meat was probably reserved for feast days, how adequate was the largely plant-based diet? The pulses would have provided protein, and cheese would probably have been eaten, to judge from the cheese-making equipment found at two of the Antonine forts. The staple wheaten bread and porridge would have provided basic carbohydrate, enlivened with various flavourings. Wine and probably ale would have provided additional nutrition, as would Figs and wild fruit in season. This fare would surely have been a luxury diet to the auxillaries of largely captive Iron Age tribes and not so very different from the basic Roman diet for the Roman legionaries. There are no complaints about the army diet on record!

Early Historic, Pictish and Norse

As yet the archaeobotanical studies from Dundurn and Easter Kinnear stand alone as revealing the plant foodstuffs from the Pictish heartland of the Highlands and lowlands north of the Forth. These studies have helped to make the Picts less enigmatic than they were once thought to be but, nonetheless, here is a gap that needs filling, when more sites become available.

The archaeobotanical work at Buiston has proved very rewarding, with the imported Coriander and Dill among the outstanding discoveries. The world was already shrinking; trade along the western seaways into Ireland and Scotland, as well as England, was well-established. As pottery is more durable than organic substances it has been found most frequently and Sally Foster (1996, p68) has mapped these finds. It can be expected that, as more high status sites of this period are excavated and subjected to bioarchaeological analysis, further evidence for trade will be uncovered.

Evidence for imports from distant parts comes from the organic dyes used for *The Book of Kells* (Meehan 1994), which may well have been produced on Iona in the seventh century. Meehan (p88) tells us that 'Organic mauves, maroons and purples may have come from the Mediterranean plant *Chrozophora tinctoria* [a formerly cultivated annual called Turnsole] . . . with a kermes red from the pregnant body of the Mediterranean insect *Kermoccus vermilio*'. The picture that has emerged of the economic life of the monastic community on Iona is of wooden buildings of timber and wattle enclosed by a bank topped with shrubs and small trees providing shelter from the fierce winds which besiege the Western Isles. The island would have been fully exploited with crops which would certainly have included Barley with its resistance to salt spray. Small herds and flocks would have grazed on the fertile pastures of what was probably a largely treeless island. Meat from domestic and wild sources was supplemented by sea foods and skins were tanned and made into shoes. Skins of young calves would have been used for vellum for manuscripts, although there is no material evidence yet for this. Metal and glass working was carried out in the monastery. This early Christian community would seem to have been largely self-sufficient, but had contacts both within Scotland and with Europe. This enabled the monks to obtain items which could not be produced on the island.

In the far north of the Scottish mainland and in the Northern Isles, it is fortunate that Norse, and pre-Norse (Pictish) sites have been dug recently with environmental archaeology as one of the main aims of the excavations. When we look at the overall pattern that environmental archaeology details for us from the pre-Norse onwards, it is continuity that is shown in the aspects of farming which we have been discussing. As was the case for the earlier Iron Age, it appears that in addition to domestic animals and crops, all the wildlife from the land, sea shore and inshore waters and additionally deeper waters, were exploited for food. The numbers recorded suggest however that these merely supplemented farm animals and cereals, to add variety, rather than their consumption as an essential part of the diet. There is the strong suggestion of a change of emphasis to fishing in the Later Norse but, as yet, we do not know how extensive that was.

We have many other questions to be answered by future work. Which plants and animals did the Norse bring with them? Did they introduce Common Oat to northern Scotland and how long did it survive in these soils which are predominantly of shell-sand before being replaced by the traditional Bristle Oat? Why did the Black Oat and Flax begin to spread in the pre-Norse period? Bristle Oat seems to have come via the Atlantic seaboard. Did Flax come from pre-Norse traders from Scandinavia? Was more grain needed to pay taxes to Pictish overlords and the growing church hierarchy? We need to fill in the considerable gaps in time and space in mainland Scotland to see if the pattern extends to areas unaffected by the Norse. Did the Norse introduce their own medicinal plants such as Garden Angelica growing in walled gardens? Did they bring their own breeds of animals as has been suggested for the Black-faced Sheep; did these mix with the existing Sheep to form new breeds? Perhaps DNA analyses could answer that question.

One thing that has become clear in this survey is that charred material and bone-rich middens are complementary to the waterlogged deposits where bones may have largely dissolved away. Waterlogged deposits preserve insects which indicate mouldering hay and decayed wood with an occasional Flea or Louse suggesting low levels of hygiene. Was this a Norse characteristic or did a similar state exist in Pictish houses? Evidence for dyeing and knitting as well as the preservation of wooden utensils, vessels and woodworking tools are another bonus from a waterlogged environment.

The quantity of imports is one of the features separating Pict from Norse. Although largely a feature of affluent farmsteads, wooden floors and the wood for the long characteristic Norse benches were all brought over from the Norse homeland. Fishing boats were imported but only painstaking excavation of boat graves will reveal their variety. The affluence of some of the farms can be guessed at from records of traded items, from post-Medieval times which are outside our remit. By the thirteenth century brightly coloured glazed pottery had become a status symbol relating to trade with England and continental Europe. What was the source of wealth? Was it the taxes imposed by the earls or did private enterprise reaping the rich sea harvest have a share in it? More house sites with household middens will be needed to answer these questions.

What becomes very apparent when we look at Old Norse farming terms and what archaeology and environmental archaeology combine to show us from the Norse period onwards is how much began or was reinforced by the Norse incomers and continued unchanged until very recently in the Northern Isles. Archaeology gives evidence for haymaking although all traces of the hay may have gone, in the shape of the tenth-century rick base at Jarlshof, identical to those used in Shetland in recent time. From botanical studies we have possible evidence for the infield and outfield system of cultivation which may have begun in response to a rapidly increasing Norse population and which continued into the nineteenth-century. The corn and malt dryers going back to the late Norse and rotary querns of Iron Age origin both continued in use until living memory. The short-lived horizontal water-mill at Orphir had its successors in Orkney, the last being the nineteenth-century Click Mill in Birsay. The soapstone baking stones at the Biggings, and their probable forerunners at Howe, replaced by iron in the fifteenth century are still used at the present time in a modified form to cook flat cakes on top of the stove. The Late Norse may have instigated the beginning of the fishing industry which continues to employ many in Shetland and its tradition of boats built in Norway.

This way of life, though exemplified in Orkney and Shetland, was echoed in the other crofting counties, Caithness, Sutherland, Ross and Cromarty. It may seem that this is the end of our survey of the changing life in Scotland but the developing towns, especially to the south and the associated rural communities tell of increasing industry in the middle ages in parts untouched by the Norse legacy. Before moving on we should perhaps consider how environmental archaeology of the Norse period should progress in the future. What should future research concentrate on? Although writing about Beachview in Birsay Bay, James Rackham's suggestions might well be applied to all pre-Norse and Norse sites. He suggests that, in order to assess the relative importance of the different resources from land and sea, the same large sample should be used to process both plant and animal material down to the smallest mesh size to retrieve the smallest item; 1-2mm for fish bones, smaller for seeds, in order to reconstruct the Norse economy. Furthermore these should be taken from a variety of different contexts to be representative of the whole site. The finds should be sufficiently numerous that 'each sample can be used as a representative sample of the individual food resources, or constitute a reliable presence or absence record'. It could be added that particular attention should be paid to distinguishing Pictish from Norse samples so that the distinction between these two cultures can be clarified.

Medieval

As is shown in Table 6, so much more is known of the archaeobiology of Aberdeen, Perth and Elgin than any other Scottish towns that they form a readily comparable group. The importance of Common Oat and Wheat is particularly striking and they seem to have largely replaced Barley, formerly the most important cereal in Scotland. Flax is present at all three, as is Weld, the dye plant. Hemp was recorded in Aberdeen and Elgin. Powerful medicinal plants were present in all: Opium Poppy in all three towns, Deadly Nightshade in Perth and Elgin, Henbane in Perth and Hemlock in Aberdeen. Although these narcotic plants now grow scattered throughout Scotland, none is native and clearly all are archaeophytes, introduced for medicinal purposes in the Medieval period or, for some, possibly even earlier. Fruit was gathered from the wild and orchard fruit was noted at Elgin. Figs and raisins were recorded at both Aberdeen and Elgin. Similar foodstuffs and other useful plants, such as mosses suitable for small-scale domestic purposes, were used in all three towns. Possible differences between affluent and less well-off areas could perhaps be ascertained if pits used exclusively by burghers could be found. These might yield a wider range of luxury foods. Evidence for imported luxuries is extensive, with dyed woollens and silk, imported pottery and other valuables, but only the figs, raisins and possibly Wheat indicate imported luxury foods.

Ian Hodgson has discussed the bones from Aberdeen, Perth and Elgin which mainly date to between the twelfth and fifteenth century. Because of the status as royal burghs, animals could only be slaughtered within the burghs and exported from them. From each of the three burghs he has shown that from age at death, a high proportion of the cattle were killed after at least three winters and many after five or six years of age. It is believed that Medieval Cattle reached optimum hide quality by five or six years old. Most of the crown's income was derived from the export of cattle hides, wool fells and wool. As Hodgson points out, Cattle provided a wide source of products: meat, milk, blood, horn, leather, bone, gut, neat's foot oil and fat for tallow candles. Scottish Cattle were smaller and more slender than those in England.

It appears that Sheep and Goats were primarily killed for wool fells rather than wool as an older kill-off pattern would then have been suggested. If milk were a primary concern they would have been slaughtered after five years of age as they became barren. Pigs were reared for varying lengths of time from less than a year to more than three years. The small numbers of Pigs has been attributed to the reduction in forests but, as permission had to be sought for pannage, this may have limited the numbers. Pigs could have been kept tethered in the backlands and fed on household scraps. Catherine Smith has commented on the small numbers of Pigs throughout Medieval Scotland. Swine were considered unclean in north-east Scotland but many religious houses kept large herds of them. It has been suggested that this aversion to pork goes back to Celtic mythology. Red Deer are predominantly of male animals and Hodgson suggested that this may have been deliberate reluctance to kill the females and so keep the breeding stock. For a period known for its hunting, numbers of Red and Roe Deer are low and it has been suggested that destruction of forests may have been a factor. Medieval Red Deer were larger than those of the present time, which subsist largely in moorland and so that does not seem the complete answer. When more high-class sites are excavated perhaps relatively higher deer numbers will be found.

Butchered bones showed that at times of scarcity Horses were eaten, even if it was only as dog food. Hodgson noted that Horses ranged in size from small pack animals to 'small, hardy riding animals'. Domestic Fowl and possibly Domestic Goose and Duck were present at Perth and eggshells were recorded from Aberdeen. Fish bones were seldom identified although fish must have been preserved and eaten a great deal especially in Lent and on Fridays in this Catholic country. Evidence from the bones bears out the written evidence that hides, woolfells and clipped wool were the main animal products exported and tannin pits add proof that this was undertaken in the towns. Hodgson suggested that the Sheep were of mixed breeds, which included the coloured Soay type. The type of Sheep present is relevant to the colour of wool produced and thus the suitability of that wool for dyeing. Large quantities of wool and cloth were retrieved from Perth High Street excavations dated to the twelfth to fourteenth centuries and some of these have been analysed by Michael Ryder. He notes that records tell us nothing of the appearance of Medieval Sheep. In the twelfth century there were clearly distinct breeds as fine woolled Sheep cost 10D each and those with coarse wool only 6D. Pigmented fibres were associated with coarse wool. From Perth High Street (AD 1150-1300) it is estimated that only 30% of the wool was dyed and that almost 60% of the remainder had some form of pigmentation.

The communal use of latrines and rubbish dumps, especially in the twelfth century when there was little class distinction in towns, means that it is not easy to distinguish between the diet of rich and poor. At Perth in particular, much industrial processing was carried out and it is not known what proportion of the beasts which were stripped of their hides and sheepskins were eaten. It is unfortunate that fish and bird bones have not, in general, been identified. Records show that the poorer people ate a great deal of fish, either fresh or salted down. Salt meat was eaten by all after the cull of animals at Martinmas (11th November) when the grass had finished growing. The presence of hay plants in the middens suggests that some animals were over wintered in the backlands.

The history of Peas and Beans in Scotland is an interesting one. They were imported in the thirteenth and fourteenth centuries but also grown on a small scale as at Edinburgh Castle before the fourteenth century. In the later fifteenth century parliament became anxious about the balance of payments and decreed that each plough team should sow Wheat, Peas and Beans. Pulses were also to be sown in small quantity in cottar's kailyards. This was quite different to the situation in England and Wales where these legumes had been grown from the Anglo-Saxon period onwards, having been introduced in the Neolithic period. The record for other cultivated vegetables is less easily established; this is due partly in difficulties of recognition. Leeks, Onions and Kale were chiefly consumed in pottage, a thick soup, which was still the staple foodstuff in England at the end of the middle ages. Pottage might be enriched with stock from boiled meat, poultry or fish. Different flavours could be achieved by the addition of wild herbs, especially those of the Umbellifer family. The wide range of potherbs and salads sown in England frequently included Parsley and some were used medicinally which were not readily distinguished in planting notes, to which we owe much of this information. As most of these would be at their best before flowering or seeding, they have not been recognised in Scotland. Seeds of cresses and sweet herbs, eaten in salads, should, however, be looked for in sewage deposits. Which other vegetables would have been used? From the records of Edinburgh Castle, we know that the wealthy ate Onions, Garlic, Leeks, Peas and Beans. Root crops were used in the late fourteenth century in France and, by the fifteenth century, Skirret, Carrot, Parsnip and Turnip had been introduced into England. We do not know how quickly these vegetables came to be used by the nobility and church dignitaries in Scotland. The headed Cabbage and Skirret are first mentioned in 1322. Harvey (1981, 1984) mentions that all ranks ate together until the end of the middle ages and so all would have partaken of pottage.

That fruit was grown in orchards is known from written evidence from a number of noble homes. Records show that Edinburgh Castle orchards grew Apples, Pears, Cherries, Strawberries and Plums. Medieval towns have produced Bullace, Damson, Wild or Cultivated Cherry and Crab or Sweet Apple. Imported fruit were dried figs and raisins. Such fruit would have been restricted to the better off as a pound of figs would have cost a labourer a day's wages.

Cheese was paid in rents but has not been recognised in the fossil record and so tends to be forgotten as an important food source in the winter months and a welcome change from salted meat and fish. In the Highlands, when the grass had grown in the high pastures, many of the cows with their calves and ewes with their lambs, were taken up to summer sheilings and their milk was turned into cheese. Perforated vessels do not seem to have survived and it seems likely that soft milk cheese was salted for the winter.

Spices were all imported, some of them at great expense, especially Mace and Nutmeg. Coriander has been found at Aberdeen and Mace at Paisley Abbey. Nutmeg has yet to be found in Scotland but is likely to be recognised if the large, whole seeds are recovered. Pepper and Cumin were paid as rents and their seeds should also be looked for. The Scots merchant Haliburton bought drugs but it is not known which they were. The most powerful ones, Opium Poppy, Deadly Nightshade, Henbane, Hemlock and Caper Spurge could all have been grown in Scottish physic gardens attached to monasteries and great houses and been collected at the appropriate time and dried for later use.

Before the great increase in tree planting during the last few centuries, much of Scotland was largely devoid of trees. Woodland clearance began and was first substantial at different times in different regions: On Orkney some 5000 and more years ago but in central Scotland only 2000-2500 years ago, before the Roman invasions. By high Medieval times, the treelessness of the Scottish Lowlands was established. Trees yielding long straight timber, suitable for roofing cathedrals, palaces and abbeys were becoming in short supply. For the building of Glasgow Cathedral in 1132, wood was taken from Luss on Loch Lomond and must have been floated down the Loch and the River Leven and up the Clyde to the Cathedral site. For St Andrews Cathedral, timber was taken from Clackmannan forest. For the peasants' wooden houses, a great deal of timber and wattle was used. Woodland was felled for ship building in Fife and Leith to build a fleet to suppress piracy. By the later fifteenth century, the government was alarmed at the lack of good timber and tenants were asked to plant woods and hedges but not to build fences; a surprisingly early conservation measure.

Cereals: Bread, Bannocks, Broth, Porridge and Ale

Six-rowed Barley was the main crop in the Scottish Neolithic period and both the Naked and Hulled types were grown, with the former predominating and the latter becoming

215

more common towards the end of the period in some areas. Rare grains of Oat, almost certainly all of them the weedy Wild Oat, appear at a few sites. Emmer Wheat was found at Skara Brae and at Boghead in the north-eastern mainland and it was grown successfully on Deeside with some Bread Wheat. There are few records of very sparse grains of Bread Wheat in Scottish prehistory and these, with all the remains thought to be that species from later periods, are in need of revision. Only then will the early history of Bread Wheat be considered as securely known.

Throughout the Bronze Age, Naked and Hulled Barley continued to be the principal grain, with some Emmer Wheat persisting in some areas favourable for its growth. Hulled Barley became predominant in the later part of the period. In the first millenium BC Spelt Wheat appears for the first time in Scottish history in the central Highlands at Oakbank Crannog where the inhabitants also grew Barley and Emmer Wheat. The site at Cyderhall in Sutherland is notable for the earliest discovery of Common Oat, along with both Naked and Hulled Barley and Emmer Wheat. The layers at Edinburgh Castle formed in the last few centuries BC produced Naked and Hulled Barley, Emmer and Bread Wheats and Oats. Both Emmer and Spelt Wheats are well known, as elsewhere, from Roman sites in Scotland, including three forts on the Antonine Wall alone. At the Scottish Roman sites they are likely to have been imports from the south. Barley found at Roman sites is more likely to have been the local crops.

Cultivation of both Emmer and Spelt Wheats died out in the early centuries after Christ if not before and in that millennium cultivated Oats and Rye began as crops. Though found at some Medieval sites and one Norse one, Rye was never a very important crop in Scotland. Both Bristle and Common Oat became very important, though the former is now of very minor significance while the latter has retained importance to this day.

Carbonised remains of cereals recovered during excavations have been familiar to Scottish archaeologists for many decades, because, just like other incompletely burnt material, they survive well in soils, pure carbon being non-biodegradeable. The strong blackness of carbon gives conspicuousness. By contrast, it is only in the last few decades, with the excavation of waterlogged sites, that the much less obvious remains of cereals such as bran have been recognised in the laboratory by careful microscopy after sieving. CD's discovery of the Wheat/Rye bran at the Bearsden Roman fort was certainly the first in Scotland and one of the very first anywhere. Needless to say, cereals are crucially important as foodstuffs for sedentary people but how exactly were the processed crops prepared by the earliest farmers and by their successors up to Medieval times — as bread, broth or porridge?

Not surprisingly for such a perishable material, no whole or pieces of loaves of bread have survived from prehistoric Scotland. Nevertheless, even the most delicate organic remains do survive, if only very rarely, and perhaps one day some early loaf, or carbonised fragments of such, will be found by some lucky archaeologist. Substantial fragments of carbonised bread has been found at Iron Age sites in central Sweden (Viklund 1994).

Regrettably, as yet no well-preserved ancient human body, like those in Denmark and England, has emerged in recent years from a Scottish bog and been subjected to careful archaeobotanical investigation (Turner 1995). If such a discovery is made, then there may be undigested bread in the stomach. Barley is unsuitable for baking into bread, as bread is normally thought of in modern times, but could have been made into bannocks, as Bere Barley still is in a small way on Orkney. The Neolithic folk grew Barley throughout Scotland and, to grind the grain, had saddle querns, which can produce a fine meal, and so they could have baked bannocks, as their descendants in later periods could also very well have done. Early ovens may be difficult to tell from kilns but a possible oven was discovered at Rinyo, on the Orcadian island of Rousay, by Gordon Childe (Childe and Grant 1946). For prehistoric people the hearth would have been the focus of cooking and Barley bannocks were produced there on flat stones. Like Barley, Oats cannot be baked into leavened bread but oatcakes could also have been made at the hearths when Oats were grown in later times.

Emmer Wheat makes an unsatisfactory loaf but both Spelt and Bread Wheats make good bread. During the Iron Age saddle querns were replaced by rotary querns which produced meal more efficiently and quickly. Cereals need not be baked into bread but cooked into broth, the thick soup for which modern Scotland is famous, just as it is even more so for the thicker, less liquid porridge. Emmer Wheat can be made into a good porridge, as CD's experiment showed, but there were not cultivated Oats in Scotland till the last 2000 years or so. When did oatmeal porridge gain its popularity? It may have been consumed since Oats were first grown but its popularity may have developed only in very recent times, indeed, after the period covered by this book. According to Alexander Fenton in his *Country Life in Scotland,* it was not until the late 1600s that improvement to the fertility of the outfields by liming increased the production of Oats. Not until the eighteenth century did oatmeal begin to replace bread and porridge of Barley, particularly in the lowlands but to a lesser extent in the Highlands and Orkney. In the far north and Northern Isles was oatmeal porridge first made by the Norse who may have increased the area of land growing Bristle Oat? To answer that question it may be necessary to analyse the burnt remains of food on soapstone potsherds.

The analysis of the coprolite from Warebeth broch on Orkney throws light on Barley broth. It is CD's interpretation that Barley had been used to thicken a meat stew. If such a thing happened some 2000 years ago then, why not from the earliest times that Barley was grown?

Regarding cereals, for Norse and Medieval times there is much of interest not just from archaeological remains but from documentary evidence for the latter period. As Duncan (1975) pointed out, the interpretation of the rural economy of Medieval Scotland, in terms of social and economic history, as yet, has hardly been written. He has, however, delved into the early documents. Until the eleventh century, he describes Scotland as a land of peasants, living in peasant towns, although there is little written evidence of any kind from the eleventh century. Towns flourished in the twelfth and thirteenth centuries but in the fourteenth century the wars against the English resulted in the destruction of Berwick, Edinburgh, Perth, Roxburgh and other smaller towns south of the Tay. In the fifteenth century these towns were rebuilt and the country gradually revitalised. Bread, pottage and Barley ale were the main means of sustenance of the poor. Bran from Rye bread has been recovered in sewage from Perth. Rye was imported from the Baltic countries, although Duncan records that it was grown in Scotland in the twelfth century and, on a small scale, in the early fourteenth century. Bread Wheat is more demanding than the other cereals, both in its demands for sunshine and fertile soils, and, north of the Tay, Duncan records Oats and Bere Barley as the only crops, although parts of sunny Moray probably grew some Bread Wheat. English Bread Wheat was imported as, for instance, from Kings Lynn but it is not known how much was grown in Scotland overall. All the bran of Bread Wheat or Rye found in sewage has so far been accompanied by Corncockle seeds, which have not been found in kilns drying locally grown Oats and Barley. The Corncockle may be an indication that the grain had been grown in England.

As Table 6 shows, Common Oat seems to have been the more prevalent of the cultivated Oats found in the Scottish towns but this may be partly due to the wetter, windier climate of the northern areas being less suitable for Common Oat. Bristle Oat seems to have become thoroughly established during the preceding period and it may be that the foreign merchants who did business in the towns were more accustomed to Common Oat, the better yielding of the two. Furthermore, the better drained, more fertile land in the south could have been used for its production. More analyses from town and country will perhaps clarify this point. Bristle Oat, though yielding a poorer harvest, gives good quality forage. Perhaps the most surprising change is how Barley seemingly became largely replaced by Oats. This may in part be due to the increasing popularity of ale, as brewing became a large-scale business in towns and monasteries. Duncan considers that up to a third of the Barley grown was used to make ale. Unless a brewery caught fire at the time when a quantity of Barley was being germinated for malt, and thus preserved, we are unlikely to be able to distinguish Barley being used for that purpose rather than any other.

As bread has been recovered only as bran fragments in dispersed sewage, we do not know its composition. White wheaten bread was expensive and mainly bought by the wealthy. Careful measurements of bran fragments would indicate whether a finely sieved or coarse wholemeal bread was consumed at any particular site. We have virtually no evidence for oaten bread; Oat bran is delicate and transparent and is therefore easily overlooked or destroyed. A little Barley bran from Perth is a good indication that that Barley bannocks were eaten. Together with oatcakes they could be baked on gridles, or flat baking stones by the hearth, to produce the traditional unleavened products. Ovens, needed for yeast cookery with Bread Wheat or Rye, were expensive to build and heat and therefore were used mainly by the burghers and the nobility.

The ideas put forward by the Dineleys suggest that brewing ale was an important feature of life in Neolithic Orkney and, if there, why not elsewhere in Britain? What is badly needed, as the Dineleys fully realise, is archaeobotanical and biochemical corroboration of their claims. As mentioned above, organic residue analyses indicate alcohol drinking in prehistoric Greece and even earlier in Iran. Much influenced by the Scottish pollen analyses, the Dineleys consider that the consumption of ale was widespread too in Bronze Age Britain and, if then, why not at all later times? Finally, there is the matter of Pictish or Danish or Viking Heather ale, first mentioned by Hector Boece, some four centuries ago, and most recently discussed by Charles Nelson (2000). If the possibility ever arises, scientific investigation is needed.

Conclusion

Had this book been written some 30 years ago it would have been a slim volume with little data to discuss, there having been very few substantial archaeobiological studies in Scotland at that time. This book has been primarily an account of the successful interplay between botany and archaeology, this concluding chapter began with reference to the great advances made in recent years and the book can end in similar vein. In 1911 in his wide survey of knowledge of the Antonine Wall, George Macdonald wrote (pp163, 165), referring to the construction of houses on the site of the Bearsden Fort, 'The fort, it is to be feared, must be regarded as lost to archaeology . . . . Twenty years ago the site was full of possibilities. Now it is unlikely we shall ever learn more.' If Sir George, as he became, could read this book the Dicksons would like to think that he would be very happy that his pessimism has proved to be unjustified and he would be gratified at the advances, in both traditional and environmental archaeology, during the renewed study of the fort. Redevelopment of the site allowed David Breeze of Historic Scotland to carry out extensive excavations in the 1970s. As discussed in detail in chapter 6, from the point of view of archaeobotany, the fort is now one of the best known in all the Roman Empire. In another 90 years time what further advances will there have been as more and more techniques are applied to elucidate the lives of the early inhabitants of Scotland?

If, as yet, little can be said about the ancient history of Scottish bread and bannocks, broth and porridge and ale, what about the two other enjoyable products which make Scotland famous on a global scale, especially in the last week of January each year, but far from only then? These are whisky, from the Gaelic usquebagh, and not an exclusively Scottish product but an Irish one too, and haggis, of disputed etymology, and again not an exclusively Scottish food but also popular in England till the eighteenth century. That neither has been discussed until the very last paragraph of a book of some 100,000 and more words strong, with much to say about drink and especially foodstuffs, is simply because archaeological investigations in Scotland have revealed nothing at all. Perhaps 25, 50 or 100 years from now these gaps will also have been filled.

PART 2: SOME PARTICULARLY NOTEWORTHY PLANTS

The plants discussed in this part are of particular importance for a variety of reasons. There are major woodland-forming trees, such as the Oaks and Scots Pine, all of which have been of great economic importance to prehistoric and later peoples. There are the crucial food plants such as the cereals, food plants collected from the wild such as Cloudberry and Hazel, imported food plants such as Fig and Mace, medicinal plants, some of which are toxic such as Deadly Nightshade, fibre plants such as Flax and Hemp, bedding and thatch plants such as Heather and Bracken, and dye plants such as Woad. For many of these economic plants a map is given, showing the distribution of each in Britain and Ireland according to presence or absence, on the basis of the 10km squares of the National Grid of the Ordnance Survey. Open circles show records made before 1950 and closed circles after 1950.

There are illustrations of most of the plants, many taken from a 1624 edition of P.A. Mattioli's *Commentarii in sex libros Pedacii Dioscoridis* issued by Gaspard Bauhin. The Italian Pierandrea Mattioli's large tome, which first appeared in 1544 was a herbal, a book on medicinal plants. Its great success led to many editions (Arber 1986). These illustrations are both artistically satisfying and of a high degree of botanical accuracy.

Both the formal and informal plant names used in this book follow where possible those in Clive Stace's *New British Flora* (1997), which is the most up-to-date standard account of plants growing wild in Britain (see Appendix 4). *Stearn's Dictionary of Plant Names for Gardeners* (1996) is a learned and readable account of the meanings of many formal names; it has been used for the explanations of the names of the discussed species. Mabberley's *The Plant-book* (1997) has also been consulted. It is an outstanding, concise source of botanical information.

Few plants do not have medicinal properties, real or imaginary. It is seldom that the precise archaeological context allows the archaeobotanist to be sure that the recovered remains had been intended for medicinal use and this applies with greater force the further back in prehistory the site being investigated. We do know however that in southern Europe such knowledge of medicinal plants was widespread and that it goes back some 4000 years in a more or less continuous tradition. Hippocrates, c.460-377 BC, is known as the father of modern medicine, and his use of medicinal plants was quoted and added to by Pliny, the Roman compiler, and others. When Europe suffered the unrest of 'the Dark Ages' this knowledge was subsequently kept alive in the Arabic cultures and later by the Christian monasteries. It was disseminated throughout Europe and copies of herbals were made and cherished by monks. William Turner's cure for baldness given in the following account of Hazel clearly derives from Pliny and Dioscorides, *c*.AD 40-90, a Greek physician in Emperor Nero's army (Gunther 1934).

In modern times much research has been done on the active ingredients of plants and many of these plants have been found to contain powerful drugs and are either still used or have been synthesised. Morphine, for instance, the most effective painkiller known to man, is still obtained from the Opium Poppy. Many other plants are still used in herbal medicine and their active ingredients and details of the ailments for which they are most suited are readily available. The books quoted here in discussions of medicinal plants are *Edible and Medicinal Plants of Britain and North Europe*, an illustrated book by Launert (1981), and Potter's *New Encyclopaedia of Botanical Drugs and Preparations*, a referenced standard work on a world-wide basis (Wren, 1988). The well-known *A Modern Herbal* (Grieve 1931) is expansive on past uses but has not been revised to take account of modern research on the often powerful constituents of these drug plants. The recent *Healing Threads* by Mary Beith (1995) discusses the traditional medicines of the Highlands and Islands of Scotland.

66 *This certainly shows a species of* Alnus *but not the British native one, which has flat-topped leaves. It could be Grey Alder (*Alnus incana*). As is true for all species of Alder, the drawing shows separate male catkins (cylindrical, mostly above) and female catkins (fat, mostly below)*

Alder (*Alnus glutinosa*)
66, 67

Alnus was the name in Latin and *glutinosa*, of course, means sticky and refers to the tiny glands which occur on the young shoots. One of some 25 species of the genus that grow in north temperate regions, this is a nitrogen-fixing, waterside tree widely tolerant of soil conditions. Wood of Alder occasionally to be found in peat-bogs is distinctly reddish, just like the growing timber, and is often taken to be Scots Pine. The map is misleading for the Northern Isles; all the present trees on Orkney are the result of planting (Bremner and Bullard 1990, Bullard 1995). However, the tree may have grown there before the prehistoric human occupation.

Both wood and charcoal of Alder have been recovered from many archaeological layers in Scotland from the Neolithic onwards. Alder responds well to coppicing and many multi-trunked trees are to be seen in wet Scottish woodland. The timber is durable under water and so has been used as piles for crannogs, as at Oakbank, and the wood makes good charcoal for gunpowder and is suitable for clogs. The bark gives a red colour in dyeing.

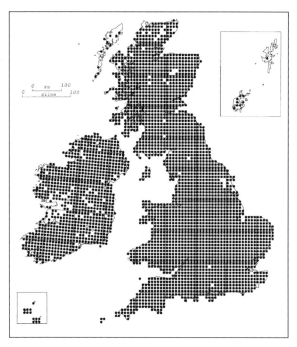

67 Map of Alder. All the localities shown in the Outer Hebrides, bar one, are planted trees, as are those in the Northern Isles

When James Robertson visited Sutherland in 1767 (Henderson and Dickson 1994) he noted the women making a black dye by adding Alder to copperas (ferrous sulphate). The leaves were used fresh or in poultices to relieve sore feet (Beith 1995). The staved bucket recovered from the broch at Howe was made of Alder. A small box with a sliding lid had been made out of a solid piece of Alder. Found at Birsay, Orcadian Mainland, it has decorated sides and as such is the only wood-carving from Scotland of the eighth to tenth centuries AD (Stevenson 1954). It contained six handles, the largest of which was made of Willow.

Alder pollen is a major component of Scottish pollen diagrams especially those from the mainland in the Oak region (**6** & **7**).

Birches (*Betula* spp)
68-70

There are three British species of the genus *Betula*, which has some 35 species in all in the Northern Hemisphere. The species, Dwarf Birch, which lives up to its name, has so far had no relevance to Scottish archaeology but the tree Birches have great importance, their remains having been found very often in excavations as wood, charcoal and bark. Downy Birch is *B. pubescens* and *B. pendula* is Silver Birch. *Betula* is the original Latin name, *pendula* refers to the hanging branches, and *pubescens* to the downiness. Their hybrid has the name *B.* x *aurata*; *aurata* means ornamented with gold.

The tree Birches are short-lived, fast-growing, come into reproduction quickly and disperse an abundance of winged fruits. Between them, they have a very broad ecology

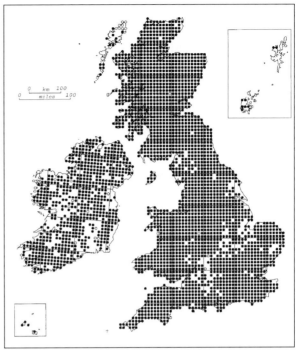

*68 A tree Birch. The drawing
shows only the pendulous male
catkins, though, like Alders,
Birches have both male and
female ones on the same tree. It
is unclear whether the drawing
represents Downy or Silver
Birch. Linnaeus did not make
the distinction; he recognised
them as one species — Betula
alba*

69 Map of Downy Birch

*70 Birch bark rolls. The longest is
45mm long. At the Norse site
of the Biggings, frequently
found pieces of Birch bark
included these rolls*

growing on many different soils. They are hardy, and Downy Birch in its subspecies *tortuosa* (a shrubby form) grows at the polar timberline in Scandinavia. It can be difficult to distinguish between Downy and Silver Birch and there has been a recent claim that Silver Birch is less frequent in Scotland than previously thought (Worrell and Malcolm 1998). See Stace (1997) for the means of separation, though the drawings of the fruits therein are very misleading. The map of Downy Birch shows how sparse the tree is at present on the Northern Isles and the Outer Hebrides.

Trees Birches grew in Scotland, if only sparsely, in Late-glacial times and quickly spread as the climate warmed up, and so they were readily exploitable when the Mesolithic colonists first arrived. The Birches can be coppiced, but they respond to pollarding very poorly. The wood can be made into household utensils, the bark into containers and into glue for fletching arrows, as the gear found with the Tyrolean Iceman shows so well. There are records of the Birch bark being eaten in Kamchatka and Fennoscandia, and infusions of leaves have been made in Europe and North America (Sturtevant 1919). Birch syrup is made commercially in Alaska and Birch wine is made commercially in the Scottish Highlands at present.

Stumps, trunks and branches of Birch are frequently encountered in eroded peat faces or by peat diggers; when on such a treeless place as the Mainland of Orkney they may cause some wonderment, as they have done for centuries (see chapter 10). Tree Birch pollen is a major component of Scottish pollen diagrams. However, pollen analysts do not distinguish the pollen of the two species of tree Birch and so the separate histories of Downy and Silver Birch can be disentangled only by identifying seeds and catkin scales.

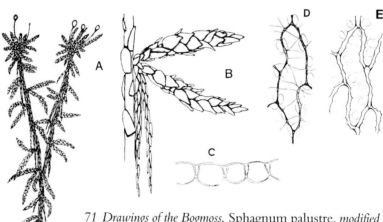

71 Drawings of the Bogmoss, Sphagnum palustre, *modified from Lewis and Anderson (1981): A. Stems showing the characteristic branching, overlapping leaves and spore capsules. B. Magnified portion showing the different leaves on the main axis and on the side branches. C. Transverse section of a branch leaf showing the differentiation into narrow and broad cells. D and E. Cells of the upper and lower surfaces of a branch leaf showing the broad, water-holding cells, with pores, and the narrow cells, which are photosynthetic*

72 Map of Bogmoss. The map shows Sphagnum palustre, *one of the Bogmosses which inhabit wet woodlands*

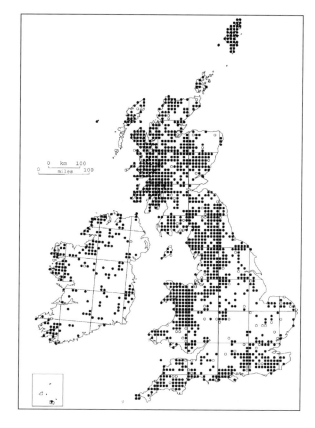

Bogmosses (*Sphagnum* spp)
71-73

Mosses of the large genus *Sphagnum* are often called Bogmoss for the very good reason that their principal habitat is those mires, which are mostly very acid, peat-forming mires, loosely referred to as bogs, where they can be major components of the vegetation. *Sphagnum* (the Greek designation of an unknown plant) is almost the only moss with a widely used common name.

Bogmosses are often recovered from archaeological contexts and a good example very relevant to this book is the occurrence of numerous leafy shoots of *Sphagnum palustre* inside the cist at Ashgrove, along with lesser amounts of *Hylocomium splendens*, a moss with no common name though it is both abundant and distinctive and has a great many archaeological records from Britain and elsewhere. This particular species of Bogmoss grows in wetlands and often in wet woodlands of Birch, Willow and Alder and occurs throughout Britain, as the map shows.

That Bogmoss should be found in a grave has immediate archaeological interest because its use as a wound dressing extends right down to the modern era. It was used in both World Wars for such a purpose. The shape and anatomy of the Bogmoss stems and leaves give it a great water-holding capacity and its chemistry is such as to increase markedly the acidity of its watery surroundings. Its efficacy as a dressing is clear, not just

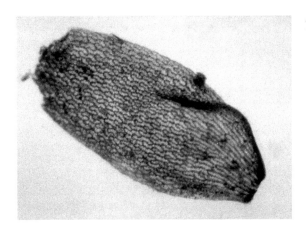

73 A single leaf of Sphagnum *from the early fifteenth century silts in the Paisley Abbey drain. The leaf is about 1mm long*

in its absorbency but because many bacteria do not thrive under strongly acidic conditions. Apart from their use as dressings, Bogmosses have been used for excretory and menstrual hygiene. Native peoples of north-western North America use Bogmosses in just these ways (Turner 1998). The Dena'ina Indians of Alaska differentiate between Red Bogmoss and White (i.e. non-red) Bogmoss; the former is used as a medicinal plant and the latter for hygiene (nappies, toilet paper and menstrual pads; Kari 1995). The deliberate selection of different species of Bogmoss for different purposes by the Indians of British Columbia has been discussed by Gottesfeld and Vitt (1996), who state (p106) that Bogmoss 'is generally considered to be superior to cloth diapers [nappies] for preventing diaper rash . . .'. Tahlan women of British Columbia 'about to be confined for childbearing, gathered and stored large quantities of Sphagnum. They used it to carpet the lodge in which the baby was to be born, to wipe the newborn baby's skin and to line the bark cradle.'(Turner 1998, p59). Bogmosses are readily available all over Scotland now and would have been even more so in the past before the many drainage schemes, both minor and major, in recent centuries. They could well have been used in the ways just described. According to Mary Beith (1995, p244), Bogmoss was used for sore feet in the Highlands where '. . . as well as alder leaves, fomentations of warm water in which sphagnum had been simmered made a popular rub for travellers' weary limbs before going to bed'.

An engaging plausibility as it may seem, and indeed to some a certainty (Darwin 1996), the thought that the young man interred in the Ashgrove cist had died of wounds staunched with Bogmoss must remain unsubstantiated until even more convincing discoveries are made. The Bogmoss from Ashgrove is not the only Bogmoss recovered from a Bronze Age burial; two cremation urns from near Edinburgh contained spores of Bogmoss that may have derived from leafy stems inserted deliberately.

Spores of the Bogmosses are very often found in greatly fluctuating amounts in analyses from peat-bogs, as in the raised bog peats at Flanders Moss and Walls Hill (**6** & **7**). There may be more than ten species growing on any one bog surface; some do not produce spores regularly but some do, while others release spores only very rarely if at all.

74 *Mass of compacted Bracken fronds from Dundurn. The smooth stems are about 10mm broad*

Bracken (*Pteridum aquilinum*)
74, 75

The name *Pteridium* combines the Greek for fern and wing, and *aquilinum* means eagle-like. This tall-growing, genetically very variable fern is often stated to be cosmopolitan and there have been many attempts to erect subspecies and other taxa below the rank of species. As the map shows, Bracken occurs throughout Britain; it is limited by frostiness, waterlogging of soil and fierce windiness. Probably in no other part of the world does Bracken flourish as it does in the highland zone of Britain. Occurring mostly as long-lived, poisonous clones, with fronds sometimes up to 2m tall, Bracken is one of the most conspicuous plants in Scotland where, especially on rough hillsides, it can grow in vast, impenetrable profusion, greatly to the detriment of grazing for Sheep and other large herbivores. Many scientists have devoted much or all of their careers in attempts to eradicate it, so far without much success. Now it is thought of as a pestilential weed not just by farmers but also conservationists, who wish to stop its invasion of species-rich pasture where it can overwhelm Orchids or other rarities. Few plants can survive under its dense canopy and the long-persistent litter of the dead fronds. By contrast in the past, not just the prehistoric past but even the very recent past, Bracken was put to a great variety of uses, which have been very thoroughly discussed by Rymer (1976) in one of the many published symposia concerning the biology and control of Bracken.

A few small pieces of frond were recovered from the Skara Brae middens and so it seems likely it had been put to some use which, however, must remain unclear. By contrast the excavation of the crannog at Oakbank in Loch Tay produced very large amounts of the fronds which had perhaps been used as bedding or thatch or both, two of the major uses to which this fern may well have been put again and again throughout prehistory and in later times. As late as 1777 John Lightfoot noted that the Highlanders (p659) '. . . thatched their houses with the stalks of this fern, and fastened them down with ropes made of either birch-bark or heath. Sometimes they used the whole plant for the same purpose but that does not make so durable a covering.'

Another example of finds of massive quantities of fronds was in the midden at Dundurn, the Pictish stronghold in Perthshire (see chapter 7). In the days when Bracken

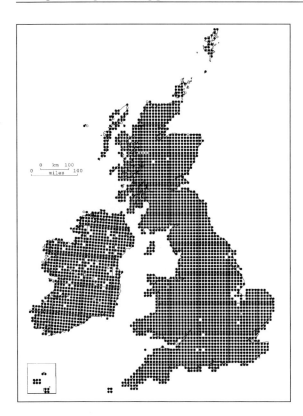

75 Map of Bracken

was much used, frequent cutting of the fronds may have helped to keep it in check; cutting has to be persistently recurrent over years to have a debilitating effect. Before Sheep became so numerous on the Scottish hillsides in the last 250 years, with a concomitant reduction in Cattle, trampling by the larger beasts would have helped keep Bracken in check.

Bracken has large, black-coloured, deep-seated rhizomes, which can be removed to the extent of tonnes per hectare. Both the fronds and the rhizomes have been, or still are, eaten by humans such as the Moaris, the First Nations of North American, Canary Islanders and the Japanese. There is, however, substantial evidence that to do so is to risk developing cancer.

Its supposed medicinal uses were engagingly listed by Rymer (1976, p170) who quoted Langham (1579):

> '. . . Burnings, Catteel galled, Festers, Gnats, Horsesicke, Kanker, Miltpaine, Mother suffocat, Nosebleeding, Purgation, Sinewes griefes, Skinne off, Sores, Wormes, Wounds . . . . '

The spores of Bracken are readily recognisable, though the too casual beginner might confuse them with those of Bogmoss and *vice versa*. Many pollen diagrams document its Holocene history, which is that of a plant benefiting from human disturbance and its curves often more or less parallel those of the pollen of Ribwort Plantain and Grasses.

228

Broad Bean (*Vicia faba*)
76, 77

This is a plant brought into cultivation millennia ago and, as engagingly discussed by Simoons (1998), subject to a Pythagorean ban which was not necessarily connected with favism, the hemolytic disease. Originally small and dark-seeded, unlike the large and light coloured seeds of modern cultivars, this is the familiar, hardy Bean very often grown in vegetable gardens and not just in recent times. It was part of the Medieval crop rotation. In 1568 the herbalist William Turner thought that 'This pulse is so well known in all countries, that it needeth no description'. *Vicia* was the Latin name for some leguminous plants, plants of the large, nitrogen-fixing family Leguminose, now more usually called Fabaceae. *Faba* was the Latin name for this very species. Broad Bean is an upright plant, unlike many of the more than fifty tendril-bearing species of the genus in Europe, which are scrambling herbs. Other vernacular names are Celtic Bean, Field Bean, Horse Bean, Fava or Faba Bean, and Tick Bean. Broad Bean and other pulses such as Pea (*Pisum sativum*) are

76 Broadbean

rich in protein. According to Zohary and Hopf (1993) the wild ancestor is still unknown but Mabberley states that it is usually considered as derived from *Vicia narbonensis,* which is found from southern Europe to Central Asia.

The Field Bean is the forerunner of the Broad Bean which evolved from it in the early Middle Ages. Field Beans are still grown in Scotland as a forage crop. The small brown beans need to be well cooked to be edible. Beans (and Peas) have been recorded in England from the Neolithic period onwards (often recorded as var. *minor*). Seeds of pulses are not usually found in quantity; because they do not require to be dried they are less likely to become accidentally charred. The two seeds from Late Norse Freswick are the first to be found in Norse sites in Scotland, although they have been recorded by Siobhán Geraghty from Norse Dublin, Ireland. Very few seeds were recovered from Edinburgh Castle AD (1000-1325); these and those from Freswick are the earliest finds to be published from Scotland. Further evidence for Norse use of these Beans comes from Knut Krzywinski who recognised the pollen from a tenth-century latrine in Bergen, Norway. He concluded that the flowers, their remains presumably still attached to young pods, had been cooked and eaten, or the pollen had been adhering to the pods. Broad Bean pods are sometimes eaten young at the present time. The flowers are insect-pollinated so little pollen is liberated into the air. Pollen analyses from rare waterlogged middens, or latrines, could produce similar evidence for Scotland. In Norse times, then, this Bean could have come direct from Norway or possibly by way of trade from the east coast of Scotland.

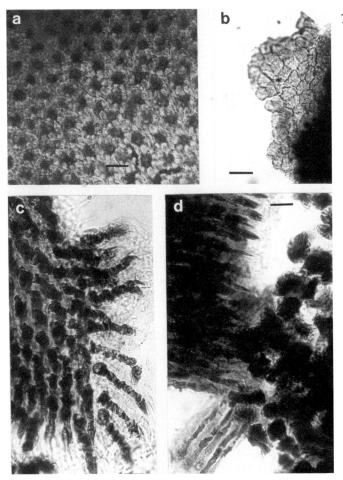

77 *Remains of Broadbean*
a. Palisade cells of seed
coat of a modern seed
b, c & d. Cuticle, palisade
and subepidermal cells of
a seed from the Bearsden
Fort

Cereals: Barley (*Hordeum vulgare*)
78-80

1498. Don Pedro de Ayala, Spanish ambassador at the court of James IV. 'On the islands there are many flocks and great quantities of barley' (Hume Brown 1891, p46).

1689. Rev Thomas Morer, English vicar. 'Their harvest is very great of oats and barly, which is the more common and flourishing grain of the country . . . Not but they have beans, pease, and some wheat likewise . . . but the oats and barly are most in request, as on which they chiefly depend: on the first for bread, on the other for drink, which is sometimes strong enough to arm 'em against the coldness of the climate. And of their barly there are two sorts; one of which has double ears, and they call it beer: this they make their malt of . . .' (Hume Brown 1891, p267).

From archaeological layers, cereals can be recovered as pollen, phytoliths, grain, bran, awns, chaff, partial or whole ears, carbonised or not, and as organic residues from, and impressions on, pottery. Carbonised cereal grains in small or large numbers have been found over and over again in archaeological sites in Scotland, no less than elsewhere.

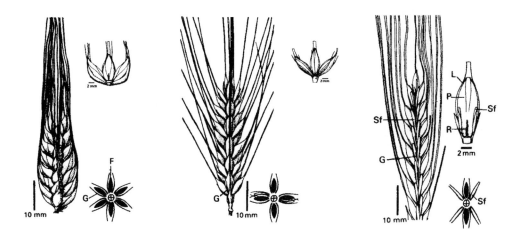

78 *Ears and spikelets of Barley modified from Bell (1998). The full length of the awns is not shown. Left: Complete ear of Six-rowed Barley, with, top, cluster of three spikelets and, bottom, spikelet layout. G=glume and F=floret. Centre: Complete ear of Bere, with, top, cluster of three spikelets and, bottom, spikelet layout. Right: Partial ear of Two-rowed Barley with, top, cluster of three spikelets and, bottom, spikelet layout. L=lemma, P=palea, R=end of axis bearing spikelets and Sf=sterile floret*

Barley is the most important cereal crop in Scotland today and so it has been throughout the thousands of years since Neolithic times. Because of their enormous economic importance cereals have been much studied, using more and more complex techniques and, as is often the case when there is a great deal of taxonomic knowledge, the classification can become highly detailed, with various opinions about the ranking of the very many forms in cultivation. Cereals are anciently domesticated, annual Grasses, which with the other Grasses, belong to the family Gramineae, now often called Poaceae.

Barleys comprise about 20 wild species as well as the cultivated species in the genus *Hordeum*, which is the original Latin name. For the crop Barleys, a modern grouping as outlined by Zohary and Hopf (1993) is as follows:

Hordeum vulgare subspecies *spontaneum* (Wild Barley, native of the Middle East)
H. vulgare subspecies *distichon* (Two-rowed Barley, originated in cultivation)
H. vulgare subspecies *vulgare* (Six-rowed Barley, originated in cultivation)

These subspecies are often given full specific rank, as in Stace (1997).

The structure of the flowers and inflorescences (heads of flowers) of Grasses is very complex. The basic structural unit of the normally many-flowered heads of cereals (and other Grasses) is called a spikelet (**78**). In cereals, the infructescences (ripened inflorescences) are referred to as ears. The seeds, often referred to as grain, are technically called caryopses (a caryopsis is a distinctive, multi-layered type of fruit peculiar to the Grasses). The grains in a spikelet are enclosed by layers of chaff (technically paleas,

231

79 Carbonised ears of Naked Six-rowed Barley from Howe Broch. Scale bar in cm

lemmas and glumes, the outermost of which may have long narrow projections called awns). If the grain is more or less fused with the chaff it is referred to as hulled and if not so fused is called naked. Wild Barley is hulled, as are most but not all of the very many cultivated forms. In Barley the spikelets are in groups of three placed alternately along the stalk. In Two-rowed Barley only the middle spikelet in each group produces a ripe grain and so the head appears to have two rows, whereas, in Six-rowed Barley, all the spikelets ripen. Apart from Oats, all the cereals discussed in this book have the spikelets arranged in dense, narrow ears. The stalk that bears the spikelets is technically called the rachis, which, when the ear is ripe, can be brittle or not. The cultivated Barleys are non-brittle; the rachis does not break into short segments.

That cereal which has been most often reported from Scottish prehistoric and historic sites is Hulled Six-rowed Barley, usually found as carbonised grain. The Barley much cultivated nowadays is Hulled Two-rowed Barley. However, a form of Six-rowed Barley called Bere is still grown on Orkney where according to Miller (1976, p150) 'Official statistics, unfortunately, do not distinguish between the old "Arctic" barley (bere or bear) and the new two-row fodder barley, but we can trace a decline from 3471 acres in 1923, when bere-meal was still a popular human food, either as bannocks or ale, to 2065 in 1939 and a mere 897 in 1960'. Even in the 1990s, Bere is still grown in small quantity for the baking of bere bannocks which are a circular, flat type of bread, peculiar to Orkney. Birsay is the remaining area where Bere Barley, sometimes called Four-rowed Barley, is still grown. According to Scott and Palmer (1987, p365) 'Bear, along with *Avena strigosa* [Bristle Oat, often called Black Oat] remained staple cereal crops in Shetland for many centuries, indeed until the first half of the present century, when both had been largely replaced by *Avena sativa* [Oat]'. On Skye in 1768 James Robertson noted '. . . very good black Oats, four row'd barley & a good quantity of

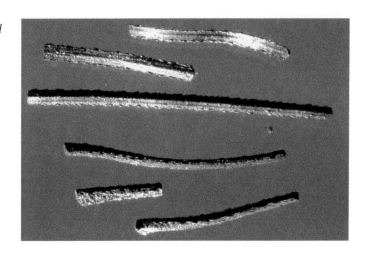

80 Fragments of carbonised awns of a Barley (top) and a Wheat (bottom), from Old Kilpatrick crannog. The longest fragment is a few cm long

potatoes . . .' (Henderson and Dickson 1994). The Barley he listed is Bere, because in Bere the heads are arranged in such a way that there appear to be four rows although all the spikelets are fertile. In his reports on the Hebrides of 1764 and 1771 the Rev John Walker noted the cultivation of Bere as well as of Bristle (Black) Oat on the many islands he visited (McKay 1980).

Barley is a hardy cereal, widely tolerant of soil conditions, including even slight salinity, but best suited to fertile, deep loams. The hardiest forms grow as far north as 70°N in Norway. Barley is crucial in the production of beer and whisky, very important activities in Scotland. Bere and Bristle Oat were the grains traditionally grown in Scotland. Oats were sown from mid-March to April and Bere from late April to May; harvesting was from September to October. Barley needs fertilising to produce good crops and was grown in the infield, the land nearest to the farmstead. After harvesting the stock was let into these arable fields which consequently were dunged; seaweed, if available, ashes and household refuse from the midden would also be added. The infield was manured annually for the Bere to ensure the best yields as tax was paid in Bere. The outfield, further from the settlement, was used to grow Bristle Oat; it only received dung if there was some to spare and was sometimes left fallow for alternate years. Bristle Oat is more weather resistant and will also ripen in the stook. It will grow in the lime-rich machair soils which predominate in the coastal settlements of the Western Isles. The better yielding Common Oat grows well in drier soils but not in shell sand where there is a manganese deficiency which needs correcting with an acid fertiliser. Consequently it was not commonly grown until improved drainage became widely practised in the eighteenth century and acid fertilisers were introduced in the nineteenth century.

Bere and Bristle Oat remained the staple cereals in much of Scotland until the nineteenth century. Bristle Oat is still grown for fodder in remote areas of Shetland (see chapter 8). Bread Wheat and Rye have been tried there but have not been successful as the summers are too cool. Poor summers and autumn gales can still ruin crops in Orkney where there is a much higher proportion of good arable land than in Shetland.

81 Oats

Cereals: Oats (*Avena* spp)
81-83

Jean Froissart, French priest, late fourteenth century. 'The Scots are bold, hardy, and much inured to war . . . each man carries a broad plate of metal . . . a little bag of oatmeal . . . they place this plate over a fire, mix with water their oatmeal . . . make a thin cake, like cracknel or biscuit . . . it is therefore no wonder that they perform a longer's days march than other soldiers' (Hume Brown 1891, p8 and 9).

Hume Brown, 1891, p98. 'All the early travellers in Scotland, we have seen, agree in stating that oatmeal was the chief fare of the lowland Scots'.

Avena, the classical name, is a genus of some 25 species, some being weeds and others cultivated. The species relevant in Scottish archaeology are Common Oat (*A. sativa,* cultivated), Bristle Oat, often called Black Oat, (*A. strigosa,* cultivated) and Wild Oat (*A. fatua*, weedy). *Sativa* means cultivated, *strigosa* means bristly and *fatua* means insipid or not good. The grains of these overlap in size and can be very difficult or impossible to differentiate, but the scars on the spikelet bases are diagnostic, if they can be seen. In the absence of this feature, many records are given merely as Oats without further precision.

Almost all discoveries of these Oats in Scotland, and all of the cultivated Oats, fall within the last 2500 years and most of them within the last 1500. Oats can grow well in cool, moist climates and Bristle Oat especially tolerates poor, exposed land. On Shetland, according to Scott and Palmer (1987, p366) '*A. strigosa* and *Hordeum vulgare* (the 'black Oats and bear' of many eighteenth- and nineteenth-century observers of the Shetland scene) had been the main cereal crops for many centuries'. *A. strigosa* could grow on impoverished soils (as it did under similar conditions in other areas of north and west Britain) and in Shetland its straw was used for thatching and basket-making. Bristle Oat

82 Carbonised Oats from Paisley Abbey. The shortest is 3.6mm and the longest 4.6mm

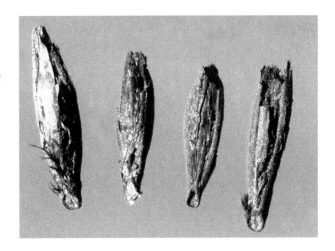

83 Carbonised florets of Wild Oat, showing the horseshoe scars, from Old Kilpatrick Crannog. The longest is about 1cm long

was grown on the poor 'outfield' while the higher-yielding *A. sativa* was reserved for the richer, manured 'infield' soils'. Rev John Walker noted the cultivation of Bristle Oat on all the many Hebridean islands he visited in 1764 and 1771 (McKay 1980).

Cultivated Oats in Scotland are famous as crucial components of porridge, brose (including Athole brose), sowans, oatcakes, haggis and crowdie or crannachan (Lockhart 1983). No whole or even fragmentary oatcake is known from any Scottish archaeological site but sooner or later one will be found.

Cereals: Rye (*Secale cereale*)
84-86

1661. John Ray, famous English naturalist. 'The Scots cannot endure to hear their country or countrymen spoken against. They have neither good bread, cheese or drink . . . They use much pottage made of cole-wort, which they call keal [kale], sometimes broth of decorticated barley . . . The ground in the valleys and plains [in the south-east] bears good corn, but especially beer-barley or bigge, and oates, but rarely wheat and rye.' (Hume Brown 1891, p231 and 232).

Secale was the Latin name for some cereal and *cereale* refers to agriculture. Rye is one of the hardiest cereals. It favours light, sandy conditions but not stiff clays or humus-rich soils. This tall cereal, scarcely grown in Scotland now, if at all, was first reported from Scottish archaeology from two Roman contexts by Knud Jessen and Hans Helbæk in 1944. These Roman finds may very well represent imports. Carbonised grains of Rye found at the later Bronze Age site at Myrehead, near

*84 Rye. As is seen in **85**, the ears of Rye are straight-sided and the awns are longer than in Mattioli's drawing*

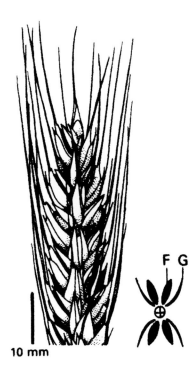

10 mm

85 Partial ear and spikelet layout of Rye from Bell (1998). F=floret and G=glume

Falkirk, were not thought of as derived from a crop (Barclay and Fairweather 1984) and Bill Boyd (1986) discussed the history of Rye further in connection with that of Ergot, a fungal parasite which infects Rye along with many other grasses. Concerning the history of Rye on the European scale Karl-Ernst Behre (1992, p141) stated 'It is difficult to prove cultivation of rye because rye is a secondary crop plant which expanded originally as weed in the cornfields and only later attained the status of a cultivated plant . . . with archaeological material it is usually impossible to distinguish between the weed and cultivated form of rye by purely morphological characteristics'. Over wide areas of Europe including Britain, Rye only became a significant crop in Medieval times (Behre 1992, as in France, Ruas 1992, and in southern Germany, Rösch *et al.*1992).

In the plant-rich samples from Medieval Perth, Mary Fraser found a mere eight carbonised grains of Rye but she failed to find it at either Elgin or Aberdeen. Subsequently, bran of Rye was also found at Perth. It has been reported from Medieval St Andrews and from a Norse site on Rousay, Orkney. Mary Fraser summed up the status of Rye as follows (p101): 'By Medieval times in England it was an important cereal on poor soils where wheat would not thrive. In Scotland, according to Duncan (1975), Rye is scarcely mentioned in the Medieval rentals but was grown on a small scale in central Scotland in the early fourteenth century. He continues: In general, therefore, wheat was grown more widely in southern Scotland, the land of open fields, where it perhaps had taken over some acreage devoted earlier (in the twelfth century) to rye; it was, however, still grown only in lesser amounts than oats and bere. North of Tay the land of smaller fields was also the land of oats and bere and almost exclusively so . . . Martin (1716) mentions rye being cultivated in the Western Isles along with barley and oats. In the eighteenth century oats and rye were sometimes sown together on poor land in the north of Scotland. However by the end of that century rye had gone out of cultivation (Handley, 1953).'

In Galloway of the late seventeenth century, Rye was grown on the higher ground; 'Symson differentiates between low country people, with an economy based on cattle, barley and long-bearded oats, and the "moor-men", living in smaller settlements and sheilings and growing crops of rye' (Donnachie and Macleod 1974). In 1768, travelling through Ardnamurchan and Moidart to Arisaig, James Robertson noted that '. . . the people are very diligent in digging and cultivating what ground there is between the rocks, they sow small black oats, four row'd barley, some rye & potatoes . . .' (Henderson and

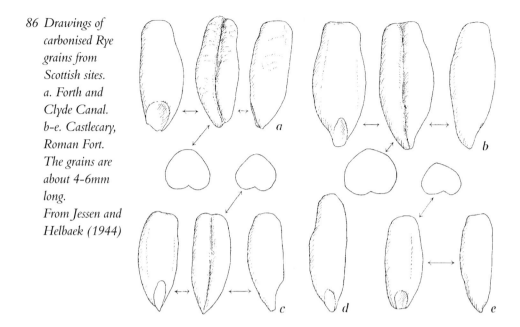

86 Drawings of carbonised Rye grains from Scottish sites.
a. Forth and Clyde Canal.
b-e. Castlecary, Roman Fort. The grains are about 4-6mm long.
From Jessen and Helbaek (1944)

Dickson 1994). Rev Walker in his economic reports on the Hebrides from the third quarter of the eighteenth century found little cultivation of Rye (McKay 1980).

This Scottish evidence of Rye cultivation is so meagre for any period including the late eighteenth century that one wonders why Robert Burns choose to compose the famous love song 'Coming through the Rye' rather than refer to Oats or Barley, though, of course, he happily remembered a night spent with Annie among the rigs of Barley!

Cereals: Wheats — Bread Wheat (*Triticum aestivum*), Emmer (*Triticum dicoccum*) and Spelt (*Triticum spelta*)
87-92

1598. Fynes Morison, English traveller. 'On the East side towards the Sea I passed Fife, a pleasant little Territory of open fields. Without inclosures, fruitfull of Corne (as bee all the partes neare Barwick [Berwick], save that they yeeld little wheate, but much Barley and Oates), and all a plaine country, but it had no Woodes at all . . .'

Fynes Morison again. 'They vulgarly eate harth [hearth] Cakes of Oates, but in Cities also have wheaten bread, which for the most part was bought by Courtiers, Gentlemen, and the best sortes of Citizens' (Hume Brown 1891, p86 and 89).

Though Barley in its varied forms is frequent in the Scottish Neolithic, the primitive Wheat called Emmer is far from unknown, as for instance from Skara Brae, the stone-built Neolithic village on Orkney, long famous not just in Scottish archaeology but throughout the world, and from Balbridie in Aberdeenshire, not so celebrated as Skara Brae but where there was an especially noteworthy wooden building in Neolithic times. Hulled and non-brittle, Emmer has long been known to have been part of the Roman military diet in

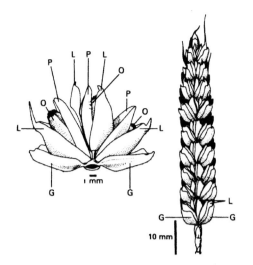

87 Complete ear and spikelet of Bread Wheat from Bell (1998). G=glume, L=lemma, O=ovary and P=palea

88 Balbridie Bread Wheat

Scotland (and, of course, not just there) as discoveries from the Antonine Wall forts testify.

Triticum is the classical Latin name for Wheat and *dicoccum* refers to the two grains that develop in each spikelet. *T. monococcum* (Einkorn, with one grain per spikelet) has no history in Scotland and a very insubstantial history in England, but *T. aestivum* (Bread Wheat, *aestivum* referring to summer) has recently been found in the Scottish Neolithic, again at Balbridie. As Zohary and Hopf (1993, p18) have put it, 'Wheats are superior to most other cereals (e.g. Maize, Rice, or Barley) in their nutritive value. The grains contain not only starch (carbohydrate content of wheat grains is 60-80%), but also significant amounts of protein (8-14%).' No whole or even fragmentary wheaten loaf of bread or, indeed any kind of bread, has ever been recovered from a Scottish archaeological site.

The far travelled herbalist, William Turner, had never seen Spelt in England but was familiar with it near Strasbourg where he says (1562, p564) '. . . there all men use it, for they grow no wheat at all. Yet I never saw fairer and pleasanter bread in any place in all my life than I have eaten there, made only of this spelt.'

90 (above) Carbonised partial ears of Emmer, from Old Kilpatrick Crannog. The longest fragment is about 2cm long

89 (above) Spelt

91 (right) Emmer. From Körber-Grohne (1994)

92 (right) Carbonised grain of Spelt from Lyne Antonine Fort. The grains are about 6mm long. Left ventral view, middle side view and right dorsal view

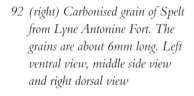

239

Spelt is a tall-growing, hulled Wheat tolerant of poor soils but not grown now as a crop in Scotland or in the rest of Britain and, from Scotland, it is known only from a small number of archaeological sites including Roman forts on the Antonine Wall such at Bearsden, Castlecary and Rough Castle. The most noteworthy record, however, is that from the Oakbank Crannog, in Loch Tay, occupied well before the Romans invaded Scotland.

Cloudberry (*Rubus chamaemorus*) 93-95

93 Cloudberry from Lightfoot's Flora Scotica *(1777): flowering shoot and a fruiting head. The flower is about two-thirds natural size and the fruit about natural size*

Rubus is the Latin name and *chamaemorus* refers to a mulberry growing close to the ground; Cloudberry is low-growing and its fruits somewhat resemble mulberries. *Rubus* is a large genus which includes Raspberry and Bramble, both of which turn up as pips very frequently in archaeological layers in Scotland and elsewhere. So far, not just in Scotland but in Britain as a whole, the very distinctive pips of Cloudberries have very seldom been found in archaeological contexts. Pips have been recovered from several Medieval towns in Norway (Griffin 1994). Half a pip was recovered from Medieval Perth by Mary Fraser and seven pips from Oakbank Crannog (Miller *at al.* 1998). Rich in vitamin C, indeed more so than in many other berries according to Kortesharju (1988), the fruits can be made into jams, desserts and a liquor, as they very frequently are in Scandinavia and Finland. Not all Finns, nor Scandinavians, nor Miller *et al.* (1998) will agree with Mabey (1996, p182) who considers that the berries '. . . make a thin marmalade, but are indifferent eating'. Quoting Carl Linnaeus's *Flora Lapponica,* Lightfoot (1777) stated that to preserve the fruit through the winter the Laplanders bury them in the snow and in the spring find them fresh and good.

Writing in his large *Flora of Alaska and Neighbouring Territories,* the Swede Eric Hulten stated 'Fruit excellent to eat when ripe, keeps without the addition of sugar over the winter and makes very good jam' (1968, p602). 'Berries including crow berries, salmon berries and cloud berries were both consumed fresh and stored for winter use'; so wrote Taylor and Sturtevant (1995, p206) referring to the native inhabitants of the Aleutian Islands. Moerman (1998) lists many North American tribes as storing the fruits frozen, or in seal oil, and he gives medical uses by the Micmacs and the Crees. Cloudberries contain two-and-a-half to three times by weight of vitamin C as does an orange (Heller 1953).

Occurring throughout the highland zone of Britain but not in Shetland or any of the

94 *Map of Cloudberry,*
a species which in
Britain is restricted
to blanket peats on
hilly ground

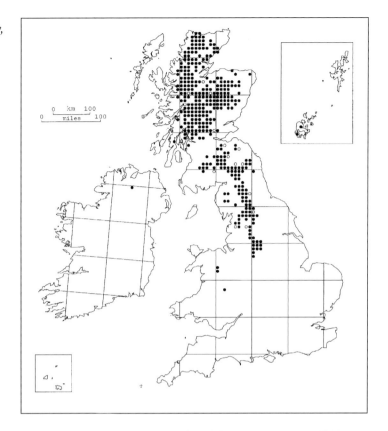

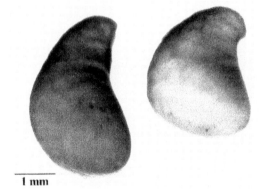

95 *Pips of Cloudberry from Oakbank*
Crannog

1 mm

Hebrides, Cloudberry appears well named because it often grows in the clouds, inhabiting as it does mires of the blanket bog type (in Britain exclusively so). Such peat-bogs develop mostly on high ground and only in areas where there are a very large number of rain days and very low annual potential water deficit. However, as Geoffrey Grigson points out, the cloud in Cloudberry derives from the Old English clud for rock or hill; were Hillberry the name it would be entirely appropriate. The pips recovered from the Oakbank Crannog imply long-range foraging by the Iron Age inhabitants; see chapter 5. Cloudberry has distinctive pollen grains but they have seldom been recorded in pollen diagrams.

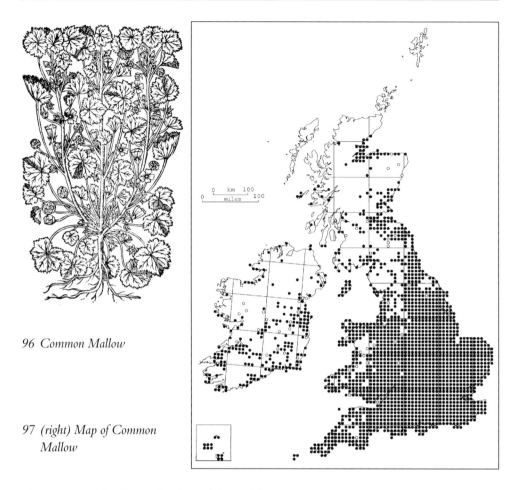

96 Common Mallow

97 (right) Map of Common Mallow

Common Mallow (*Malva sylvestris*)
96-98

Some 12 species of the genus grow in Europe but only three as wild plants in Scotland where none may be native but are likely to be archaeophytes, that is to say introduced before AD 1500. The map clearly shows that Common Mallow avoids much of Scotland and lives up to its name only in the south-east; the further south one goes in Europe the commoner it becomes along roadsides and in waste places. Like other members of the family Malvaceae, Common Mallow has large and heavily ornamented pollen grains and these were found on the slides prepared from the Bearsden ditch, although only from the Roman layer and not the post-Roman part.

The name *Malva* was used by Pliny who extols the medicinal virtues of the plant. It seems probable the Common Mallow was grown for a special purpose. He states that anyone taking half a cyathus of Mallow juice daily would be immune to all diseases. Perhaps the plant was being taken as a prophylactic. Some Common Mallow a day keeps the doctor away! Common Mallow is still used, in herbal medicine, both internally and externally for its mucilaginous qualities. It is known that the Romans collected the seeds,

98 A pollen grain of Common Mallow from the Roman in-fill of the east annexe ditch at the Bearsden Fort. The pollen grains of this species are large, over 100 microns in diameter

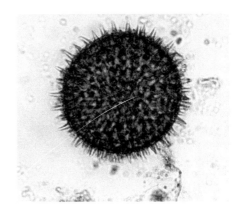

because an earthenware vessel containing 30,000 Common Mallow seeds was found in a Roman cellar of second-century date in Germany, and bronze ampulla of the Roman period at Uitgeest in the Netherlands contained seeds of Common Mallow as well as Radish, Celery and Wild Marjoram (Buurman 1988).

Coriander (*Coriandrum sativum*) and Dill (*Anethum graveolens*) 99-103

Coriander is an umbellifer, a member of the family Umbelliferae, or as it is more usually called now the Apiaceae. Like its fellows Celery, Parsley, Lovage, Sweet Cecily and many others, it is strongly aromatic. Crushed leaves smell like Bed Bugs, so it is said, but one hopes few people in Britain or elsewhere these days will be able to use this attribute as an aid to identification. *Coriandrum* is the ancient Greek name and *sativum* means cultivated. The map shows a scatter of records from across Britain with few in Scotland; these represent only temporary establishments resulting from lost culinary seed.

Somewhat unusually for the family, Coriander has almost spherical fruits. When dry, they show most distinctly the sinuous stripes, which are very recognisable even if only fragments of the fruits are found, as is mostly the case. The first Scottish archaeological record is that from the Bearsden Roman fort.

The Roman Cookery of Apicius gives recipes for *Fish stewed with Coriander, Parsnips in Coriander Chive Sauce* and for both *Truffles* and *Lentils and Chestnuts* in *Coriander Wine Sauce* (Edwards 1984*)*. Perhaps the Bearsden Romans ate similar dishes though truffles may never have reached the northwest frontier of the

99 Coriander

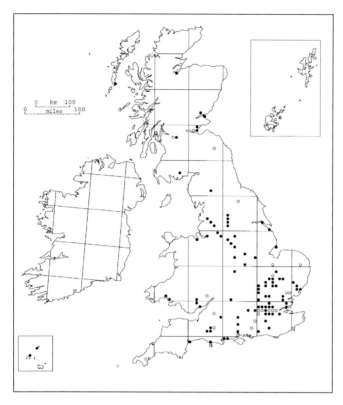

100 (left) Map of Coriander. The records are of short-lived occurrences of plants escaped from cultivation

101 (below left) Remains of Coriander from the Bearsden Fort. This is part of the wall of a seed showing the diagnostic zig-zag pattern

0   0.5mm

Roman Empire. At any rate this detachment of troops and the other members of the Roman army in Britain may well have used Coriander for flavouring their food, whether it was cordon bleu or military stodge. Its use began much earlier than the period of the Roman Empire as the seeds found in Tutankhamun's tomb show.

Like Coriander, Dill is an annual member of the Apiaceae. *Anethum* is the Greek name and *graveolens* means heavily scented. Fragments of the fruits were recovered from the Bearsden sewage. In 1629 Parkinson put the uses well, as follows: 'The leaves of Dill are much used in some places with fish, as they doe Fenell; but because it is so strong many doe refuse to use it. It is also, put among pickled Cowcumbers, wherewith it doth very well agree, gluing unto the cold fruit a pretty spicie taste or rellish. It being stronger than Fenell, is of more force to expell winde in the

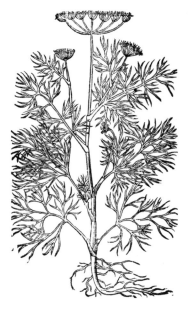

102 (left) Dill

103 (right) Remains of Dill from the Bearsden Fort. The scale bar is 0.5mm

body. Some use to eate the seed to stay the Hickocke. [hiccups].'

Satisfying as it is that Coriander and Dill should turn up in Roman layers in Scotland, perhaps it should not be thought very surprising. It is even more satisfying and perhaps not to have been totally expected that both have been recovered from Dark Age deposits in lowland Scotland. The crannog at Buiston yielded both, as did a pit at Whithorn. Coriander also was among the plant remains from Medieval Aberdeen.

Corncockle (*Agrostemma githago*)
104-106

Tall, slender and not much branched, Corncockle was formerly a weed of cereal fields and has large seeds, about the same size as cereal grains. Attractive in their pinkness, its large flowers make it a very ornamental garden plant. *Agrostemma* comes from the Greek *agros* meaning field and *stemma* meaning crown or garland. The etymology of *githago* is obscure, according to Hooker's *The Student's Flora of the British Isles* (1884).

Though often recovered only as fragments from archaeological layers, the black, knobbly seeds are very readily recognisable. Such fragments were extracted from the Roman sewage at Bearsden and had earlier been found at both Birrens and Newstead. It seems that Corncockle came as a contaminant of imported grain. In England Corncockle is known from the Iron Age onwards, but in Scottish archaeology there have been no discoveries earlier than Roman times. The seeds were recovered from all three Medieval sites investigated by Mary Fraser: Perth, Aberdeen and Elgin. Medieval cornfields were pink with Corncockle, yellow with Corn Marigold, blue with Cornflower and red with Poppies (Greig 1988). With a wide tolerance of soils (other than waterlogged ones) that supported cereals, often Wheat and Rye (Firbank 1988), Corncockle was a troublesome

104   (above) Corncockle

105   *(above right) Map of Corncockle. Until the nineteenth century, Corncockle was a serious weed of cornfields. Being a tall annual with attractive flowers it is often grown in gardens or the seeds scattered in the wild by conservationists. These are the plants which have given rise to many of the recent records. The seeds are about 3.5mm long*

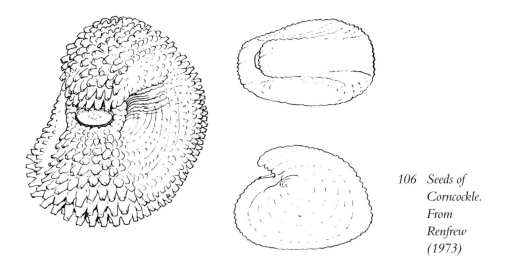

106   *Seeds of Corncockle. From Renfrew (1973)*

weed until the improvements in seed cleaning such as the nineteenth-century invention of the cockler which could separate seeds of Corncockle from cereal grains. By the mid-twentieth century it was a great rarity in Britain and has not been seen as a cereal weed here for several decades, though it can be so found still in central Europe as in the Vinschgau, in Südtirol. Not being destroyed by heating, a toxic saponin, githagen, in the seeds makes bread unpalatable.

Crab Apple (*Malus sylvestris*)
107-109

That prehistoric Europeans exploited Crab Apples has been known ever since the excavations last century of the lake villages in Switzerland and surrounding countries; Neolithic folk halved and quartered, then dried, the fruits for later consumption. Fresh Crab Apples make very unpleasant eating but drying renders them palatable (Dr Barrie Juniper, personal communication). Only in recent years have pips been recovered from Scottish prehistoric sites, but the use

107 Apple. This is a Sweet Apple, not a Crab Apple which has much smaller fruits and is often thorny

was evidently widespread because the discoveries come not just from the mainland but the Hebrides and from Orkney too, such as at Skara Brae. Pollen of '*Malus sylvestris*' has been recorded in several samples from Monolith 1 of the re-excavation of Star Carr in Yorkshire; the sediment had formed around 8500 BC. It is clear that the Crab Apple grew in Britain as early as Mesolithic times (Dark 1998).

Malus comes from the Greek for apple and the epithet *sylvestris* means growing in woods or simply wild, both appropriate for this small tree which often grows as singletons. Crab Apple has been little studied in Scotland and a glance through county *Floras* clearly shows that many botanists are confused about the identification and status of the tree. The map, therefore, has its limitations, possibly severe. Round the edges of some of the islands in Loch Lomond there are Crab Apple trees typically thorny with small fruits. Its present range may not extend to the Outer or Northern Isles, although one specimen has been found on Shetland, and there are few records from north of the Great Glen. In 1767 James Robertson noted a '*Pyrus malus*/Crab-tree or Wilding' in a small wood at the head of Loch Broom (Henderson and Dickson 1994, p56). This scarcity makes one wonder about the native status of the tree on the islands and in the far north, and perhaps even Scotland as a whole. Did prehistoric people take Crab Apples with them wherever they colonised, just as they took cereals? For this speculation to be true then the Neolithic inhabitants of Orkney and northern Scotland must have grown the Crab Apples from pips because propagation from cuttings or suckers would have been very difficult or more likely impossible. Cultivated Apples are propagated by grafting, a technique known at least as far back as Roman times or earlier.

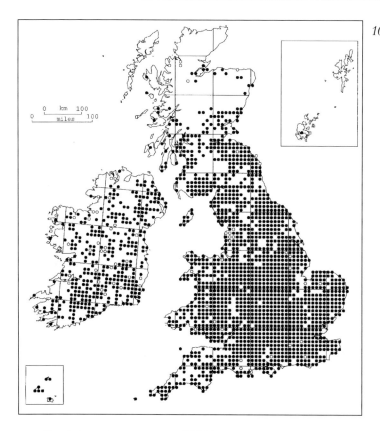

108 Map of Crab Apple. It does not draw a reliable separation of Crab and Sweet Apple which field botanists readily confuse if the trees are not fruiting. Discarded Sweet Apple pips voided or thrown away with cores, often grow up on waste ground and roadsides. Such growth accounts for many of the records

109 Two pips of Crab Apple from Skara Brae. The bigger one is 5.2 x 2.9mm

One of five *Malus* species in Europe and of about 33 species in all from the north temperate zone, the Crab Apple almost certainly has nothing to do with the ancestry of the thousands of cultivars of the familiar, much eaten Sweet Apple, even though that species may have been in cultivation for millennia. The records of *Malus* from several Roman sites in England cannot be separated into Crab Apple and Sweet Apple on the basis of their pips, the only remains to have been found (CD 1994). There are more than 2000 cultivars of Apple in cultivation in Britain alone. The geographical origin of the Sweet Apple is probably Kazakhstan through to western China (Juniper 1998).

With regard to medicinal uses John Lightfoot (1777, p258) claimed that 'Its juice, or *crab-vinegar,* applied outwardly is good to cure spasms, cramps, strains, etc.'.

Deadly Nightshade (*Atropa belladonna*) and Henbane (*Hyoscyamus niger*)
110-113

These two poisonous, sometimes lethal, plants are alien in Scotland and indeed are archaeophytes, that is to say they were brought here by humans before AD 1500 (Dickson 1998). Atropos was one of the three Fates, a deadly one. Belladonna, of course, means beautiful lady and refers to the use of the juice to dilate the pupils. *Hyoscyamus* is Greek meaning Pigbean and *niger* means black. In southern Europe there are also White Henbane and Golden Henbane. All these herbaceous plants belong to the Solanaceae, a family which also includes the Potato and the Tomato and which is well known for the many toxic alkaloids. Deadly Nightshade is a perennial with a very persistent rootstock, often growing in shady places on base-rich soil, whereas Henbane is an annual of sunny, often base-rich ground. The seeds of Henbane are long viable in the soil. A strong affinity of both these plants for old castles and abbeys has been discussed by Conolly (1994). Deadly Nightshade is a rarity in Scotland now, with Henbane not much commoner, as the maps show.

110   Deadly Nightshade. The drawing of the fruit, right below middle, is misleading; Deadly Nightshade has soft, dark-coloured berries, not dry, circumcissile capsules which are the fruits of Henbane

Mary Fraser and David Robinson found seeds of Henbane in the Medieval layers from Perth and seeds of Deadly Nightshade from both Medieval Perth and Elgin. Henbane has also been recovered from the Roman fort at Elginhaugh, Norse and Late Norse deposits on Orkney, and from layers at Edinburgh Castle dated to AD 100-300. Seeds of Henbane have often turned up at settlement sites elsewhere in Europe as in Finland from sites of Viking to nineteenth-century age (Lempiänen 1991) and at Keil in north-western Germany (Wiethold 1995).

Henbane is mentioned again and again in old herbals, as the tabulation in John Harvey's *Medieval Gardens* makes clear. Seeds of a species of Henbane were found with other medicinal plants in the ancient necropolis at Saqqâra in Egypt (Manniche 1993). Henbane is used not only in European medicine but in Chinese too (Keys 1976). Because of its narcotic effects, it was used for anaesthesia. According to Wren (1988, p143) 'The alkaloid hyoscine is used very widely, as a pre-operative medication, to prevent travel sickness and for many other purposes'. Smoked like tobacco, Henbane has been used as a

111 (left) Map of Deadly Nightshade. The plant is certainly an archaeophytic alien in Scotland

112 (above) Henbane

remedy for toothache (Vickery 1995). The alkaloid atropine has medicinal applications, but the Nightshade can live up to its name Deadly; the consumption of several of the purple-black berries is enough to kill a child. Both plants are rarities in Scotland and so are unlikely to cause much harm but not no harm, as two residents of Edinburgh know having eaten 'Bramble' jelly, made of Deadly Nightshade berries.

Fig (*Ficus carica*)
114-116

Ficus is the Latin name for the Fig and *carica* refers to Caria, a part of ancient Asia Minor. Figs have been cultivated for millennia but not for sure for very long in Britain where the earliest certain growing of this small, variable tree is from the early 1400s AD. No matter how plausible it may seem, the often repeated assertion in the horticultural and archaeobotanical literature that the Romans grew Figs in Britain needs substantiation (Dickson and Dickson 1996). There are very many records of Fig pips from Roman military and urban sites in Britain but their abundance and widespread localities are not

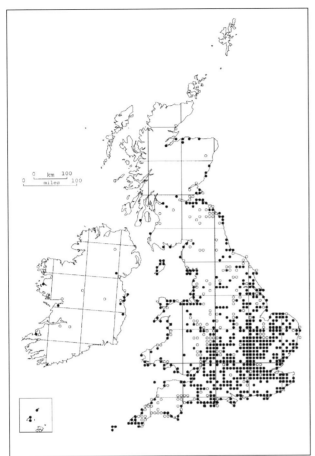

113 (left) Map of Henbane

114 (above) Fig

proof that Figs were grown here. A regular part of the military diet throughout the Empire, Figs were exported from the Mediterranean countries in the dried state in which their high sugar content prevented rotting unless they were wetted.

A single Fig can contain over 1000 pips. An understanding of the complex reproductive biology of the Fig reveals that fully ripened pips are only formed when the indispensable, tiny, pollinating wasp and pollen-bearing trees are present. Neither condition is met when Figs are grown in Britain and consequently no pips form fully and no edible fruit is produced. Growing on trees in Britain those Figs which swell to become edible are formed on parthenocarpic varieties. Such Figs have dispensed with the sexual process and develop no fertile pips. This is somewhat like cultivated Bananas, which have no seed, or seedless Grapes and Oranges (but only if the somewhat arcane botanical complexities are ignored as they have been here).

The first Figs recovered from a Scottish site were those from the Bearsden fort on the Antonine Wall. Subsequently pips have been recorded from the Agricolan fort at Elginhaugh and from Medieval Scottish sites too, notably Paisley Abbey and Kirkwall. Fig pips, like Tomato seeds, pass freely through the human gut unharmed and grow well if the appropriate conditions are reached after expulsion. Archaeological pips are very strongly

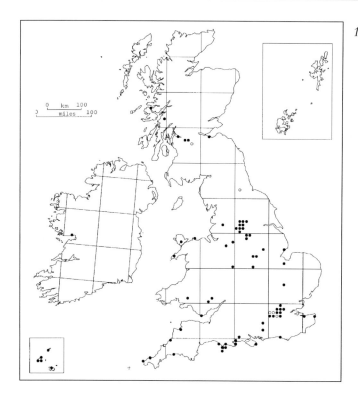

115 Map of Fig. Many of the records are from urban, waterside situations which point to pips having survived sewage treatment and then germinated, as in Sheffield, Glasgow and Edinburgh. Such trees can survive for long periods but they never produce ripe fruits with fertile pips, there being no pollen nor pollinators in Britain

116 Fig pips from Paisley Abbey. The largest are about 1.5mm across

connected with sewage, as indeed were those few wild Fig trees which grow in Britain today having survived the perils of sewage treatment and thereafter the difficulties of establishment. The sole wild, self-sown Fig in Glasgow survived the record spell of low air temperatures (to -20° C) over Christmas 1995; it has not been known even to attempt fruiting unlike those 35 trees along the River Don in Sheffield which try but there the fruits can never ripen.

There is as yet only one discovery of prehistoric fig pips from Britain. The site is Hengistbury on the coast of Hampshire and the age is late Iron Age. Perhaps this was as one would have expected, but it is still a fine addition to knowledge. Among plant remains seemingly from the poorly documented 1906 excavation of the Old Kilpatrick crannog in the intertidal zone of the Clyde estuary were a few fig pips, kept in Kelvingrove Museum in Glasgow. From a crannog they could have dated from around 2000 years ago and it would have been most interesting should the age have proved to be pre-Roman but any ancient date would have been notable. The pips were sacrificed for accelerator dating and the age turned out to be AD 1900! Perhaps they had been part of an excavator's lunch, or came down the Clyde as sewage from the Glasgow conurbation. The map shows wild Figs, not planted trees, and many of these occurrences are connected with sewage, as their precise habitats make clear.

That Figs '. . . provoke a man to stool and purge the kidneys . . .' is a comment by William Turner (1562) but, as he was well aware, long before his time Dioscorides and Galen had written in similar vein.

Flax (*Linum usitatissimum*)
117, 118

117   Flax

Linum is the Latin name and *usitatissimum* means most useful. *Linum* is a big genus with many species growing in the Mediterranean area. Very anciently cultivated, Flax is grown both for fibre, made into linen, and seeds (linseed) which are rich in oil. At the present time Flax for fibre and linseed is grown as two separate crops. Flax has been bred to produce a long-stemmed plant for fibre and was grown extensively in Scotland including Orkney from the eighteenth to nineteenth centuries. Flax has recently been reintroduced into Scotland as part of the agricultural diversity programme. It requires fertile well-drained soils with freedom from heavy rains and frosts and the plant does not compete well with weeds. The separation of its fibres for linen is time consuming.

To indicate the complexity of the processing, the following method is extracted from J.P. Wild's account on Flax processing. To give the best quality fibre, the plant must be pulled before the seeds are fully ripe. The separation of the bast fibres (those used for linen) takes several operations and Flax is the most difficult fibre to prepare. The stems must be retted to loosen the outer bark by bacterial decay. This is achieved by soaking in water in retting pits for two or three weeks, weighed down to keep the fibres submerged. The stalks are then drawn across a hackle (heckle) board, which has rows of different-sized iron spikes, to remove the remains of the stem, leaving the bast fibres ready for spinning.

Flax fibres, like those of Hemp, do not preserve well but the stem fragments may be sought in ancient retting pits. Such a pit, of Bronze Age date, has been found in southern England and an eighteenth-century one by Loch Tay in Perthshire has recently been

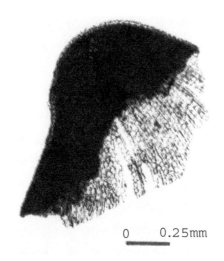

0   0.25mm

*118 Remains of Flax from the Bearsden
Fort. One end of a broken seed*

investigated by Jennifer Miller. There is little archaeological evidence that is undoubtedly linked with Flax production; spindle whorls to spin Flax are similar to those used for wool. Long iron heckle teeth have been occasionally preserved, as at Jarlshof, but these may have been used for combing wool.

Plant oils do not become rancid as do animal oils, and linseed contains 35-40% oil. The discovery of a burnt clump of seeds from a Norse site in Limerick, Ireland, suggests pressing for oil. It would be interesting to analyse the fabric of Norse pottery lamps to identify the oil used in them. Before the Norse period, Flax seeds have usually been found only in small numbers, as at Balbridie (Neolithic, the earliest Scottish record), Oakbank Crannog and Crosskirk Broch. Finds around hearths are thought to represent domestic use. Linseed can be used as a laxative, the oil-rich seeds retain heat well for poultices and this use goes back over 2000 years. Flax stems hung up to dry after retting are likely to have dropped their seeds and be found in various contexts. Careful analyses of these contexts may help to decide for which purpose the plant was being grown.

The pre-Norse evidence is interesting. Flax seeds were recorded from a pre-Norse building of probable fifth- to sixth-century date at Howe; they were not found in earlier Iron Age levels. The Pictish Freswick also produced seed. At Pool, Flax did not appear until the Pictish/Norse transition, which suggests that Flax came in with the Norse farmers. Was Flax reintroduced from the south or from Norway before the Norse settled in Mainland Orkney and Caithness? If so, what was it used for? It seems unlikely that the complex processing for linen was attempted without the help of the Norse, experienced in its manufacture in their homeland.

The large quantity of seeds from the Norse, especially Pool and Saevar Howe, and Later Norse sites, at Earl's Bu, Beachview and Freswick, all suggest linen production. Instead of a relatively few seeds brought in to hearth areas for domestic use, larger quantities are found in different contexts. Glass linen smoothers have been found on Norse sites in Scotland. Corrosion products sometimes preserve adherent fabric; a belt buckle in a Viking grave at Kneep had linen fabric attached. Swedish graves have yielded scraps of fine linen attached to brooches. Pleated linen undergarments were worn by Scandinavian women and it is thought that they were woven from Flax grown on the farms.

Guelder Rose (*Viburnum opulus*)
119-121

In Britain there are two indigenous species of the genus *Viburnum*, the Guelder Rose and the Wayfaring Tree. Both are tall shrubs and the Guelder Rose grows throughout except for the Outer Hebrides and the Northern Isles, whereas the Wayfaring Tree is strongly southern and lime-loving, even in Europe as a whole. Pollen analysis has revealed that Guelder Rose was present in Scotland since Late-glacial times (Godwin 1975). There have been only two discoveries, both prehistoric, of *Viburnum* wood from archaeological contexts in Scotland. The first, made last century, was the uppermost 27cm of an arrow shaft, still with the flint arrowhead attached; it came from a peat-bog at Fyvie in Aberdeenshire (Anderson 1876). The second was made much more recently. It is a single piece of wood from the midden at Skara Brae; unfortunately its very small size precludes recognition as having been a part of any sort of

119 Guelder Rose

artefact. The anatomy of *Viburnum* wood is very distinctive but it can be difficult to separate the two species in question. However, on grounds of plant geography and soil requirements, in all likelihood the species in question for these Scottish discoveries is the Guelder Rose.

Only at a small number of places have prehistoric arrow shafts been discovered. In all of Europe there are about ten such localities. A considerable variety of woods have been used: Alder (only one tentative identification), Ash, Cornelian Cherry, Hazel, Scots Pine, Spindle Tree, Willow, Yew and, as just stated, *Viburnum*, from Fyvie, but significantly not just there. The Tyrolean Iceman had a quiver containing 14 arrows all with shafts made of the Wayfaring Tree. The burial of the Iron Age prince from Hochdorf in southern Germany contained 21 shafts, four of them being *Viburnum*, and from the Mesolithic at Holmegaard in Sjaeland, Denmark, there were several shafts, all of the Guelder Rose. *Viburnum* has thus been recorded from different places and at very different periods all across Europe. It would seem that species of *Viburnum* were the favoured shrubs for making arrow shafts. Certainly in Scotland, all through prehistory Hazel and Willow would have been much more readily available than *Viburnum*. Why *Viburnum*? Both species readily produce straight, smooth branches of the appropriate length and thickness and the wood is hard. Highbush Cranberry of north-western North America is *Viburnum edule*, with edible fruits, but it often has a straggling habit which perhaps precluded the local Indians from using it for arrow shafts. The Tlingit Indians made their shafts from Yellow Cedar, according to Suttles (1990). The diversity of different woods used for shafts in European prehistory is paralleled by the list of no fewer than 15 given by Roger Ascham (1545) in the earliest British book on toxophily.

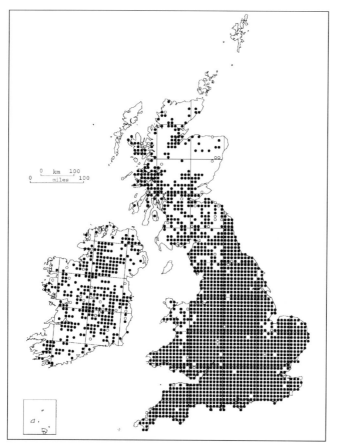

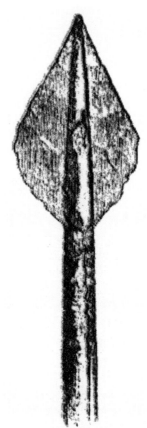

120   *(left) Map of Guelder Rose*
121   *(right) Arrow from Fyvie*

The fruits of Guelder Rose are edible. However, no seeds have ever turned up in Scottish archaeological contexts. *Viburnum* pollen is seldom found.

Hawthorn (*Crataegus monogyna*)
122-124

Crataegus is the Greek name alluding to strength and *monogyna* refers to one pistil. This is one of only two native trees of the genus in Britain and the only one found in Scotland. There are some 200 other members of the genus in north temperate regions. With its very name deriving from the Anglo-Saxon for hedge-thorn, Hawthorn is very familiar as hedging and has been by far and away the most commonly used plant in rural Scotland for such a purpose. From the bottom of the well at Bar Hill on the Antonine Wall, Macdonald and Park (1906, p91) recovered 'A twig of hawthorn [that] looked as if it had been but a

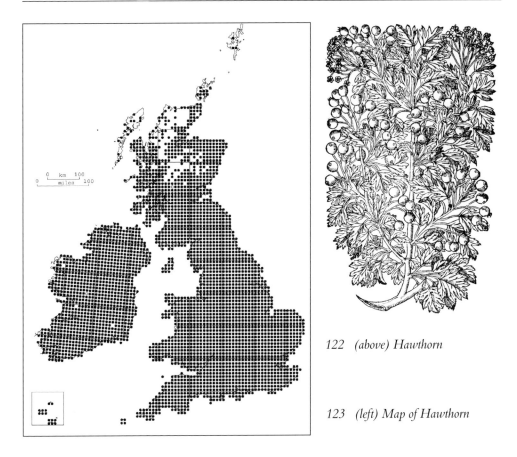

122 (above) Hawthorn

123 (left) Map of Hawthorn

few months broken from the branch'. At a re-excavation of the fort several decades later, at the bottom of a ditch there were many large, cut pieces of Hawthorn, one complete with epiphytic moss. Their shapes are strongly suggestive of growth as a hedge (Boyd 1984c). This is a unique discovery in British archaeology.

In the Highlands a decoction was used for sore throats and an infusion for control of blood pressure (Beith 1995).

Hazel (*Corylus avellana*)
125-128

Carbonised remains of Hazelnuts are recovered again and again from Mesolithic sites and not just from sites of that early period but from many of those of later prehistoric and historic times. Before cereal cultivation, undoubtedly the most important plant food throughout north-western Europe were the nuts of this often many-stemmed, tall bush or small tree. The nuts are rich in oil, protein, starch and sugar, with vitamins B1, C and trace elements.

Hazel is one of only three species of *Corylus* indigenous in Europe and the only one indigenous in north-western Europe, though the Filbert (*C. maxima* a native of the

257

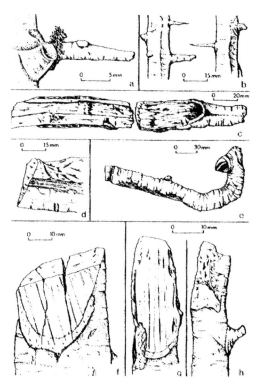

124 Branch fragments of Hawthorn from the Bar Hill Fort. a and b. Branches with spines and one with moss. c to h. Fragments showing tear wounds, unnaturally crooked growth, and cut ends. From Boyd (1984)

Balkans and Romania) with its somewhat larger nuts is cultivated commercially in Kent and elsewhere. *Corylus* is the Greek name for the plant and *avellana* refers to Avella Vecchia, a town near Naples, famous for its fruit trees. Mattioli's illustration is of Filbert not Hazel, as the large bracts round the nuts indicates.

As the map shows, Hazel grows as a native throughout Britain and Ireland, but it may be locally scarce and unproductive. On Orkney there are a mere three bushes, all in sheltered positions on the Isle of Hoy. They are lingering remnants of the former, prehistoric abundance and similarly on Shetland Hazel is 'Now exceedingly rare and known from only two sites'. (Scott and Palmer 1987, p109). These very sparse Hazels on the Northern Isles do not produce nuts under present conditions. The Hazel scrub found here and there on the Western Isles can produce nuts in certain years. Many Hazels and Filberts in the Grey Squirrel's territory of southern Britain produce nuts abundantly, but Oliver Rackham (1986) claims that there Hazel is a seriously threatened tree because these alien Squirrels take all the nuts before they ripen.

Often found on well-drained soils, Hazel can grow on a wide range of soil types except the most acidic. Pollen analysis clearly shows that in the early Holocene Hazel was much more abundant than now. With the then unleached soils providing very suitable habitats, Hazel was at first free of overshadowing by taller trees until Oak and Elm spread. Growing under well-illuminated conditions, Hazel would have provided good crops of nuts if there were no late frosts in early spring. Whether, as some believe, there was a relationship between fire, either natural or man-made, and the spread and abundance of Hazel is an idea difficult to investigate. Sociable nutting events have taken place into the modern era, as related by Rackham (1986) and Mabey (1996). However, even given that Hazel grew vigorously during the somewhat warmer summers of several thousand years ago, it is hard to believe that many of its branches were so massive as to support a large lady harvester metres above the ground during a jolly Mesolithic nutting party, as shown in Finlayson's *Wild Harvesters The First People in Scotland* (1998). In any case, the nuts form at the tips of slender branches well out of reach and so climbing would have been of little use.

The nuts can be stored in the ground, below the frost level, in suitable containers that

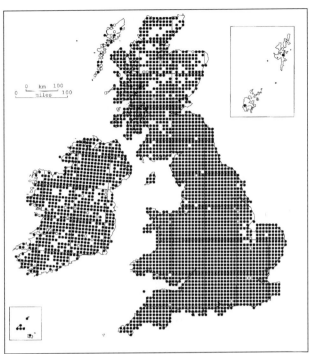

125 Hazel. The large bracts
       seen in this illustration
       indicate that the shrub
       drawn was Filbert rather
       than the Hazel native in
       Britain

126 Map of Hazel

  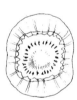 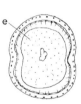

127 Hazelnuts. From
       Renfrew (1973).
       e=endosperm

exclude pests, as has been suggested occurred at Mount Sandel, Ireland, in Mesolithic times (Woodman 1985). On germination in spring the shells split precisely into halves and the seedlings can even be eaten, as children do in Norway. Unless large numbers of germinated shells are found, as in Medieval Bergen (Krzywinski *et al.*1983), there is no evidence that prehistoric man took advantage of such early green shoots. Recently it has been speculated that the Mesolithic inhabitants of Colonsay collected great quantities of nuts and after roasting them may have made the kernels into a paste for ease of storage (Finlayson 1998). Why such a practice would have eased any storage problem is hard to see.

John Lightfoot (1777, p587) stated unexplicitly with regard to locality '. . . there are instances of their [the kernels] having been made into bread'. Hazel was not just of interest to prehistoric and later peoples as food but also as a very important tree for small scale constructional purposes because it coppices so well. Cutting down close to soil level encourages the growth of many long, straight branches, which do not break easily when

128   Coppiced Hazel

used for making wattles for wattle-and-daub walls, as well as for fences and hurdles. Hazel can be and has been sustainably coppiced for several thousand years for these useful stems. In England this form of woodland management goes back at least as far as the Neolithic period at the Somerset Levels.

With regard to medicinal uses, according to Launert (1981) the active principles are essential oil, myricitoside and palmitic acid, which stimulate the circulation and bile production. However, scepticism will attach perhaps to the claim by William Turner (1551, p288) that 'The ashes of burned nuts with hog's grease or bear's grease, laid upon the head from which the hair falleth off, it will restore the hair again'.

Pollen of Hazel is important in Scottish pollen diagrams especially, but not only those covering the first half of the Holocene. Figures **6-10** show pollen called 'Hazel-type'. The problem is that the pollen of Hazel is very similar to that of Bog Myrtle and most pollen analysts do not make the distinction. A shrub often reaching about 1m, Bog Myrtle is locally abundant in Scottish peatlands but absent from, or sparse in, some areas.

Heather (*Calluna vulgaris*)
129-131

The generic name comes from the Greek to cleanse, referring to the use of members of the Heather family as brooms. *Vulgaris*, of course, means common. Heather grows throughout Britain and Ireland and over much of Europe and becomes sparse to the south, under the Mediterranean climate, and to the east, with increasing continentality. This shrub, usually short-lived (only a few decades) and low-growing (usually less than 1m tall), has a strongly acidifying effect on the underlying soil and can produce a thick, slowly decomposing layer of very infertile humus. Heather can grow prostrate, as it does on the very windswept hillsides of the Northern Isles. It has colonised the remotest Scottish islands such as St Kilda.

Highly resistant to the fires which kill many other heathland plants, Heather has long

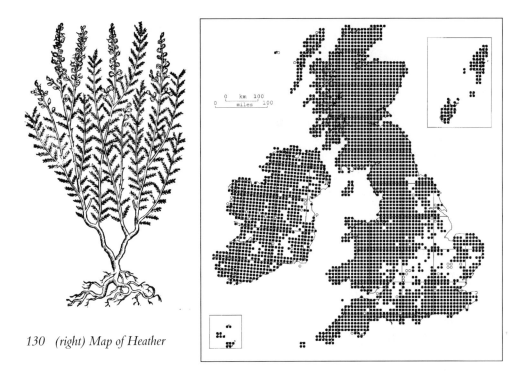

130 (right) Map of Heather

129 (above left) Heather is not the easiest plant to draw but the artist has caught the characteristic look — the crooked woody stems, the tiny leaves and distinctive flowers. Pieces of leafy twigs and of woody stems with knot holes and wrinkles, and the flowers too are often extracted from peats and archaeological samples

been managed by burning, which is a practice called muirburn in Scotland. The resulting young, leafy shoots are palatable to Sheep and Red Deer, and particularly to Red Grouse. Extensive areas of Heather heathland on Scottish hillsides, especially in the eastern Highlands, are the product of this management and, on the cessation of muirburn, the heathlands can quickly be colonised by Birch and Oak, if there are nearby seed sources and the grazing regime is not too intense.

Heather has romantic connotations in Scotland, being an informal emblem in addition to the more formal royal Thistle. Occasionally there are white-flowered plants (lucky white Heather) among those with the usual purple flowers. In late summer the flowers are much visited by Bees for nectar which makes very fine honey. Among the other many uses of Heather are thatching, bedding, basketry, brewing and dyeing. In Sutherland in 1767 James Robertson saw women making a yellow dye from Heather tops (Henderson and Dickson 1994). Heather's properties as bedding seem near miraculous. According to Mary Beith (1995, p222) the late sixteenth-century Scots historian George Buchanan stated that Heather '. . . may vie in softness with the finest down, while in salubriousness it far exceeds it . . . so that those who, lie down languid and weary in the evening, arise in the morning vigorous and sprightly'.

131 Remains of Heather basket from the later Phase 7 of Howe Broch. The scale is 20cm. With suggested reconstruction from early twentieth-century examples

Heather, reputedly, had at least one other wonderful attribute. Charles Nelson (2000, p30) quoted the sixteenth-century writer Dr John Bellenden as follows: 'This herbe . . . namit hadder . . . in the moneth of July has ane floure of purpure hew, also sweit as huny. The Pichtis maid of this herbe, sum time, ane richt delicius and hailsum drink. Noctheless, the maner of the making of it is perist, be exterminioun of the said Pichtis out of Scotland; for they schew nevir the craft of making this drink bot to thair ain blud.'

Remains of Heather have been found repeatedly in Scottish archaeological contexts. However, it should be made clear that the 'heather' rope from Skara Brae was made from Crowberry and not Heather (as stated by Darwin 1996) and that the Heather ale, deduced from pollen analysis of pot sherds, from the Neolithic on Rum, needs re-evaluation.

Perusal of figures **6-10** is enough to show how important Heather is in Scottish pollen diagrams especially in the last few to several thousand years.

Hemp (*Cannabis sativa*)
132

As explained by Stearn, *Cannabis* is the Latin name derived from a language of Central Asia or the Near East and giving rise to both the words canvas and hemp. The first claim of the recognition of Hemp in Scottish archaeology was made in 1875 by A.J. Warden who had opened cists at Barnhill Links near Broughty Ferry. In one he found that the limbs appeared '. . . at first sight to be closely tied or wound round by some fibrous substance somewhat resembling a tarred hemp string'. There are no corroboratory details but, intriguingly, there is now another claim for Hemp in prehistoric Scotland. Michael Ryder (1999) made diameter measurements of the fibres in cloth and string and thought Hemp more likely than Flax. His material came from a Bronze Age site at St Andrews. Next, there are the lengths of hempen rope from the Roman fort at Bar Hill, mentioned in chapter 1.

Apart from trying to identify fibres, the history of Hemp in Scotland can be investigated by archival research and by recognising its pollen, which is very similar to that of Hops. Graeme Whittington and Kevin Edwards have done both. To understand why Hemp is so elusive in the subfossil record its culture and uses need to be comprehended.

Like Flax, the cultivation and processing of which have been described above, it is grown as an annual crop on rich soils. Seeds are stripped off in early autumn and the stems retted in pits, although there is an old practice of leaving the stems until winter begins for dew-retting, a slow but effective method of loosening the bast fibres. It is not known if this was practised in Scotland. The rest of the preparation is similar to that of Flax. Both pollen and seeds, however, have been recovered and, together with historical evidence, they indicate an industry widespread in both time and space. In the eighteenth century Hemp was still being cultivated in the Outer Hebrides, Islay and in Galloway. Place name evidence incorporating Hemp in the name comes from many parts including Caithness, Fife, East Lothian, Selkirk and Ayrshire.

132 Hemp

They do not, however, inform us when Hemp was introduced and for how long it was cultivated. Either Hemp fibre or canvas was imported, especially in the sixteenth century, and Whittington and Edwards point out that local production of canvas could have been from imported fibre.

Pollen sequences were analysed by Whittington and Edwards through the deposits in two lochs in Fife, a county of fertile soils with a long history of arable farming. Both sites showed cereal pollen, Hemp and weeds of cultivation as well as pastureland plants. The rise in Hemp at Black Loch begins in the eleventh century and falls in the thirteenth or fourteenth century. There are dating problems at Kilconquhar Loch, but Hemp was present continuously from the end of the sixteenth to the eighteenth century. Whittington and Edwards suggested that the reason for the differences lies in their two locations. Kilconquhar Loch is close to the East Neuk fishing ports where there may well have been a heavy demand for canvas, rope and fishing nets. Where rare seeds are found, as in late thirteenth- or early fourteenth-century Aberdeen and fourteenth- and fifteenth-century Elgin, were they chance finds still attached to fibre which was being retted or was Hemp being grown for the oil in its seeds or its therapeutic effects? Its usefulness as a drug plant was known in Scotland by the seventeenth century and, as it was already known to ancient civilisations, it is probable that its medicinal properties were also known in Scotland long before that. Dried flowering tops and seeds of the female plants contain the dark resin which is extracted for its sedative, analgesic and anti-inflammatory uses. Because *Cannabis* also has hallucinogenic properties it is at present prohibited to grow it in Britain. Unless the resin were also to be found it is unlikely that the finds of seeds would indicate whether it was grown for fibre, oil or medicine.

133   Lesser Celandine; the drawing clearly shows the root tubers

Lesser Celandine (*Ranunculus ficaria*)
133-135

This well-known, small spring-flowering Buttercup is one of the more surprising species to have turned up in recent years in prehistoric contexts across western and northern Europe including Scotland. The recovered parts are neither pollen nor seeds but the club- or spindle-shaped root tubers are up to 1cm long (tubers are swollen roots adapted for food storage). *Ranunculus* is the Latin name, from the diminutive of *rana*, a frog, because many species of the genus grow in damp places and *ficaria* is a Medieval plant name probably from *Ficus*, the Fig, with reference to the tubers are somewhat resembling little figs. A taller plant strongly connected with human habitations and with an archaeological history of some interest, the Greater Celandine, is an unrelated plant of the Poppy family.

Often growing in woods, though not on the most acid soils, Lesser Celandine also flourishes on damp ground of grasslands and riverbanks. It occurs throughout the British Isles including the remotest islands, such as Foula, Fair Isle, the Flannan Isles, and St Kilda, where no trees cast any shade and never have done for tens of thousands of years. On Orkney where there is virtually no semi-natural woodland it grows in 'mainly damp and shady places' (Bullard 1995). Attractive in its bright yellow flowers, it is occasionally planted, sometimes in a form with many petals (*flore pleno*). On the Faroes it is an alien and, having been planted as a medicinal herb in churchyards, it is called kirkjubøólja (Ostenfeld and Gröntved 1934; Rasmussen 1989).

This is a particularly noteworthy plant as its ancient and modern uses are quite different. The plant contains saponins, protoanemin, anemonin and tannins. It is astringent and the saponins are fungicidal. It was recorded by Theophrastus (370-285 BC) and in the first century AD Dioscorides recommended the juice of the plant for purging the head and to use as a gargle. In the late sixteenth century 'the doctrine of signatures' became fashionable and plants were thought to show a divinely-inspired resemblance to the part of the body they were intended to cure. The tubers of Lesser Celandine look somewhat like haemorrhoids and so the plant was used to treat piles so successfully that it became known as Pilewort. This must be one of the very few instances where, purely by chance, the plant does resemble the complaint it is most suited to treat. We can assume that before the late sixteenth century, the plant would still have been used because Dioscorides recommended it; herbals were then still based on classical authors' uses. Some 2500 species strong, the Buttercup family has few food plants but many members contain suites of toxins and the frequently cultivated Monk's-hood is often referred to as the most poisonous plant in Europe. Some archaeologists have claimed that the tubers of

134 (left) Map of Lesser
     Celandine
135 (above) Tubers of Lesser
     Celandine from Howe
     Broch. The longest is
     about 10mm

Lesser Celandine were eaten; see the account of Skara Brae in chapter 3.

According to Sturtevan (1919), Linnaeus stated that the young leaves can be eaten with other potherbs.

Mace (*Myristica fragans*)
136, 137

The generic name *Myristica* comes from the Greek myristikos 'fit for anointing'. A tree reaching 20m, *M. fragrans* is a one of about 80 species in the genus from south-east Asia and Australia. Each fruit gives both a single nutmeg, the seed proper, and mace, botanically called an aril, an external appendage eaten by pigeons which in so doing disperse the seeds. The original area of the Nutmeg is Maluku (Mollucas or Spice Islands), part of Indonesia. Though still frequently used as spices, nutmeg and mace formerly had a culinary and medicinal, and consequently commercial, importance very much greater than now. According to Balick and Cox (1996, p137) '. . . nutmegs that cost the Dutch $1 in Banda could be resold for $30,000 in Amsterdam', and according to Milton (1999) in sixteenth-century London nutmegs had a mark up of 60,000%. They and other spices, such as

265

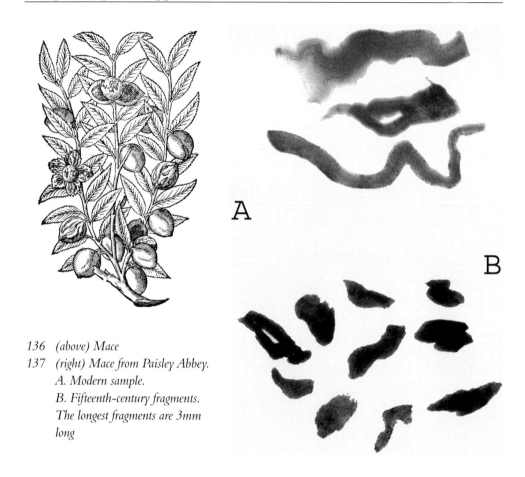

136   (above) Mace
137   (right) Mace from Paisley Abbey.
       A. Modern sample.
       B. Fifteenth-century fragments.
       The longest fragments are 3mm
       long

pepper, cinnamon and cloves, were very profitable cargoes carried by the Dutch East India Company's ships such as had been intended for the ill-fated Batavia wrecked off the west coast of Australia in 1629 (Godard 1993). Long before the Dutch, the Portugese had exploited the Banda Islands, the sole small part of Maluku where Nutmeg trees grew. The tempting, but inconclusive, evidence for Nutmeg and Mace in southern Europe in Classical times has been discussed by Innes Miller (1969). According to Flach and Willink (1989, p193) 'The first record in Europe, in Constantinople, dates from AD 540. At the end of the twelfth century the species was generally known in Europe'. In 1386 in *The Canterbury Tales* Chaucer wrote about putting nutmeg in ale. It was and is still used as seasoning of meat stuffings, egg and cheese dishes, sauces, soups and vegetables. Extracts are used in the canning industry and in cosmetics.

CD's recovery of fragments of mace from the silted-up fifteenth-century drains below Paisley Abbey is the first and so far only discovery in world archaeology. What a picture is conjured up! The fruits had grown on the Banda Islands, been harvested, separated into nutmeg and mace, exported all the way from south-east Asia to Europe, perhaps first to the Low Countries, then across the North Sea perhaps to Leith, then to the kitchen of the Abbey and finally entered the drains after flavouring some meal or drinks of the monks resident in one of the wealthier clerical communities in Scotland.

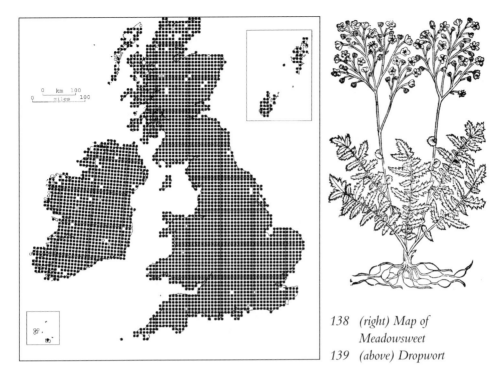

138 (right) Map of
      Meadowsweet
139 (above) Dropwort

In discussing medical uses in Maluku now, Van Gils and Cox (1994) are very cautious about ascribing to nutmeg any psychoactive properties. Though mentioning toxicity, they make no comment about any ecbolic results implied or claimed outright by some such as Bianchini *et al.* (1976) '. . . one has to glance through Victorian cookery books giving very big quantities of nutmeg to understand the enormously high rate of miscarriages at that time'. Flach and Willink state that the consumption of two ground nutmegs can cause death. Stressing serious side effects, Liener stated (1969, p413) 'The nutmeg has been used as a panacea for a wide variety of ailments including toothache, dysentery, rheumatism, halitosis, and for inducing abortions'. An essential oil, myristicin, is the toxic substance. Perhaps misled by the illustration in the earlier editions of Mattioli, Turner (1568) thought that Mace was the flower of Nux myristica and considered that 'Mace . . . is much binding and very spicy'.

Archaeobotany has produced other evidence of the importation of species from faraway places. From Medieval Kiel in north-western Germany, Wiethold (1995) found Pepper (from southern India) and Malagueta Pepper (from West Africa).

Meadowsweet (*Filipendula ulmaria*) and Dropwort (*F. vulgaris*)
138-140

In Britain many plants have lots of common names; see Geoffrey Grigson's book for lists and very readable discussions. Some of the vernacular names for *Filipendula ulmaria* used in Britain and elsewhere in Northern Europe indicate the archaeological interest of this

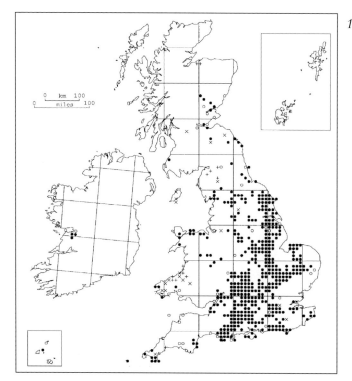

140   Map of Dropwort.
Vertical crosses show
records of planted
occurrences recorded
before 1950 and
diagonal crosses after
1950

plant: Lady of the Meadow; Queen of the Meadow; Blackin-girse (Shetland); Yule-girse (Orkney); Meadwort (Somerset) and Meadurt (southern Scotland); mjödört (Sweden, with different spellings in Norway and the Faeroe Islands). The Scandinavian names mean mead plant, i.e. the plant used to flavour mead, fermented honey, as surely must the two given above from Somerset and southern Scotland. William Turner (1568) gives the name as 'medewurte'.

Filipendula comes from the Latin a thread and hanging. This refers to the root tubers of Dropwort (*F. vulgaris*), a southern lime-lover, as the map shows, is the only other indigenous member of the genus in Northern Europe. *Ulmaria* refers to the leaflets' resemblance to the leaves of Elm (*Ulmus*).

Linnaeus called the plant *Spiraea Ulmaria* and in the first part of that old binomial resides yet more archaeological interest because the term aspirin is derived from it. Many know about salicylic acid being prepared from the bark of Willow (*Salix*), but it was from Meadowsweet flower buds that the preparation was first made. The *a* of the name *aspirin* comes from *acetylsalicylic acid* and the *spir* from *Spiraea*. William Turner had nothing of note to say about Meadowsweet, but John Gerard (1633) stated 'It is reported that the floures boiled in wine and drunke do maketh the heart merrie'. In the Highlands and Islands, according to Mary Beith (1995, p236), Meadowsweet was 'Traditionally used for treating feavers and headaches, its Gaelic name, meaning Cu-Chulainn's belt, comes from a story about the great Celtic hero. Ill with a fierce fever, Cu-Chulainn was cured by being bathed in meadowsweet.' With regard to folk medicine in Central Europe, Weber (1995) lists diuretic, sudorific and astringent effects. He also mentions that in Siberia the plants were

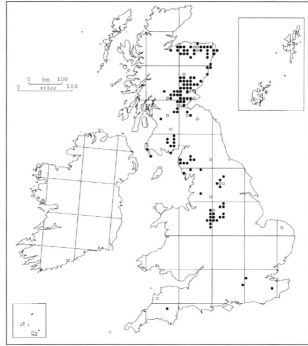

141 (above) Monk's Rhubarb.
From Lousley and Kent
(1981)

142 (left) Map of Monk's
Rhubarb

eaten and the rhizomes made into a porridge.

The first recognition of *Filipendula* pollen from a Scottish archaeological context was made by CD when pollen analysing the contents of the Bronze Age cist at Ashgrove in Fife. The use of the generic name alone is deliberate; the pollen of the two species cannot be readily distinguished. In the Scottish context, pollen is much more likely to have derived from Meadowsweet, a tall and abundant plant of fens, than from Dropwort, a low-growing plant of well-drained ground and of very local current occurrence in Scotland and of restricted past occurrence too because of its soil requirements. Meadowsweet has a long flowering season from early summer through to autumn. It does not produce nectar but the flowers are visited by bees to collect pollen. Its pollen is a well-known component, sometimes minor, sometimes major, of honey in Britain and elsewhere (Deans 1957, Maurizio 1971, Fossel 1974). The attractiveness of Meadowsweet for honey bees is made very clear by this translation from Norwegian: 'In Ostfold and Vestfold they used to rub beehives with leaves or flowers of Meadowsweet to induce a swarm to enter the hive. This is an old practice and derives from the time when people used straw hives but even today it has not completely died out . . . If you rub your hands and clothes with the flowers it calms the bees during handling.' (Hoeg, 1974, p362). See chapter 4, Pollen Analyses and Burial Practices, for the discussion of the significance of Meadowsweet pollen in Scottish prehistory.

No remains of Dropwort have been identified from Scotland or the rest of Britain. However, from central Sweden, Roger Engelmark (1984) found the carbonised root tubers as grave goods from Iron Age cemeteries.

269

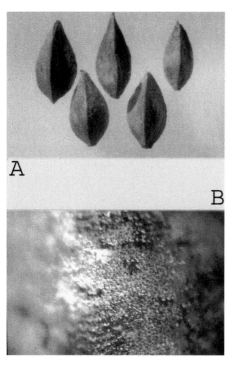

A

B

143   Remains of Monk's Rhubarb from
Paisley Abbey. A. Five seeds. B. Seed
surface much magnified to show
characteristic pattern. The longest seed is
almost 3mm long

Monk's rhubarb (*Rumex pseudoalpinus*)
141-143

Rumex was the Latin name and *alpinus* refers to the Alps, where this tall perennial Dock with very broad leaves is abundant by roadsides and around farms, and *pseudo*, of course, means false. It has long been realised that this species is an introduction in Britain, as the common name hints. It has edible leaves, cooked or raw. The rhizomes, underground creeping stems, have been used as a purgative.

In their book on *Docks and Knotweeds of the British Isles,* Lousley and Kent state (p118) 'This species was formerly used for medicinal and veterinary purposes and is still valued in the Alps for the treatment of sore places on the udders of cows in the mountain pastures. It is probable that it was for such uses as this that Monk's Rhubarb was dispersed among the northern farming communities in Britain rather than, as is often suggested, because the large leaves were used for wrapping up butter.'

Whatever had been the use made by the inhabitants of Paisley Abbey, seeds recovered from the drains below that establishment were, like Mace, a very satisfying discovery (CD 1996). The seeds have not been recognised from any other British archaeological layer or from layers in continental Europe. The Cluniac Crossraguel Abbey was a sister house of Paisley Abbey. It is situated beside the main road (A77) between Maybole and Kirkoswald, Ayrshire. In 1983 JHD found Monk's Rhubarb growing on the roadside verge by the Abbey. Perhaps it had survived from ancient cultivation, but it was unfortunately destroyed by road widening some years later. The map shows that this archaeophyte has become established in widespread areas of upland Britain, especially eastern Scotland.

Mosses (especially the weft- and fan-forming spp)
144-146

Large species of mosses have been recovered time and again from archaeological contexts, often in both diversity and abundance. The Pictish site at Dundurn in the central Highlands is a good example. Interpreted as flooring material dumped on a midden, the

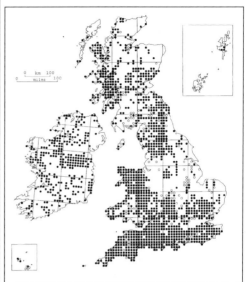

144 *(left) Map of* Hylocomium splendens

145 *(below) Map of* Neckera complanata

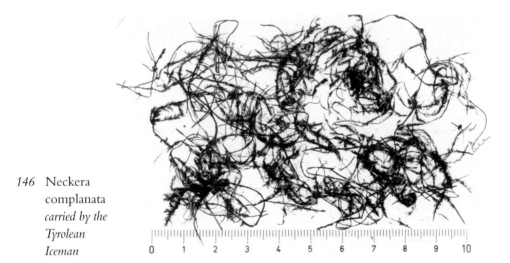

146 Neckera
complanata
carried by the
Tyrolean
Iceman

richly organic layer with much Bracken yielded 15 species of mosses, 10 of which are woodland plants, including two species of *Neckera*, *N. complanata* and *N. crispa*. The generic name commemorates the German botanist Noel Joseph de Necker, *complanata* means flattened and *crispa* refers to the crisped appearance of the leaves.

As mentioned in the account of Bogmoss, few mosses have vernacular names and the species of *Neckera* are not among them. *Neckera complanata* has exceptional archaeological interest because of its deliberate, selective use as part of the boat caulking technique in Bronze Age Yorkshire and both *Neckera* spp were carried by the Tyrolean Iceman for some

271

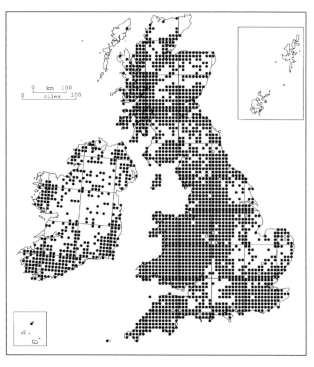

147   Sessile Oak. The leaf bases indicate Sessile rather than Pedunculate Oak. The catkins are male and no female ones are shown

148   Map of Sessile Oak

purpose that may never be known with certainty (JHD 2000b). These happen to be three particular examples with which JHD has been involved. However, there are a great many more archaeological discoveries from across Europe and from all periods back to the Neolithic. These two species of *Neckera,* which have a life form called fan (Bates 1998), and other large mosses such as *Hylocomium splendens* and *Rhytidiadelphus* spp (which have the life form called weft) can be gathered in large masses, easily freed of impurities such as any adhering soil and are highly suitable for packing, stuffing and wiping. Such mosses have been found in many ancient cess-pits in both Britain and Scandinavia. Viking and Medieval towns were very mossy places. *Hylocomium splendens* is perhaps the most frequently encountered moss species in archaeological layers in Britain and elsewhere in Europe (JHD 1973, 1986). The maps indicate how easily available these mosses would have been to anyone wishing to use them for whatever purposes.

Oaks (*Quercus* spp)
147-149

Quercus was the Latin name for these trees, some deciduous and some evergreen, which number about 400 species, growing very largely in north temperate regions. In Britain there are only two indigenous species: the Pedunculate Oak with stalked acorns (*Q. robur;*

149 *Ring of Oak trunks with an inside diameter of 1.50m at the west end of Mugdock Wood. The tree would have been first coppiced 500 years or more ago*

robur having been the Latin word for Oak-wood with the connotation of strength) and the Sessile Oak, with stalkless acorns (Q. *petraea*; *petraea* meaning rock-loving). The map shows the spread of Sessile Oak but it should be realised that the natural patterns of the two Oaks have been much changed by planting and hybridisation. The absence from the Northern Isles now may be due to ancient overexploitation. Bennett *et al.* (1992) considered that the Oak or Oaks grew on Shetland several thousand years ago; the two species cannot be separated on pollen characteristics.

The Oaks are potentially very long-lived trees providing very good timber and both can be coppiced and pollarded; in Scotland there is abundant evidence of coppicing but very little of pollarding. A few of the coppiced Oaks at Mugdock Wood, north of Glasgow, are massive enough to indicate that the cutting down started in Medieval times (Stevenson 1990) and, on the basis of annual ring counts, some of the very ancient looking, romantically-shaped Oaks in the wood pasture at Cadzow, near Hamilton, are several hundred years old, having germinated from acorns in Medieval times (Dougall and Dickson 1997, 1999). At both these places, as is typical of the Oaks in Scotland, many of the trees have characters of both the species and can be considered hybrids (Q. x *rosacea*; *rosacea* meaning rose-like). As discussed cogently by Oliver Rackham (1980), there is no need to question the native status of Pedunculate Oak in Scotland, as had been asserted by Anderson (1967).

With wide tolerance of soil type, the Oaks are capable of growing on soils of poor nutrient status and of low reaction. The fruit is the familiar acorn but not so familiar, perhaps, is the fruiting behaviour. Any stand of Oaks only produces heavy crops every six or seven years, with some of the intervening years being totally barren.

With its usually clear-cut annual rings and distinctive pattern of other anatomical features (the grain), wood of Oak is readily recognisable. Wood and charcoal of Oak are recovered over and over again from Scottish archaeological layers but there are very few discoveries of acorns or their cups, or cupules in the botanical jargon. From the Mesolithic site at Glen Lussa in the north of the Inner Hebridean Island of Jura, John Mercer (1974) reported a few burnt acorn 'husks' with many fragments of Hazel shells and a solitary

Bramble pip. It is tempting to wonder if the Mesolithic folk had been using acorns as food. Had that been the case then roasting would have been required to reduce the bitterness from the abundant tannin.

As the noted plant ecologist A.G. Tansley put it (1952, p18), 'Oak combines the qualities of hardness, weight, suppleness, and toughness in a remarkable degree. It is very durable even under water . . . It is also easily worked and its surface is of considerable beauty.' Apart from the fine timber for constructing ships and buildings and for making furniture, Oak has or had a variety of uses: charcoal for smelting, bark for tanning leather and dyeing (production of pyroligneous acid). British prehistoric canoes are overwhelmingly of Oak (Mowat 1996). The plough stilt from the Milton Loch crannog of the second century AD was of Oak (Pigott 1955).

150   Opium Poppy

Opium Poppy (*Papaver somniferum*)
150-152

The three seeds of this infamous plant from the Oakbank Crannog prove its occurrence in Scotland in prehistoric times, long before the Roman occupation of Scotland, but it is a plant much better known from later deposits of Roman and Medieval age. *Papaver* is the Latin name for the plant and *somniferum* refers to the sleep-inducing properties which arise from opium, a suite of more than 30 alkaloids including morphine and codeine, present in the latex of the fruit walls and other parts of the plant. Morphine is 4-21% by weight of opium. Opium, it should be stressed, does not occur in the seeds which, however, are rich in oil and are often used to sprinkle over bread. However, opium adheres in small amounts to the surface of the seeds and, even after baking, still occurs in trace amounts.

Like many cultivated plants Opium Poppy is very variable and its taxonomy is not straight forward (Kadereit 1986). There is Opium Poppy in the strict sense, subspecies *somniferum,* which is known only in cultivation or escaped therefrom. In addition there is subspecies *setigerum,* which may deserve full species rank. It is a weed readily found around the Mediterranean, particularly in the west, and in Morocco and Macaronesia (the Canary Islands, Madeira and Azores).

Opium Poppy grows best on rich, circumneutral soils. Unlike other Poppies, the capsular fruits do not open to allow dispersal of the often 7,000 or more seeds but birds can break their way in, or decay of the fruit wall will release the seeds. The map shows its very widespread occurrence in Britain. Its commonness does not result from an illicit desire to cultivate a drug plant but from the fashion for growing many very decorative cultivars in gardens from where the seeds reach waste ground on which the plant can established itself at least temporarily.

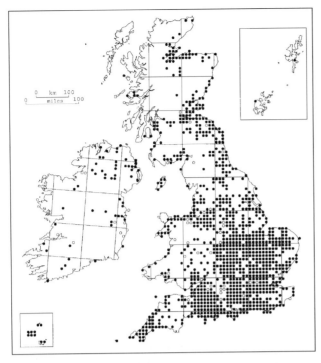

151 (left) Map of Opium Poppy which is an archaeophytic alien. The records derive from seeds having grown up on waste ground and in and around gardens where the plants had been grown for the decorative rather than narcotic qualities

152 (below) Seeds of Opium Poppy from a well in the Roman fort at Welzheim in southern Germany. From Körber-Grohne et al. (1983). The seeds are about 1mm long

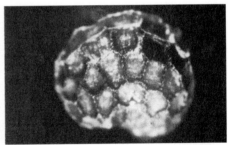

Ramsons (*Allium ursinum*)
153-155

Allium is the classical Latin name for Garlic and *ursinum* refers to bears, and the combination *Allium ursinum* occurs in Pliny. Also known as Wild Garlic, Ramsons often grows in large, dense stands on damp but well-drained and fertile soils in woods and other shady places. Both pollen and seeds of Ramsons have been recorded from Neolithic Switzerland and in Denmark an impression of a fruiting head was found on prehistoric pot. The plant may be used as food as the flavour of both leaves and bulbs is similar to that of onions. If eaten in large quantities it is poisonous to stock. It is worth noting that Ramsons has similar properties to those of the cultivated Garlic; the uses of Garlic as a medicinal plant go back at least 4000 years. Garlic bulbs possess many complex chemicals including a volatile oil containing alicin which is reputed to have antibiotic, hypotensive and antithrombic effects. Garlic and related plants have been considered not just as aphrodisiacs or stimulating and

275

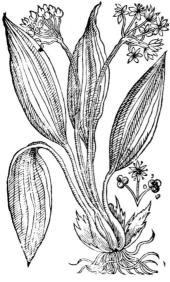

153 (above) Ramsons

154 (right) Map of Ramsons

155 (left) Carbonised bulbs of Ramsons from the Fairy Knowe Broch. The bulbs are about 2 to 3cm long

strengthening agents, but have also been subject to 'anti-allium sentiments' (Simoons 1998).

On the Isle of Skye Ramsons was used as a potherb, an infusion was taken internally for the 'stone', it was considered good for purifying the blood and was used as a drawing poultice (Beith 1995).

The bulbs of Ramsons store the carbohydrate, fructan. Because of their subterranean growth any accidental removal of the bulbs into a dwelling seems improbable and so the discovery by William Boyd of carbonised bulbs from the broch at Fairy Knowe in Stirlingshire is very remarkable and unique in archaeology. As the map shows, Ramsons would have been readily available to the early inhabitants of Scotland in most areas, though not in much of the Highlands or Orkney.

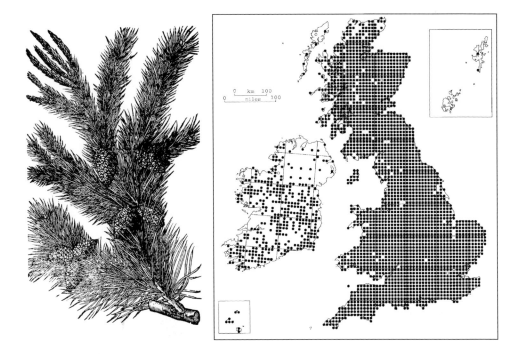

156 (left) Scots Pine. The drawing clearly shows the two needles (leaves) per short shoot and the typical small cones

157 (right) The map shows all records of Scots Pine in the British Isles. The last native Scots Pines disappeared from Ireland a few thousand years ago and from England too, unless scattered trees growing on bogs are descendants of native stock. The vast majority of records from throughout Britain and Ireland are of planted trees or escapes from cultivation (by seed)

Scots pine (*Pinus sylvestris*)
156-160

Growing from the northwest Highlands of Scotland all the way to eastern Siberia, Scots Pine is the most widely distributed of all the nearly 100 species of Pine, most of which inhabit the Northern Hemisphere. *Pinus* is the original Latin name and *sylvestris* means of the woods or merely wild, as in the Spanish 'flores sylvestres' meaning wild flowers. Some taxonomists have considered the pyramidal-shaped, short-leaved and short-coned trees in Scotland to be distinct and have called them subspecies *scotica*.

Capable of growing into a tree of over 30m though not especially long-lived, Scots Pine produces useful timber. It can flourish on a variety of soil types but is most usual on nutrient poor and strongly acidic, coarse mineral soils or peats. Success of regeneration by seed is encouraged by fires that have bared and fertilised the soil. To coppice a Scots Pine is to kill it. The map shows Scots Pine as growing all over Britain including even Shetland but the vast majority of the dots represent planted trees or their escaped offspring. The only remaining indigenous Scots Pines are those in the scattered remnant woodlands in

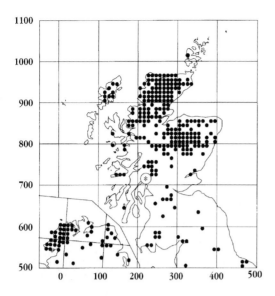

158 Map of ancient Scots Pine stumps in peat. The encircled asterisk shows the location of the stumps at Loch Sloy. Modified from Bennett (1995)

159 (below) This is the dated stump from Loch Sloy. However hard the wood is and however recent the stump appears, this tree was growing about 2750 BC. From Wylie and Dickson 1988

the Scottish Highlands. The southernmost, few and very spread out native trees are in Glen Falloch at the head of Loch Lomond where, as elsewhere, without protection from Sheep and Red Deer, regeneration is suppressed.

Often looking of very recent growth, stumps and logs of this tree are familiar in eroded peat bogs throughout much of Scotland, especially the Highlands, and have engendered much comment from many authors including the perplexed Herbert Maxwell (1915, p162) who thought that 'One of the darkest enigmas of natural science is presented in the remains of pine forest buried under such a dismal treeless expanse as the Moor of Rannoch, and on the Highland hills up to and beyond 2000 feet altitude . . .'. Certainly such places in the Highlands can be a very impressive sight but now the darkness has vanished and there is great understanding of the age of these remains and of the ecological conditions under which the woodlands grew. Fresh as they may seem, nonetheless, the vast majority of the stumps are more than 4000 years old, as radiocarbon dating has

160   *Ancient Scots Pine stumps exposed by peat erosion at 670m a.s.l. on Coire Riabach,
Banffshire. Such dramatic sights of tree remains entombed in peat have caused wonder for
many years, such as more than two centuries ago when the Rev Christopher Tait (1794)
investigated the raised bogs in the Upper Forth Valley. This photograph was taken by Francis
Lewis (1906) who studied Scottish peat stratigraphy; he wrongly thought that peat which we
now know formed within the last 11,250 years (The Holocene, the post-glacial period)
encompassed glacial stages*

repeatedly shown. With the pollen and macroscopic fossil analyses by Hilary Birks (1975) setting a high standard, there have been various investigations showing in detail that the precise nature of the tree-bearing peat had not been too acidic or infertile.

Pollen of Scots Pine is found in all long sequences of peat and mud that have been investigated in Scotland, and sometimes the amounts are large and sometimes small (**6-10**). In the case of low or very low percentages particularly, the interpretation in terms of immediately local, regional or distant growth can be very difficult. Of all the indigenous trees in Scotland, Scots Pine has the most complex history. The scattered much reduced native Scots Pine woodlands, often referred to as the former Caledonian Forest or the Great Wood of Caledon (a romantic, misleading name; Breeze 1992, JHD 1992), contain trees of different origins and histories. Those from Wester Ross, for instance, are genetically different from those in the Cairngorm region (Perks and Ennos 1999). In the last few decades, there have been several summaries of the Scottish history of Scots Pine and the most recent summary being that of Bennett (1995). The last word on the Late-glacial and Holocene history of Scots Pine has yet to be said.

The timber has been used for boat and house building and furniture making, and pieces of the resin-rich root wood for tapers. At Oakbank Crannog, only one small chip of Scots Pine was found apart from tapers; the resinous nature of Pine wood allows a long

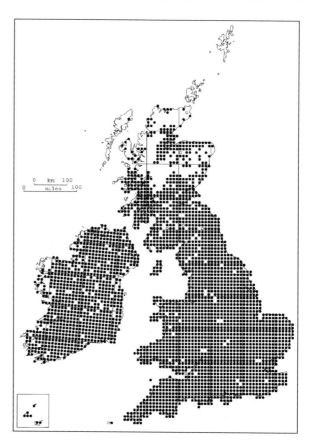

161 *(above) Sloe. The drawing shows the leaves and fruits well but omits any thorns. However, the degree of thorniness varies greatly*

162 *(left) Map of Sloe*

slow burn (Sands 1997). In Wester Ross, John Lightfoot (1777) saw fishermen making ropes from the inner bark. That author thought (p558) 'few trees have been apply'd to more uses than this'. The bark of Scots Pine has been eaten in Fennoscandia (Sturtevant 1919). From the Highlands and islands particularly, wood and charcoal of Scots Pine have frequently extracted from archaeological layers from the Neolithic onwards.

Sloe (*Prunus spinosa*)
161-163

This densely growing, spiny, early-flowering shrub inhabits all of Britain except the Northern Isles and the Outer Hebrides; the records from the Outer Hebrides shown on the map are known to be based on planted trees. *Prunus*, the Latin name, is a genus of more than 200 species including many bearing edible fruits: almonds, apricots, cherries, peaches and plums. Some of the side branches of Sloe become thorns, and so hence *spinosa*. Botanically the fruit of the Sloe is exactly like a small plum, though bitter to the taste, unlike the lusciousness of the many different sorts of Plums proper. However, Sloe fruits are famous for their use as a flavouring for alcohol such as gin or, as John Lightfoot put it (1777, p255), 'and the fruit will make a very grateful and fragrant wine'. Preparations of Sloe were used to treat asthma, scabies and relaxed throats (Beith 1995).

Remains of Sloe, often called Blackthorn, are well known from prehistoric sites across Europe. Usually the parts found are the stones of the fruits, as from a Neolithic site at Balfarg, in Fife, and from the crannogs at Old Kilpatrick in the Clyde Estuary and Oakbank in Loch Tay. Wood and charcoal has been recovered, as from the Skara Brae middens and the Bronze Age site at Ardnave on Islay. It is very evident from these and many other recoveries from archaeological sites that the fruits of the Sloe were often gathered from the wild. Did prehistoric people eat the fruits of the Sloe despite the bitterness? One of the most surprising discoveries of Sloe concerns the Tyrolean Iceman, who was well-clothed and equipped even with a framed rucksack, though little remained of that, and whatever the contents may have been they are unknown. Beside the body of this Neolithic man there was a single whole fruit, not just the stone, but also with the adherent soft tissue intact (Spindler 1994, Oeggl and Schoch 1995). Had he been carrying dried fruit as part of his provisions?

163 Stone of Sloe, opened by a Bank Vole, from Old Kilpatrick Crannog. The stone is about 1cm long

The point is that drying produces palatability. Pat Wiltshire (1992) showed that drying and then wetting removes the astringency and produces a taste like stewed plums.

Walnut (*Juglans regia*)
164, 165

Juglans is the original Latin name and *regia* means royal. This is the only European species of the genus of some 21 species. It is not a Scottish or indeed an English native. The etymology of the name Walnut is of interest. Herbert Maxwell pointed out (1915, p130): 'The very name we have given it forbids us to claim the walnut as a native of the British Isles, for in Anglo-Saxon speech it was *weah nut*, the foreign nut . . .'. This begs the question of whether the name was devised in England or was already in use by the invading Anglo-Saxons. No matter, because the alien status of the tree in Britain is not in doubt.

Not just the tallest Walnut growing in Britain at present (in Perthshire) but a large proportion of the tallest British trees are in Scotland (Mitchell 1996). But in northern Britain this tree, which thrives and fruits heavily in southern Europe, fruits poorly if at all. Alan Mitchell (1996, p246) stated 'Like the sweet chestnut, the fruit is in need of hotter summers to ripen fully than it can have in Britain, and to reach the size the Romans were used to . . .'. The map indicates only planted trees in Scotland; nobody has ever reported a self-sown tree north of the Border. Most Scottish Floras do not even mention Walnut. The splendid *Flora of Moray, Nairn & East Inverness* by Mary McCallum Webster (1978) is an exception. She states merely 'Planted' apart from listing localities, some of them being

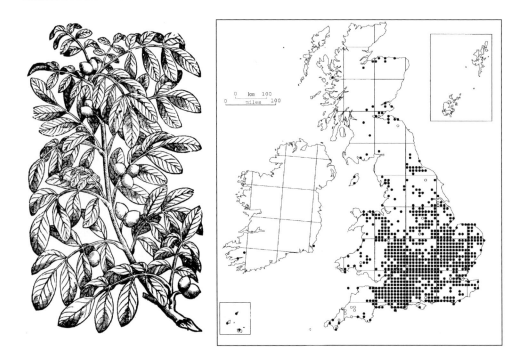

164   (left) Walnut

165   (right) Map of Walnut. All the Scottish records are of planted trees. There appear never to have
      been any records of germinated seeds growing into trees in the wild in Scotland

the grounds of grand dwellings.

In the light of this unsatisfactory cropping in Scotland, it is of interest that, at the Roman fort at Bar Hill on the Antonine Wall, excavation of the well produced '. . . one or two walnuts — apparently grown in an uncongenial climate, as they were stunted and had no kernels . . .' (Macdonald and Park 1906, p129). This should not be taken as an indication of local growth of the tree, since it is much more likely that the shells were discarded remnants of imported fruit from points further south, perhaps England or even further afield. Mary Fraser (1981) found remains of Walnut fruits at Medieval Perth and Elgin; these, too, are likely to have been imports. CD recovered shell fragments from the drain beneath Paisley Abbey.

Woad (*Istatis tintoria*)
166

'Ancient Britons never hit on anything as good as woad to fit on . . .' (two lines from 'Woad', sung to the tune Men of Harlech, Glasgow University Student Song Book 1953). This is part of the common knowledge that the Celts were said by the Romans to have painted or tattooed their skins with the blue dye derived from Woad. As Caesar stated in

De Bello Gallico (Book V, 14), 'All the Britons, indeed, dye themselves with woad, which produces a blue colour, and makes their appearance in battle more terrible' (Van der Veen *et al.* 1993).

Archaeobotany, whether north or south of the Border, has yet to throw any strong light on this matter, although Alan Hall (1995) has found pod fragments from a pit fill of late first century AD at Dragonby, near Scunthorpe, South Humberside. Tattoos on very ancient mummies can survive very well, as the simple therapeutic designs on the 5300 year old Tyrolean Iceman show (Egg *et al.* 1993). Only a well-preserved bog body of the correct period from some suitable peatland might throw light on the matter. [The surviving upper half of Lindow Man has no epidermal decoration and, sadly, no such corpse has yet been found in Scotland during the last few decades, the period of environmental archaeology. The discovery of a tattooed Pict grappling with a Roman centurian in his No.1 uniform would be most welcome. JHD would like to be that archaeobotanist first on the scene.]

166   Woad

Isatis is the classical Greek name and *tinctoria* refers to dyeing. Remains of Woad have yet to be found in Scotland, although it appears to have been imported in the twelfth century. Records show further imports at the end of the fifteenth century and again in 1612, with a number of other dyeplants, as listed by Su Grierson. It is likely to have been imported in the form of balls of crushed leaves; fragments of Woad stems have been found in Viking York. Woad appears to have been imported into Aberdeen and sent to Dundee to colour cloth which was being manufactured there.

As it is one of the few readily available plants that yield a good blue dye, it would have been much sought after. It grows well in sunny eastern Scotland but needs a rich soil. It is surprising that it was not cultivated there rather than imported, although it was grown in the Haddington district in the nineteenth century. The dye substance is indigotin, the same substance as in indigo, which was imported into Scotland from the seventeenth century, and which cannot be distinguished from Woad on fabric analysis. The complex processes involved in dyeing with Woad suggest that it was not used to dye fabric in Scotland until commercial dyeing was undertaken in towns.

Yew (*Taxus baccata*)
167-169

Many thousands of words have been written in articles and in books devoted to this low-growing, often planted even if sombre, evergreen tree, which is encrusted with legends. The ancient, fragmented tree, at least 2000 years old, at Fortingall in Perthshire, is part of

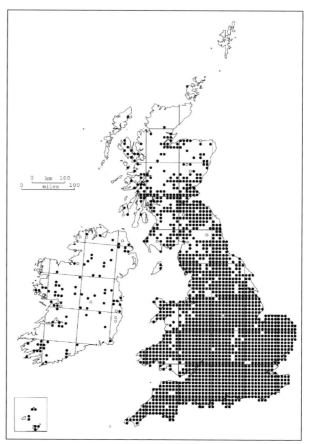

167 *(above) Yew. Yew is another tree with separate male and female plants but the drawing shows both male (left) and seeds (mainly to the right). The tuft of short leaves (top left) is an aberration of some kind*

168 *(above right) Map of Yew. The vast majority of the Scottish localities are of planted trees or escapes from cultivation*

the tree's romantic fascination; it is claimed to be 5000 years old (Chetan and Brueton 1994) or even 'could be over 8000 years' (Bellamy 1998) which becomes 'possibly 9000' in Lewington and Parker (1999). *Taxus* is a small genus and *T. baccata* is the only species indigenous in Europe. *Taxus* was the Latin name and *baccata* means berry-like; the seeds have a scarlet, fleshy appendage (an aril), which is not poisonous though other parts of the tree are toxic because of alkaloids.

There are few places in Scotland where stands of Yew are growing wild, that is to say not obviously planted or self-sown from nearby planted trees. The vast majority of records shown on the map derive from planted trees. JHD (1994a and b) has questioned the evidence for its native status in Scotland, although there are ancient occurrences of the easily identifiable wood and charcoal and even of the not so easily recognisable pollen (listed in JHD 1994a). One such discovery is the pins made of Yew that were recovered from the six- to ninth-centuries AD layers in a ditch on Iona (Barber 1981), another is the sword of Bronze Age date from Grotsetter, Orkney (Stevenson 1960) and yet another is

169   Fortingall tree as published in Pennant's 1774 volume

the longbow broken more than 5500 BC and found sticking out of peat at Rotten Bottom in the Tweedsmuir Hills (Sheridan 1996). Because of its strong, springy wood, Yew makes the best long bows and most, but not all, ancient bows from across Europe are made of that wood, such as the bow found with the Tyrolean Iceman and the two of Neolithic age from the Somerset Levels (Clark 1963). The Tlingit Indians of north-western North America made bows of the local Pacific Yew but also of Western Hemlock (Suttles 1990). Pacific Yew is called 'bow plant' by a number of First Peoples in that region (Turner 1998).

The Medieval Welsh made bows out of Elm, but longbows of Yew were those that were so effective in warfare, as the French and Scots found out to their cost in their clashes with the English (Bradbury 1985). Nonetheless, the inhabitants of Scotland had a long tradition of archery as the Pictish symbol stones alone show. The Picts used both shortbows and crossbows (Sutherland 1995).

The Yew may be an ancient introduction in Scotland. The status of the tree needs to be tested by analyses of long pollen sequences, going back to the earliest Holocene, before any likelihood of human planting, from those places such as the Loch Linnhe area where there are wild-looking populations (Dickson 1994a).

As Sands (1997) showed, many different types of wood were used in the construction of the Oakbank Crannog which was situated only about 4km from Fortingall. Scaife recognised one pollen grain of Yew from his analyses of the floor deposits. However, a single grain could have come a very long way. Had Sands found timber of Yew, that would have been a fascinating discovery because of the nearby ancient tree, but he did not.

Appendix 1: Archaeobotany

Nomenclature and level of identification

Unambiguous and recognised throughout the scientific world, Latinised names (formal binomials) are usually used in biological reports written for archaeologists. They are given here as Appendices 4 and 5 for those plants and animals referred to in the text as English names. The level of identification possible for plant remains varies according to the type of material as well as the state of preservation. Seeds of a given species can often be distinguished from those of related species. For simplicity of description, the term 'seeds' covers not just seeds but other structures which function as seeds but which in a strict botanical sense are fruits. Any researcher attempting critical 'seed' identification should be well acquainted with the distinction.

The first part of a binomial is the name of the genus and always begins with a capital letter; the second part is the name of the species and begins with a lower case letter. For instance, well-preserved seeds of Creeping Buttercup (*Ranunculus repens*) can be distinguished from those of Meadow Buttercup (*Ranunculus acris*). Very poorly preserved Buttercup seeds may only be identified as *Ranunculus* sp where sp is the accepted abbreviation for species singular and spp is species plural. Wood and charcoal can usually be identified to the generic level, sometimes even to the species level. The flora of Scotland has only a few indigenous trees. Wych Elm (of the genus *Ulmus*, containing about 18 species) and Scots Pine (of the genus *Pinus*, of more than 90 species) are the only species of their respective genera native in Scotland. Wood or charcoal identified as these genera can therefore reasonably be taken to represent Wych Elm or Scots Pine but there is the problem of North American driftwood in western and northern coastal sites and of imported wood particularly in Roman sites.

In the most formal botanical usages, the binomial is followed by the authority, the person or persons who erected the name. *Ficus carica* L. is the Fig. L. stands for Linnaeus, the eighteenth-century plant taxonomist. Many of the formal names of the most familiar plants have Linnaeus as the authority, as can be seen in Appendix 4.

In order to cover these various levels of identification, the word taxon (pl. taxa) can be used. Taxon means any taxonomic category. It covers identifications to the family level, as in Buttercup family (the Ranunculaceae), to the generic level, as for instance Buttercup and to the specific level, as for Creeping Buttercup. Designation to a wider category 'type' or 'group' is sometimes all that is possible for certain pollen grains such as when a number of possible genera or species are involved. The 'Meadow Buttercup group' covers 12 species of the genus *Ranunculus*; this group is itself a subcategory of the 'Meadow Buttercup type', which includes five genera of Ranunculaceae.

The abbreviation *cf.* is used where an identification is tentative, usually either because the poor condition of the remains has restricted confidence or the recovered remains are insufficient to separate closely related species definitively. The degree of identification of plant material depends partly on the level of experience of the specialist and partly on the item to be identified. Whatever the level of skill of the researcher, comprehensive reference collections are needed both for pollen and all the various types of larger plant remains. The wise trainee apprentices him or herself to an established group, whilst building up both collections and expertise. When preparing reference material it must be borne in mind that herbarium sheets and seeds from botanical gardens are not necessarily correctly named. Unripe seeds, which may well be the only ones present on herbarium sheets, appear greenish or shrunken.

The processes of collecting, sieving, identifying and evaluating the plant material needs a fuller account than is possible here. The booklet *Handbook for Archaeologists No. 4 Archaeobotany* by James Grieg (1989) is most useful, not least in its list of reference manuals and research papers, only a small proportion of which are listed in the bibliography of the present book. The following sections amplify some important points. Other books and papers concerning pollen analysis are mentioned below. The recent book in German *Archäobotanik* by Jacomet and Kreuz (1999) is an authoritative, comprehensive survey.

Large (macroscopic) remains of plants

Sampling

It should already be apparent that environmental archaeology is time-consuming and consequently expensive. Initial costing of the project is therefore agreed after consultation with the archaeologist. Environmental archaeologists should, if at all possible, take their own samples or closely supervise the sampler. In light, especially sandy, soils modern seeds can travel down to lower levels and samples of the topmost levels should also be collected if such contamination is suspected. In loose building rubble, small rodents such as Mice and Voles store seeds well underground. Presumably cached by such a creature, seeds of Broad-leaved Dock found 2m below the surface of a broch on Orkney proved to be modern. With or without the prickly exterior covering, seeds of that plant deliberately left out in the Dicksons' pantry were soon removed by Field Mice. A Norman introduction in Britain, Rabbits can cause marked disturbance by their burrowing, as JHD saw along with Paul Mellar's excavators in the Mesolithic shell heaps on Oronsay.

Sieving the samples on site is not recommended, but can be essential if weight or space is a limiting factor in delivering material to the laboratory. Contamination by wind-blown plant material and abandoned remains of messy diggers' lunches can become an unhelpful complication.

Samples of charred remains and wood

Large samples, frequently of silt or clay, require special treatment. Machines of the Siraf type recirculating pumped water using basically an oil drum and a series of sieves can be made or purchased. As samples may be of about 20l, the amount of inorganic residue generated is considerable. These machines do not collect all the burnt fragments, as experimental work by Dominique de Moulins (1996) has recently shown. A proportion of each dried residue should therefore also be checked.

It is self-evident that the material from different contexts within a site may reveal different aspects of the inhabitants' economy. The very wet climate over much of Scotland will have mitigated against the use of storage pits for grain. Pits such as cess-pits and wells are likely to contain their original rubbish derived from a number of sources. Ditches can contain a natural infilling, rubbish or a mixture. If pits or ditches have remained waterlogged they should be sampled as for other waterlogged material. The contents of ovens, hearths and corn dryers will reveal remains of crops at different stages of preparation. Their analysis can indicate whether the processing was carried out before or after threshing. From the contents of a domestic oven the purity of a crop to be consumed can be deduced. Floor deposits can reveal crop cleaning processes; postholes can also contain this evidence, even when the floor appears clean, since burnt or rotten posts may have left spaces into which seeds could have percolated.

In order to gain a comprehensive view of the plant use at a site, a large number of samples may need to be taken. Good advice on sampling strategies was given by Van der Veen and Fjeller (1982). Later sub-sampling or even the selection of random samples may be needed.

The sparseness of cereal remains on many Scottish sites means that many or large samples may be needed in order to decide what had been a major and what a subsidiary crop.

The identification of cereal grains and chaff can be difficult. It is not easy to simulate the burning of ancient cereal grains and so reference grains may not resemble those which have survived burning in the past. Stephanie Jacomet's book (1987) is very useful for wheat and barley grains and chaff. As a result of the 1992 London Museum workshop, further information has been published on wheat identification. Wheats are particularly difficult to identify and it may take the specialist several years before a sufficient range of material has been encountered to enable confident identification. The recognition of Oat grains to the species level does not seem possible; by comparing well-preserved chaff fragments with the detailed drawings in Jane Renfrew's book (1973) it may, however, be feasible to identify the Oats to the species on the basis of the chaff identification. Oily seeds such as linseed can be distorted during the charring process. To help cope with these difficulties, meetings with other plant specialists are invaluable for the beginner.

If a house site is sampled for carbonised wood, charcoal should be collected from all features, so as to give as comprehensive a basis as possible for deducing the composition of the former woodland. Single larger pieces should be bagged and labelled separately, to avoid unnecessary duplication of work, since the brittleness of charcoal makes subsequent fragmentation into many pieces only too easy. The temptation to help loosen clayey material by breaking it up by hand whilst sieving must be resisted, otherwise charcoal and other fragile material may be shattered.

The temptation to take 'spot' samples should also be resisted, unless, for instance, an ear of burnt grain is noted. Such remains will suffer less damage if a quantity of the substrate is collected and the whole placed in a rigid container, remembering that damp samples cause cardboard containers to disintegrate. Tissue paper or other padding, inner and outer permanent labels are, of course, essential.

Whereas charcoal and other burnt plant materials need to be dried out before they can be identified, wood must normally be kept damp, ideally in double polythene bags, and kept fungus-free by adding a preservative or by storing at a low temperature, preferably below 4°C. Needless to say, paper and card labels soon disintegrate.

Waterlogged samples

If a site has remained waterlogged and is well sealed in from later activity, samples are best taken in a vertical column, from a cleaned face, into a metal box hammered into the section. If the column is from a ditch the apparently inorganic base should also be sampled. Boxes become very heavy when full and short boxes of about 25cm in length are easier to manoeuvre. It is all too easy to label the box inadequately; it is, of course, essential to label top and bottom and depths from the ground level. Secure polythene wrapping, firmly taped, is needed to prevent subsequent drying out. Pollen samples can be taken in the laboratory from the monolith when changes in stratigraphy can be more easily evaluated than on site on a dark and rainy day! It is surprising how quickly such columns will dry out in a centrally heated building. Such desiccation vitiates sampling and the teasing apart of possible bedding planes to remove wood and leaves, especially fragile moss stems, for instance, before sieving.

The depth of material removed for each sample depends on changes in the stratigraphy. About 5-10cm in depth should be selected initially with the volume depending on the richness of the seed content. Some muds and silts will break down in water, but samples containing humic matter will generally need soaking in very dilute sodium or potassium hydroxide to break up the material so that the resultant sieved material is clearly separated. Calcareous samples can be broken down in dilute hydrochloric acid. It is advisable first to break up material by hand to remove larger charcoal, wood fragments and other identifiable material. A known volume should be broken down and the sorting process described below repeated after sieving until ideally no more plant taxa are recorded. If clayey or silty material is being sieved, a sink trap becomes essential to avoid blocking the drains.

A series of sieves will probably be needed. A range of sieves of between 4 and 0.3mm mesh diameter are generally used. The sieved material should be searched systematically. A perspex trough with a grid etched on the base has been found useful. Remains considered identifiable can be removed with fine forceps or a paintbrush. The fine fraction may prove sterile or may contain innumerable tiny Rush seeds or other minute plant remains. The number of these and other superabundant seeds can be estimated by noting the proportion of the material searched. These, with other small translucent seeds, should be placed on a slide with warmed glycerine jelly beneath a sealed coverslip for later identification using a high power microscope. Round paint palettes of plastic or porcelain divided into three or four divisions are useful for initially segregating the remains. They can be covered with a half petri dish. A drop of dilute formalin will help to inhibit fungal growth. Many delicate remains will distort on drying out; glycerine can be added to prevent drying but it does tend to obscure the cell pattern. The cells are most clearly seen when the seed surface is drying.

Damp filter paper is a useful base on which to examine seeds.

Microscopes and identification

A low power stereomicroscope, with a cool light source, such as fibre-optic lighting, is used to examine the material, and identified seeds may be stored in small vials. A mixture of glycerol, ethanol and formalin can be used for permanent storage, together with an indelibly marked label. This can be stored inside the vial but the modern adhesives of paper labels are not durable and a more permanent adhesive tape may be needed for outer labels.

A high power microscope will be needed to identify small transparent seeds and other translucent plant material. For charred material, especially charcoal, a special microscope with direct illumination is needed. A magnification of about x200 is most useful, but x100 and x300 are sometimes used.

Softer parts of seeds may disappear in the sub-fossil state; for instance the style base, stalk and epidermal cells of Buttercup seeds are lost. Reference seeds can be treated by heating in water or dilute alkali and the softer parts scraped away to simulate the subfossils. In addition to reference collections, various manuals are routinely consulted. No single book covers the details needed for all taxa. Beijerinck's *Zadenatlas der Nederlandsch Flora* (1947) has drawings of the Dutch flora, which is very similar to that of lowland Britain. The drawings in such texts are usually of seeds in the pristine state but subfossils may lack hairs and other fragile parts. The Russian seed atlas by Katz and colleagues (1965) includes some useful drawings of subfossil seeds. The volumes begun by Berggren (1969, 1981) and based on the Scandinavian flora have photographs with very detailed descriptions. *Botanical macro-remains* (Schoch *et al.* 1988) is based on 168 species of the fruits and seeds which commonly occur in Swiss lake deposits and so it is of only limited use to those working on the British flora. A good feature of the book, however, is its stereo-scan photos, which include useful enlargements of the cell patterns. The list of reference books and papers could be greatly extended; German research papers are often particularly well illustrated and those by Knörzer usually contain useful discussions of the identifications.

Remains of mosses are frequently recovered from peats, lake muds and water-logged archaeological layers; remains of liverworts are very infrequent and carbonised material of either is very rare. Detached leaves and leafy stems can often be identified to the species level. For British material the identification manuals by Smith (1978, 1990) and Paton (1999) are useful, although confirmation is required by examination of well-authenticated herbarium specimens. Further details of methods and a discussion of the environmental inferences are given by JHD (1973, 1986).

Small reference seeds, such as those of Grasses, may need pre-treating chemically and mounting on microscope slides. The papers by Udelgard Körber-Grohne (1964, 1991) are invaluable in this respect. As grasses are such an important part of the flora, because they occupy a diversity of habitats, they must be identified to enable the fullest ecological deductions to be made. Ground-up cereal bran may give valuable dietary evidence, and may, if found in rubbish pits, indicate dispersed faeces. Reference slides of chemically treated cereal grains can be prepared for comparison. A simple method is given in CD's 1987 paper; the more lengthy preparation detailed by Körber-Grohne keeps the grains whole. The rather durable nutlets of Sedges can sometimes also be identified to the species level and the presence of turf can often be determined by the identification of grassland sedges. Nilsson and Hjelmquist's illustrated paper (1967) describes most of the commonly encountered species. The detail of the cell pattern needs a microscope with direct illumination. Such a microscope will also be found useful when identifying other opaque seeds.

Sir Harry Godwin's *History of the British Flora* is invaluable, not least for its background to vegetational change and the Quaternary history of individual species. The second edition published in 1975 predates most of the recent archaeobotanical work in Britain. Records of identifications of individual species and their archaeological sites throughout Britain are held in a database at the Environmental Archaeology Unit of York University.

Microscopic remains of plants

Sampling for pollen analysis

The precise aim of the pollen analysis should be discussed with the archaeologist before the samples are taken. A regional pollen diagram may be required from a nearby lake or bog for recording a large pollen catchment area. The larger the basin the greater the area represented. Sampling should avoid inflow and outflow channels and marginal vegetation, and help from an experienced person will be needed for the crucial selection of the sampling site as many months of work will be spent on the analyses. Many peat bogs have been cut over extensively in the past and such diggings may have been subsequently re-colonised by plants; clearly such places should be avoided for sampling.

Whether the pollen is to be extracted in the form of long columns from a peat borer or from a monolith from a cut face, indelible labelling, both inside and outside a sealed polythene wrapping, is essential. Such samples should ideally be kept at low temperatures, below 4°C to inhibit fungal infection and prevent them drying out. The preparation of all samples for pollen analysis requires a modern fume cupboard as hazardous chemicals such as concentrated sulphuric acid and hydrofluoric acid are used. The sampling interval and the thickness of the individual samples depend on the precise objectives of the analysis. Widely spaced samples will give a general, overall picture whereas very thin contiguous samples may be needed to reveal the details of woodland clearance and agricultural activity.

Identification, counting and interpretation

The identification of pollen grains and spores requires an extensive reference collection of herbaceous pollen and spores, in addition to tree and shrub pollen types. Peter Moore and colleagues' book (1991) gives clear indications as to what types can be identified (**170**). *The Northwest European Pollen Flora* (Punt *et al.* several volumes, 1976 onwards) indicates that many pollen grains can be determined to the species level, given an extensive reference collection and a microscope with a good oil immersion lens. Cereal pollen, especially that of Barley, may be difficult to distinguish from that of certain wild grasses. Measurements and differences in the surface sculpturing of both wild grass and cereal species are given by S.-T. Andersen; CD's 1988 paper summarises his data.

The number of grains needing to be counted for a statistically acceptable result

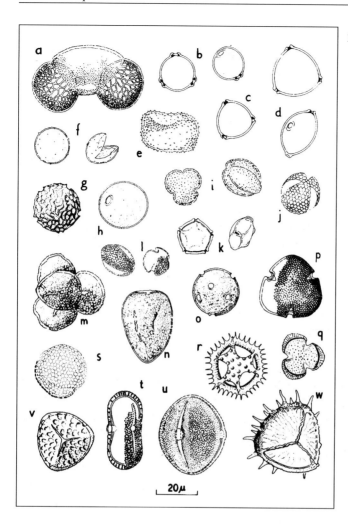

170 *Drawings of pollen grains and spores frequently recognised in samples from British peats, lake muds and archaeological layers.*
a. Scots Pine, b. Tree Birch, c. Dwarf Birch, d. Hazel, e. Yew, f. Juniper, g. Wych Elm, h. Poaceae (Grasses), i. Oak, j. Ash, k. Alder, l. Willow, m. Heather, n. Cyperaceae (Sedges and related plants), o. Ribwort Plantain, p. Small-leaved Lime, q. Mugwort, r. Dandelion-type, s. Pondweed, Hogweed-type, u. Common Rockrose, v. Bogmoss, w. Lesser Clubmoss.
1 micron = one thousandth of a mm.
From Pigott and Pigott (1959)

depends on the number of taxa recorded. If there are about 20 taxa present, 150-200 grains may suffice. However, there may be as many as 100 taxa in a sample and a count of 1000 grains would then be advisable. Usually a total of about 500 grains will give a reliable result. Scanning under low power magnification may produce rare grains otherwise not recorded. During pollen counting, any charcoal fragments present should be noted and distinguished as wood or herbaceous charcoal. Fragments of charcoal below about 3mm in diameter may have blown in from fires in and around settlements and do not necessarily relate to woodland clearance.

Usually the sites of regional pollen diagrams are too far away from the settlement site to provide evidence of arable farming. Cereal flowers are mostly self-pollinating and some arable weeds are insect-pollinated and release very little pollen dispersed into the atmosphere. The analysis of a small pollen catchment area close to the settlement such as a ditch or similar deposit may be needed to detect possible arable cultivation. Although Scotland now has distinct arable areas mainly in the sunnier south and east of the country, it seems probable that earlier farming was mixed arable and pastoral.

Phytoliths

Phytoliths or grass opals are microscopic particles of hydrated silica from the cells of plants, mainly but not only of Grasses (**171**). They may remain after other traces of plants have disappeared. However, their value in distinguishing one cereal such as Wheats and Barleys from another seems very limited (Lentfer *et al.* 1997). Only a very few studies of phytoliths pertaining to Scottish archaeology have been published and their results are very minor (Johnston 1965, Proudfoot 1978, Powers 1997, Powers *et al.* 1989), despite the optimistic conclusions by Powers (1992). In the very recent study by J.-L. Scwhenninger (in Pearson *et al.*1999) of the site at Dun Vulan, South Uist, not a single plant identification was made from phytoliths but it is claimed (p340) that the phytoliths suggest '. . . the processing and burning of primarily herbaceous plant material as distinct from woody combustibles and, because of the presence of diatoms, that the burnt material derived from '. . . marine or freshwater environments, most probably marshy machair type habitats'. Diatoms can be identified to the species from their siliceous shells and hence palaeoenvironmental deductions can be made but in the absence of botanical precision from phytoliths it is hard to see how such studies will ever prove valuable in environmental archaeology in Scotland or in other temperate countries. Phytolith analyses have much greater value in tropical areas (Pearsall 1989, 1994).

Archaeological sites

The pollen preserved in former land surfaces beneath burial mounds and field walls, for instance, may indicate the vegetation that covered the site before settlement began. Such pollen and that from ditches, turf lines and other largely inorganic deposits is frequently degraded and difficult to count. The interpretation of pollen from a soil profile is quite different to that of pollen profile from lake muds or peats, because the pollen is liable to have been moved up and down due to percolation of rainwater and biological action, especially earthworm activity. Samples should be taken as vertical columns. Sampling from archaeological sites and their interpretation are fully covered in *The Palynology of Archaeological Sites* by Geoffrey Dimbleby (1985).

Turves

Well-preserved turves which have remained permanently waterlogged may contain the local vegetational history covering tens of years before the turf was removed. An excellent example of this potential is revealed from a ditch at the Roman fort at Bar Hill, west-central Scotland, analysed by Bill Boyd (1984). Analyses of contiguous samples may be needed to show rapid clearance phases. These particular analyses are detailed in the section on pre-Roman woodland clearance (chapter 6).

Coprolites

Whether of human origin or not, coprolites (fossil or subfossil faeces or dung in discreet lumps) can be an informative source of pollen. They may not necessarily have remained waterlogged but have often been recovered from well-stratified horizons. Their preparatory treatment for pollen analysis is similar to that of other pollen samples from more usual organic materials. The results may well record the local vegetation, from

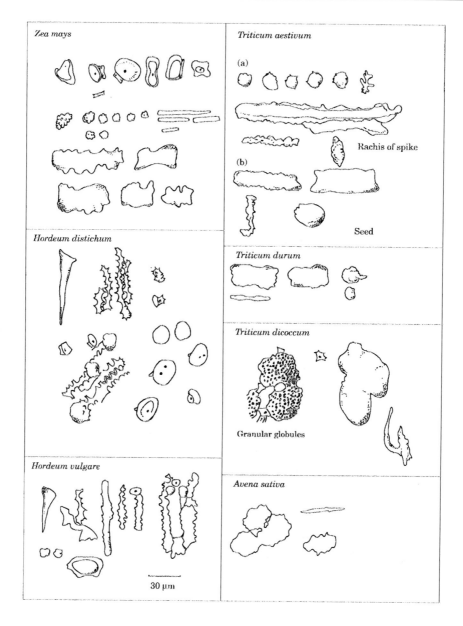

171 Phytoliths. From Lentfer, Boyd and Gojak (1997)

pollen in the water drunk near to the settlement. The chemical signatures of ancient faeces can persist in archaeological layers, as can the undigested coarse plant remains, in a dispersed state without the least sign of any definite faecal mass. Few botanical analyses of coprolites and disintegrated faeces have yet been carried out in Scotland but the results are substantial. Intestinal parasite eggs may be preserved in coprolites and these can be identified.

Appendix 2: Archaeozoology

The earliest settlers in Scotland had no knowledge of cereals and their diet seems to have been largely meat- or fish-based. Changes in diet over time are an important part of our understanding of humankind's relation to the environment. Information on the animal part of the diet is therefore included where available. Unfortunately, the acid soils of much of Scotland have not preserved bones and there are therefore many gaps in our knowledge of prehistoric diets. On the basis of bones, shells and coarse plant remains, the precise proportions of plant and of animal foods consumed can only be a matter of speculation. Now, however, analyses of the stable isotopes of carbon and nitrogen in organic tissues are giving a new insight into this important subject (Ambrose 1993, O'Connell and Hedges 1999). No such work has, as yet, been carried out on Scottish samples.

The identification and study of bones, shells and other animal remains is the work of the archaeozoologist. The vast animal kingdom requires specialisation and usually mammal, fish and bird bones are examined by different specialists. In dry calcareous sites, land snails may survive where all other organic material has perished. Beetles may provide the key to past temperatures as these insects respond more quickly to climatic change than plants, due to their ease of mobility. Flies and their pupae may indicate putrid conditions. Fleas and other ectoparasites as well as internal parasites can be identified and provide intimate details of the lives of humans and their animals.

Archaeozoologists will prefer to take their own samples, but bones are often collected from residues. A sub-sample of 1kg may be used for paraffin flotation of beetle remains; these are commonly found in house deposits and other richly organic refuse. *Zooarchaeology* by Reitz and Wing (1999) deals with all vertebrates and larger invertebrates such as molluscs and crustaceans but not insects.

Appendix 3: Dating

Radiocarbon

Radiocarbon dating is well-known as the main dating system used by archaeologists. Since the 1960s it has become evident that there are long-term fluctuations in the atmospheric content of radiocarbon leading to systematic errors in dating. Fortunately it is possible to recalculate radiocarbon dates in accordance with the calendar years revealed by the annual rings laid down in wood of trees such as Oak. Computer programmes can now be applied to correct the dates, and OxCal has been adopted in this book; other programmes are also commonly used. Dates are given in radiocarbon years BP (before 1950, 'the present') and as calibrated calendar years as cal BC or cal AD.

Several grams of organic material, plant material or bone, are needed for dating by the originally devised method. A single season's growth, such as that afforded by a cereal hoard, will usually give a more accurate date than wood or charcoal, especially that of long-lived trees such as Oak. Accelerator mass spectrometer (AMS) dating can be done on very small amounts of organic material. A single charred cereal grain or three or four seeds is sufficient.

In dating peat samples there is the problem of potential contamination when there has been root penetration from a higher level. It may be necessary to separate out material which was undoubtedly contemporary, such as Bogmoss leaves, and obtain an AMS dating on them. Careful scrutiny of the pollen washings should reveal the presence of roots and rootlets which may be contemporary or not. All radiocarbon dates are statistical estimates and cannot be used to separate close events especially within 50 and 100 years.

Tree rings

Excellent accounts of this method of dating are to be found in the handbook *Dendrochronological Dating* (Eckstein 1984) and the book *A Slice Through Time* (Baillie 1995). A useful brief account on selection and sampling of timber has been given by Ruth Morgan (1975). The method is based on sequencing tree-ring widths across an adequate sample of wood which can be matched to chronologies that have been established in Britain and continental Europe. Long-term chronologies for Oaks in central and western Europe go back to around 5300 BC. As previously stated, tree-ring dating is used to correct the anomalies of radiocarbon dating.

Tree-ring dating is appropriate on Oak wood when a long sequence of growth rings is available, including sapwood, and if possible bark. For suitable wood, the dendrochronologist can provide a precise felling date; further interpretation is possible from multiple samples. The number of rings needed depends on a number of factors, for instance 60 rings may be insufficient to fit the wood definitely within a known chronology. Sampling should cover the maximum ring pattern. Two good examples of dendrochronological dating relevant to Scotland are those for Busiton Crannog (see chapter 7) and the Bishop's Castle attached to Glasgow Cathedral. For the former there are dates of AD 594, 609, 613 and 620 and the latter AD 1191 (Anonymous 2000).

Appendix 4: List of formal names of plants discussed in the text

Adder's-tongue — *Ophioglossum* spp

Alder — *Alnus glutinosa* (L.) Gaertn.

Almond — *Prunus dulcis* L.

Alpine Clubmoss — *Diphasiastrum alpinum* (L.) Holub

American Larch — *Larix laricina* (Du Roi) Koch

Annual Knawel — *Scleranthus annuus* L

Annual Meadow-grass — *Poa annua* L.

Ash — *Fraxinus excelsior* L

Aspen — *Populus tremula* L.

Barley — *Hordeum vulgare* L

Beech — *Fagus sylvatica* L.

Bell Heather — *Erica cinerea* L.

Bent — *Agrostis* spp

Bere — *Hordeum vulgare* subspecies *vulgare* L.

Bilberry — *Vaccinium myrtillus* L.

Birch — *Betula* spp

Bird Cherry — *Prunus padus* L.

Bittersweet — *Solanum nigrum* L.

Arctic Bearberry — *Arctostaphylos alpinus* (L.) Spreng.

Black-bindweed — *Fallopia convolvulus* (L.) Á. Löve

Black-mulberry — *Morus nigra* L.

Black-mustard — *Brassica nigra* L.

Black-oat — *Avena strigosa* L.

Black-poplar — *Populus nigra* L.

Bladderwrack — *Fucus vesiculosus* L.

Blue Skullcap — *Scutellaria lateriflora* L.

Blinks — *Montia fontana* L.

Brazilwood — *Caesalpinia sappan* L.

Bluebell — *Hyacinthoides non-scripta* (L.) Chouard ex Rothm

Bogmoss — *Sphagnum* spp

Bog Bilberry — *Vaccinium uliginosum* L.

Bog Myrtle — *Myrica gale* L.

Bog Pondweed — *Potamogeton polygonifolius* Pourret

Bottle Sedge — *Carex rostrata* Stokes / *Carex vesicaria* L.

Box — *Buxus sempervirens* L.

Bracken — *Pteridium aquilinum* (L.) Kuhn

Bramble — *Rubus fruticosus* L.

Bread Wheat — *Triticum aestivum* L.

Bristle Oat — *Avena strigosa* Schreb. / *Avena strigosa* Schreber

Broad Bean — *Vicia faba* L.

Dryopteris dilatata (Hoffm.) A. Gray

Broad Buckler-fern — *Dryopteris dilatata* (Hoffm.) A.Gray

Broad-leaved Dock — *Rumex obtusifolius* L.

Broad-leaved Lime — *Tilia platyphyllos* Scop.

Brome — *Bromus* spp

Buckthorn — *Frangula alnus* Miller / *Rhamnus cathartica* L.

Buckwheat — *Fagopyrum esculentum* Moench / *Prunus domestica* ssp *insititia* (L.) Bonnier & Layens

Bullace — *Prunus domestica* ssp *insititia* (L.) Bonnier & Layens

Bulrush — *Typha latifolia* L.

Bur-reed — *Sparganium* spp

Buttercups — *Ranunculus* spp

Cabbage — *Brassica oleracea* L

Caper Spurge — *Euphorbia lathyris* L.

Caraway — *Carum carvi* L.

Carnation Sedge — *Carex panicea* L.

Carrot — *Daucus carota* ssp *sativus* (Hoffm.) Arcang.

Cat's-ear — *Hypochaeris radicata* L.

Cat-tail — *Typha latifolia* L.

Celery — *Apium graveolens* L.

Charlock — *Sinapis arvensis* L.

Chestnut — *Castanea sativa* Mill.

Chick Pea — *Cicer arietinum* L.

Chickweed — *Stellaria media* L.

Chives — *Allium schoenoprasum* L.

Cinnamon — *Cinnamomum zeylandicum* Nees

Cinquefoil-type — *Potentilla* spp

Cloudberry — *Rubus chamaemorus* L.

Clovers — *Trifolium* spp

Cloves — *Eugenia caryophyllus* Thunb

Common Bistort — *Persicaria bistorta* (L.) Samp

Common Club-rush — *Schoenoplectus lacustris* (L.) Palla

Common Hairmoss — *Polytrichum commune* Hedw

Common Mallow — *Malva sylvestris* L

Common Mouse-ear — *Cerastium fontanum* Baumg

Common Oat — *Avena sativa* L.

Common Reed — *Phragmites australis* (Cav.) Trin. ex Steud.

Common Rock-rose	*Helianthemum nummilarium* (L.) Miller	Flote-grass	*Glyceria* spp
Common Scurvygrass	*Cochlearia officinalis* L	Floating Sweet-grass	*Glyceria fluitans* (L.) R.Br.
Common Sedge	*Carex ovalis* Gooden.	Forget-me-not	*Myosotis* spp
Common Sorrel	*Rumex acetosa* L	Fungi	*Daedalea quercina* Fr., *Fomes*
Common Spike-rush	*Eleocharis palustris* (L.) Roem. & Schult.		*fomentarius* (L.ex Fr.) Kickx *Fomes ignarius* (L. ex Fr.) Kickx
Common Whitebeam	*Sorbus aria* (L.) Crantz	Galangal	*Alpinia officinarum* Hance
Compact Rush	*Juncus conglomeratus* L	Garden Angelica	*Angelica archangelica* L.
Coriander	*Coriandrum sativum* L	Garlic	*Allium sativum* L.
Cork Oak	*Quercus suber* L.	Gean	*Prunus avium* L.
Corncockle	*Agrostemma githago* L.	Ginger	*Zingiber officinale* Rosc
Cornflower	*Centaurea cyanus* L.	Golden Henbane	*Hyoscyamus aureus* L.
Corn Marigold	*Chrysanthemum segetum* L.	Goosefoot	*Galium aparine* L.
Cornelian Cherry	*Cornus mas* L.	Grape-vine	*Vitis vinifera* L.
Corn Spurrey	*Spergula arvensis* L.	Grasses	Poaceae (= Gramineae)
Cottongrass	*Eriophorum* spp	Great Pignut	*Bunium bulbocastanum* L.
Cowberry	*Vaccinium vitis-idaea* L.	Greater Bird's-foot-trefoil	*Lotus pedunculatus* Cav.
Cow Parsley	*Anthriscus sylvestris* L.	Greater Celandine	*Chelidonium majus* L.
Creeping Willow	*Salix repens* L.,	Greater Plantain	*Plantago major* L.
Cumin	*Cuminum cyminum* L.	Greater Stichwort	*Stellaria holostea* L.
Damson	*Prunus domestica* ssp *institia* (L.) Bonnier & Layens	Greater Tussock-sedge	*Carex paniculata* L.
		Greater Woodrush	*Luzula sylvatica* L.
Danewort	*Sambucus ebulus* L.	Guelder Rose	*Viburnum opulus* L.
Deadly Nightshade	*Atropa belladonna* L.	Gypsywort	*Lycopus europaeus* L.
Dead-nettle	*Lamium* spp	Harebell	*Campanula rotundifolia* L.
Devil's-bit Scabious	*Succisa pratensis* Moench	Hawkbit	*Leontodon* spp
Dewberry	*Rubus caesius* L.	Hawthorn	*Crataegus monogyna* Jacq.
Dill	*Anethum graveolens* L.	Hazel	*Corylus avellana* L.
Dockens	*Rumex* ssp	Hazel-type pollen	*Corylus avellana* or
Dog Rose	*Rosa canina* L.		*Myrica gale* L.
Dog's-mercury	*Mercurialis perennis* L.	Heath-grass	*Danthonia decumbens* (L.) DC
Dogwood	*Cornus sanguinea* L.	Heath Rush	*Juncus squarrosus* L.
Downy Birch	*Betula pubescens* Ehrh.	Heather	*Calluna vulgaris* (L.) Hull
Dropwort	*Filipendula vulgaris* Moench	Hemlock	*Conium maculatum* L.
Dwarf Birch	*Betula nana* L.	Hemp.	*Cannabis sativa* L.
Dyer's-rocket	*Reseda luteola* L.	Hemp-nettle	*Galeopsis* spp
Einkorn	*Triticum monococcum* L.	Henbane	*Hyoscyamus niger* L.
Elm	*Ulmus* spp	Highbush Cranberry	*Viburnum edule* (Michx.) Raf
Emmer	*Triticum dicoccum* L.	Hog's Fennel	*Peucedanum officinale* L.
Enchanter's-nightshade	*Circaea lutetiana* L.	Hogweed	*Heracleum sphondylium* L.
Elder	*Sambucus nigra* L.	Holly	*Ilex aquifolium* L.
False Oat-grass	*Arrhenatherum elatius* (L.) P.Beauv. ex J.S.& C.Presl	Honeysuckle	*Lonicera periclymenum* L
		Hops	*Humulus lupulus* L.
Fat-hen	*Chenopodium album* L.	Hornbeam	*Carpinus betulus* L.
Fennel	*Foeniculum vulgare* Mill.	Hulled Barley	*Hordeum vulgare*
Ferns	Filicales	Issler's Clubmoss	*Diphasiastrum complanatum* spp *issleri* (Rouy) Jermy
Field Bean	*Vicia faba* L.		
Field Horsetail	*Equisetum arvense* L.	Iris	*Iris* spp
Field Madder	*Sherardia arvensis* L.	Ivy	*Hedera helix* L.
Field Maple	*Acer campestre* L.	Jointed Rush	*Juncus articulatus* L.
Field Woundwort	*Stachys arvensis* L.	Juniper	*Juniperus communis* L.
Fig	*Ficus carica* L.	Kale	*Brassica oleracea* var. *viridis* L.
Figwort family	Schrophulariaceae	Knotted Wrack	*Ascophyllum nodosum* (L.) Le Jol.
Filbert	*Corylus maxima* Mill.		
Fir	*Abies* spp	Knotgrass	*Polygonum aviculare* L.
Flat Wrack	*Fucus spiralis* L.	Lady-fern	*Athyrium felix-femina* (L.) Roth
Flax	*Linum usitatissimum* L.		

Lady's-mantle	*Alchemilla* spp
Leek	*Allium porrum* L.
Lentil	*Lens culinaris* Medikus
Lesser Celandine	*Ranunculus ficaria* L.
Lesser Clubmoss	*Selaginella selaginoides* (L.) Link
Lesser Spearwort	*Ranunculus flammula* L.
Lime	*Tilia* spp
Linseed	*Linum usitatissimum* L.
Lovage	*Levisticum officinale* Koch
Louseworts	*Pedicularis* spp
Lyme-grass	*Leymus arenarius* (L.) Hochst.
Mace	*Myristica fragrans* Houtt.
Madder	*Rubia tinctoria* L.
Malagueta Pepper	*Aframomum melegueta* Schumann
Mare's-tail	*Hippuris vulgaris* L.
Marsh Cinquefoil	*Potentilla palustris* (L.) Scop.
Marsh Lousewort	*Pedicularis palustris* L.
Marsh Marigold	*Caltha palustris* L.
Marsh Pennywort	*Hydrocotyle vulgaris* L.
Marsh Violet	*Viola palustris* L.
Marsh Woundwort	*Stachys palustris* L.
Mat-grass	*Nardus stricta* L.
Meadow Buttercup	*Ranunculus repens* L.
Meadow-grasses	*Poa* spp
Meadowsweet	*Filipendula ulmaria* (L.) Maxim.
Meadow Vetchling	*Lathyrus pratensis* L.
Midland Hawthorn	*Crataegus laevigata* (Poir.) DC.
Monk's-rhubarb	*Rumex pseudoalpinus* Hoefft
Moonwort	*Botrychium lunaria* (L.) Sw.
Mosses	*Hylocomium splendens* (Hedw.) B., S. & G., *Neckera complanata* Hedw., *Neckera crispa* Hedw., *Rhytidiadelphus squarrosus* (Hedw.) Warnst.
Mugwort	*Artemisia* spp
Naked Barley	*Hordeum vulgare*
Nettle	*Urtica* spp
Nipplewort	*Lapsana communis* L.
Northern Dock	*Rumex longifolius* DC
Norway Maple	*Acer platanoides* L.
Nutmeg	*Myrisitca fragans* Houtt.
Oak	*Quercus* spp
Oats	*Avena* spp
Olive	*Olea europaea* L.
Onion	*Allium cepa* L.
Opium Poppy	*Papaver somniferum* L.
Orache	*Atriplex* spp
Pacific Yew	*Taxus brevifolia* Nutt.
Pale Persicaria	*Persicaria lapathifolia* (L.) Gray
Pale Sedge	*Carex pallescens* L
Parsley	*Petroselinum crispum* Hoffm.
Parsley-piert	*Aphanes* spp
Parsnip	*Pastinaca sativa* L.
Pea	*Pisum sativum* L.
Peach	*Prunus persica* (L.) Batsch

Pepper	*Piper nigrum* L.
Pignut	*Conopodium majus* L.
Pine	*Pinus* spp
Plum	*Prunus domestica* ssp *domestica* L.
Poplar	*Populus* spp
Poppy	*Papaver* spp
Puffball	*Bovista nigrescens*
Purple Moor-grass	*Molinia caerulea* (L.) Moench
Purging Flax	*Linum catharticum* L.
Ragged-Robin	*Lychnis flos-cuculi* L.
Ramsons	*Allium ursinum* L.
Raspberry	*Rubus idaeus* L.
Red Campion	*Silene dioica* (L.) Clairv.
Red Fescue	*Festuca rubra* L.
Red Dead-nettle	*Lamium purpureum* L.
Redshank	*Persicaria maculosa* Gray
Reed	*Phragmites australis* Trin.
Reed Canary-grass	*Phalaris arundinacea* L.
Remote Sedge	*Carex remota* L.
Ribwort Plantain	*Plantago lanceolata* L.
Rue	*Ruta* spp
Rice	*Oryza sativa* L.
Rosebay Willowherb	*Chamerion angustifolium* (Raf.) Raf.
Roseroot	*Sedum roseum* (L.) Scop.
Rough-stalked Meadow-grass	*Poa trivialis* L.
Rowan	*Sorbus aucuparia* L.
Royal Fern	*Osmunda regalis* L.
Rush	*Juncus* spp
Rye	*Secale cereale* L.
Saffron	*Crocus sativus* L.
Sallow	*Salix cinerea* L.
Salmonberry	*Rubus spectabilis* Pursh
Sand Leek	*Allium scorodoprasum* L.
Savin	*Juniperus sabina* L.
Scarlet Pimpernel	*Anagallis arvensis* L.
Scentless Mayweed	*Tripleurospermum inodorum* (L.) Schultz-Bip.
Scots Lovage	*Ligusticum scoticum* L.
Scots Pine	*Pinus sylvestris* L.
Sea-buckthorn	*Hippophae rhamnoides* L.
Sea Mayweed	*Tripleurospermum maritimum* (L.) Koch
Sea Plantain	*Plantago maritima* L.
Sedges	*Carex* spp
Sedge Family	*Cyperaceae*
Selfheal	*Prunella vulgaris* L.
Sheep's Sorrel	*Rumex acetosella* L.
Shepherd's-purse	*Capsella bursa-pastoris* L.
Silverweed	*Potentilla anserina* L.
Sharp-flowered Rush	*Juncus acutiflorus* L.
Shoreweed	*Littorella aquatica* (L.) Asch.
Silver Birch	*Betula pendula* Roth
Six-rowed Barley	*Hordeum vulgare* subspecies *vulgare*
Skirret	*Sium sisarum* L.
Skullcap	*Scutellaria galericulata* L.

Sloe	*Prunus spinosa* L.	Water Starwort	*Callitriche* spp
Small-leaved Lime	*Tilia cordata* Mill.	Wayfaring Tree	*Viburnum lantana* L.
Small Nettle	*Urtica urens* L.	Weld	*Reseda luteola* L.
Smooth Meadow-grass	*Poa pratensis* L.	Western Hemlock	*Tsuga heterophylla* (Raf.) Sarg.
Smooth Tare	*Vicia tetrasperma* (L.) Schreb.	Weymouth Pine	*Pinus strobus* L.
Soft Rush	*Juncus effusus* L.	White Clover	*Trifolium repens* L.
Speedwell	*Veronica* spp	White Henbane	*Hyoscyamus albus* L.
Spelt	*Triticum spelta* L.	White Horehound	*Marrubium vulgare* L.
Spindle Tree	*Euonymus europaeus* L.	White Waterlily	*Nymphaea alba* L.
Spiny Sow-thistle	*Sonchus asper* (L.) Hill	Willow	*Salix* spp
Spruce	*Picea* spp	Wild Carrot	*Daucus carota* ssp *carota* L.
Stag-horn Clubmoss	*Lycopodium clavatum* L.	Wild Celery	*Apium graveolens* L.
Stinging nettle	*Urtica dioica* L.	Wild Flag	*Iris setosa* Pall.
Stinking Chamomile	*Anthemis cotula* L.	Wild Garlic	*Allium ursinum* L.
Stone Bramble	*Rubus saxatilis* L.	Wild Cherry	*Prunus avium* L.
Stone Pine	*Pinus pinea* L.	Wild Oat	*Avena fatua* L.
Sugar	*Saccharum officinarum* L.	Wild Pear	*Prunus communis* L.
Sweet Apple	*Malus domestica* Borkh.	Wild Radish	*Raphanus raphanistruim* L.
Sweet Cicely	*Myrrhis odorata* Scop.	Wild Service-tree	*Sorbus terminalis* (L.) Crantz
Sycamore	*Acer pseudoplatanus* L.	Wild Strawberry	*Fragaria fesca* L.
Tamarack	*Larix laricina* (Du Roi) K. Koch	Wild Turnip	*Brassica rapa* spp *sylvestris* (L.) Janchen
Terebinth	*Pistacia terebinthus* L.	Willow-herbs	*Epilobium* spp
Toad Rush	*Juncus bufonius* L.	Winter-cress	*Barbarea* spp
Tormentil	*Potentilla erecta* L.	Woad	*Isatis tinctoria* L.
Truffle	*Tuber* or other Tuberales	Wood Anemone	*Anemone sylvatica* L.
Two-rowed Barley	*Hordeum distichon* L.	Wood Avens	*Geum urbanum* L.
Tufted Hair-grass	*Deschampsia caespitosa* (L.) P.Beauv.	Wood Dock	*Rumex sanguineus* L.
		Wood Forget-me-not	*Myosotis sylvatica* Hoffm.
Turnsole	*Chrozophora tinctoria* (L.) Rafin.	Woodrushes	*Luzula* spp
		Wych Elm	*Ulmus glabra* Hudson
Vanilla	*Vanilla planifolia* Andr.	Yarrow	*Achillea millefolium* L.
Vetch/Vetchling	*Vicia/Lathyrus* spp	Yellow Cedar	*Chamaecyparis nootkatensis* (Lamb.) Spach
Walnut	*Juglans regia* L.		
Water Chestnut	*Trapa natans* L.	Yellow Iris	*Iris pseudacorus* L.
Water Crowfoot	*Ranunculus* subg. *Batrachium*	Yew	*Taxus baccata* L.
Water Pepper	*Persicaria hydropiper* (L.) Spach	Yorkshire Fog	*Holcus lanatus* L.

Appendix 5: List of formal names of animals discussed in the text

The names, both formal and informal, have been taken from Muss and Dahlstrom, P. (1981) for fish, from Tebble (1976) and Campbell and Nichols (1980) for molluscs and other marine life, from Corbet and Ovenden (1980) and Van Den Brink (1967) for mammals, from Chinery (1979) for insects and from Howard and Moore (1994) for birds.

Angel Shark	*Squatina squatina*	Eider	*Somateria mollissima*
Aurochs	*Bos taurus*	Elk	*Alces alces*
Badger	*Meles meles*	Fallow Deer	*Dama dama*
Ballan Wrass	*Labrus bergylta*	Field Mouse	*Apodemus sylvaticus*
Baltic Tellin	*Macoma balthica*	Flat Periwinkle	*Littorina littoralis*
Bank Vole	*Clethrionomys glareolus*	Flea	*Pulex irritans*
Barnacle Goose	*Branta leucopsis*	Flounder	*Platichthys flesus*
Bass	*Dicentrarchus labrax*	Fox	*Vulpes vulpes*
Beaver	*Castor fiber*	Feral Pigeon	*Columba livia*
Bed Bug	*Cimex lectularius*	Fulmar	*Fulmarus glacialis*
Black Sea-bream	*Spondyliosoma cantharus*	Gannet	*Morus bassanus*
Brown Bear	*Ursus arctos*	Golden Eagle	*Aquila chrysaetos*
Bumble Bee	*Bombus terrestris*	Golden Plover	*Pluvialis apricaria*
Capercaillie	*Tetrao urogallus*	Goldeneye	*Bucephala clangula*
Clam	*Pecten maximus*	Goshawk	*Accipiter gentilis*
Cod	*Gadus morhua*	Great Auk	*Pinguinus impennis*
Common Cockle	*Cerastoderma edule*	Great Black-backed Gull	*Larus marinus*
Common Crane	*Grus grus*	Great Northern Diver	*Gavia immer*
Common Limpet	*Patella vulgata*	Great Skua	*Catharacta skua*
Common Seal	*Phoca vitulina*	Grey Seal	*Halichoerus grypus*
Common Tern	*Sterna hirundo*	Greylag Goose	*Anser anser*
Conger Eel	*Conger conger*	Guillemot	*Uria aalge*
Coot	*Fulica atra*	Gull	*Larus* spp
Cormorant	*Phalacrocorax carbo*	Haddock	*Melanogrammus aeglefinus*
Corncrake	*Crex crex*	Hake	*Merlucius merlucius*
Curlew	*Numenius arquata*	Halibut	*Hippoglossus hippoglossus*
Dalmation Pelican	*Pelecanus crispus*	Hare	*Lepus capensis*
Dogfish (Lesser Spotted)	*Scyliorhinus canicula*	Hedgehog	*Erinaceus europaeus*
Domestic Cat	*Felis catus*	Herring	*Clupea harengus*
Domestic Dog	*Canis domesticus*	Honey Bee	*Apis melifera*
Domestic Duck	*Anas domesticus*	Horse	*Equus* spp
Domestic Fowl	*Gallus domesticus*	Horse Mussel	*Modiolus modiolus*
Domestic Goose	*Anser domesticus*	Iceland Mussel	*Arctica islandica*
Domestic Pidgeon	*Columba livia*	Jack Snipe	*Lymnocrytes minimus*
Domestic Pig	*Sus domesticus*	Kestrel	*Falco tinnunculus*
Edible Crab	*Cancer pagurus*	Killer Whale	*Orcinus orca*
Eel	*Anguilla anguilla*	Knot	*Calidris canutus*

Lesser Black-backed Gull	*Larus fuscus*	Roundworm	*Ascaris lumbricoides*
Limpet	*Patella* sp	Saithe	*Pollachius virens*
Ling	*Molva molva*	Salmon	*Salmo salar*
Little Auk	*Alle alle*	Scallop (Queen)	*Chlamys opercularis*
Lobster	*Homarus gammarus*	Sea Bream	*Pagellus bogaraveo*
Louse	*Pediculus humanus*	Sea Trout	*Salmo trutta*
Lynx	*Lynx lynx*	Sea Urchin	*Echinus esculentus*
Mackerel	*Somber scombrus*	Shag	*Phalacrocorax aristotelis*
Mallard	*Anas platyrhynchos*	Shrew	*Sorex* spp
Manx Shearwater	*Puffinus puffinus*	Soay Sheep	*Ovis aries*
Mountain Hare	*Lepus timidus*	Song Thrush	*Turdus philomelos*
Mullet	*Chelon labrosus*	Sperm Whale	*Physeter catodon*
Mussel	*Mytilus edulis*	Spiny Dogfish	*Squalus acanthias*
Norway Lobster	*Nephrops norvegicus*	Starling	*Sturnus vulgaris*
Orkney Vole	*Microtus arvalis orcadensis*	Stork	*Ciconnia* spp
Otter	*Lutra lutra*	Sturgeon	*Acipenser sturio*
Peafowl	*Pavo cristatus*	Tern	*Sterna* spp
Periwinkle	*Littorina littorea*	Thorn-backed Ray	*Raja clavata*
Pine Marten	*Martes martes*	Tope	*Galeorhinus galeus*
Plaice	*Pleuronectes platessa*	Torsk	*Brosme brosme*
Polecat	*Putorius putorius*	Trout	*Salmo trutta*
Pollack	*Pollachius pollachius*	Turbot	*Scophthalmus maximus*
Puffin	*Fratercula arctica*	Turnstone	*Arenaria interpres*
Quail	*Coturnix coturnix*	Walrus	*Odobenus rosmarus*
Rabbit	*Oryctolagus cuniculus*	Water Rail	*Rallus aquaticus*
Raven	*Corvus corax*	Whelk	*Buccinium undatum*
Ray	*Raja* sp	Whipworm	*Trichuris trichiura*
Razorbill	*Alca torda*	White Stork	*Ciconia ciconia*
Razor Shell	*Ensis siliqua*	Whiting	*Merlangius merlangus*
Red Deer	*Cervus elaphus*	White-tailed Eagle	*Haliaeetus albicilla*
Red Grouse	*Lagopus lagopus*	Whooper Swan	*Cygnus cygnus*
Red Kite	*Milvus milvus*	Widgeon	*Anas penelope*
Red-throated Diver	*Gavia stellata*	Wild Boar	*Sus scrofa*
Reindeer	*Ranifer tarandus*	Wild Cat	*Felis sivestris*
Rock Dove	*Columba livia*	Wild Horse	*Equus caballus*
Rockling	*Ciliata mustela*	Wolf	*Canis lupus*
Roe Deer	*Capreolous capreolus*	Wrasse	*Crenilabrus melops*
Rook	*Corvus frugilegus*		

References

Aaby, B. 1976. Cyclic climatic variations in climate over the past 5500 yr. reflected in raised bogs. *Nature* 263, 281-284.

Acts of Parliament of Scotland. Volume 1, 1124-1423 includes Assisa de Tollensis David 1 1124-1153.

Alcock, L., Alcock, E. A. and Driscoll, S. T. 1984. Reconnaissance excavations on Early Historic fortifications and other royal sites in Scotland, 1974-84: 3, Excavations at Dundurn, Strathearn, Perthshire, 1976-77. *Proceedings of the Society of Antiquaries of Scotland* 119, 189-226.

Ambrose, S.H. 1993. Isotopic analyses of palaeodiets: methodological and interpretative considerations. Pages 59-130 in Sandford, M.K. (ed) *Investigations of Ancient Human Tissues*. Langhorne: Gordon Breach Science Publishers.

Andersen, S. H. 1987. Tybrind Vig: a submerged Ertebølle Settlement, in Denmark. Pages 253-280 in Coles, J.M. and Lawson, A.J. (eds) *European Wetlands in Prehistory*. Oxford: Clarendon Press.

Andersen, S. T. 1979. Identification of wild grass and cereal pollen. *Danmarks Geologiske Undersøgelse, Arbog (1978)*, 69-92.

Anderson, A. O. and Anderson, M. O. 1991. *Adomnan's Life of Columba*. Oxford: Clarendon Press.

Anderson, J. 1876. Notice of a flint arrow-head in the shaft, found in a moss at Fyvie, Aberdeenshire. *Proceedings of the Society of Antiquaries of Scotland* 11, 508-513.

Anderson, M.L. 1967. *A History of Scottish Forestry*. Edinburgh: Oliver & Boyd.

Anonymous. 2000. Tree-Rings make a date for the Bishop's Castle, Glasgow. *Newsletter of the West of Scotland Archaeology Service* 4, 5.

Arber, A. 1986. *Herbals Their Origin and Evolution*. Cambridge University Press. Third edition.

Ascham, R. 1545. *Toxophilus*. Reprint of the 1788 edition by R. Marsh; Wrexham.

Ashmore, P. J. 1996. *Neolithic and Bronze Age Scotland*. London: Batsford.

Austin, T. 1888. *Two fifteenth century cookery-books*. London: The Early English Text Society 91.

Aveling, E. 1997. Birch tar chewing gum. *British Archaeological Reports* 21, 6.

Baillie, M. 1988. Marker dates — Turning prehistory into history. *Archaeology in Ireland* 2, 154-155.

Baillie, M. 1989. Do Irish Bog Oaks Date the Shang Dynasty? *Current Archaeology* 117, 310-13.

Baillie, M. G. L. 1995. *A Slice through Time Dendrochronology and Precision Dating*. London: Batsford.

Baillie, M.G.L. 1999. *Exodus to Arthur Catastrophic Encounters with Comets*. London, Batsford.

Bakels, C. 1988. Hekelingen, a Neolithic site in the swamps of the Maas estuary. Pages 155-61 in Küster, H.(ed) *Der Prähistorische Mensch und seine Umwelt*. (= Forschungen und) Bericht zur Vor-und Fruhgeshichte in Baden-Wurttemburg). 31.

Balick, M.J. and Cox, P.A. 1996. *Plants, People, and Culture. The Science of Ethnobotany*. New York: Freeman.

Ballin Smith, B. 1994. *Howe: Four Millennia of Orkney Prehistory*. Edinburgh: Society of Antiquaries of Scotland Monograph No. 9.

Balls, E.K. 1962. *Early Uses of California Plants*. Berkeley, University of California Press.

Barber, J. W. 1981 Excavations on Iona, 1979. *Proceedings of the Society of Antiquaries of Scotland* 111, 282-386.

Barber, J. 1997. *The Archaeological Investigation of a Prehistoric Landscape: Excavations on Arran 1978-1981*. Edinburgh: Scottish Trust for Archaeological Research.

Barber, J.W. and Crone, B.A. 1993 Crannogs: a diminishing resource? A survey of the crannogs of southwest Scotland and excavations at Buiston crannog. *Antiquity* 67, 520-33

Barber, K.E. 1981. *Peat Stratigraphy and Climatic Change: a Palaeoecological Test of the Theory of Cyclic Peat Bog Regeneration*. Rotterdam: A.A. Balkema.

Barber, K.E. 1982. Peat-bog stratigraphy as a proxy climate record. Pages 103-13 in, A F Harding (ed) *Climatic change in later Pre-history*. Edinburgh University Press

Barclay, G.J. 1997. The Neolithic. Pages 127-148 in Edwards, K.J. and Ralston, I.B.M(eds) *Scotland: Environment and Archaeology, 8000 BC – AD 1000*. Chichester: John Wiley & Sons.

Barclay, G. J. and Fairweather, A.D. 1984. Rye and Ergot in the Scottish later Bronze Age. *Antiquity* 58, 126.

Barrett, J.H. 1997. Fish trade in Norse Orkney and Caithness: a zooarchaeological approach. *Antiquity* 71, 616-38.

Bates, J.W. 1998. Is 'life-form' a useful concept in bryophyte ecology? *Oikos* 82, 233-237.

Batey, C. E. and Morris, C. D. 1992. Earl's Bu, Orphir, Orkney: Excavation of a Norse Horizontal Mill. Pages 33-42 in C. D. Morris and D. J. Rackham (eds) *Norse and Later Settlement and Subsistence in the North Atlantic.* Glasgow: Department of Archaeology and the University of Glasgow.

Batey, C. E., Jesch, J. and Morris, C. D. 1993. *The Viking Age in Caithness, Orkney and the North Atlantic.* Edinburgh University Press.

Beijerinck, W. 1947. *Zadenatlas der Nederlandsch Flora.* Wageningen: Veenman.

Beith, M. 1995. *Healing Threads: Traditional Medicines of the Highlands and Islands.* Edinburgh: Polygon.

Bell, B. and Dickson, C. 1989. Excavations at Warebeth (Stromness Cemetery) Broch, Orkney. *Proceedings of the Society of Antiquaries of Scotland* 119, 101-31.

Bellamy, D. 1998. Is this the oldest tree in the world? *The Times Weekend* October 3 1998.

Bennett, K.D. 1995. Post-glacial dynamics of pine (*Pinus sylvestris* L.). Pages 23-29 in J.R.Aldous (ed) *Our Pinewood Heritage.* Edinburgh: Forestry Commission.

Bennett, K.D., Boreham, S., Sharp, M.J. and Switsur, V.R. 19992. Holocene history of environment, vegetation and human settlement on Catta Ness, Lunnasting, Shetland. *Journal of Ecology* 80, 241-273.

Berggren, G. 1969. *Atlas of Seeds and Small Fruits of Northwest-European Plant Species with Morphological Descriptions, Pt. 2 Cyperaceae.* Stockholm: Swedish Museum of Natural History.

Berggren, G. 1981. *Atlas of Seeds and Small Fruits of Northwest-European Plant Species with Morphological Descriptions. Part 3 Salicaceae-Cruciferae.* Stockholm: Arlöv.

Bianchi, F., Corbetta, F. and Pistola, M. 1976. *Fruits of the Earth.* London, Cassell.

Bigelow, G.F. 1985. Sandwick, Unst and late Norse Shetland Economy. Pages 95-127 in Smith, B. *Shetland Archaeology. New Work in Shetland in the 1970s.* Lerwick: Shetland Times.

Birks, H.H. 1975. Pine. Studies in the vegetational history of Scotland. *Philosophical Transactions of the Royal Society of London B* 270, 181-226.

Birks, H.J.B. 1991. Floristic and Vegetational History of the Outer Hebrides. Pages 38-48 in Pankhurst, R. J. *Flora of the Outer Hebrides.* London: Natural History Museum Publications.

Birks, H.J.B. 1994. Did Icelandic eruptions influence the post-glacial vegetational history of the British Isles? *Trends in Ecology and Evolution* 9, 312-14.

Birks, H.J.B. 1997. Scottish biodiversity in a historical context. Pages 21-35 in Fleming, L.V *et al.* (eds) Edinburgh: The Stationary Office.

Birks, H.J.B. and Madsen, B. J. 1979. Flandrian vegetational history of Little Loch Roag, Isle of Lewis. *Journal of Ecology* 67, 825-42.

Blackford, J.J., Edwards, K.J., Dugmore, A.J., Cook, G.T. and Buckland, P.C. 1992. Icelandic volcanic ash and the mid-Holocene Scots pine (*Pinus sylvestris*) pollen decline in northern Scotland. *The Holocene* 2, 260-265.

Boardman, S. and Dickson, C. 1995. Botanical remains from the inner ditch, in Keppie, L. J. F., Baillie, G. B., Dunwell, A. J., McBrien, J. H. and Speller, K. Some excavations on the line of the Antonine Wall 1985-93. *Proceedings of the Society of Antiquaries of Scotland* 125, 601-71.

Bohncke, S. 1983. The pollen analysis of deposits in a food vessel from the henge monument at North Mains. Pages 178-80 in Barclay, G. J. Sites of the third millennium BC to the first millennium AD at North Mains, Strathallan, Perthshire. *Proceedings of the Society of Antiquaries of Scotland* 113, 122-281.

Bond, J.M. 1998. Beyond the fringe? Recognising change and adaptation in Pictish and Norse Orkney. Pages 81-90 in Mills, C.M. and Coles, G. (eds) *Life on the Edge Human Settlement and Marginality.* Symposia for the Association for Environmental Archaeology No. 13. Oxford: Oxbow Books.

Bond, J.M. and Hunter, J. R. 1987. Flax-growing in Orkney from the Norse period to the eighteenth century. *Proceedings of the Society of Antiquaries of Scotland* 117, 175-81.

Bonsall, C. 1996. The Obanian Problem Coastal Adaptation in the Mesolithic of Western Scotland Pages 183-97 in Pollard, T. and Morrison, A.(eds) *The Early Prehistory of Scotland.* Edinburgh University Press.

Bottema, S. 1975. The interpretation of pollen spectra from prehistoric settlements (with special reference to Liguliflorae). *Palaeohistoria* 17,17-35.

Bouchardy, C. and Moutou, F. 1989. *Observing British and European Mammals.* London: British Museum (Natural History).

Boyd, W. E. 1984a. Environmental changes and Iron Age land management in the area of the Antonine Wall, Central Scotland: a summary. *Glasgow Archaeological Journal* 11, 75-81.

Boyd, W.E. 1984b. Stranger than truth. *Circaea* 2, 5.

Boyd, W.E. 1984c. Prehistoric hedges: Roman Iron Age hedges from Bar Hill. *Scottish Archaeological Review* 3, 32-34.

Boyd, W.E. 1985a. Palaeobotanical evidence from Mollins. *Britannia* 16, 37-48.

Boyd, W.E. 1985b. Botanical remains of edible plants from an Iron Age broch, Fairy Knowe, Buchlyvie, Stirling. *Forth Naturalist and Historian* 7, 77-83.

Boyd, W. E. 1985c. The problem of the time span represented by pollen spectra in podzol turves, with examples from the Roman sites at Bar Hill and Mollins, central Scotland. BAR 266, 189-196.

Boyd, W. E. 1986. Botanical fossils from Medieval and post-Medieval Glasgow. *Glasgow Archaeological Society Bulletin* 22, 3-5.

Boyd, W. E. 1986. Rye and ergot in the ancient history of Scotland. *Antiquity* 60, 45-48.

Boyd, W. E. 1988. Cereals in Scottish antiquity. *Circaea* 5, 101-110.

Bradbury, J. 1985. *The Medieval Archer*. Woodbridge: The Boydell Press.

Breeze, D. J. 1982. *The Northern Frontiers of Roman Britain*. Batsford, London.

Breeze, D. J. 1985. Roman forces and native populations. *Proceedings of the Society of Antiquaries of Scotland* 115, 223-8.

Breeze, D. J. 1992. The great myth of Caledon. *Scottish Journal of Forestry* 46, 331-335.

Bremner, A.H. and Bullard, E.R. 1990. *Trees & Shrubs on Orkney*. The Authors: Kirkwall.

Buckland, P. C. Sadler, J. P. and Smith, D. N. 1993. An Insect's Eye-View of the Norse Farm. Pages 506-27 in Batey, C .E., Jesch, J. and Morris, C.D. (eds) *The Viking Age in Caithness, Orkney and the North Atlantic*. Edinburgh University Press.

Bullard, E.R. 1995. *Wildflowers in Orkney*. Kirkwall, privately published.

Bunting, M. J. 1994. Vegetation History of Orkney: pollen records from two small basins in west Mainland. *New Phytologist* 128, 771-92.

Buurman, J. 1988. Roman medicine from Uitgeest. Pages 341- 351 in Küster, H. (ed.) *Der prähistorische Mensch und Seine Umwelt*. Stuttgart, H Konrad Thiess Verlag.

Cadell, H.M. 1913. *The Story of the Forth*. Glasgow: Maclehose and Sons.

Campbell A.C. & Nichols, J. 1980 *The Seashore & Shallow Seas of Britain & Europe*. Hamlyn.

Carter, S. P., McCullagh, R. P. J. and MacSween, A. 1995. The Iron Age in Shetland: excavations at five sites threatened by coastal erosion. *Proceedings of the Society of Antiquaries of Scotland* 125, 429-82.

Charman, D.J., West, S., and Kelly, A. 1995. Environmental change and tephra deposition: the Strath of Kildonan, Northern Scotland. *Journal of Archaeological Science* 22, 799-809.

Chaucer, G. 1951. *The Canterbury tales*. Translated into modern English by N. Coghill Harmondsworth: Penguin.

Chetan, A. and Brueton, D. 1994. *The Sacred Yew*. London: Arkana.

Childe, V.G. 1956. Maes Howe. *Proceedings of the Society of Antiquaries of Scotland* 88, 155-172.

Childe, V.G. and Grant, W.G. 1946. A Stone Age settlement at the Braes of Rinyo. Rousay, Orkney. *Proceedings of the Society of Antiquaries of Scotland* 81, 16-42.

Chinery, M. 1979 *A Field Guide to the Insects of Britain and Northern Europe*. London: Collins.

Christie, J. 1864. Account of the opening of an ancient cist in the parish of Cabbach, Aberdeenshire. *Proceedings of the Society of Antiquaries of Scotland* 5, 362-363.

Clapham, A. J. and Scaife, R. G. 1988. A pollen and plant macrofossil investigation of Oakbank crannog, Loch Tay, Scotland. Pages 293-325 in Murphy, P. and French, C.(eds) *The Exploitation of Wetlands*. Oxford: British Archaeological Reports. British Series 186.

Clark, J.G.D. 1963. Neolithic bows from the Somerset Levels, England, and the prehistory of archery in Northwestern Europe. *Proceedings of the Prehistoric Society* 29, 50-98.

Clarke, D.V. 1998. The environment and economy of Skara Brae. Pages 8-19 in R.A.Lambert (ed) *Species History in Scotland*. Scottish Cultural Press.

Clarke, D. V. and Sharples, N. 1985. Settlements and Subsistence in the Third Millennium BC. Pages 54-82 in Renfrew, C.(ed) *The Prehistory of Orkney*. Edinburgh University Press.

Coleman, R.J. 1996. Burbage plots of Medieval Perth. *Proceedings of the Society of Antiquaries of Scotland* 126, 689-732.

Coles, B. and Coles, J. 1989. *People of the Wetlands. Bogs, Bodies and Lake Dwellings*. London: Thames & Hudson.

Coles, J. 1973. *Archaeology by Experiment*. London: Hutchinson.

Coles, J. M. 1971. The early settlement of Scotland: excavations at Morton, Fife. *Proceedings of the Prehistoric Society* 37, 284-366.

Coles, J. and Coles, B. 1996. *Enlarging the Past. The Contribution of Wetland Archaeology*. Edinburgh: Society of Antiquaries of Scotland Monograph Series Number 11.

Coles, J. M., Hibbert, F. A. and Orme, B. J. 1973. Prehistoric Roads and Tracks in Somerset, England: 3. The Sweet Track. *Proceeding of the Prehistoric Society* 39, 256-93.

Coles, J. M. and Orme, B.J. 1983. *Homo sapiens* or *Castor fiber*? *Antiquity* 57. 95-102.

Collingwood, R.G. and Wright, R.P. 1994. *The Roman Inscriptions of Britain. Volume II Instrumentum Domesticum*. Stroud: Alan Sutton Publishing.

Comrie, J. D. 1932. *History of Scottish Medicine, Volume 1*. London: The Wellcome Historical Medical Museum, 2nd ed.

Connolly, A. 1994. Castles and abbeys in Wales: refugia for 'Medieval' medicinal plants. Pages 628-637 in J.H.Dickson and R.R. Mill (eds) *Plants and People Economic Botany in Northern Europe AD 800-1800. Botanical Journal of Scotland* 46, 521-706.

Cooper, M.R. and Johnson, A.W. 1998. *Poisonous Plants and Fungi in Britain.* London; the Stationary Office.

Corbet, G. & Ovenden, D. 1980 *The Mammals of Britain & Europe.* Collins.

Coulton, G.C. 1933 *Scottish Abbeys and Social Life.* Cambridge University Press.

Cowie, T. G. and Shepherd, I.A.G. The Bronze Age. Pages 151- 168 in K.J. Edwards and I.B. Ralston (editors) *Scotland: Environment and Archaeology. 8000 BC - AD 1000.* Chichester: John Wiley & Sons.

Cranwell, L. 1953. New Zealand Pollen Studies The Monocotyledons. *Bulletin of the Auckland Institute and Museum* 3, 1-89.

Crawford, B. E. 1987 *Scandinavian Scotland.* Leicester University Press.

Crawford, B. E. and Ballin Smith, B. 1998. *The Biggings, Papa Stour, Shetland. The history and excavation of a Royal Norwegian Farm.* Edinburgh: Society of Antiquaries of Scotland Monograph No 10.

Crewe, C. 1975. Birrens charcoal summary. Pages 269-273 in Robertson, A.S. *Birrens (Blatobulgium).* Edinburgh: T. & A. Constable.

Crone, B. A. 1993. Crannogs and chronologies. *Proceedings of the Society of Antiquaries of Scotland* 123, 245-54.

Crum, H.A. and Anderson, L.E. 1981. *Mosses of Eastern North America. Volume 1.* New York: Columbia University Press.

Curle, C. L. 1982. *Pictish and Norse finds from the Brough of Birsay 1934-74.* Edinburgh: Society of Antiquaries of Scotland Monograph No.1.

Curle, J. 1911. *A Roman Frontier Post and its People: The Fort at Newstead in the Parish of Melrose.* Glasgow: Maclehose.

Dark, P. 1998. Lake-edge Sequences: Results and Interpretation of the Lake-edge Sequences. Pages 125-146 and pages 153-161 in Mellars, P. (ed) *Star Carr in Context.* Cambridge, Macdonald Institute Monographs.

Darwin, T. 1996. The *Scots Herbal: The Plant Lore of Scotland.* Edinburgh: Mercat Press.

Davies, R. W. 1971. The Roman military diet. *Britannia* 2, 122-42.

Dawson, A. G. 1992. *Ice Age Earth. Late Quaternary Geology and Climate.* London: Routledge.

Dawson, W. R. 1931 *A Leechbook of the fifteenth century.* London: MacMillan.

Deans, A. S. C. 1957. Survey of British honeys. *Bee Research Association Report* 142.

De Moulins, D. 1996. Sieving experiment: the controlled recovery of charred plant remains from modern and archaeological samples. Pages 153-6 in Behre, K-E. and. Oeggl, K(eds). Early Farming in the Old World. *Vegetational History and Archaeobotany Special Volume.*

Dencker, J. 1997. Stone Age settlements in the middle of nature's larder. Pages 87-91 in Pedersen, L *et al.* (eds) *The Danish Storebælt since the Ice Age.* Copenhagen: A/S Storebælt Fixed Link.

Dickson, C. A. 1970. The study of plant macrofossils in British Quaternary deposits. Pages 233-254 in Walker, D .and West, R G (eds) *Studies in the Vegetational History of the British Isles.* Cambridge University Press.

Dickson, C. 1983. Appendix 3. Fruits, seeds and charcoal from Ardnave, Islay. Pages 358-60 in Ritchie, G. and Welfare, H. Excavations at Ardnave, Islay. *Proceedings of the Society of Antiquaries of Scotland* 113, 302-366.

Dickson, C. 1987. The macroscopic plant remains. Pages 137-142 in Hedges, J. *Bu, Gurness and the Brochs of Orkney.* Oxford: BAR British Seriies 163.

Dickson, C. 1990. Experimental Processing and Cooking of Emmer and Spelt Wheats and the Roman Army Diet. Pages 33-39 in Robinson, D. E. (ed) *Experimentation and Reconstruction in Environmental Archaeology.* Symposia for the Association of Environmental Archaeology No. 9. Oxford: Oxbow Books.

Dickson, C. 1995. Plant remains. Pages 410-417 in Terry, J. Excavation at Lintshie Gutter Unenclosed Platform Settlement, Crawford, Lanarkshire, 1991. *Proceedings of the Society of Antiquaries of Scotland* 125, 369-427.

Dickson, C. A. 1987. The identification of cereals from ancient bran fragments. *Circaea* 4, 95-102.

Dickson, C. 1988. Distinguishing cereal from wild grass pollen: some limitations. *Circaea* 5, 67-71.

Dickson, C. 1989. The Roman army diet in Britain and Germany. *Dissertationes Botanicae* 133, 135-54.

Dickson, C. 1990. Experimental processing and cooking of Emmer and Spelt Wheats and the Roman army diet. Pages 33-39 in Robinson, D.E.(ed) *Experimentation and Reconstruction in Environmental Archaeology.* Oxford: Oxbow Books.

Dickson, C. 1994. Macroscopic fossils of garden plants from British Roman and Medieval deposits. Pages 47-71 in Moe, D. *et al.* editors *Garden History: Garden Plants, Species, Forms and Varieties.* Pact 42.

Dickson, C. 1995. Plant remains. Pages 410-417 in Terry, J. Excavations at Lintshie GutterUnencloseed Platform Settlement, Crawford, Lanarkshire. *Proceedings of the Society of Antiquaries of Scotland* 125, 369-427.

Dickson, C. 1996. Food, medicinal and other plants from the fifteenth-century drains of Paisley Abbey, Scotland. Pages 25-31 in Behre, K-E and Oeggl, K.(eds). Early Farming in the Old World. *Vegetational History and Archaeobotany Special Volume.*

Dickson, C. 2000. Food, Medicinal & Other Plants from the Drain. Pages 213-224 in J.Malden (ed) *The Monastery and Abbey of Paisley*. Renfrewshire Local History Forum.

Dickson, C. forthcoming 'The plant remains' in *Skara Brae* Clarke, D.V.C. and Shepherd, A.N. Historic Scotland/ National Museums of Scotland.

Dickson, C.A. and Dickson, J.H.1984. The botany of the Crosskirk Broch site. Pages 147-155 in Fairhurst, H. *Excavations at Crosskirk Broch, Caithness*. Society of Antiquaries of Edinburgh Monograph No.3.

Dickson, C., Dickson, J.H. and Breeze, D. 1979. Flour or bread in a Roman military ditch at Bearsden, Scotland. *Antiquity* 53, 437-442.

Dickson, J.H. 1973. *Bryophytes of the Pleistocene*. Cambridge University Press.

Dickson, J.H. 1978. Bronze Age Mead. *Antiquity* 52, 108-13.

Dickson, J.H. 1979. *The Botany of Brochs*. Pages 62-65 in Thoms, L.M *Early Man in the Scottish Landscape*. Edinburgh Univeristy Press.

Dickson, J.H. 1980. *Glasgow Region Field Guide*. Quaternary Research Association.

Dickson, J.H.1984. Monk's Rhubarb (*Rumex alpinus* L.) in Ayrshire. *Glasgow Naturalist* 5, 482.

Dickson, J.H. 1986. Bryophyte Analysis. Pages 627-43 in Berglund, B.(ed) *Handbook of Palaeoecology and Palaeohydrology*. Chichester: John Wiley.

Dickson, J.H. 1992a. North American driftwood, especially *Picea* (spruce) from archaeological sites in the Hebrides and Northern Isles of Scotland. *Review of Palaeobotany and Palynology* 73, 49-56.

Dickson, J.H.1992b. Scottish Woodlands: Their Ancient Past and Precarious Present *Botanical Journal of Scotland* 46, 155-165.

Dickson, J.H. 1994a. The Yew tree (*Taxus baccata* L.) in Scotland — Native or early introduction or both? *Scottish Forestry* 48, 252-259.

Dickson, J.H. 1994b. Further notes on Yew. *Scottish Forestry* 48, 271.

Dickson, J.H. 1998. Plant introductions in Scotland. Pages 38-44 in Lambert, R. A. *Species History in Scotland*. Scottish Cultural Press, Edinburgh.

Dickson, J.H. 2000. Some Especially Noteworthy Plants from the Drain. Pages 225-2230 in J. Malden (ed) *The Monastery and Abbey of Paisley*. Renfrewshire Local History Forum.

Dickson, J.H. and Brough, D. W. 1989. Biological Studies of a Pictish Midden.. *Dissertationes Botanicae* 133, 155-66.

Dickson, J.H. and Dickson, C. 1996. Ancient and Modern Occurrences of Common Fig (Ficus carica L.) in the British Isles. *Quaternary Science Reviews* 15, 623-633.

Dickson, J.H. and Gauld, W. W. 1986. Mark Jamieson's Physic Plants. *Scottish Medical Journal* 32, 60-62.

Dickson, J.H., Macpherson, P. and Watson, K. 2000a. *The Changing Flora of Glasgow*. Edinburgh University Press.

Dickson, J.H., Oeggl, K., Holden, T.G., Handley, L.L., O'Connell, T. and Preston, T. 2000b. The Omnivorous Tyrolean Iceman: Colon Contents (Meat, Cereals, Pollen, Moss and Whipworm) and Stable Isotope Analyses. *Philosophical Transactions of the Royal Society B*.

Dimbleby, G. W. 1985. *The Palynology of Archaeological Sites*. London: Academic Press.

Dineley, M. and Dineley, G. 2000a. From grain to ale: Skara Brae, a case study. In Ritchie, A. (ed.) Neolithic Orkney Conference.

Dineley, M. and Dineley, G. 2000b. Neolithic ale: barley as a source of malt sugars for fermentation. In Fairbairn, A. (ed.) Conference on plants, NSG, Oxbow Books.

Dockrill, S.J. and Bond, J.M, 1996. *Old Scatness/Jarlshof Environs Project, pt. 1: Old Scatness Broch Excavations, 1-21*, Shetland Amenity Trust and University of Bradford.

Dockrill, S.J., Bond, J. M., Milles, A., Simpson, I., and Ambers, J. 1994. Tofts Ness, Sanday, Orkney. An integrated study of a buried Orcadian landscape. Pages 115-32 in R. Luff and P. Rowley-Conwy eds *Whither Environmental Archaeology?* Oxfords: Oxbow Books.

Donald, A.P. 1981. A Pollen Diagram from Pitbladdo, Fife. *Transactions of the Botanical Society of Edinburgh* 43, 281-9.

Dougall, M and Dickson, J. 1997. The Old Managed Oaks in the Glasgow Area. Pages 76-85 in Smout, T. C. (ed) *Scottish Woodland History*. Edinburgh: Scottish Cultural Press.

Dougall, M. and Dickson, J.H. The ancient oaks of Cadzow. *The Glasgow Naturalist* 23, 29-35.

Driscoll, S.T. 1997. A Pictish settlement in north-east Fife: the Scottish Field School of Archaeology excavations at Easter Kinnear. *Tayside and Fife Archaeological Journal* 3, 74-118.

Driscoll, S.T. and Yeoman, P.A. 1997. *Excavations within Edinburgh Castle in 1988-91*. Edinburgh: Society of Antiquaries of Scotland Monograph No.12.

Dugmore, A. 1989. Icelandic volcanic ash in Scotland. *Scottish Geographical Magazine* 105, 68-72.

Dumayne, L. 1993a. Invader or native? — vegetation clearance in northern Britian during Romano-British times. *Vegetation History and Archaeobotany* 2, 29-36.

Dumayne, L. 1993b. Iron Age and Roman Vegetation clearance in Northern Britain: further evidence. *Botanical Journal of Scotland* 46, 385-392.

Dumayne-Peaty, L. 1998. Human impact on the environment during the Iron Age and Romano-British times: Palynological evidence from three sites near the Antonine Wall, Great Britain. *Journal of Archaeological Science* 25, 203-214.

Duncan, A. M. M. 1975. *Scotland: the Making of the Kingdom.* Volume 1. Edinburgh: Oliver and Boyd.

Earwood, C. 1990. The wooden artefacts from Loch Glashan crannog. *Proceedings of the Society of Antiquaries of Scotland* 121, 231-40.

Edwards, J. 1984. *The Roman Cookery of Apicius.* London: Rider.

Edwards, K. J. 1996. A Mesolithic of the Western and Northern Isles of Scotland? Evidence from pollen and charcoal. Pages 23-38 in Pollard, T. and Morrison, A.(eds) *The Early Prehistory of Scotland.* Edinburgh University Press.

Egg, M., Goedecker-Ciolek, R., Groeman-Van Waateringe, W. and Spindler, K. 1993. Die Gletschermumie vom ende der Steinzeit aus den Ötztaler Alpen. *Jahrbuch des Römischen-Germanischen Zentralmuseums* 39, 1-128.

Elliot, W. 1991. Animal footprints on Roman bricks from Newstead. *Proceedings of the Society of Antiquaries of Scotland* 121, 223-226.

Ellis, E.A. 1965. *The Broads.* London: Collins.

Englemark, R. 1984. Two useful plants from iron Age graves in Central Sweden. *Archaeology and Environment* I2, 87-92.

Englemark, R. and Viklund, K. 1988. Forhistorisk 'popcorn'. *Populär Arkeologi* 2,11.

Evans, J. G. 1983 Appendix 2 Mollusca and other invertebrates from Ardnave, Islay. Pages 358-60 in Ritchie, G. & Welfare, H. Excavations at Ardnave, Islay. *Proceedings of the Society of Antiquaries of Scotland* 113, 302-366.

Ewart, G. and Triscott, J.1996. Archaeological excavations at Castle Sween, Knapdale, Argyll 7 Bute, 1989-90. *Proceedings of the Society of Antiquaries of Scotland* 126, 517-557.

Faegri, K. 1961. Palynology of a bumble-bee nest. *Veröffentlichungen des Geobotanischen Institutes der Eidgenössischen Technischen Hochschule. Stiftung Rübel in Zürich* 37, 60-67.

Fagan, B. 2000. *Floods, Famines and Emperors.* London: Pimlico.

Fairhurst, H. 1984 *Excavations at Crosskirk Broch, Caithness.* Edinburgh: Society of Antiquaries of Scotland Monograph No. 3.

Fairweather, A. D. and Ralston, I. B. M. 1993. The Neolithic timber hall at Balbridie, Grampion Region, Scotland: the building, the dates, the plant macrofossils. *Antiquity* 67, 313-23.

Fenton, A. S. 1978. *The Northern Isles: Orkney and Shetland.* Edinburgh: John Donald.

Fenton, A. S. 1987. *Country Life in Scotland Our Rural Past.* Edinburgh: John Donald.

Finlayson, B. 1998. *Wild Harvesters. The First people in Scotland.* Edinburgh: Canongate Books.

Finlayson, B. and Edwards, K. J. 1997. The Mesolithic Pages 109-126 in Edwards, K. J. and Ralston, I. B. M. (eds) *Scotland: Environment and Archaeology, 8000 BC- AD 1000.* Chichester, John Wiley.

Firbank, L.G. 1988. *Agrostemma githago* L. *Journal of Ecology* 76, 1232-1246.

Flach, M. and Willink, M.J. 1989. Myristica fragrans Houtt. Pages 192-196 in Westphal, E. and Jansen, P.C.M. (eds) *Plant Resources of South-East Asia.* Wageningen, Pudoc.

Ford, B. and Robinson, D. 1987. Moss. Pages 153-155 in Holdsworth, P. *Excavations at Medieval Burgh of Perth 1979-1981.* Society of Antiquaries of Scotland Monograph 5.

Fossel, A. 1974. Die Bienenweide der Ostalpen, dargestellt am Beispiel des steirschen Ennstalles. *Mitteilungen naturwissenchaft Ver Steiermark* 104, 87-118.

Fossitt, J. A. 1996. Late Quaternary vegetation history of the Western Isles of Scotland. *New Phytologist* 132, 171-96.

Foster, S. M. 1996. *Picts, Gaels and Scots.* London: Batsford.

Foulis, J. 1792. An inquiry inrto the beverage of the Ancient Caledonians, and other northern nations, at their feasts; and their drinking vessels. *Archaeologia Scotia* 1, 12-25

Fraser, G. K. and Godwin, H. 1955. Two Scottish pollen diagrams, Carnwath Moss, Lanarkshire and Strichen Moss, Aberdeenshire. *New Phytologist* 54, 216-21.

Fraser, M. J. 1981. *A study of the botanical material from three Medieval Scottish sites.* M. Sc. Thesis University of Glasgow.

Frohne, D. and Pfänder, H.J. 1983. *A Colour Atlas of Poisonous Plants.* Wolfe, Stuttgart.

Geikie, J. 1866. On the buried forests snd peat mosses of Scotland, and the changes of climate they indicate. *Transactions of the Royal Society of Edinburgh* 24, 363-384.

Geikie, J. 1897. *The Great Ice Age and its Relation to the Antiquity of Man.* London: Edward Standford.

Gerard, J. 1633. *The Herball or Generall Historie of Plantes,* enlarged and amended by T. Johnson. Facsimile edition, 1975 New York: Dover.

Geraghty, S. 1996. *Viking Dublin: Botanical Evidence from Fishamble Street.* National Museum of Ireland, Royal Irish Academy Series C, 2.

Glob, P.V. 1973. *The Mound People.* London: Faber and Faber.

Godard, P. 1993. *The First and Last Voyage of the Batavia.* Perth: Abrolhos Publishing PTY. Ltd.

Godmunsson, G. 1996. Gathering and processing of lyme-grass (*Elymus arenarius* L.) in Iceland. *Vegetation History and Archaeobotany* 5, 13-23.

Godwin, H. 1975. *History of the British Flora.* Cambridge University Press, 2nd ed.

Goodwin, K. and Huntley, J. P. 1991.The Waterlogged Plant Remains and Woodland Management Studies. Pages 54-64 in McCarthy, M. R. The structural sequence and environmental remains from Castle Street, Carlisle. *Cumberland and Westmorland Antiquarian and Archaeological Society Research Series No. 5.*

Gottesfeld, L.M. and Vitt, D.H. 1996. The selection of *Sphagnum* for diapers by indigenous North Americans. *Evansia* 13, 103-106.

Gramsch, B. and Kloss, K. 1989. Excavations near Friesack: an Early Mesolithic Marshland Site in the Northern Plain of Central Europe. Pages 313-24 in Bonsack, C. (ed) *The Mesolithic in Europe.* Edinburgh: John Donald.

Greig, J. 1988. Traditional cornfield weeds — where are they now? *Plants Today* 1, 183-191.

Greig, J. 1989. Handbooks for Archaeologists, 1989. No. 4 *Archaeobotany.* Strasbourg: European Science Foundation. No. 2 *Dendrochronological dating.* No. 3 *Radiocarbon dating.*

Grierson, S. 1986. *The Colour Cauldron. The History and Use of Natural Dyes in Scotland.* Perth: Privately published, Newmiln Farm, Tibbermore.

Grieve, M. 1931. *A Modern Herbal.* London: Jonathan Cape.

Griffin, K. 1988. Plant remains. Pages 15-108 in Schia, E (ed) *De arkeologiske utgravninger; Gamlebyen, Oslo.* Bind 5. Oslo: Alvheim and Eide.

Griffin, K. 1994. The usage of wild berries and other fruits in the Medieval and post-Medieval households in Norway. *Botanical Journal of Scotland* 46, 521-526.

Griffin, K. and Sandvik, P. U. 1991. Plant remains from Medieval Trondheim, Norway. In Hajnalova, E (ed) Palaeoethnobotany and Archaeology, Nitra: *Acta Disciplinaria Archaeologica*,111-2.

Grigson, G. 1987. *The Englishman's Flora.* London: J.M.Dent & Sons.

Grove, J. M. 1988. *The Little Ice Age.* London: Methuen.

Gunther, E. 1973. *Ethnobotany of Western Washington.* Seattle: University of Washington Press.

Gunther, R. T. 1934. *The Greek Herbal of Dioscorides.* Oxford University Press.

Haggarty, A. and Haggarty, G. 1983. Excavations at Rispain Camp, Whithorn 1978-1981. *Transactions of the Dumfriesshire & Galloway Natural History & Antiquarian Society* 58, 21-51.

Hall, A. 1995. Archaeobotanical evidence for woad *Isatis tinctoria* L. from Medieval England and Ireland. Pages 33-38 in Kroll, H. and Pasternak, R. (eds) *Res Archaeobotanicae — Symposium Kiel.* Kiel: Christian-Albrecht-Universität.

Hall, A. 1996. A survey of palaeobotanical evidence for dyeing and mordanting from British archaeological excavations. *Quaternary Science Reviews* 15, 635-640.

Hall, A. R. and Kenward, H. K. 1990. Environmental Evidence from the Colonia: General Accident and Rougier Street. The Archaeology of York 14: The Past Environment of York, CBA London.

Hall, A., Tomlinson, P., Hall, R., Taylor, G. and Walton, P. 1984. Dye plants from Viking York. *Antiquity* 58, 58-60.

Hall, V. A., Pilcher, J.R. and MacCormac, F.G. 1994. Icelandic volcanic ash and the mid-Holocene Scots pine (*Pinus sylvestris*) decline in the north of Ireland: no correlation. *The Holocene* 4, 79-83.

Hamilton, J.R.C. 1956. *Excavations at Jahlshof, Shetland.* Edinburgh: Ministry of Works Archaeological Report 1. HMSO.

Hamilton, J.R.C. 1968. *Excavations at Clickhimin*, Shetland. Edinburgh: Ministry of Works Archaeological Report 6. HMSO.

Handley, J.E. 1953. *Scottish Farming in the Eighteenth Century.* London, Faber and Faber.

Hanson, W. S. 1997. The Roman presence: Brief Interludes. Pages 195-216 in Edwards, K. J. and Ralston, I. B. M. *Scotland: Environment and Archaeology, 8000 BC-AD 1000.* Wiley, Chichester.

Hanson, W. S. forthcoming Elginhaugh: *A Flavian Fort and its Annexe.* London: Roman Society.

Hanson, W.S. and Yeoman, P.A. 1988. *Elginhaugh A Roman Fort and its Environs.* Edinburgh: Historic Buildings and Monuments.

Harman, M. 1983. Animal remains from Ardnave, Islay Pages 343-50 in Ritchie, J.N.G. and Welfare, H. Excavations at Ardnave, Islay. *Proceedings of the Society of Antiquaries of Scotland* 113, 302-366.

Harvey, J. 1981. *Mediaeval Gardens.* London: Batsford.

Harvey, J. H. 1984. Vegetables in the middle ages. *Garden History* 12, 89-99.

Haslam, S. 1972. *Phragmites communis* Trin. *Journal of Ecology* 60, 573-584.

Hedges, J. W. 1983. Trial excavations on Pictish and Viking settlements at Saevar Howe, Birsay, Orkney. *Glasgow Archaeological Journal* 10, 73-124.

Hedges, J. W. 1986. Bronze Age structures at Tougs, Burra Isle, Shetland. *Glasgow Archaeological Journal* 13, 1-43.

Hedges, J. W. 1987. *Bu, Gurness and the Brochs of Orkney Pt. 1 Bu*. Oxford: BAR British Series 163.

Heer, O. 1866. Treatise on the Plants of the Lake Dwellings in Keller, F. *The Lake Dwellings of Switzerland and other Parts of Europe*. London.

Heller, H.1953. *Wild Edible and Poisonous Plants of Alaska*. College: United States Department of Alaska.

Henderson, D. M. and Dickson, J. H. 1994. *A Naturalist in the Highlands*. Edinburgh: Scottish Academic Press.

Henshall, A.S. and Wallace, J.C. 1965. The excavation of a chambered cairn at Embo, Sutherland. *Proceedings of the Society of Antiquarties of Scotland* 96, 9-36.

Herodotus 1996. *The Histories*. Harmondsworth: Penguin.

Hill, P. 1996. *Whithorn and St Ninian: The Excavation of a Monastic town, 1984-91*. Stroud: Sutton.

Hoeg, A. 1974. *Planter og Tradisjon*. Oslo: Universitetsforlaget.

Holden, T.G. 1996. The plants and the people from Buiston Crannog, Ayrshire, Scotland. *Antiquity* 70, 954-9.

Hillman, G. C., Mason, S., de Moulins, D. and Nesbit, M. 1996. Identification of archaeological remains of Wheat: the 1992 London workshop. *Circaea* 12, 195-209.

Hinton, P. 1991. Weed associates of recently grown *Avena strigosa* Schreber from Shetland, Scotland. *Circaea* 1, 49-54.

Hirons, K. R. and Edwards, K. J. 1990. Pollen and related studies at Kinloch, Isle of Rhum, Scotland, with particular reference to possible early human impacts on vegetation. *New Phytologist* 116, 715-27.

Hodgson, G. W. I. 1983. The animal remains from Medieval sites within three burghs on the eastern Scottish Seaboard in Proudfoot, B. (ed) *Site, Economy and Environment*. Oxford: BAR International Series 173.

Holdsworth, P. 1987. *Excavations in the Medieval Burgh of Perth, 1979-81*. Edinburgh: Society of Antiquaries of Scotland Monograph No. 5.

Hooker, J.D. 1884. *The Student's Flora of the British Isles*. London: Macmillan.

Howard, R and Moore A. 1994 . *A Complete Checklist of the Birds of the World*. Second Edition. Academic Press.

Hulten, E. 1968. *Flora of Alaska and Neighbouring Territories A Manual of the Vascular Plants*. Cambridge University Press.

Hume Brown, P. 1891. *Early Travellers in Scotland*. Edinburgh: David Douglas.

Hunter, J.R. 1986. *Rescue excavations on the Brough of Birsay 1974- 82*. Edinburgh: Society of Antiquaries of Scotland Monograph No. 4.

Hunter, M. 1996. *Jo: Ben's Orkney*. Place of publication unstated.

Innes, C. 1860. *Scotland in the Middle Ages*. Edinburgh: Edmonston and Douglas.

Innes Miller, J. 1969. *The Spice Trade of the Roman Empire*. Oxford: Clarendon Press.

Jacomet, S. 1987 *Prähistorische Getreidefunde*. Basel: Botanisches Institut der Universität.

Jacomet, S. and Kreuz, a. 1999. *Archäobotanik*. Stuttgart: Eugen Ulmer.

Jane, F.W. 1970. *The Structure of Wood*. London: A. & C. Black, 2nd ed.

Jessen, K. and Helbæk, H. 1944. Cereals in Great Britain and Ireland in prehistoric and early historic times. *Det Kongelige Danske Videnskabernes Selskab Biologiske Skrifrter* III, 2.

Johansen, J. 1994. Medicinal and Other Useful Plants in the Faroe Islands before AD 1800. Pages 611-16 in Dickson, J.H. and Mill, R.R. (eds) *Plants and People Economic Botany in Northern Europe AD 800-1800*. *Botanical Journal of Scotland* 46.

Johnstone, P. 1980. *The Sea-craft of Prehistory*. London: Routledge and Paul.

Jones, A.K.G. 1990. Experiments with Fish Bones and Otoliths: Implications for the Reconstruction of Past Diet and Economy. Pages 143-46 in Robinson, D.E. (ed) *Experimentation and Reconstruction in Environmental Archaeology*. Oxford: Oxbow Books.

Juniper, B. 1998. Tracing the Origins of the Apple. *St Catherine's Year 1998*, 20-23. (Year Book of St Catherine's College, University of Oxford).

Kadereit, J. 1986. *Papaver somniferum* L. (Papaveraceae): A triploid hybrid? *Botanische Jahrbuch Systematische*. 106, 221-244.

Kaland, S.H.H. 1993. The Settlement of Westness, Rousay, 308-39 in Batey, C.E., Jesch, J. and Morris, C.D. (eds) *The Viking Age in Caithness, Orkney and the North Atlantic*. Edinburgh University Press.

Kari, P.R. 1995. *Tanaina Plantlore* Anchorage: Alaska Natural History Association.

Katz, N. J., Katz, S. V. and Kipiani, M. G. 1965. *Atlas and Keys of Fruits and Seeds Occurring in the Quaternary deposits of the USSR* (in Russian). Moscow: Nauka.

Keatinge, T. and Dickson, J.H. 1979. Mid-Flandrian changes in vegetation on Mainland Orkney. *New Phytologist* 82, 585-612.

Kenward, H.K., Hall, A.R. and Jones, A.K.G. 1980. A tested set of techniques for the extraction of plant and animal macrofossils from waterlogged archaeological deposits. *Science and Archaeology* 22, 3-15.

Keys, D. 1999. *Catastrophe: An Investigation into the origins of the Modern World*. London: Century.

Keys, J.D. 1976. *Chinese Herbs*. Rutland, Vermont, C.E.Tuttle.

Kitchener, A. C. 1998. Extinctions, Introductions and Colonisations of Scottish Mammals and birds since the Last Ice Age. Pages 63-92 in Lambert, R. A. (ed) *Species History in Scotland*. Edinburgh: Scottish Cultural Press.

Knights, B. A., Dickson, C. A., Dickson, J. H. and Breeze, D. J. 1983. Evidence Concerning the Roman Military Diet at Bearsden, Scotland, in the second Century AD. *Journal of Archaeological Science* 10, 139-52.

Körber-Grohne, U. 1964. *Bestimmungschlüssel für subfossile Juncus-Samen und Gramineen-Früchte. Probleme der Küstenforschung im Südlichen Nordseegebiet,* 7. Hildesheim: Lax.

Körber-Grohne, U. 1991. *Identification key for subfossil Gramineae fruits. Probleme der Küstenforschung im Südlichen Nordseegebiet,* 18. Hildesheim: Lax.

Körber-Grohne, U., Kokjabi, M., Piening, U. and Planck, D. 1983. *Flora and Fauna im Osykastell von Welzheim*. Stuttgart: Konrad Theiss Verlag.

Kortesajarhu, J. 1988. The Golden Berry of the Bogs. Pages 155-157 in Neuvonen, V. M. *et al.* (eds) *Finland Land of Natural Beauty*. Helsinki, Oy Valitut Palat.

Krzywinski, K., Fjelldal, S. and Solvedt, S. E-C. 1983. Recent palaeoethnobotanical work at the Medieval excavation at Bryggen, Bergen, Norway. Pages 145-69 in Proudfoot, B.(ed). *Site, Environment and Economy*. BAR International Series 173.

Kuijper, W. J. and Turner, H. 1992. Diet of a Roman centurion at Alphen aan den Rijn, in the first century AD. *Review of Palaeobotany and Palynology* 73, 187-204.

Ladurie, E. Le Roy. 1972. *Times of Feast, Times of Famine A History of Climate since the year 1000*. London; George Allen & Unwin.

Lamb, H. H. 1982. *Climate History and the Modern World*. London: Methuen.

Lambert, C. A. 1964. Appendix IV The plant remains from Cist 1 in Henshall, A.S. A dagger grave and other cist burials at Ashgrove, Methilhill, Fife. *Proceedings of the Society of Antiquaries of Scotland* 97, 166-79.

Langham, W. 1579. *The garden of health, conteyning the sundry rare and hidden virtues and properties of all kindes of simples and plants*. London.

Launert, E. 1981. *Edible and Medicinal Plants of Britain and Northern Europe*. London, Hamlyn.

Law, C. 1998. The Uses and Fire-ecology of Reedswamp Vegetation. Pages 197-206 in Mellars, P. (ed) *Star Carr in Context*. Cambridge, Macdonald Institute Monographs.

Lempiänen, T. 1991. Past occurrences of Hyoscyamus niger L. in Finalnd according to macrofossil finds. *Annales Botanici Fennici* 28, 261-271.

Lentfer, C.J., Boyd, W.E. and Gojak, D. 1997. Hope Farm Windmill: phytolith analysis of cereals in early colonial Australia. *Journal of Archaeological Science* 24, 841–856.

Lees, J. C. 1878. *The Abbey of Paisley*. Paisley: Gardner.

Leiner, I.E. 1969. *Toxic Constituents of Plant Foodstuffs*. London: Academic Press.

Lewington, A. and Parker, E. 1999. *Ancient Trees*. London: Collins and Brown.

Lewis, J.H. 1996. Excavations at St Andrews, Castlecliff, 1988-90. *Proceedings of the Society of Antiquaries of Scotland* 126, 605-688.

Lightfoot, J. 1777. *Flora Scotica* Volume 1. London: B.White.

Linnaeus, C. 1737. *Flora Lapponica*. Amsterdam.

Linskens, H.F. and Jorde, W. 1997. Pollen as food and medicine — a review. *Economic Botany* 51, 78-87.

Lockhart, G.W. 1983. *The Scot and his Oats*. Barr: Luath Press.

Lousley, J. E. and Kent, D.H. 1981. *Docks and Knotweeds of the British Isles*. London: Botanical Society of the British Isles.

Lowe, J. 1993. Isolating the climatic factors in early and mid-Holocene palaeobotanical records from Scotland. In Chambers, F.M. (ed.) *Climate Change and Human Impact on the Landscape*.

Lynch, M., Spearman, M. and Stell, G. 1988. *The Scottish Medieval Town*. Edinburgh: Donald.

Mabberley, D. J. 1997. *The plant-book. A portable dictionary of the vascular plants*. Cambridge University Press, 2nd edition.

Mabey, R. 1996. *Flora Britannica*. London: Sinclair-Stevenson.

Malden, J.1995. The Cluniac Monastery of Paisley: a preliminary investigation. *Proceedings of the Society of Antiquaries of Scotland* 125, 1193-1194.

Malden, J. 2000. *The Monastery & Abbey of Paisley*. Renfrewshire Local History Forum.

McCarthy, M. R. 1991. The structural sequence and environmental remains from Castle Street, Carlisle: excavations 1981-2. *Cumberland and Westmorland Antiquarian and Archaeological Society Research Series No. 5.*

McCormick, F. 1992. Early faunal evidence for dairying. *Oxford Journal of Archaeology* 11, 211-219.

McCormick, F. and Buckland, P.C. 1997. The Vertebrate Fauna. Pages 83-103 in K.J. Edwards, and Ralston, I.B.M. (eds) *Scotland: Environment and Archaeology, 8000 BC - AD 1000*. Chichester: Wiley.

MacDonald, G. 1911. *The Roman Wall in Scotland*. Glasgow, James Maclehose.

MacDonald, G. and Curle, A. O. 1929. The Roman Fort at Mumrills. *Proceedings of the Society of Antiquaries of Scotland* 63, 396-569.

McGovern, P.E., Glusker, D.L, Exner, L.J. and Voigt. M.M. 1992. Neolithic resinated wine. *Nature* 360, 24-25.

McGrail, S. 1987. *Ancient Boats in North-West Europe: the Archaeology of Water Transport to AD 1500.* London: Longman.

MacIvor, I., Thomas, M.C., and Breeze, D.J. 1981. Excavations on the Antonine Wall fort of Rough Castle, Stirlingshire, 1957-61. *Proceedings of the Society of Antiquaries of Scotland* 110, 230-285.

McKay, M.M. 1980. *The Rev. Dr. John Walker's Report on the Hebrides of 1764 and 1771.* Edinburgh, John Donald.

MacKie, E. W. 1974. *Dun Mor Vaul An Iron Age Broch on Tiree.* Glasgow: University of Glasgow.

MacLaren, A. 1974. A Norse House on Drimore Machair, South Uist. *Glasgow Archaeological Journal* 3, 9-18.

McLaren, F. S., Evans, J. and Hillman, G. C. 1991. Identification of charred seeds from SW Asia. Pages 796-806 in Pernica, E. and Wagner, G. A.(eds) Archaeometry '90. Proceedings of the 26th International Symposium on Archaeometry, Heidelberg 1990.

Maclean, A. C. and Rowley-Conwy, P. A. 1984. The carbonised material in Burl, H.A.W. Report on the excavation of a Neolithic mound at Boghead, Speymouth Forest, Fochabers, Moray, 1972 and 1974. *Proceedings of the Society of Antiquaries of Scotland* 114, 69-71.

Manniche, L. 1993. *An Ancient Egyptian Herbal.* British Museum Press. London.

Marren, P. 1990. *Woodland Heritage.* Newton Abbot: David & Charles.

Martin, A. E. 1966. Infra-red instrumentation and techniques. Elsevier, Amsterdam.

Martin, M. 1716. *A Description of the Western Isles of Scotland.* Facsimile of the second edition. Edinburgh: Mercat Press.

Mattioli, P.A. 1624. *Commentarii im libros sex pedacii Dioscoridis anazarbei de medica materia. Media Caesarei et Ferdinandi Archiducis Austriæ quæ extant Omnia a Casparo Bauhino.* Basel.

Maurizio, A. 1971. Le spectre pollinique des miels Luxembourgeois. *Apidologie* 2, 221-238.

Maxwell, H. 1915. *Trees: A Woodland Notebook.* Glasgow: Maclehose.

Meehan, B. 1994. *The Book of Kells.* London: Thames and Hudson.

Mellars, P. A. 1987. *Excavations on Oronsay: Prehistoric Human Ecology on a Small Island.* Edinburgh University Press.

Mellars, P. and Dark, P. 1998. *Star Carr in Context.* Cambridge: Macdonald Institute Monographs.

Mercer, J. A. 1974. Regression-time Stone-workers Camp, 33ft OD, Lussa River, Isle of Jura. *Proceedings of the Society of Antiquaries of Scotland* 103, 1-33.

Milles, A. 1986. Comparative analysis of charred plant remains from Ness of Gruting. Pages 123-4 in Whittle, A., Keith-Lucas, M., Milles, A., Noddle, B., Rees, S. and Romans, J. *Scord of Brouster. An Early Agricultural Settlement on Shetland.* Oxford University Archaeological Monograph 9.

Miller, R. 1976. *Orkney.* London: B.T.Batsford.

Milton, G. 1999. *Nathaniel's Nutmeg.* London, Hodder and Stoughton.

Moerman, D.E. 1998. *Native American Ethnobotany.* Portland: Timber Press.

Moffett, L. 1991. Pignut tubers from a Bronze Age cremation at barrow Hills, Oxfordshire, and the importnace of vegetable tibers in the prehistoric period. *Journal of Archaeological Science* 18, 187-191.

Moffett, L., Robinson, M. A., Straker, V., 1989. Cereals, fruit and nuts: charred plant remains from Neolithic sites in England and Wales and the Neolithic economy. In Milles, A., Williams, D. and Gardner, N., (eds) *The Beginning of Agriculture.* BAR International Series 496. Oxford.

Mitchell, A. 1996. *Trees of Britain.* London: HarperCollins.

Moe, D. 1998.Natural scientific methods, a potential, or more needed in future archaeology? *Archaeologica Baltica* 3, 103-108.

Monk, M. A. and Pals, J. P. 1985. Part 2 Charred plant remains. Pages 79-81 in Woodman, P. C. *Excavations at Mount Sandel 1973-77.* Belfast: HMSO.

Moore, P.D. 1978. Bronze Age honey. *Nature* 276, 443.

Moore, P.D. 1994. Flowers and funerals. Nature 369, 308-309.

Moore, P. D., Webb, J. and Collinson, M. C. 1991. *Pollen Analysis, a Laboratory Manual.* Oxford: Blackwell, 2nd ed.

Morgan, R. A. 1975. The Selection and Sampling of Timber from Archaeological sites for Identification and Tree-ring analysis. *Journal of Archaeological Science* 2, 221-30.

Morris, C. D. 1989. *The Birsay Bay Project 1 Coastal Sites beside the Brough Road, Birsay, Orkney. Excavations 1976-19872. Volume 1.* University of Durham Monograph Series 1.

Morris, C. D. 1996. *The Birsay Bay Project Volume 2 Sites in Birsay Village and the Brough of Birsay, Orkney.* University of Durham Monograph Series 2.

Morris, C. D., Batey, C. E. and Rackham, D. J. 1995. *Freswick Links, Caithness. Excavation and Survey of a Norse Settlement.* North Atlantic Biocultural Organisation Monograph 1 / Highland Archaeological Monograph 1.

Morrison, I. 1985. *Landscape with Lake Dwellings: The Crannogs of Scotland.* Edinburgh University Press.

Mowat, R.J.C. 1996. *The Logboats of Scotland.* Oxford: Oxbow Books.

Munro, R. 1882. *Ancient Scottish Lake-dwellings or Crannogs.* Edinburgh: David Douglas.

Murray, H.K. and Murray, J. C. 1993. Excavations at Rattray, Aberdeenshire. A Scottish Deserted Burgh. *Medieval Archaeology* 37, 109-218.

Murray, H.K., Murray, J. C., Shepherd, A.N. and Shepherd, I.A.G. 1992. Evidence of agricultural activity of the later second millennium BC at Rattray, Aberdeenshire. *Proceedings of the Society of Antiquaries of Scotland* 122, 113-125.

Murray, J.C. 1982, *Excavations in the Medieval Burgh of Aberdeen 1973-81.* Edinburgh: Society of Antiquaries of Scotland Monograph Series No. 2.

Muss, B.J. & Dahlstrom, P. 1981 *Collins Guide to the Sea Fishes of Britain & North-Western Europe.* Collins, Glasgow.

Nairne, D. 1891. Notes on the Highland woods. Ancient and modern. *Transactions of the Gaelic Society* 17, 170-221.

Nelson, E.C. 2000. Viking ale and the quest for the impossible: some marginalia leading, perhaps, to 'the most powerfullest drink ever known'. *Yearbook of the Heather Society* 2000, 25-33.

Nichols, G. 1999. Kwaday Dän Sinchì ('Long Ago Person Found'). *Canadian Archaeological Association Newsletter* 19, 14-18.

Nilsson, O. and Hjelmquist, H. 1967. Studies on the nutlet structure of South Scandinavian species of *Carex. Botaniske Notiser* 120, 460-85.

O'Connell, T.C. and Hedges, R.E.M. 1999. Investigations into the effect of diet on modern human hair isotopic values. *American Journal of Physical Anthropology* 108, 409-425.

Oeggl, K. and Schoch, W. 1995. Neolithic plant remains discovered together with a mummified corpse('Homo tyrolensis') in the Tyrolean Alps. Pages 229-238 in Kroll, H. and Pasternak, R. (eds) *Res archaeobotanicae.* Kiel, Institut für Ur- und Frügeschichte der Christian-Albrecht-Universität.

Ostenfeld, C.H. and Gröntved, J. 1934. *The Flora of Iceland and the Færoes.* London: Williams and Norgate.

Owen, O. 1993. Tuquoy, Westray, Orkney. 'A Challenge for the future'. Pages 318-39 in Batey, C.E. , Jesch, J. and Morris, C.D. (eds) *The Viking Age in Caithness, Orkney and the North Atlantic.* Edinburgh University Press.

Palsson, H. and Edwards, P. 1981. *Orkneyinga Saga: the History of the Earls of Orkney.* Harmondsworth: Penguin.

Parkinson, J. 1629. *Paradisi in Sole Paradisus Terrestris.* London.

Parry, M.L.1975. Secular climatic change and marginal land. *Transactions of the Institute of British Geographers* 64, 1-13.

Paton, J.A. 1999. *The Liverwort Flora of the British Isles.* Colchester: Harley Books.

Pearsall, D. 1989. *Paleoethnobotany A Handbook of Procedures.* San Diego: Academic Publishers.

Pearsall, D. 1994. *Investigating New World tropical agriculture: contributions from phytolith anaylsis.* Pages 115-138 in Hather, J.G. *Tropical Archaeobotany Applications and Developments.* London: Routledge.

Pearson, M.P., Sharples, N., Mulville, J. and Smith, H. 1999. *Between Land and Sea Excavations at Dun Vulan, South Uist.* Sheffield Academic Press.

Pedersen, L., Fischer, A. and Aaby, B. 1997. *The Danish Storebælt since the Ice Age.* Copenhagen: A/S Storebælt Fixed Link.

Peglar, S. 1978. A Radiocarbon-dated pollen diagram from Loch of Winless, Caithness, north east Scotland. *New Phytolologist.* 82, 245-63.

Pennant, T. 1774. *A Tour in Scotland in 1769.* Chester: Monk.

Perks, M.P. and Ennos, R.A. 1999. Analysis of genetic variation for quantitative characters between and within four native populations of Scots Pine (*Pinus sylvestris*). *Botanical Journal of Scotland* 51, 103-110.

Pernicka & Wagner G.A eds. Basel: Birkhauser Verlag. Archaeometry '90, Proceedings of the 26th International Symposium on Archaeometry, Heidelberg 1990, 796-806.

Pigott, C.D. and Huntley, J. 1981. Factors controlling the distribution of *Tilia cordata* at the northern limits of its geographical range III. Nature and causes of seed sterility. *New Phytologist* 87, 817-839.

Pigott, C. M. 1953. Milton Loch Crannog 1: a native house of the second century AD in Kirkcudbrightshire. *Proceedings of the Society of Antiquaries of Scotland* 87, 134-52.

Pojar, J. and MacKinnon, A. 1994. *Plants of the Pacific Northwest Coast.* Vancouver: Lone Pine.

Pollard, T. and Morrison, A. 1996. *The Early Prehistory of Scotland.* Edinburgh University Press.

Pollock, R.W. 1992 The excavation of a souterrain and roundhouse at Cyderhall, Sutherland. *Proceedings of the Society of Antiquaries of Scotland* 122, 149-60.

Powers, A.H. 1992. Great expectations: a short historical review of European phytolith systematics. Pages 15-35 in Rapp, G. and Muholland, S. C. (eds) *Phytolith Systematics Emerging Issues.* New York: Plenum Press.

Powers, A.H. 1997. Phytolith report. Microfiche in Driscoll, S.T. and Yeoman, P.A. (eds) *Excavations within Edinburgh Castle in 1988-91.* Society of Antiquaries of Scotland Monograph No. 12.

Powers, A.H., Padmore, J. and Gilbertson, D.D. 1989. Studies of late prehistoric and modern opal phytoliths from coastal sand dunes and machair in north-west Britain. *Journal of Archaeological Science* 16, 27-45.

Proudfoot, E.V.W. 1978. Camelon native site. *Proceedings of the Society of Antiquaries of Scotland* 109, 112-8.

Punt, W. *et al.* 1976 onwards. *The Northwest European Pollen Flora*. Amsterdam: Elsevier.

Rackham, D. J., Stallibrass, S.M. and Allison, E.P. 1991. The animal and bird bones. Pages 73-88 in McCarthy, M. R. The structural sequence and environmental remains from Castle St, Carlisle: excavations 1981-2. *Cumberland and Westmorland Antiquarian and Archaeological Society Research Series No. 5*

Rackham, O. 1986. *The History of the Countryside*. London: J.M. Dent & Sons.

Ramsay, S. 1995. Woodland clearance in west-central Scotland during the past 3000 years. Ph.D Thesis, University of Glasgow.

Ramsay, S. 1996. Human impact on the vegtetation around Walls Hill. Pages 59-63 in Alexander, D. (ed) *Prehistoric Renfrewshire* Renfrewshire Local History Forum.

Ramsay, S. and Dickson, J.H. 1997. Vegetational History of Central Scotland. *Botanical Journal of Scotland* 49, 141-150.

Rasmussen, S. 1989. An inventory of herbaceous plants in Faroese gardens. Pages 67- 79 in Højgaard, A. *et al.* (eds) *A century of tree-planting in the Faroe Islands*. Tórshavn, Faroes.

Renfrew, J.M. 1973. *Palaeoethnobotany*. London: Methuen.

Rideout, J.S. 1995. Carn Dubh, Moulin, Perthshire: survey and excavation of an archaeological landscape 1987-90. *Proceedings of the Society of Antiquaries of Scotland* 125, 139-95.

Rideout, J.S., Owen, O. A. and Halpin, A. 1992. *Hillforts of Southern Scotland*. Edinburgh: Archaeological Operations and Conservation.

Rietz, E.J. and Wing, E. S. 1999. *Zooarchaeology*. Cambridge University Press.

Ritchie, A. 1983. Excavation of a Neolithic farmstead at Knap of Howar, Papa Westray, Orkney. *Proceedings of the Society of Antiquaries of Scotland* 113, 40-121.

Ritchie, A. 1993. *Viking Scotland*. London: Batsford.

Ritchie, A. *Ancient Orkney*. London: Batsford.

Ritchie, G. and Welfare, H. 1983. Excavations at Ardnave, Islay. *Proceedings of the Society of Antiquaries of Scotland* 113, 302-66.

Ritchie, J.N.G. 1988. *Brochs of Scotland*. Aylesbury: Shire Publications.

Ritchie, J. N. G. 1981. Excavations at Machrins, Colonsay. *Proceedings of the Society of Antiquaries of Scotland* 11, 263-281.

Roberts, A.J., Russell, C., Walker, G.J. and Hirby, K.J. 1992. Reional variation in the origin, extent and composition of Scottish woodland. *Botanical Journal of Scotland* 46, 167-189.

Robinson, D. E. 1983. Possible Mesolithic activity in the west of Arran: evidence from peat deposits. *Glasgow Archaeological Journal* 10, 1-11.

Robinson, D. 1983. Pollen and plant macrofossil analysis of deposits from the Iron Age ditched enclosure at Shiels, Govan, Glasgow. Pages 123-134 in Jones, M. *Integrating the Subsistence Economy*. Oxford: British Archaeological Reports.

Robinson, D.E. 1986. Clubmosses from Medieval Perth. *Antiquity* 60, 49-50.

Robinson, D.E. and Dickson, J.H. 1988. Vegetational history and land-use: radiocarbon-dated pollen diagram from Machrie Moor, Arran, Scotland. *New Phytologist* 109, 223-251.

Rösch, M., Jacomet, S. and Karg, S. 1992. The history of cereals in the region of the former Duchy of Swabia (*Herzogtum Schawben*) from the Roman to the Post-Medieval period: results of archaeobotanical research. *Vegetation History and Archaeobotany* 1, 193-231.

Ruas, M-P. 1992. The archaeobotanical record of cultivated and collected plants of economic importance from Medieval sites in France. *Review of Palaeobotany and Palynolgy* 73, 301-314.

Russell, N.J., Hamilton-Dyer, S., McCormick, F., Boardman, S., Crone, B. A. and Carter, S. 1993. Economic and environmental evidence for the shell midden. Pages 34-6 & fiche in

Connock, K.D., Finlayson, B.and Mills, C.M. Excavation of a shell midden site at Carding Mill Bay near Oban, Scotland. *Glasgow Archaeological Journal* 17, 25-38.

Russell-White, C. J. 1995. The excavation of a Neolithic and Iron Age settlement at Wardend of Durris, Aberdeenshire. *Proceedings of the Society of Antiquaries of Scotland* 125, 9-27.

Ryder, M.L.1999. Probable fibres of Hemp (*Cannabis sativa* L.) in Bronze Age Scotland. *Environmental Archaeology* 4, 93-95.

Rymer, L. 1976. The history and ethnobotany of bracken. *Botanical Journal of the Linnean Society* 73, 152-176.

Sands, R. 1997. *Prehistoric Woodworking The Analysis and Interpretation of Bronze Age and Iron Age Toolmarks*. London: Institute of Archaeology.

Schoch, W.H., Pawlik, B. and Schweingrüber, F.H. 1988. *Botanical Macro-remains*. Stuttgart: Haupt.

314

Schweingrüber, F. H. 1982. *Microscopic Wood Anatomy*. Teufen: Fluck-Wirth.

Schweingrüber, F.H. 1990. *Anatomy of European Woods*. Berne: Haupt.

Scott, J. G. 1960. Loch Glashan. *Discovery and Excavation in Scotland* 8-9.

Scott, J.G. 1996. The ditched enclosure at Sheils, Govan, Glasgow. Pages 65-70 in Alexander, D. (ed) *Prehistoric Renfrewshire*. Renfrewshire Local History Forum.

Scott, M. 1991. The Flowering of Scotland. Pages 43-53 in Magnusson, M. and White, G. (eds) *The Nature of Scotland. Landscape, Wildlife and People*. Edinburgh: Cannongate.

Scott, W. and Palmer, R. 1987. *The Flowering Plants and Ferns of the Shetland Islands*. Lerwick: The Shetland Times.

Scourse, J.D. 1991. Late Quaternary stratigraphy and palaeobotany of the Isle of Scilly. *Philosophical Transactions of the Royal Society of London B* 334, 405-448.

Seaward, M.R.D. 1976. Observations on the bracken component of the pre-Hadrianic deposits at Vindolanda, Northumberland. *Botanical Journal of the Linnean Society* 73, 177-185.

Severin, T. 1978. *The Brendan Voyage*. London: Hutchinson.

Shepherd, I. A. G. and Tuckwell, A. N. 1979. Traces of beaker-period cultivation at Rosinish, Benbecula. *Proceedings of the Society of Antiquaries of Scotland* 108, 108-13.

Sheridan, A. 1996. The oldest bow and other objects. *Current Archaeology* 149,188-190.

Sibbald, R. 1684. *Scotia Illustrata*. Edinburgh: James Kniblo.

Sibbald, R. 1711. *Conjectures concerning the Roman Ports, Colonies, and Forts, in the Firths*. Edinburgh: Andrew Symson.

Simoons, F.J. 1998. *Plants of Life Plants of Death*. Madison: University of Wisconsin Press.

Small, J. 1883. *A Description of the Isles of Orkney*. Reprint of the 1693 book by James Wallace. Edinburgh: W. Brown.

Smith, A.G. 1981. The Neolithic. Pages 82-114 in Simmons, I.G. and Tooley, M.J. (eds) *The Environment and British Prehistory*. London: Duckworth.

Smith, A. J. E. 1978. *The Moss Flora of Britain and Ireland*. Cambridge University Press.

Smith, A. J. E. 1990. *The Liverworts of Britain and Ireland*. Cambridge University Press.

Smith, A. N. 1995. The excavation of Neolithic, Bronze Age and Early Historic features near Ratho, Edinburgh. *Proceedings of the Society of Antiquaries of Edinburgh* 125, 69-138.

Smith, J.A. 1871. Notice of excavations in a broch and adjacent tumulus near Lerwick, in the parish of Dundrossness, Zetland. *Proceedings of the Society of Antiquaries of Scotland* 9, 212-219.

Smout, T.C. 1969. *A History of the Scottish People 1560-1830*. Glasgow: Collins.

Sneader, W. 1985. *Drug Discovery: The Evolution of Modern Medicine*. John Wiley, Chichester.

Spindler, K. 1994. *The Man in the Ice*. Weidenfeld and Nicolson, London.

Stace, C. 1997. *New Flora of the British Isles*. Cambridge University Press, 2nd edition.

Stearn, W.T. 1996. *Stearn's Dictionary of Plant Names for Gardeners*. London: Cassell.

Steer, K.A. and Feacham, R.W. 1954. The Roman Fort and Temporary Camp at Oakwood, Selkirkshire. *Proceedings of the Society of Antiquaries of Scotland* 86, 81-105.

Steven, H.M. and Carlisle, A. 1959. *The Native Pinewoods of Scotland*. Edinburgh: Oliver and Boyd.

Stevenson, J.F. 1990. How ancient is the woodland of Mugdock? *Scottish Forestry* 44, 161-172.

Stevenson, R.B.K. 1954.Celtic carved box from Orkney. *Proceedings of the Society of Antiquaries of Scotland* 86, 187-190.

Stevenson, R.B.K. 1960. A wooden sword of the Late Bronze Age. *Proceedings of the Society of Antiquaries of Scotland* 91, 191-193.

Stuart, J. 1865. Notices of a group of artificial islands in the Loch of Dowalton, Wigtonshire, and other artificial islands or 'crannogs' throughout Scotland. *Proceedings of the Society of Antiquaries of Scotland* 6, 114-178.

Sturtevant, E.L. 1919. Sturtevant's Notes on Edible Plants. *Annual Report of the New York Experimental Station* 2, part II.

Sutherland, E. 1994. *In Search of the Picts*. London: Constable.

Suttles, W. 1990. *Handbook of North American Indians. Volume 7. Northwest Coast*. Washington: Smithsonian Institution.

Tait, C. 1794. An account of the peat-mosses of Kincardine and Flanders in Perthshire. *Transactions of the Royal Society of Edinburgh* 3, 266-279.

Tansley, A.G. 1952. *Oaks and Oak Woods*. London: Methuen.

Taylor, C.F. and Sturtevant, W. C. 1995. *The Native Americans The Indigenous Peoples of North America*. London: Salamander Books.

Tebble, N. 1976 *British Bivalve Seashells* HMSO.

Terry, J. 1993. Excavation of a farmstead enclosure, Uppercleuch, in Annandale, Dumfries and Galloway. *Transactions of the Dumfriesshire & Galloway Natural History and Antiquarian Society* 68, 53-74.

Terry, J. 1995. Excavation at Lintshie Gutter Unenclosed Platform Settlement, Crawford, Lanarkshire. 1991. *Proceedings of the Society of Antiquaries of Scotland* 125, 369-427.

Thomas, G.D. 1988. Excavations at the Roman civil settlement at Inveresk, 1976-77. *Proceedings of the Society of Antiquaries of Scotland* 118, 139-176.

Thomsen, T. 1929. Egekistfundet fra Egtved, fra den Aeldere Bronze Alder. *Nordisk Fortidsminder* 2, 165-214

Thornton, I. 1996. *Krakatau.* Harvard University Press.

Tipping, R. 1994. The form and fate of Scotland's woodlands. *Proceedings of the Society of Antiquaries of Scotland,* 124, 1-54.

Tipping, R. 1994. 'Ritual' Floral Tributes in the Scottish Bronze Age - Palynological Evidence. *Journal of Archaeological Science* 21, 133-39.

Tipping, R. 1995. The pollen evidence. Pages 223-231 in S. Stevenson The excavation of a kerbed cairn at Beech Hill House, Coupar Angus, Perthshire. *Proceedings of the Society of Antiquaries of Scotland* 125, 197-235.

Tipping, R. 1996. Microscopic Charcoal Records, Inferred Human Activity and Climate Change in the Mesolithic of Northernmost Scotland. Pages 39-61 in Pollard, T. and Morrison, A. (eds) *The Early Prehistory of Scotland.* Edinburgh University Press.

Tomlinson, P. 1985a. Use of vegetative plant remains in the identification of dye plants from waterlogged ninth-tenth century AD deposits at York. *Journal of Archaeological Science* 12, 269-83.

Tomlinson, P. 1985b. An aid to the identification of fossil buds, bud-scales and catkin-bracts of British trees and shrubs. *Circaea* 3, 45-130.

Tomlinson, P. 1991. Vegetative plant remains from waterlogged deposits identified at York. Pages 109-19 in Renfrew, J.(ed) *New Light on Early Farming.* Edinburgh University Press.

Turner, J. 1965. A contribution to the history of forest clearance. *Proceedings of the Royal Society B* 161, 343-354.

Turner, N.J. 1998. *Plant Technology of First Peoples in British Columbia.* Vancouver: UBC Press.

Turner, R.C. 1995. Recent research into British bog bodies. Pages 108-122 in Turner, R.C. and Scaife, R.G. (eds) *Bog Bodies New Discoveries and Perspectives.* London: British Museum Press.

Turner, V. 1997. *Ancient Shetland.* London: Shetland.

Turner, W. 1551. *A New Herball. Part I.* Republished by Cambridge University Press in 1995, edited by G.T.L. Chapman and M.N. Tweddle.

Turner, W. 1562 and 1568. *A New Herball. Parts II and III..* Republished by Cambridge University Press in 1995, edited by G.T.L. Chapman, F. McCombie and A.U.Wesencraft.

Tzedakis, Y. and Martlew, H. 1999. *Minoans and Myceneans Flavours of Their Time.* Athens: Greek Ministry of Culture.

Van Den Brink , F.H. 1967 *A Field Guide to the Mammals of Europe.* Collins, London

Van der Veen, M. 1992. *Crop Husbandry Regimes An Archaeobotanical Study of Farming in northern England 1000 BC -AD 500.* Sheffield: J.R.Collis.

Van der Veen, M. and Fjeller, N. 1982. Sampling seeds. *Journal of Archaeological Science* 9, 287-98.

Van der Veen, M., Hall, A.R. and May, J. 1993. Woad and the Britons painted blue. *Oxford Journal of Archaeology* 12, 367-371.

Van Geel, B., Buurman, J. and Waterbolk, H.T. 1996. Archaeological and palaeoecological indications of an abrupt climate change in The Netherlands, and evidence for climatological teleconnections around 2650 BP. Journal, of Quaternary Science 11, 451-460.

Van Gils, C. and Cox, P.A. 1994. Ethnobotany of nutmeg in the Spice Islands. *Journal of Ethnopharmacology* 42, 117-124.

Van Ziest, W. and Casparie, W. A. 1974. Niederwil, a palaeobotanical study of a Swiss Neolithic lake shore settlement. *Geologie en Mijnbouw* 53 415-28.

Vencl, S. 1994. The archaeology of thirst. *Journal of European Archaeology* 2, 299-326.

Vickery, R. 1995. *Oxford Dictionary of Plant-lore.* Oxford University Press.

Viklund, K. 1994, The long history of Swedish bread. *Laborativ Arkeologi* I7, 30-36.

Wallace, J. 1693. *A Description of the Isles of Orkney.* Edinburgh.

Warden, A.J. 1875. Notice of stone cists, etc, found at Barnhill near Broughty Ferry. *Proceedings of the Society of Antiquaries of Scotland* 11, 310-312.

Watling, R. 1975. Prehistoric puffballs. *Bulletin of the British Mycological Society* 9, 112-4, 112-114.

Weber, B. 1994. Iron Age Combs: Analyses of Raw material. Pages 190-3 in Ambrosiani, B. and Clarke, H. (eds) *Development Around the Baltic and the North Sea in the Viking Age.* Birka Studies 4, The Twelfth Viking Congress, Stockholm.

Weber, H.E. 1995. *Gustav Hegi Illustrierte Flora von Mitteleuropa.* Band IV Teil 2A. Berlin: Blackwell.

Wiethold, J. 1995. Plant remains from town deposits and cesspits of Medieval and post-Medieval Kiel (Schleswig-Holstein, Germany). Pages 359-384 in Kroll, H. and Pasternak, R. (eds) *Res Archaeobotanicae* Kiel: Oetker-Voges Verlag.

Whittington, G. 1993. Palynological investigations at two Bronze Age burial sites in Fife. *Proceedings of the Society of Antiquaries of Scotland* 123, 211-213.

Whittington, G. and Edwards, K. J. 1990. The cultivation and utilisation of hemp in Scotland. *Scottish Geographical Magazine* 106, 167-73.

Whittington, G. and Edwards, K.J. 1993. *Ubi solitudinem faciunt pacem appelant:* the Romans in Scotland, a Palaeoenvironmental Contribution. *Britannia* 24, 13-25.

Whittington, G. and Edwards, K.J. 1997. Climate Change. Page 11-22 in Edwards, K.J. and Ralston, I.B.M. (eds) *Scotland: Environment and Archaeology, 8000 BC -AD1000.* Chichester: John Wiley & Sons.

Whittington, G., Edwards, K. J. and Cundill, P. R. 1991. Late- and Post-glacial vegetational change at Black Loch, Fife, eastern Scotland — a multiple core approach. *New Phytologist* 118, 147-66.

Whittle, A., Keith-Lucas, M., Milles, A., Noddle, B., Rees, S. and Romans, J.C.C. 1987. *An Early Agricultural Settlement on Shetland.* Oxford University Committee for Archaeology Monograph No.9.

Wickham-Jones, C.R. 1994. *Scotland's First Settlers.* London: Batsford.

Wild, J. P. 1970. *Textile manufacture in the northern Roman Provinces.* Cambridge University Press.

Wilkins, D.A. 1984. The Flandrian woods of Lewis (Scotland). *Journal of Ecology,* 72, 251-8.

Wilson, G. 1975. The botanical setting of the Roman fort at Birrens, Dumfriesshire. Pages 259-268 in. Robertson, A.S *Birrens (Blatobulgium).* Edinburgh: T. and A. Constable.

Wiltshire, P. E. J. 1992. The effect of food processing on the palatability of wild fruits with high tannin content. Pages 385-397 in Kroll, H. and Pasternak, H.(eds). *Res Archaeobotanicae* International Workgroup for Palaeoethnobotany. Proceedings of the 9th Symposium Kiel (1992).

Woodman, P. C. 1985. *Excavations at Mount Sandel 1973-77.* Belfast: HMSO.

Worrell, R. and Malcolm, D.C. 1998. Anomalies in the distribution of Silver Birch (*Betula pendula* Roth) in Scotland. *Botanical Journal of Scotland* 50, 1-10.

Wren, R. C. 1988. *Potter's New encyclopaedia of Botanical Drugs and Preparations* (rewritten by Williamson, E. M. and Evans, F. J.). Saffron Walden: Daniel.

Wylie, D.D. and Dickson, J.H.1998. The Holocene history of Scots Pine (*Pinus sylvestris* L.) at Loch Sloy, Scottish Highlands. *Glasgow Naturalist* 23, 16-23.

Yalden, D. 1999. *The History of British Mammals.* London: T & AD Poyser Natural History. *istory of British mammals.*

Yanovsky, E. 1936. Flowering Plants of the North American Indians. *United States Department of Agriculture Miscellaneous Publications 23, 1-83.*

Yeoman, P. 1984. Excavation at Castlehill of Strachan, 1980-81. *Proceedings of the Society of Antiquaries of Scotland* 114, 315-64.

Yeoman, P. 1995. *Medieval Scotland.* London: Batsford.

Ziegler, P. 1969. *The Black Death.* Stroud: Sutton Publishing Ltd.

Zohary, D. and Hopf, M. 1993. *Domestication of Plants in the Old World: The Origin and Spread of Cultivated Plants in West Asia, Europe, and the Nile Valley.* Oxford: Clarendon Press. 2nd edition.

Zvelebil, M. 1994. Plant Use in the Mesolithic and its Role in the Transition to Farming. *Proceedings of the Prehistoric Society* 60, 35-74.

Index

In this index all sites have been listed that have trees, tall shrubs and all those plants of economic importance. Animals have not been indexed. **Bold** type indicates the page of an illustration.

Abercairney **181**, 203
Aberdeen 179, 186-189, 213, 245, 245
Alder 12, 14, 18, 19, 24-30, 32, 34, 38, 41, 45, 59, 64, 66, 67, 69, 71, 73-75, 89, 91- **93**, 95, 98, 107, 108, 110, 111,113, 116, 125, 127, 129, 132, 135, 136, 140. 141, 146, 157, 185, 194, 196, 202, 207, **221**, **222**
Ale/beer 82, 84, 196, 208, 210, 215, 217-219, 262
Antonine Wall 91, 114, **115**, **116**, 219
Apple 43, 123, 124, 190, 196, 215
ard/ard marks 76
Ardnave 69, **71**
Arran 29, 32, 35, 36, 47, 69, 81
Ash 12, 14, 19, 29, 32, 35, 38, 55, 64 –67, 69, 75, 107, 110, 111, 11, 125, 126, 130, 134-136, 140-142, 157, 162, 170, 173, 194, 196, 202
Ashgrove **71**, 79, **80,** 89, 207, 226
Aspen 108, 110
Aspirin 268

Balbridie 49, 67, 68, 207, 237
bannocks 105, 168, 215, 217
Bar Hill 14, **115**, 122, 123, 256, 257, 282
Barley 16, 18, 19, 50, 51, 59, 61, 62, 67, 69, 70, 73, 75, 76, 77, 89, 92, 96, 100, 105, 107-109, 110, 112, 116, 117, 122, 123, 125, 127, 131, 132, 138, 140, 142, 146-149, 151-154, 158, 159, 162, 165, 167, 168, 172, 173, 175, 176, 180, 182, 184, 190, 191, 192, 196, 201-203, 202, 210, 211, 213, 216-218, 230, **231-233**, 235, 237
Barvas Machair **145**, 172
basket **98**
beakers 79, **80,** 84

Bearsden **115**, 117-126, 209, 210, 219, 242, 243, 251, **254**
Beech 14, 18, 19, 63, 130, 170, 207
Beech Hill House **71**, 79, 82
Beach View **157**, 158, 160
Benbecula **71**, 76
Ben Lawers 31, **92**
Berriedale **65**
berries 45, 46, 99, 122
Bilberry 63, 122, 123, 181, 189, 190, 196
Birches 12, 14, 18, 19, 23-30, 32, 34, 35, 37, 39, 41, 57, 59, 62–64, 66, 67, 69, 71, 73, 74, 85, 92, 95, 106-108, 110, 111, 113, 115, 125-127, 131, 134-136, 140, 142, 146, 147, 157, 162, 170, 173, 185, 186, 192, 194, 196, 201, 202, 206, 207, 222, **223**, 224
Bird-cherry 48, 64-66, 73, 74, 89, 93, 133, 190, 207
Birrens 19, **115**
Birsay Bay **145**, 212, 156-161
Black Loch **115**, 116, 117, 263
Black Mustard 137, 138, 140
Boghead 49, 50, 67, 216
Bogmosses 24–28, 75, 79, 81, 126, 133, 198, **224**, 225, 226
Bog Myrtle 189
Bones 14, 15, 16, 18, 19, 34, 36, 42, 43, 49, 50, 52, 60, 62, 63, 76, 77, 102, 103, 105, 107, 113, 119, 123, 124, 131, 133, 135, 138-140, 149, 154, 157, 159-161, 163-165, 171, 173, 185, 189, 190, 191, 192, 202, 213, 295, 151
Bullace 190, 215
Buckquoy 156, **157**, 160
Bracken 12, 13, 24–28, 36, 69, 79, 81, 90, 93, 105, 121, 126, 130, 133, 182, 185, 205, 210, **227**, **228**
bracket fungi 13

Bramble 48, 57, 64, 69, 90, 93, 122, 123, 133, 134, 137, 142, 188, 190, 196
bran 119, **122**, 131, 136, 189, 190, 216, 236
bread 119, 168, 215, 217, 218
Bread Wheat 19, 67, 75, 108, 110, 112, 121, 132, 140, 149, 190, 191, 202, 207, 216, 218, 237, **238**
brewhouse 58
Broad Bean 118, 124, 184, 191, 214, **229**, **230**
brochs 12, 86, 94-108,
broth 97, 215, 219
Brough of Birsay **145**, 156, 158, 161
bucket 98, 172
Buiston 12, 88, **129**, 131-133, 208, 245
Bullace 215
burnt mounds 78

Caper Spurge 190, 198, 215
Capo **181**, 203
Carlisle **115**,123
Carn Dubh **71**, 109
Carnwath **71**, 74
Carstairs **71**, 74
Castlecary **115**, 122, 123, 240
Castledykes 18, 19, **115**
Castlehill of Strachan 181, 201, 202
Castle Sween 181, 202, 203
Cereals 16, 19, 48, 50, 59, 62, 68, 70, 81, 86, 89, 91-93, 134, 135, 142, 211, 215-218, 230-239
charcoal 34, 35, 40, 57, 59, 64, 69, 70, 74, 75, 89, 95, 106-111, 113, 132, 136, 138, 139, 157, 163, 182, 201, 207
chewing gum 205
Cherry 215
cists 78, **80, 82**, 208, 262
climatic change 20, 84, 85, 207

Cloudberry 93, 20, **240**, **240**
Common Mallow 125, 126, 210, **242**, **243**
Common Whitebeam 16
coprolites 104, **105**, 131, 217, 293, 294
coprosterols 119
Coriander 118,123, 133, 137, 189, 210, 215, **243**, **244**
Cork Oak 170
Corncockle 16, 19, 181, 184, 245, **246**, 247
Crab Apple 48, 66, 67, **247**, **248**, 249
crannogs 12, 19, 86-**95**, 208, 209
Crosskirk **87**, 108
Crowberry 55, 58, 158, 159, 168
Cyderhall **71**, **87**, 108,109

Dalgety Bay **71**,79, 82
Dead-nettle 101
Deadly Nightshade 190, 213, 215, **249**, 250
digging stick 45
Dill 118, 123, 133, 137, 210, 244, **245**
Dog Rose 90, 190
Drimore Machair 172, 173
Dropwort 78, **267**, **268**
Dundurn 128-131, **130**, 210, 227, 270
dung 98, 99
Dun Mor Vaul **87**, 107
dyeing 184, 188
Dyer's Rocket 184, 188, 190

Earl's Bu **145**, 150, 151
Easter Kinnear **129**, 131, 140-142, 210
Edinburgh Castle **87**, 112, 113, **129**, 139, 140, **181**, 190, 215
Elder 124, 134, 138, 184, 190, 196
Elgin 179, 190,191, 213, 245, 249, 282
Elginhaugh **115**,123, 127
Elm 12, 14, 18, 19, 29, 34, 35, 38, 47, 48, 64, 67, 140
Elm decline 47, 48, 64, 185
Embo 49, 63
Emmer 19, 50, 67, 69, 70, 76, 89, 94, 107-109, 112, 119-121, 123, 216, 237, **239**

Fannyside Moss **115**
Fathen 158, 188, 204
Fairy Knowe 87, 108, **276**
Fig 90, 91, 122, 123, 181, 189, 190, 194, 196, 199, 204, 210, 213, 215, 249, **251**, **252**
Fir 19, 66

fire 32, 40, 41, 97-99, 100, 258, 260, 261
Flanders Moss 20, 24-28, 49, 226
Firewood/fuel 53, 57, 73, 100, 121, 125, 142, 158, 173
Flax 67, 94, 97, 108, 109, 112, 133, 140, 142, 149, 151, 151, 154, 158, 159, 164, 165, 172, 173, 176, 183, 184, 188, 190, 191, 194, 198, 211, 213, **253**, **254**
flour 119, 120
Freswick **145**, 146-150, 174, 229
Friesack 32, 45

Garden Angelica 178, 211
Garlic 142, 196, 214, 273
Gorse 196
Grape/raisins 123, 124, 189, 190, 199, 213, 215
Greater Celandine 198, 199
Guelder Rose 43, 64-66, **255**, **256**

Hadrian's Wall **115**, 122
Haggis 219, 235
Hairmoss 13, 16, 133, **134**, 184
Hawthorn 14, 48, 65, 66, 110, 135, 136, 185, 194, 202, 256, **257**, **258**
Hazel/Hazelnuts 12, 13, 14, 18, 19, 23-30, 32, 34, 36-39, 41-46, 48, 56, 59, 62-64, 67, 69, 71, 73-75, 85, 86, 89, 95, 98, 107-112, 116, 122, 123, 125-127, 129, 130-134, 139, 146, 157, 163, 169, 185, 188, 192, 194, 196, 201, 202, 204, 206, 207, 257-**260,**
Heather 12, 13, 18, 19, 24-29, 36, 40, 52, 55, 64, 75, 98, 100, 105-107, 113, 116, 125, 126, 132, 135, 138, 140-142, 147, 151, 154, 159, 173, 174, 182, 185, 192, 193, 201, 210, 218, 260, **261**, **262**
Hemlock 127, 138, 198, 199, 213, 215
Hemp 15, 213, 262, **263**
Henbane 112, 123, 127, 158, 177, 213, 215, 249, **250**, **251**
Hog's Fennel 123
Holly 19, 126, 134, 135
Hornbeam 19, 202
Howe 49, 65, **87**, 94-**98**, **99**-103, 106, **129**, 142, 154-156, 174, 212, 221, **145**, 168

Iceman 13, 208, 253, 271, 281, 283. 285
Inveresk **115**,126
Iona 128, 129. 133-136,
Ivy 34, 38, 126, 157

Jarlshof 19, **71**, 77, **87**, 106, 107, 144, **145**, 163, 164
Juniper 30, 32, 64-66, 95, 102, 108, 157, 176, 177
Jura 35

Kale 197, 214, 235
Kilns 203
Kirkintilloch **115**, 117
Kirkwall **181**, 194, 251
Knap of Howar 49, 59-62, x207

Larch 57, 98, 162, 107
Lentil 123, 124
Lesser Celandine 101, 102, 177, **264**, **265**
Letham Moss **115**
Lime 19, 79, 80, 81, 207, 208
Linseed 105, 118, 123
Lintshie Gutter 70, **71-73**, 74, 75, 207
Little Ice Age 21
Loanleven **71**, 79, 82
Loch a'Phuinnd 28, 49
Loch Garten 26, 29, 49
Loch Glashan 133
Lochlee 12, 13, 91, **129**, 131
Loch of Skaill 64, 65

Mace 199, 215, 265, **266**, 267
Machrie Moor 29, 69, **71**, 78
Machrins 173, 174
Macroscopic remains (macros) 287
Maes Howe 19, 65
Maple 162
mead 208, 268
Meadowsweet 78-84, 208, **267**, **268**, 269
medicinal plants 54, 55, 100, 101, 102, 121, 124, 125, 138, 176-178, 198, 199
Medieval Warm Period 21
microscopes 290
Midland Hawthorn 123
mill 150, 151
Milton Loch 19, 86, **88**, 92,
Mollins **115**
Monk's Rhubarb **269**, **270**
Morton 32, 36
mosses 13, 79, 83, 117, 126, 131, 133, 190, 213, 270, **271**
Mount Sandel 32, 41-43
Mumrills 16, **115**, 122, 123

names (nomenclature) 286
Ness of Gruting 50, **71**, 77
Newstead 15, **115**
Northern Isles 29, 36, 49, 104-107

North Mains **71**,79, 82
Northton 49, 63
Nutmeg 199, 215, 265, 266

Oaks 14, 18, 19, 22-29, 34, 35, 38,
   39, 41, 63, 64, 66, 67, 71, 74, 77,
   81, 84, 85, 89, 92, 107-109, 115,
   116, 126, 127, 129, 130-132, 134-
   136, 139, 142, 147, 152, 157, 162,
   163, 166, 169, 185, 192-194, 196,
   202, 207, 209, **272**, **273**
Oakbank **87**, 91-95, 131, 208, 221,
   227, 240, 274, 281
Oakwood 18, **115**
Oatcakes 168, 234, 235, 237
Oats 75, 89, 97, 108, 109, 111, 112,
   131, 132, 138, 140, 142, 149, 151-
   154, 158, 159, 162, 163, 165, 167,
   168, 172-176, 180, 182, 186, 188,
   190, 191, 192, 196, 201, 202, 203,
   211, 213, 216-218, 232, **234**, **235**
Oban 32, **33**
Old Kilpatrick **87**, 89, 91, **235**, 252
Old Scatness 165
Onions 189, 196, 214
Opium Poppy 94, 118, 123, 189, 198,
   199, 209, 213, 215, **274**, **275**
organic residues 208
Oronsay 32, 34, 35

Paisley Abbey **181**, 194-200, **234**,
   251, **266**, **270**
Papa Westray 49, 59
Pear 123, 215
Peas 124, 140, 191, 214
Peat/peat-bogs 37-40, 106, 121, 125,
   144, 146, 147, 157, 158, 163, 168,
   173, 196, 210, 241, 278
Perth 179-186, 213, 214, 236, 245,
   282
phytoliths 18, 63, 293, **294**
ploughs 136
Plum 113, 215
Point of Buckquoy **71**, 76
pollen analysis 24-29, 78-84, 291, **292**
Pool 49, 143, 145, 152-153,
Poplar 18,19,45,63, 77, 95, 127, 135
porridge 82, 121, 215, 217, 219
Puffball 13, 15, 55, 57

querns 77, 86, 94, 97, 104, 120, 173,
   212
Quoyloo Meadow 27, 29, 49, 64

Radiocarbon dating 296
Ramsons 108, 275, **276**
Raspberry 48, 69, 73, 93, 122, 123,
   133, 142, 181, 190, 196

Ratho 49
Rattray **71**, 75, 193, 194
rhizomes 53-55, 228
Ribwort Plantain 18, 24-29, 47, 64,
   69, 70, 75, 116, 126, 141, 146,
   158
Rinyo 49, 58
Rispain Camp **87**, 110
Robert's Haven 151, **145**, 174
Roman forts 15 – 19, 114-127
Rotten Bottom 56
Rough Castle 19, 114, **115**, 122, 242
Rowan 14, 16, 18, 32, 34, 38, 48, 64,
   69, 71, 73, 75, 95, 108, 125, 130,
   133, 135, 136, 140, 142, 146, 158,
   159, 184, 190, 192, 196, 202, 207
Rum 32-34
Rye 92, 119, 123, 152, 180, 181, 192,
   202, **235-237**,

Saevar Howe **157**, 160
sampling 287-289
Sandfjold **71**, 79
Sandwick 164, 165
Savin 102, 177
Scord of Brouster 62, 207
Scots Pine 12, 19, 23-30, 32, 37-40,
   63, 64, 67, 74, 85, 95, 107, 142,
   146, 147, 157, 166, 169, 185, 194,
   277-279, 280, 286
seaweed 52, 158, 159, 168
Service-tree 18
Sheils **87**, 109,110
Sheep's Sorrel 101, 102
Silverweed 46, 205
Skara Brae 13, 14, 48-59, 64-67, 76,
   x206, 207, 216, 227, 237, 247,
   281
Sketewan **71**, 79, 82
Skull-cap 101
Sloe 35, 48, 65, 66, 69, 90, 93, 123,
   192, 196, **280**, **281**,
South Uist 32, 3848-59
Spelt 19, 89, 94, 110, 119-121, 123,
   209, 216, 237,238, **239**, 240
spices 128, 131, 176-178, 199, 215
Spruce 57, 64, 66, 95,106, 125, 158,
   162, 172
St Andrews **181**, 192, 236
Stable isotopes 205
Star Carr 33, 36, 40
Stone Pine 124
Summer Savory 124

Tamarack 66
Thatch 107
The Biggins **145**, 165-172, 212,
The Dunion **87**, 110, 111

The Storebælt 32, 42-44
Tofts Ness 49, 51, 62, **71**, 76, 207
Toquoy **145** 162-163
Tougs **71**, 78
trackway 76
tree rings 296
turf 52, 53, 70, 76, 90, 98, 99, 100,
   101, 117, 121, 125, 156, 157, 168,
   203, 209, 293
Turnip 182, 215
Turnsole 210
Tybrind Vig 32, 43

Upper Cleuch **87**, 110
Upper Kenly Farm **71**, 83

volcanic eruptions 21, 22, 24, 84, 208

Walls Hill 25, 49, **115**, 226
Walnut 122, 124, 178, 184, 196, 281,
   282
Warebeth **88**, 104, 105, 217
wattle 90, 93, 125, 127, 129, 136, 140,
   185, 210, 260
Wayfaring Tree 64,
Weld 213
Westbank **71**, 79, 82, **83**
Westness 151
Weymouth Pine 57, 66
Wheats 16, 92, 94, 119, 127, 180, 188,
   192, 196, 213, 237, **238**, **239**, 240
wheel 75
whisky 219
White Horehound 125
Whithorn 128, 136-139, **137, 141**,
   181, 200, 201, 245
Wild Celery 123
Wild Cherry 43, 48, 64-66, 69, 73,
   74, 89, 90, 110, 111, 113, 123,
   125, 131, 136, 140, 141, 181, 190,
   196, 207
Wild Strawberry 93, 122, 158, 190
Willow 12, 14, 18, 19, 24-28, 30, 32,
   34, 35, 37, 41, 56, 59, 63, 64, 66,
   67, 69, 73-75 74, 77, 95, 98, 106-
   108, 110, 111, 113, 116, 125, 126,
   131, 134, 136, 140, 146, 147, 156,
   157, 162, 163, 173, 186, 194, 207
wine 123, 210
Woad 199, 282, **283**
Wych Elm **24-28**, 30, 41, 46, 47, 66,
   74, 92, 130, 141, 142, 286

Yellow Iris 54, 56
Yew 56, 135, 207, 283, **284**, 285
yoke 75